A COMPLETE GUIDE

FROGS

OF SOUTHERN AFRICA

Louis du Preez
Vincent Carruthers

With advice from
Marius Burger
Alan Channing
Michael Cunningham
Atherton de Villiers
James Harvey
Angelo Lambiris
Les Minter
Neville Passmore
Andrew Turner
Adam Shuttleworth

ACKNOWLEDGEMENTS

The authors thank the following for their assistance and comments on the manuscript, as well as for making photographs and other material available for inclusion in this work:

Marion Anstis, Linda Basson, Mike Bates, Richard Boycott, Don Broadley, Marietjie Brown, Marius Burger, Jane Carruthers, Alan Channing, Jenny Channing, Werner Conradie, Mike Cooper, Gail and David Cretchley, Michael Cunningham, Carina de Beer, Roger de la Harpe, Atherton de Villiers, Bob Drewes, Christa du Preez, Johann du Preez, Ansel Fong, Renaud Fulconis, André Geldenhuys, Attie Gerber, Marika Gericke, Mariska Greef, Mike Griffen, Wulf Haacke, Clem Haagner, James Harvey, Kate Henderson, Francois Jacobs, Michael Jennions, Donnavan Kruger, Angelo Lambiris, Marleen le Roux, John Leyden, Johan Marais, John Measey, Micaelo Menegon, Leon Meyer, Ian Michler, Les Minter, Christa Morrison, Doug Newman, Oscar Olien, Neville Passmore, Anton Pauw, Martin Pickersgill, John Poynton, Tony Reumerman, Dominic Rollinson, Arné Schiøtz, Warren Schmidt, Liz Scott, Adam Shuttleworth, Chris Stuart, Jeanne Tarrant, Krystal Tolley, Rob Toms, Andrew Turner, Eddie van Dijk, James Vonesh, Ché Weldon, Adam Yates and Breda Zimkus; Bayworld, Port Elizabeth; Natal Museum, Pietermaritzburg; National Museum, Bloemfontein; Transvaal Museum, Pretoria; Wilderness Safaris; Zambian Wildlife Authority.

The majority of tadpole mouthpart drawings were kindly supplied by Angelo Lambiris.

Sound recordings were gratefully received from: P. Bishop, Richard Boycott, Harold Braack, Marius Burger, Alan Channing, Mike Cherry, Michael Cunningham, Atherton de Villiers, Andreas Elepfandt, Michael Jennions, Les Minter, David Moyer, Neville Passmore, Mike Picker, Martin Pickersgill, Bob Sternstedt, Rob Toms and Andrew Turner.

Pippa Parker is thanked for managing the publication, Janice Evans for the design of the book, and Helen de Villiers and Cynthia Kemp for their painstaking editing and proofreading.

Part of the cost of this book was generously sponsored by the North-West University and the authors are particularly indebted to the rector, Professor Annette Combrink for her support in this regard.

Published by Struik Nature
(an imprint of Random House Struik (Pty) Ltd)
1st Floor, Wembley Square 2, Solan Street,
Cape Town, 8001 South Africa
PO Box 1144, Cape Town, 8000 South Africa
Company Reg. No. 1966/003153/07

Visit www.randomstruik.co.za and join the
Struik Nature Club for updates, news,
events and special offers.

First published in 2009
2 3 4 5 6 7 8 9 10

Publishing manager: Pippa Parker
Managing editor: Helen de Villiers
Editor and proofreader: Cynthia Kemp
Designer: Janice Evans
Cartographer and illustrator: Susan van Biljon
Deep-etching of images by Korck Publishing

Reproduction: Hirt & Carter Cape (Pty) Ltd
Printed and bound: 1010 Printing International Ltd, China

ISBN 978 1 77007 446 0 (softcover edition)
ISBN 978 1 77007 808 6 (limited hardcover edition)

Front cover: Yellow-striped Reed Frog
Hyperolius semidiscus. *(Vincent Carruthers)*
Right: Table Mountain Ghost Frog
Heleophryne rosei. *(Anton Pauw)*

NORTH-WEST UNIVERSITY
YUNIBESITI YA BOKONE-BOPHIRIMA
NOORDWES-UNIVERSITEIT
POTCHEFSTROOM CAMPUS

CONTENTS

Delicate Leaf-folding Frog

Water Lily Frog

CONTENTS OF CD

SOUTHERN AFRICAN FROG CALLS

BIBLIOGRAPHY

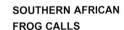

INTRODUCTION

Identification, classification, taxonomy and evolution

'These foul and loathsome animals are abhorrent because of their cold body, pale colour, cartilaginous skeleton, filthy skin, fierce aspect, calculating eye, offensive smell, harsh voice, squalid habitation, and terrible venom; and so their Creator has not exerted his powers to make many of them.'

Carolus Linnaeus (father of modern taxonomy and one of the great naturalists of his time), referring to amphibians, 1758

Harmless, colourful, melodious and ecologically vital, frogs are the antithesis of Linnaeus's disdain. Some 6 000 species of amphibians are known worldwide and more are discovered every year. At the same time, the decline and extinction of species is occurring at a disturbingly high rate, indicating widespread environmental malaise.

This field guide describes the species found in southern Africa south of the Zambezi, Okavango and Cunene rivers and introduces the reader to their biological and conservation significance. All southern African species formally described before June 2009 are included, and subsequent discoveries or descriptions will be made available on the website **http://www.nwu.ac.za/p/z/frogbook.html** in the same page format as published in this book. The taxonomy and classification used here follows that of *The Amphibian Tree of Life* by Frost *et al.* 2006.

DISTINGUISHING CHARACTERS OF FROGS AND TADPOLES

Most people are familiar with the general appearance of frogs and tadpoles, but considerable variation exists between species. Frogs vary in size from the West African Goliath Frog, *Conraua goliath*, with feet as large as the palm of a human hand and weighing more than 3 kg, to the smallest species, a Cuban frog, *Eleutherodactylus iberia* which is only 8.5 mm long. In southern Africa the largest species is the Giant Bullfrog, *Pyxicephalus adspersus* (page 414) and the smallest is the Northern Moss Frog, *Arthroleptella subvoce* (page 358). Substantial variation may occur even within members of a single species. Colour and pattern, in particular, may differ from one frog to another within a species while, conversely, two different species are sometimes so similar in colour that they are indistinguishable on the basis of appearance alone.

Often the most dependable method of distinguishing between similar species or identifying unknown tadpoles is laboratory analysis of DNA. However, this technique falls outside the scope of this book, the main purpose of which is to enable identification of living frogs in their natural habitats. Reliable identification of frogs in the field depends on a combination of different characters. These are illustrated diagrammatically on the following two pages. All of these characters should be considered in order to reach a confident decision when identifying a specimen. Where possible, more than one specimen from a population should be examined to establish the degree of variation that might occur. On p.10, a step-by-step process is described and this should be followed when identifying a frog or tadpole.

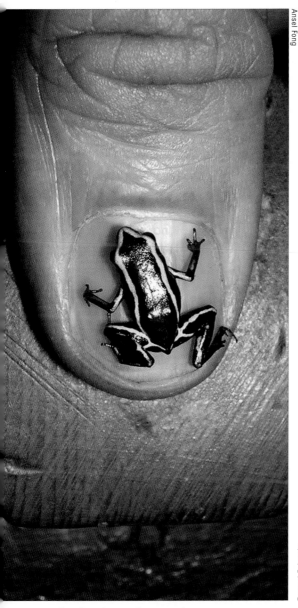

Smallest known frog species:
Eleutherodactylus iberia *from Cuba.*

Largest known frog species: Conraua goliath *from Gabon.*

Ansel Fong

Renaud Fulconis

CHARACTERS FOR IDENTIFYING ADULT FROGS

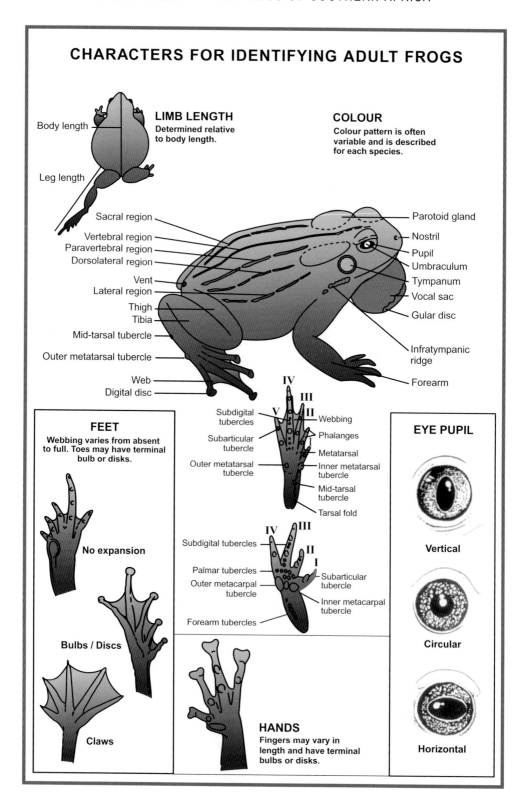

Body length

Leg length

LIMB LENGTH
Determined relative
to body length.

COLOUR
Colour pattern is often
variable and is described
for each species.

Sacral region
Vertebral region
Paravertebral region
Dorsolateral region
Vent
Lateral region
Thigh
Tibia
Mid-tarsal tubercle
Outer metatarsal tubercle
Web
Digital disc

Parotoid gland
Nostril
Pupil
Umbraculum
Tympanum
Vocal sac
Gular disc
Infratympanic ridge
Forearm

FEET
Webbing varies from absent
to full. Toes may have terminal
bulb or disks.

No expansion

Bulbs / Discs

Claws

IV
III
II
V
Subdigital tubercles
Subarticular tubercle
Outer metatarsal tubercle
Webbing
Phalanges
Metatarsal
Inner metatarsal tubercle
Mid-tarsal tubercle
Tarsal fold

IV
III
II
I
Subdigital tubercles
Palmar tubercles
Outer metacarpal tubercle
Forearm tubercles
Subarticular tubercle
Inner metacarpal tubercle

HANDS
Fingers may vary in
length and have terminal
bulbs or disks.

EYE PUPIL

Vertical

Circular

Horizontal

CHARACTERS FOR IDENTIFYING TADPOLES

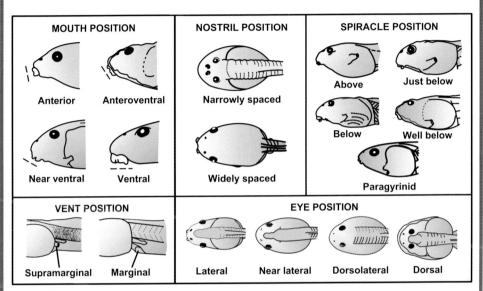

MOUTH POSITION

Anterior   Anteroventral

Near ventral   Ventral

NOSTRIL POSITION

Narrowly spaced

Widely spaced

SPIRACLE POSITION

Above   Just below

Below   Well below

Paragyrinid

VENT POSITION

Supramarginal   Marginal

EYE POSITION

Lateral   Near lateral   Dorsolateral   Dorsal

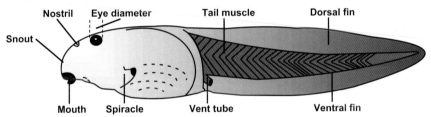

Nostril   Eye diameter   Tail muscle   Dorsal fin

Snout

Mouth   Spiracle   Vent tube   Ventral fin

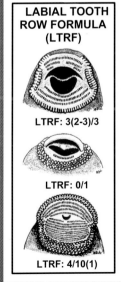

LABIAL TOOTH ROW FORMULA (LTRF)

LTRF: 3(2-3)/3

LTRF: 0/1

LTRF: 4/10(1)

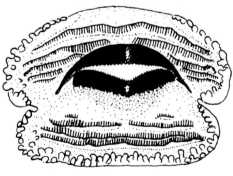

The LTRF formula here is: 5(2-5)/4(1-2), indicating that there are five rows in the upper jaw, of which rows 2-5 are divided, and 4 rows in the lower jaw, of which rows 1 and 2 are divided.

Modified from Anstis, M. (2002) *Tadpoles of South-eastern Australia a guide with keys.* New Holland Publishers, Sydney, Australia.

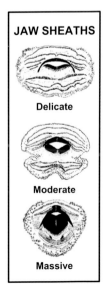

JAW SHEATHS

Delicate

Moderate

Massive

HOW TO USE THIS BOOK

Every southern African species of frog (and most of their tadpoles) is individually described and illustrated in this book. Descriptions are grouped by genus and each genus is introduced on facing, tinted pages, which include a key to the species in that genus. Where a genus comprises only one species, the genus and species descriptions are combined. Reliable identification of specimens can best be achieved by following this step-by step process:

1 Work through the FIELD KEY TO THE GENERA OF ADULT FROGS (pages 68–74) to determine the genus to which the specimen belongs.

2 Turn to the relevant genus description page and check whether the specimen conforms to the points listed in the DISTINCTIVE CHARACTERS box. If not, retrace the selections made in the key process.

3 Work through the KEY TO SPECIES on the genus page to identify the species.

4 Turn to the relevant species description page and ensure that the following questions are answered positively:

A Was the specimen found within the distribution range indicated in the **map**?

B Is the general appearance similar to the photographs and **description**, remembering that colour and patterns can vary considerably?

C Does the specimen conform to all of the points in the **KEY ID POINTS** box?

D Was it found in or near the type of **habitat** described?

E Is it approximately the same length as the **average length bar**? **Note:** smaller than average juveniles are often encountered.

F If the frog was heard calling, does the call heard match the **call description** given for each species, as well as the **sound spectrogram** (pages 464–481)? Guidance on the interpretation of spectrograms is given.

G The most reliable method of field identification is to match the call to the corresponding recorded call on the accompanying **CD**, as indicated by the TRACK LIST OF SOUTHERN AFRICAN FROG CALLS (pages 482–483).

5 Tadpole identification follows a similar series of steps, starting with the FIELD KEY TO THE FAMILIES AND GENERA OF TADPOLES (pages 75–79).

6 Information about the **biology** and **ecology** of amphibians is given on pages 30–66 and contributes to a better understanding of the complexity, fascination and importance of amphibian life in southern Africa.

7 The GLOSSARY (pages 460–463) will assist with unfamiliar terms.

8 A comprehensive BIBLIOGRAPHY of literature relevant to southern African amphibians is available on the accompanying CD.

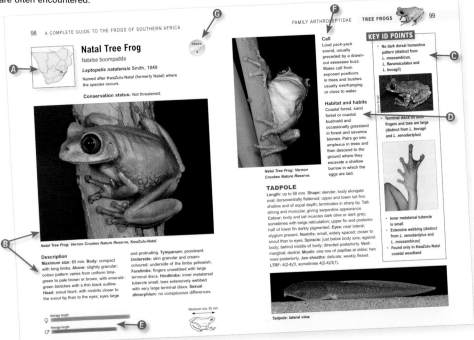

98   A COMPLETE GUIDE TO THE FROGS OF SOUTHERN AFRICA

Natal Tree Frog
Natalse boompadda

Leptopelis natalensis Smith, 1849

Named after KwaZulu-Natal (formerly Natal) where the species occurs.

Conservation status: Not threatened.

Natal Tree Frog: Vernon Crookes Nature Reserve, KwaZulu-Natal.

Description
Maximum size: 65 mm. **Body:** compact with long limbs. **Above:** slightly granular; colour pattern varies from uniform lime-green to pale brown or brown, with emerald-green blotches with a thin black outline. **Head:** snout blunt, with nostrils closer to the snout tip than to the eyes; eyes large and protruding. **Tympanum:** prominent. **Underside:** skin granular and cream-coloured; underside of the limbs yellowish. **Forelimbs:** fingers unwebbed with large terminal discs. **Hindlimbs:** inner metatarsal tubercle small; toes extensively webbed with very large terminal discs. **Sexual dimorphism:** no conspicuous differences.

Average length ♀
Average length ♂

Maximum size: 65 mm

FAMILY ARTHROLEPTIDAE   TREE FROGS   99

Call
Loud yack-yack sound, usually preceded by a drawn-out eeeeeee buzz. Males call from exposed positions in trees and bushes usually overhanging or close to water.

Habitat and habits
Coastal forest, sand forest or coastal bushveld and occasionally grassland in forest and savanna biomes. Pairs go into amplexus in trees and then descend to the ground where they excavate a shallow burrow in which the eggs are laid.

Natal Tree Frog: Vernon Crookes Nature Reserve.

TADPOLE
Length: up to 50 mm. **Shape:** slender; body elongate oval; dorsoventrally flattened; upper and lower tail fins shallow and of equal depth; terminates in sharp tip. **Tail:** strong and muscular, giving serpentine appearance. **Colour:** body and tail muscles dark olive or dark grey; sometimes with beige reticulation; upper fin and posterior half of lower fin darkly pigmented. **Eyes:** near lateral; elygium present. **Nostrils:** small, widely spaced; closer to snout than to eyes. **Spiracle:** just below body axis; against body; behind middle of body; directed posteriorly. **Vent:** marginal; dextral. **Mouth:** one row of papillae at sides; two rows posteriorly. **Jaw sheaths:** delicate; weakly flexed. LTRF: 4(2-4)/3, sometimes 4(2-4)/3(1).

Tadpole: lateral view.

KEY ID POINTS

- No dark dorsal horseshoe pattern (distinct from *L. mossambicus*, *L. flavomaculatus* and *L. bocagii*)
- Terminal discs on both fingers and toes are large (distinct from *L. bocagii* and *L. xenodactylus*)
- Inner metatarsal tubercle is small
- Extensive webbing (distinct from *L. xenodactylus* and *L. mossambicus*)
- Found only in KwaZulu-Natal coastal woodland

CLASSIFICATION AND TAXONOMY

Classification is the process by which organisms are grouped systematically. Species in which there are indicators of a common evolutionary ancestor are grouped as genera. Genera sharing a common ancestor are assembled as families, families similarly as orders, orders as classes, and classes as phyla. Taxonomy is the science of assigning organisms to their positions within this classification system and naming them according to tightly prescribed principles developed originally in the 18th century by Carolus Linnaeus.

CLASSIFICATION OF FROGS WITHIN THE ANIMAL KINGDOM	
PHYLUM	The animal kingdom is divided into 25 phyla. Frogs belong in the phylum Chordata – animals with a notachord and a hollow dorsal nerve cord. Most familiar animals belong to the sub-phylum Vertebrata (vertebrates).
CLASS	There are 9 classes of vertebrates. Frogs belong to the class Amphibia. (Other classes are Reptiles, Birds, Mammals and 5 classes of Fish.)
ORDER	Amphibians are divided into 3 orders comprising about 6 000 species: Anura (frogs), Urodela (salamanders and newts) and Apoda (caecilians). Only 1 of these, the Anura, occurs in southern Africa.
FAMILY	There are 32 families of frogs in the world, 13 of which are represented in southern Africa.
GENUS	About 270 genera of frogs exist worldwide; 33 occur in southern Africa.
SPECIES	Worldwide, there are about 5 200 described species of frogs and 157 of these are found in southern Africa.

The phylum Chordata (LATIN *chorda* = rope or cord)

Chordate animals have an axial notachord. The phylum includes certain worm-like and primitive aquatic animals, but the most familiar Chordata are the vertebrates which, in addition to amphibians, include fish, reptiles, birds and mammals.

The class Amphibia (GREEGREEK *amphi* = double; bios = life)

Amphibians are a group of vertebrate animals characterised by having two distinct phases in their lives. Although there are many exceptions, the two phases generally comprise an aquatic, larval stage – the tadpole – and a terrestrial, reproductive adult stage. Different species use a variety of strategies to protect themselves from desiccation and exposure to a harsh environment. They lay eggs without shells and these are fertilised externally as they are being laid.

Amphibians are the evolutionary ancestors of all terrestrial vertebrates – reptiles, birds, mammals and modern amphibians. In prehistoric times they were more prolific and diverse, but today only three orders remain. No marine amphibians are known.

The order Anura (GREEGREEK *an* = absent; oura = tail)

These are the frogs with which most people in southern Africa are familiar. The order Anura is the only amphibian order that occurs in southern Africa. The adult form is a squat tetrapod that loses its tail when it metamorphoses from the larval tadpole. Many of the common species have well-developed hindlegs, giving rise to the alternative name for this order, **Salienta** (LATIN *saliens* = leaping).

Anura is the largest order of amphibians, with more than 5 200 species known worldwide. The order has adapted to almost every habitat type, from rain forest to desert, and occurs on every continent and large island except Antarctica.

Unlike the other orders, the Anura have the ability to vocalise and this is an important aspect of their reproductive biology (see pages 40 and 43–45).

The order Urodela (GREEGREEK *ouros* = tail; *delos* = evident)

The order includes the salamanders and newts. They retain a tail throughout the larval and adult stages, and the alternative Latin name, **Caudata**, means 'with a tail'. There are about 550 species, all of which occur in the northern hemisphere. Most are about 150 mm in length but the Japanese and Chinese giant salamanders may exceed 1.5 m. Unlike frogs, the front and hindlegs are of equal size and positioned at right angles to the elongated body. In some species the limbs may be rudimentary or absent altogether. The Urodela are voiceless.

Marbled Newt, Triturus marmoratus: *an example of the Urodela.*

The order Apoda (GREEGREEK *a* = without; *poda* = feet)

Caecilians are naked, legless, tail-less amphibians. To date, only 173 species have been described. They occur in the tropical forests of South America, Africa and South East Asia and the biggest species may reach a length of 1.5 m. Almost all species are burrowers. Their eyes are rudimentary or absent and they have a pair of small sensory tentacles on the head to help them navigate underground where they prey on small invertebrates in the soil. The alternative name for the order is **Gymnophiona** (GREEK *gymnos* = naked; *phiona* = snake-like) but they differ from snakes and lizards by having no tail and having a terminal anus. Unlike other amphibians, fertilisation occurs internally. Eggs are usually laid in moist soil near water and, while some larvae are aquatic, most complete their entire development inside the egg. Some species guard their eggs by curling up around them.

Sao Tome Caecilian
Schistometopum thomense:
an example of the Apoda.
Eyes are rudimentary or absent.

Marius Burger

Marius Burger

Anuran families

The Anura are divided into 32 families worldwide, of which 13 are represented in southern Africa. In the past, taxonomists used skeletal and external morphological characters to classify frogs, and species were assembled into families because they appeared to be anatomically similar. Modern classification, however, relies extensively on mitochondrial DNA analysis to determine the genetic associations that make up families. In 2006 a group of international taxonomists led by Darrel Frost presented a major taxonomic revision of the world's amphibians based on modern genetics. This work, *The Amphibian Tree of Life*, demonstrates that species that look similar are not necessarily closely related, and that many of the old assumptions that defined certain families were incorrect. The new classification by Frost *et al.* is a working hypothesis, and may require changes in the future as new information becomes available.

After consultation with several prominent herpetologists around the globe, the authors of this field guide chose to follow Frost *et al.* because their work contributes significantly to scientific understanding of amphibian evolution and genetic relationships. For the fieldworker, however, the new classification of families may compound the difficulties of identification because several families include genera that are so diverse in appearance that they cannot easily be recognised as a single family. As an aid to the reader, therefore, pictures of typical representatives of each genus appear at the top corner of each species description.

Genera

The 13 families of southern African frogs are divided into 34 genera, each of which has a common ancestry indicated by its DNA. Although families are not always identifiable by external appearance, genera exhibit certain morphological or ecological characteristics that allow them to be identified in the field.

AN EXPLANATION OF THE TERMS 'FROGS' AND 'TOADS'

For many centuries the name 'toad' was applied to the European species of the genus *Bufo* while 'frog' was the common term for other Anura, mostly of the genus *Rana*. The two are easily distinguishable in Europe and were originally regarded as two types of reptile, like lizards or snakes. As scientific taxonomy progressed in the 18th and 19th centuries, frogs and toads were reclassified as two families of amphibians, a separate class from reptiles. In southern Africa there are 13 amphibian families (see pages 19–29). Toads are one of the frog families, along with the Rain Frog family, Ghost Frogs, Reed Frogs and others. It is therefore incorrect to separate frogs from toads; one is a family (toads) within an order (frogs).

Mascarene Grass Frog: a typical frog.

Guttural Toad: toads are one of the many frog families.

Species

The basic building block of the classification system is the species. In southern Africa 160 species of frogs have been described and new ones are discovered regularly as new habitats are explored and techniques for identifying species are improved.

In amphibians and other sexually reproducing animals, a species is defined as a population of animals capable of producing viable offspring by breeding among themselves but not with other species. Speciation usually occurs when a group of animals is genetically separated from other members of its species as a result of geographical, ecological or climatic change. Thus isolated, the group evolves independently inherited characteristics and becomes a separate allopatric species.

In some circumstances, groups within a species may become isolated. In time, each segregated group may show slight morphological differences yet still retain the ability to interbreed if reconnected. Such groups are considered to be **subspecies**.

In other instances, for example Painted Reed Frogs, the species is widely distributed and groups of frogs in different parts of the range show different local colour patterns. Some taxonomists accord subspecific status to the different geographically located colour forms, but there are no clear-cut boundaries between each form and breeding is continuous throughout the range. Such situations are better referred to as **clines** or **clinal population groups** than as subspecies.

SCIENTIFIC NOMENCLATURE

One of the most important aspects of taxonomy is the description and naming of species. A description is based on a **type specimen** – that is, a single specimen or small collection, usually preserved and lodged in a museum or recognised repository where scientists may have access to it in order to study it.

The scientific name of each species follows the binomial system first introduced by Carolus Linnaeus in 1735. It comprises two Latinised words, the first of which is used for all members of the genus, and the other identifies the species. The same specific name may be used in different genera (for example, *Pyxicephalus adspersus* and *Breviceps adspersus*) but in combination with a generic name, each is unique. A third Latinised name may be added to denote a subspecies. Generic, specific and subspecific names are customarily italicised, and the generic name is spelt with an initial capital letter. Family, order and class names are not italicised.

The full scientific name also includes the name of the person who first described the species for science and the date of the description. If the species is reassigned to another genus after its original description, the first describer's name appears in brackets. For example, the correct scientific name of the Painted Reed Frog is *Hyperolius marmoratus* Rapp, 1842, and the Clicking Stream Frog is named *Strongylopus grayii* (Smith, 1849). In the second example, 'Smith, 1849' is bracketed because Smith originally named the species *Rana grayii*. When the name of a genus is given without reference to any particular species, the name of the person who described the genus is given, as well as the date of description.

Strict principles apply to the naming of species and this is supervised by the International Code of Zoological Nomenclature. Once accepted in the scientific literature, a name is used universally in all countries irrespective of local language, as shown below:

GENUS	SPECIES	SUBSPECIES	DESCRIBER	DESCRIPTION DATE
Hildebrandtia	*ornata*	*ornata*	(Peters)	1878

EVOLUTION OF AMPHIBIANS

Amphibians were the first vertebrates to emerge from the water and exploit the terrestrial landscape more than 350 million years ago. The process entailed substantial physiological changes including the development of a skeleton capable of supporting the weight of the body in air, and the evolution of lungs that could inhale and absorb free oxygen from the atmosphere. These early amphibians were the common ancestors of all terrestrial vertebrates – mammals, birds, reptiles and modern amphibians.

The fossil record of frog evolution is imperfect, but tail-less anurans appear to have emerged during the Triassic prior to the dinosaurs. Southern African anurans can be traced to this period. *Vulcanobatrachus mandelae*, a frog not unlike the modern Platanna, existed in the part of Gondwana that is now southern Africa 120 million years ago. The main developments in the evolution of southern African amphibians are shown on the next two pages.

Fossil frog Vulcanobatrachus mandelai *from the Cretaceous deposits in the Marydale District, Northern Cape, about 120 million years ago.*

Fossil tadpole from Europe: the soft body parts of tadpoles rarely fossilise and our knowledge of tadpole evolution is therefore limited.

EVOLUTION

Early tetrapod evolution and descent of amphibians

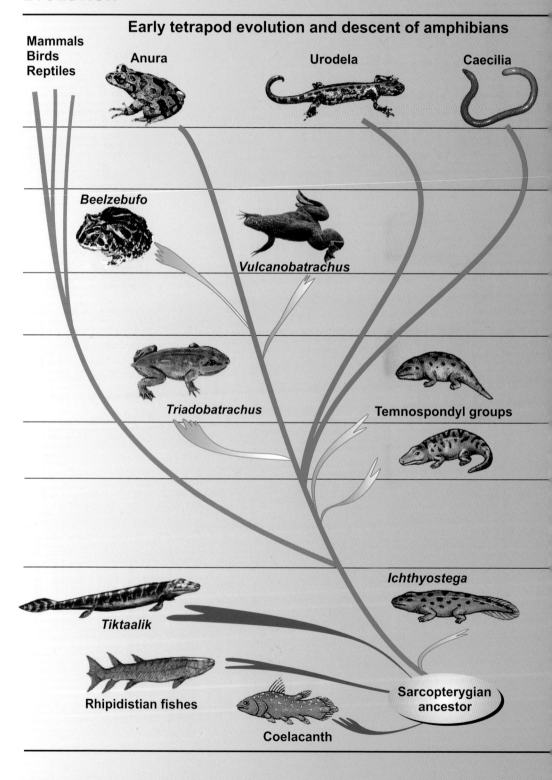

Mammals
Birds
Reptiles

Anura

Urodela

Caecilia

Beelzebufo

Vulcanobatrachus

Triadobatrachus

Temnospondyl groups

Ichthyostega

Tiktaalik

Rhipidistian fishes

Coelacanth

Sarcopterygian ancestor

ERA	PERIOD	MYA*	CONDITIONS	AMPHIBIAN EVOLUTION
CENOZOIC	NEOGENE (QUATERNARY)	0	Human evolution; possible start of *sixth mass extinction* of living species.	*Xenopus* changes little physically, but colonises diverse aquatic habitats; other southern African species radiate; frog populations decline globally.
CENOZOIC	PALAEOGENE (TERTIARY)	23	Modern reptiles and mammals evolve; global cooling.	Emergence in Namibia of *Xenopus stromeri* (similar to the modern platanna *Xenopus laevis*).
MESOZOIC	CRETACEOUS	65	Breakup of Gondwana (65 mya); massive asteroid impact contributes to the *fifth mass extinction* of living species, and demise of dinosaurs; primitive birds emerge.	Xenopoides-like *Vulcanobatrachus* (primitive antecedents of genus *Xenopus*) dated to about 120 mya; fossil *Beelzebufo*, discovered in Madagascar, indicates that the island may have been connected to South America as late as 60 mya (after separating from Africa about 80 mya).
MESOZOIC	JURASSIC	145	Large dinosaurs emerge; reptiles proliferate throughout Africa.	True Anurans begin to radiate throughout the world.
MESOZOIC	TRIASSIC	200	*Fourth mass extinction* of living species (probably caused by asteroid impact); global warming; demise of mammal-like reptiles.	Tail-less Gondwana amphibian, *Triadobatrachus* (fossil found in Madagascar) pre-dates break-up of Gondwana (65 mya) and has more vertebrae than true Anurans – indicating possible ancestor of today's southern hemisphere frogs.
PALAEOZOIC	PERMIAN	251	Reptiles become dominant species; *third mass extinction* of living species (caused by seismic activity).	Gondwana fossils (such as the Temnospondyl groups found in fossil record of Australia and southern Africa) diversify further – identifiable as ancestors of modern amphibians.
PALAEOZOIC	CARBONIFEROUS	299	Northern hemisphere warm and wet (mosses and ferns flourish), southern hemisphere arid; global cooling.	Amphibians dominate the landscape, some resembling crocodiles several metres long; adapt to terrestrial conditions with greater agility and extensive webbing on the feet; skin develops as a respiratory organ; at least 15 amphibian orders known from this period, but unclear which evolve to become today's three orders.
PALAEOZOIC	DEVONIAN	359	Mild global temperature; fluctuating wet and dry periods; *second mass extinction* of living species (caused by multiple asteroid impacts followed by rapid radiation); all vertebrates aquatic – confined to swamps and shallow seas and thus vulnerable to desiccation in low water levels.	Terrestrial vertebrates descend from a Sarcopterygian ancestor (lobed fin fish); fossilised fins of Rhipidistian fishes similar to the limbs of early amphibians, and indicate probable ability to inhabit terrestrial environments. *Tiktaalik* has neck and possibly primitive lungs – develops ability to support itself on robust weight-bearing, articulated fins (375 mya); earliest amphibian in fossil record is *Ichthyostega*, a 1.5 m long monitor-like creature, dating from about 367 mya, which can 'walk' in swamps – this adaptation probably leads to ability to inhabit terrestrial environments.
		416		
			* million years ago	

SYSTEMATIC LIST OF SOUTHERN AFRICAN FROGS

Scientific and common names of species

The following tables list the 13 families, 33 genera and 157 species of frogs that occur in Namibia, Botswana, South Africa, Zimbabwe, Swaziland, Lesotho and Mozambique south of the Zambezi River. Family headings are colour-coded to correspond with the coloured tabs that appear at the top, right-hand corner of the descriptive pages. A small illustration of a typical member of the family or genus is included in the tab and a page reference to the descriptive page is given.

The scientific name appears in the first column of the table. This is followed in the next two columns by the standard common English and Afrikaans names. Unlike birds or mammals, few frogs have widely known common names. In the past, authors often used names of their own or local popular names, which frequently led to duplication or confusion. In 1979, after wide discussion and research, *South African Frogs* (Passmore and Carruthers) assigned standard English names to all South African species. These, together with standard Afrikaans names, were reviewed and formalised in the *Atlas and Red Data Book of the Frogs of South Africa, Lesotho and Swaziland* (Minter *et al.* 2004) and those names have been retained here. Where species have not been included in the *Atlas*, English names have been taken from 'Amphibian Species of the World' **http://research.amnh.org/ herpetology/amphibia/index.php** and Afrikaans names have had to be created.

The final column in the table lists the common names that have been used in earlier publications so that they can be cross-referenced to the modern literature.

Image provided by Iziko Museums of Cape Town

PIONEER OF SOUTHERN AFRICAN FROGS

The first scientific work on southern African frogs was published in 1849 by Dr Andrew Smith in his monumental multi-volume *The Zoology of South Africa,* illustrated by George Henry Ford. It contained detailed descriptions and paintings of the 26 species of South African frogs then known, 14 of which Smith had discovered himself.

Andrew Smith was a Scottish military doctor who resided at the Cape from 1821 to 1839. Under the patronage of the governor Lord Charles Somerset he founded the South African Museum. He was also an explorer and diplomat for the colonial government and took an expedition north of the Vaal River to meet African leaders including Mzilikazi.

Scientific name	Standard English name	Standard Afrikaans name	Other published names
FAMILY ARTHROLEPTIDAE **Squeakers and Tree Frogs** (pp.80–101)			
Genus ***Arthroleptis***	Squeakers	*Kikkers*	
Arthroleptis stenodactylus	Shovel-footed Squeaker	*Graafpootkikker*	Common Squeaker, Dune Squeaker, Kihengo Screeching Frog, Narrow-footed Humus Frog, Savanna Squeaking Frog, Shovel-footed Bush Squeaker, *Duinkikker, Duinekikker*
Arthroleptis troglodytes	Cave Squeaker	*Grotkikker*	Poynton's Humus Frog, Rock Humus Frog, South Rhodesia Screeching Frog, Troglodyte Humus Frog, Troglodyte Squeaker
Arthroleptis xenodactyloides	Dwarf Squeaker	*Dwergkikker*	Chirinda Cricket Frog, Chirinda Screeching Frog, Dwarf Squeaker, Hewitt's Bush Squeaker, Hewitt's Humus Frog, Nyika Squeaker
Arthroleptis wahlbergii	Bush Squeaker	*Boskikker*	Wahlberg's Forest Frog, Wahlberg's Frog, Wahlberg's Humus Frog
Genus ***Leptopelis***	Tree Frogs	*Boompaddas*	
Leptopelis bocagii	Bocage's Tree Frog	*Bocage se boompadda*	Bocage's Burrowing Frog, Bocage's Burrowing Leaf Frog, Bocage's Frog, Horseshoe Forest Treefrog
Leptopelis broadleyi	Broadley's Tree Frog	*Broadley se boompadda*	Bagamoyo Forest Treefrog, Broadley's Tree Frog, Triad Tree Frog
Leptopelis flavomaculatus	Yellow-spotted Tree Frog	*Geelspikkelboompadda*	Brown Forest Treefrog, Brown-backed Tree Frog, Johnston's Treefrog
Leptopelis mossambicus	Brown-backed Tree Frog	*Bruinrugboompadda*	Mozambique Tree Frog, Mossambique Forest Treefrog
Leptopelis natalensis	Natal Tree Frog	*Natalse boompadda*	Forest Tree Frog, Natal Forest Treefrog, Raucous Tree Frog, *Woudboompadda*
Leptopelis xenodactylus	Long-toed Tree Frog	*Langtoonboompadda*	Natal Tree Frog, Weza Forest Treefrog

Scientific name	Standard English name	Standard Afrikaans name	Other published names
FAMILY BREVICIPITIDAE **Rain Frogs** (pp.102–135)			
Genus ***Breviceps***	Rain Frogs	*Reënpaddas*	
Breviceps acutirostris	Strawberry Rain Frog	*Aarbeireënpadda*	Cape Short-headed Frog, *Pienkreënpadda, Aarbei-blaasoppadda*
Breviceps adspersus	Bushveld Rain Frog	*Bosveldreënpadda*	Bushveld Rain Frog, Common Rain Frog, Common Short-headed Frog, Peters' Rain Frog, South African Short-head, Transvaal Rain Frog, Transvaal Short-headed Frog, *Blaasop, Transvaal blaasop*
Breviceps bagginsi	Bilbo's Rain Frog	*Bilbo se reënpadda*	*Bilbo se blaasoppadda*

Scientific name	Common name	Afrikaans name	Other names
Breviceps fuscus	Plain Rain Frog	Swartreënpadda	Black Rain Frog, Brown Short-headed Frog, Gewone Janblom, Blaasoppadda, Knysnablaasop
Breviceps gibbosus	Cape Rain Frog	Kaapse reënpadda	Cape Short-head, South African Short-headed Frog, Giant Rain Frog, Headless Frog, Hunched Toad, Linnaeus' Rainfrog, Cape Rain Frog, Linnaeus' Short-headed Frog, Rain Frog, Short-headed Frog, South African Rain Frog, Verruculose Rainfrog, Verruculose Short-headed Frog, blaasop, Jan Blom, Kaapse Janblom, Kaapse blaasoppadda, Aartappelpadda
Breviceps macrops	Desert Rain Frog	Woestynreënpadda	Boulenger's Short-headed Frog, Web-footed Rain Frog, Melkpadda, Woestynblaasoppadda
Breviceps montanus	Cape Mountain Rain Frog	Kaapse bergreënpadda	Mountain Blaasop, Mountain Rain Frog, Mountain Short-headed Frog, Kaapse bergblaasoppadda
Breviceps mossambicus	Mozambique Rain Frog	Mosambiekse reënpadda	Flat-faced Frog, Flat-faced Rain Frog, Moçambique Rain Frog, Mozambique Rain Frog, Mozambique Short-headed Frog, Mosambiek blaasop
Breviceps namaquensis	Namaqua Rain Frog	Namakwareënpadda	Namaqua Short-headed Frog, Namakwa blaasoppadda, Blaasoppadda
Breviceps poweri	Power's Rain Frog	Power se reënpadda	Power's Short-headed Frog
Breviceps rosei	Sand Rain Frog	Rose se reënpadda	Rose's Rain Frog, Rose's Rainfrog, Rose's Short-headed Frog, Sand Rain Frog, Rose se blaasoppadda, Rose's blaasop, Sandblaasoppadda, Sandreënpadda
Breviceps sopranus	Whistling Rain Frog	Fluitreënpadda	Fluitende blaasoppadda
Breviceps sylvestris	Northern Forest Rain Frog	Transvaal woudreënpadda	Forest Rain Frog, Forest Short-headed Frog, Transvaal Forest Rain Fog, Transvaal woudblaasoppadda
Breviceps verrucosus	Plaintive Rain Frog	Klareënpadda	Natal Short-headed Frog, Fluitblaasoppadda, Klaende reënpadda, Klaende blaasoppadda
Genus Probreviceps	Forest Rain Frogs	Woudreënpaddas	Primitive Rain Frogs
Probreviceps rhodesianus	Highland Forest Rain Frog	Hoëveldse woudreënpadda	Highland Primitive Rain Frog, Zimbabwe Big-fingered Frog

FAMILY BUFONIDAE
Toads (pp. 136–195)

Scientific name	Common name	Afrikaans name	Other names
Genus Amietophrynus	Typical Toads	Gewone-skurwepaddas	
Amietophrynus garmani	Eastern Olive Toad	Olyfskurwepadda	Garman's Toad, Olive Toad, Northern Mottled Toad, Light-nosed Toad, Garman's Square-marked Toad, Garman's Square-backed Toad, Eastern Olive Toad
Amietophrynus gutturalis	Guttural Toad	Gorrelskurwepadda	Common African Toad, Flat-backed Toad, Greater Cross-marked Toad, Guttural Toad, Leopard Toad, Lobatsi Toad, Marbled Toad, Common Toad, Square-marked Toad

Amietophrynus lemairii	Lemaire's Toad	*Lemaire se skurwepadda*	Lemaire's Toad, Pweto Toad, Yellow Swamp Toad
Amietophrynus maculatus	Flat-backed Toad	*Gestreepte skurwepadda*	Flat-backed Toad, Hallowell's Toad, Lesser Cross-marked Toad, Lesser Square-marked Toad, Merten's Striped Toad, Striped Toad
Amietophrynus pantherinus	Western Leopard Toad	*Westelike luiperdskurwepadda*	August Frog, Cape Toad, Leopard Toad, Panther Toad, Southern Panther Toad
Amietophrynus pardalis	Eastern Leopard Toad	*Oostelike luiperdskurwepadda*	August Toad, Gleniffer Toad, Leopard Toad, Snoring Toad
Amietophrynus poweri	Western Olive Toad	*Power se skurwepadda*	Common Lowveld Toad, Power's Toad, Kimberley Toad
Amietophrynus rangeri	Raucous Toad	*Lawaaiskurwepadda*	Kei Road Toad, Ranger's Toad, *Lawaaipadda*
Genus **Poyntonophrynus**	Pygmy Toads	**Dwergskurwepaddas**	
Poyntonophrynus beiranus	Beira Pygmy Toad	*Beira-dwergskurwepadda*	Beira's Toad, Beira Toad
Poyntonophrynus damaranus	Damaraland Pygmy Toad	*Damara-dwergskurwepadda*	
Poyntonophrynus dombensis	Dombe Pygmy Toad	*Dombe-dwergskurwepadda*	Dombe Toad
Poyntonophrynus fenoulheti	Northern Pygmy Toad	*Noordelike dwergskurwepadda*	Fenoulheti's Pygmy Toad, Fenoulhet's Toad, Grindley's Pygmy Toad, Newington Toad, Transvaal Dwarf Toad, Transvaal Pygmy Toad
Poyntonophrynus hoeschi	Hoesch's Pygmy Toad	*Hoesch se dwergskurwepadda*	Okahandja Toad, Hoesch's Toad
Poyntonophrynus kavangensis	Kavango Pygmy Toad	*Kavango-dwergskurwepadda*	Kavanga Toad, Kavango Toad, Khwai River Toad
Poyntonophrynus vertebralis	Southern Pygmy Toad	*Suidelike dwergskurwepadda*	African Dwarf Toad, Flat Toad, Pygmy Toad
Genus **Vandijkophrynus**	Van Dijk's Toads	**Van Dijk skurwepaddas**	
Vandijkophrynus amatolicus	Amatola Toad	*Amatola-skurwepadda*	
Vandijkophrynus angusticeps	Cape Sand Toad	*Sandskurwepadda*	Sand Toad, Common Cape Toad, Narrow-headed Toad
Vandijkophrynus gariepensis	Karoo Toad	*Karooskurwepadda*	*Pispadda*
Vandijkophrynus inyangae	Inyanga Toad	*Inyanga-skurwepadda*	Inyangani Toad
Vandijkophrynus robinsoni	Paradise Toad	*Paradyskloof-skurwepadda*	
Genus **Capensibufo**	Mountain Toadlets	**Bergskurwepaddas**	
Capensibufo rosei	Rose's Mountain Toadlet	*Rose se bergskurwepadda*	Cape Mountain Toad, Muizenberg Cape Toad, Rose's Mountain Toad, Rose's Toad, Striped Mountain Toad, *Rose se skurwepaddatjie*
Capensibufo tradouwi	Tradouw Mountain Toadlet	*Tradouw-bergskurwepadda*	Cape Mountain Toad, Swellendam Cape Toad, Tradouw Mountain Toad, Tradouw's Toad

Genus *Schismaderma*	**Red Toad**	**Rooiskurwepadda**	
Schismaderma carens	Red Toad	Rooiskurwepadda	
Genus *Mertensophryne*	**Forest Toads**	**Woudskurwepaddas**	
Mertensophryne anotis	Chirinda Toad	Chirinda-woudskurwepadda	Chirinda Forest Toad, Boulenger's Earless Toad, Mashonaland Toad

FAMILY HELEOPHRYNIDAE
Ghost Frogs (pp.196–213)

Genus *Hadromophryne*	**Cascade Frog**	**Snelstroompadda**	
Hadromophryne natalensis	Natal Cascade Frog	Natalse snelstroompadda	Natal Ghost Frog, Heleo Frog, Natal Torrent Frog, Southeastern Ghost Frog, Southeastern Torrent Frog
Genus *Heleophryne*	**Ghost Frogs**	**Spookpaddas**	
Heleophryne depressa	Cederberg Ghost Frog	Sederbergspookpadda	
Heleophryne hewitti	Hewitt's Ghost Frog	Hewitt se spookpadda	Hewitt's African Ghost Frog, *Elandsberg-spookpadda*
Heleophryne orientalis	Eastern Ghost Frog	Oostelike spookpadda	East Cape Ghost Frog, East Cape Torrent Frog
Heleophryne purcelli	Cape Ghost Frog	Kaapse spookpadda	
Heleophryne regis	Southern Ghost Frog	Suidelike spookpadda	Rex's Ghost Frog, Rex's Torrent Frog, Royal Ghost Frog, Southern Ghost Frog
Heleophryne rosei	Table Mountain Ghost Frog	Tafelberg-spookpadda	Ghost Frog, Rose's Ghost Frog, Rose's Torrent Frog, Skeleton Gorge Ghost Frog, Thumbed Ghost Frog

FAMILY HEMISOTIDAE
Shovel-nosed Frogs (pp.214–221)

Genus *Hemisus*	**Shovel-nosed Frogs**	**Graafneuspaddas**	
Hemisus guineensis	Guinea Shovel-nosed Frog	Guinee-graafneuspadda	Broadleys Shovel-nosed Frog, Guinea Shovelsnout Frog, Guinea Shovel-snouted Frog, Pig-nosed Frog
Hemisus guttatus	Spotted Shovel-nosed Frog	Gespikkelde graafneuspadda	Spotted Burrowing Frog, Spotted Pig-nosed Frog, Spotted Shovelnose Frog, Spotted Shovel-snouted Frog, Spotted Snout-burrower, *Gespikkelde spitsbekpadda*

Scientific name	Common name	Afrikaans	Other names
Hemisus marmoratus	Mottled Shovel-nosed Frog	*Marmergraafneuspadda*	Marbled Pig-nosed Frog, Marbled Shovelnose Frog, Marbled Shovel-snouted Frog, Marbled Snout-burrower, Mottled Burrowing Frog, Mottled Shovel-nosed Frog, Pig-nosed Frog, Shovel-nosed Burrowing Frog, *Gemarmerde graafneuspadda*

FAMILY HYPEROLIIDAE
Reed Frogs (pp.222–280)

Scientific name	Common name	Afrikaans	Other names
Genus *Afrixalus*	**Leaf-folding Frogs**	**Blaarvoupaddas**	
Afrixalus crotalus	Snoring Leaf-folding Frog	*Snorkblaarvoupadda*	*Blaarnespadda*
Afrixalus aureus	Golden Leaf-folding Frog	*Goueblaarvoupadda*	Golden Dwarf Reed Frog, Golden Banana Frog, Golden Spiny Reed Frog, Golden Dwarf Leaf-folding Frog
Afrixalus delicatus	Delicate Leaf-folding Frog	*Delikate blaarvoupadda*	Pickersgill's Banana Frog, Delicate Spiny Reed Frog, *Sierlike blaarnespadda*
Afrixalus fornasinii	Greater Leaf-folding Frog	*Grootblaarvoupadda*	Brown and White Spiny Reed Frog, Brown-striped Spiny Reed Frog, Fornasini's Banana Frog, Fornasini's Spiny Reed Frog, Mozambique Banana Frog, Silver-banded Banana Frog, Spiny Reed Frog, Zaire Banana Frog, *Grootblaarpadda*
Afrixalus knysnae	Knysna Leaf-folding Frog	*Knysna-blaarvoupadda*	Knysna Banana Frog, Knysna Spiny Reed Frog, *Knysna-blaarpadda*
Afrixalus spinifrons	Natal Leaf-folding Frog	*Natalse blaarvoupadda*	Golden Spiny Reed Frog, Natal Banana Frog, Natal Spiny Reed Frog, *Natalse blaarnespadda*, Intermediate Spiny Reed Frog
Genus *Hyperolius*	**Reed Frogs**	**Rietpaddas**	
Hyperolius poweri	Power's Sharp-nosed Reed Frog	*Power se skerpneusrietpadda*	Brown Long Reed Frog, Green Long Reed Frog, Günther's Sharp-nosed Reed Frog, Long Reed Frog, Sharp-nosed Reed Frog
Hyperolius argus	Argus Reed Frog	*Argus-rietpadda*	Argus Sedge Frog, Argus-eyed Frog, Argus-spotted Sedge Frog, Boror Reed Frog, Golden Sedge Frog, Golden Spotted Reed Frog, Yellow Spotted Reed Frog, *Argusrietpaddatjie*
Hyperolius benguellensis	Bocage's Sharp-nosed Reed Frog	*Bocage se skerpneusrietpadda*	Benguella Reed Frog
Hyperolius horstockii	Arum Lily Frog	*Aronskelkrietpadda*	Arum Frog, Horstock's Arum Frog, Horstock's Reed Frog, Yellow-striped Reed Frog, *Varkblompadda*
Hyperolius marginatus	Marginated Reed Frog	*Rooiflankrietpadda*	Silver-striped Sedge Frog, Margined Sedge Frog
Hyperolius marmoratus	Painted Reed Frog	*Skilderbontrietpadda*	Ahl's African Reed Frog, Aposematic Reed Frog, Black and White Striped Reed Frog, Marbled Reed Frog, Marbled Rush Frog, Sangeve Reed Frog, Spotted Tree Frog, Striped Reed Frog, Striped Rush Frog, Variegated Rush Frog, White-lipped Reed Frog, *Gestreepte rietpaddatjie*, *Geverfde rietpadda*
Hyperolius mitchelli	Mitchell's Reed Frog	*Mitchell se rietpadda*	

Hyperolius nasutus	Long Reed Frog	*Langneusrietpadda*	Longnose Reed Frog, Long-nosed Reed Frog, Sharp-nosed Reed Frog, Sharp-and-blunt-snouted Sedge Frog
Hyperolius parallelus	Angolan Reed Frog	*Angolese rietpadda*	
Hyperolius parkeri	Parker's Reed Frog	*Parker se rietpadda*	Brown Sedge Frog, Green Sedge Frog
Hyperolius pickersgilli	Pickersgill's Reed Frog	*Pickersgill se rietpadda*	Avoca Reed Frog
Hyperolius pusillus	Water Lily Frog	*Waterleliepadda*	Dwarf Reed Frog, Lily Pad Frog, Translucent Tree Frog, Transparent Pygmy Sedge Frog, Water Lily Reed Frog, Water Lily Reed Frog
Hyperolius rhodesianus	Laurent's Reed Frog	*Laurent se rietpadda*	
Hyperolius semidiscus	Yellow-striped Reed Frog	*Geelstreeprietpadda*	
Hyperolius swynnertoni	Swynnerton's Reed Frog	*Swynnerton se rietpadda*	Broadley's Forest Treefrog, Broadley's Tree Frog
Hyperolius tuberilinguis	Tinker Reed Frog	*Groenrietpadda*	Green Reed Frog, Smith's Reed Frog, Straw Sedge Frog, Green Sedge Frog, Yellow-green Reed Frog
Genus Kassina	**Kassinas**	***Vleipaddas***	
Kassina maculata	Red-legged Kassina	*Rooibeenvleipadda*	Brown-spotted Tree Frog, Red-legged Pan Frog, Spotted Hylambates, Spotted Kassina, Spotted Kassin's Frog, Spotted Running Frog, Vlei Frog
Kassina senegalensis	Bubbling Kassina	*Borrelvleipadda*	Burbling Kassina, Running Frog, Senegal Frog, Senegal Kassina, Senegal Kassin's Frog, Senegal Land Frog, Senegal Running Frog
Genus Semnodactylus	**Rattling Frog**	***Ratelpadda***	
Semnodactylus wealii	Rattling Frog	*Ratelpadda*	Long-toed Running Frog, Rattling Kassina, Weale's Frog, Weale's Kassina, Weale's Kassina, Weale's Kassin's Frog, Weale's Frog, Weale's Running Frog

FAMILY MICROHYLIDAE
Rubber Frogs (pp.281–289)

Genus *Phrynomantis*	Rubber Frogs	*Rubberpaddas*	
Phrynomantis affinis	Spotted Rubber Frog	*Gespikkelde rubberpadda*	Northern Red-spotted Frog, Pweto Snake-necked Frog, Red-spotted Frog, *Spikkelrubberpadda*
Phrynomantis annectens	Marbled Rubber Frog	*Marmerrubberpadda*	Red-spotted Namibia Frog, Red Marbled Frog, Cape Snake-necked Frog, Red-spotted Frog, *Marmerpadda*
Phrynomantis bifasciatus	Banded Rubber Frog	*Gebande rubberpadda*	Red-banded Frog, Red-banded Rubber Frog, South African Snake-necked Frog, Two-banded Frog, Two-striped Frog

FAMILY PHRYNOBATRACHIDAE
Puddle Frogs (pp.290–299)

Genus Phrynobatrachus	Puddle Frogs	Modderpaddas	
Phrynobatrachus acridoides	East African Puddle Frog	Oostelike modderpadda	Cope's Toad Frog, Eastern Puddle Frog, Mababe Toad-frog, Small Puddle Frog, Zanzibar Puddle Frog, Zanzibar River Frog
Phrynobatrachus mababiensis	Dwarf Puddle Frog	Dwergmodderpadda	Chitiala Frog, Common Cricket Frog, Mababe Puddle Frog, Mababe River Frog, Mababi Puddle Frog
Phrynobatrachus natalensis	Snoring Puddle Frog	Snorkmodderpadda	Auata River Frog, Typical toad Frog, Murle River Frog, Natal Frog, Natal Puddle Frog, Natal River Frog, Puddle Frog, Scortecci's River Frog, Smith's Frog, Toad Frog
Phrynobatrachus parvulus	Small Puddle Frog	Kleinmodderpadda	Dwarf Puddle Frog, Loanda River Frog

FAMILY PTYCHADENIDAE
Grass Frogs (pp.300–327)

Genus Hildebrandtia	Ornate Frogs	Skilderbontpaddas	
Hildebrandtia ornata	Ornate Frog	Skilderbontpadda	African Ornate Frog, Black-throated Pyxie, Budgett's Burrowing Frog, Common Ornate Frog, Moeru Frog, Ornate Burrowing Frog, Ornate Pyxie, Southern Ornate Frog
Genus Ptychadena	Grass Frogs	Graspaddas	
Ptychadena anchietae	Plain Grass Frog	Rooiruggraspadda	Anchieta's Frog, Anchieta's Ridged Frog, Benguella Grassland Frog, Long-legged Grass Frog, Northern Rana, Savanna Ridged Frog
Ptychadena guibei	Guibe's Grass Frog	Guibé se graspadda	Guibe's Yellow Bellied Grass Frog, Guibe's Grassland Frog, Guibe's Ridged Frog
Ptychadena mapacha	Mapacha Grass Frog	Mapacha-graspadda	Mapacha Ridged Frog
Ptychadena mascareniensis	Mascarene Grass Frog	Maskareense graspadda	Broad-banded Rana, Broad-banded Ridged Frog, Mascarene Frog, Mascarene Grassland Frog, Mascarene Ridged Frog, Mascarene Rocket Frog
Ptychadena mossambica	Broad-banded Grass Frog	Breëbandgraspadda	Broad-banded Grass Frog, Moçambique Ridged Frog, Mozambique Grass Frog, Mozambique Grassland Frog, Mozambique Ridged Frog, Single-striped Grass Frog
Ptychadena oxyrhynchus	Sharp-nosed Grass Frog	Skerpneusgraspadda	Gevlekte graspadda

Ptychadena porosissima	Striped Grass Frog	*Gestreepte graspadda*	Ethiopia Grassland Frog, Grassland Ridged Frog, Steindachner's Frog, Three-striped Grass Frog, Three-striped Rana
Ptychadena schillukorum	Schilluk Grass Frog	*Schilluk-graspadda*	Sudan Grassland Frog, Schilluk Ridged Frog
Ptychadena subpunctata	Speckled-bellied Grass Frog	*Spikkelpens-graspadda*	African Spotted Frog, Bocage's Grass Frog, Bocage's Grassland Frog, Spotted Grass Frog, Spot-bellied Ridged Frog, Spotted Ridged Frog
Ptychadena taenioscelis	Dwarf Grass Frog	*Kleingraspadda*	Dwarf Rana, Lukula Grassland Frog, Small Ridged Frog, Spotted Throated Ridged Frog, Stripe-legged Frog
Ptychadena uzungwensis	Udzungwa Grass Frog	*Udzungwa-graspadda*	Udzungwa Ridged Frog, Uzungwe Grass Frog, Uzungwe Grassland Frog, Uzungwe Ridged Frog

FAMILY PIPIDAE
Platannas (pp.328–337)

Genus Xenopus	Platannas	Platannas	
Xenopus gilli	Cape Platanna	*Kaapse platanna*	Cape Clawed Frog, Gill's Clawed Frog, Gill's Clawed Toad, Gill's Frog, Gill's Platanna
Xenopus laevis	Common Platanna	*Gewone platanna*	African Clawed Frog, African Clawed Toad, Clawed Frog, Clawed Toad, Common Clawed Frog, Common Clawed Frog, Common Clawed Toad, Platanna, Smooth Clawed Frog, Upland Clawed Frog, Upland Clawed Frog
Xenopus muelleri	Müller's Platanna	*Geelpensplatanna*	Müller's Clawed Frog, Müller's Clawed Frog, Müller's Clawed Toad, Muller's Smooth Clawed Frog, Northern Platanna, Sago-bellied Clawed Frog, Sago-bellied Clawed Toad, Sago-bellied Platanna, Savanna Clawed Frog, Tropical Platanna, Yellow-bellied Platanna, *Tropiese platanna*
Xenopus petersii	Peters's Platanna	*Peters se platanna*	Peters' Clawed Frog

FAMILY PYXICEPHALIDAE
African Common Frogs (pp.338–449)

Genus Anhydrophryne	Chirping Frogs	Kwetterpaddas	
Anhydrophryne hewitti	Natal Chirping Frog	*Natalse kwetterpadda*	Hewitt's Frog, Yellow Bandit Frog, Hewitt's Moss Frog, Natal Moss Frog
Anhydrophryne ngongoniensis	Mistbelt Chirping Frog	*Misbeltkwetterpadda*	Natal Bandit Frog, Ngongoni Moss Frog, Mistbelt Moss Frog
Anhydrophryne rattrayi	Hogsback Chirping Frog	*Hogsback-kwetterpadda*	Hogsback Frog, Rattray's Forest Frog, Rattray's Frog

Genus	Moss Frogs	Mospaddas	
Arthroleptella			
Arthroleptella bicolor	Bainskloof Moss Frog	Bainskloof-mospadda	Bainskloof Chirping Frog
Arthroleptella drewesii	Drewes's Moss Frog	Drewes se mospadda	Drewes' Chirping Frog
Arthroleptella landdrosia	Landdroskop Moss Frog	Landdroskop-mospadda	Landdros Moss Frog, Landdroskop Chirping Frog
Arthroleptella lightfooti	Cape Peninsula Moss Frog	Skiereilandmospadda	Brown Bandit Frog, Cape Chirping Frog, Cape Peninsula Chirping Frog, Chirping Frog, Cricket Frog, Lightfoot's Frog, Lightfoot's Moss Frog, Tiny Chirping Frog, Skiereiland mospaddatjie
Arthroleptella rugosa	Rough Moss Frog	Skurwe-mospadda	
Arthroleptella subvoce	Northern Moss Frog	Noordelike mospadda	
Arthroleptella villiersi	De Villiers's Moss Frog	De Villiers se mospadda	De Villiers' Chirping Frog
Genus Cacosternum	Cacos	Blikslanertjies	
Cacosternum boettgeri	Boettger's Caco	Gewone blikslanertjie	Boettger's Caco, Boettger's Dainty Frog, Boettger's Frog, Boettger's Froglet, Boettger's Metal Frog, Common Caco, Common Dainty Frog, Dainty Frog
Cacosternum capense	Cape Caco	Kaapse blikslanertjie	Cape Caco, Cape Dainty Frog, Cape Froglet, Cape Metal Frog, Cross-marked Frog, Dainty Frog
Cacosternum karooicum	Karoo Caco	Karooblikslanertjie	Karoo Dainty Frog
Cacosternum namaquense	Namaqua Caco	Namakwa-blikslanertjie	
Cacosternum nanum	Bronze Caco	Bronsblikslanertjie	
Cacosternum parvum	Mountain Caco	Bergblikslanertjie	
Cacosternum platys	Flat Caco	Platblikslanertjie	Smooth Dainty Frog
Cacosternum poyntoni	Poynton's Caco	Poynton se blikslanertjie	Nursery Metal Frog
Cacosternum striatum	Striped Caco	Gestreepte blikslanertjie	Striped Metal Frog
Cacosternum sp. A	Rhythmic Caco	Ritmiese blikslanertjie	
Cacosternum sp. B	KwaZulu Caco	KwaZululblikslanertjie	
Genus Microbatrachella	Micro Frog	Mikropadda	
Microbatrachella capensis	Micro Frog	Mikropadda	Cape Flats Frog
Genus Natalobatrachus	Kloof Frog	Kloofpadda	
Natalobatrachus bonebergi	Kloof Frog	Kloofpadda	Boneberg's Frog, Gloomy Kloof Frog, Natal Diving Frog, Natal Frog

Genus Poyntonia	Marsh Frog	Moeraspadda	
Poyntonia paludicola	Montane Marsh Frog	Bergmoeraspadda	Kogelberg Reserve Frog
Genus Amietia	**River Frogs**	**Rivierpaddas**	
Amietia quecketti	Common River Frog	Gewone rivierpadda	Common Rana, Angola River Frog, Dusky-throated Frog, Angola Frog, Northern Rana, Nutt's Frog, Chapin's Frog
Amietia dracomontana	Drakensberg River Frog	Drakensberg-rivierpadda	Drakensberg Frog, Sani Pass Frog, Drakensberg River Frog
Amietia fuscigula	Cape River Frog	Kaapse rivierpadda	Dark-throated River Frog, Dusky-throated River Frog, Dark-throated Frog, Cape Rana, Brown-throated Frog
Amietia inyangae	Inyanga River Frog	Inyanga-rivierpadda	
Amietia umbraculata	Maluti River Frog	Maluti rivierpadda	Water Rana, Water Frog, Ice Frog, Umbraculate Frog, Umzimkulu River Leopard Frog, Grootbek rivierpadda
Amietia vandijki	Van Dijk's River Frog	Van Dijk se rivierpadda	
Amietia vertebralis	Phofung River Frog	Phofung rivierpadda	Berg Stream Frog, Drakensberg Frog, Drakensberg Rana, Drakensberg Stream Frog, Natal Drakensberg Frog
Genus Pyxicephalus	**Bullfrogs**	**Brulpaddas**	
Pyxicephalus adspersus	Giant Bullfrog	Grootbrulpadda	African Bullfrog, Bullfrog, Giant Pyxie, Giant Pyxie, Highveld Bullfrog, South African Speckled Frog, Tschudi's African Bullfrog
Pyxicephalus edulis	African Bullfrog	Kleinbrulpadda	Lesser Bull-frog, Peter's Bullfrog, Edible Frog, Edible Bullfrog
Genus Strongylopus	**Stream Frogs**	**Langtoonpaddas**	
Strongylopus bonaespei	Banded Stream Frog	Gebande langtoonpadda	Banded Sand Frog, Mountain Frog, Jonkersberg Frog
Strongylopus fasciatus	Striped Stream Frog	Gestreepte langtoonpadda	Long-toed Frog, Long-toed Grass Frog, Striped Grass Frog, Striped Grass Frog, Striped Long-toed Frog, Striped Rana, Tanganyika Striped Grass Frog
Strongylopus grayii	Clicking Stream Frog	Kliklangtoonpadda	Gray's Frog, Gray's Grass Frog, Gray's Spotted Frog, Gray's Stream Frog, Spotted Rana
Strongylopus rhodesianus	Chimanimani Stream Frog	Chimanimani-langtoonpadda	Hewitt's Long-toed Frog
Strongylopus springbokensis	Namaqua Stream Frog	Namakwa-langtoonpadda	Springbok Frog
Strongylopus wageri	Plain Stream Frog	Wager se langtoonpadda	Plain Rana, Natal Upland Frog, Wager's Stream Frog
Genus Tomopterna	**Sand Frogs**	**Sandpaddas**	
Tomopterna cryptotis	Tremelo Sand Frog	Trillersandpadda	Catequero Bullfrog, Common Burrowing Frog, Cryptic Sand Frog, Striped Burrowing Frog, Striped Pyxie, Striped Sand Frog

Scientific name	Common name	Afrikaans name	Other names
Tomopterna damarensis	Damaraland Sand Frog	Damara-sandpadda	
Tomopterna delalandii	Cape Sand Frog	Gestreepte sandpadda	African Bullfrog, Cape Burrowing Frog, Delalande's Burrowing Bullfrog, Delalande's Burrowing Frog, Delalande's Dwarf Bullfrog, Delalande's Frog, Delalande's Pyxie, Pyxie, Striped Pyxie
Tomopterna krugerensis	Knocking Sand Frog	Sandveld-sandpadda	Kruger Bullfrog, Kruger Burrowing Frog, Sandveld Pyxie
Tomopterna marmorata	Russet-backed Sand Frog	Rooirugsandpadda	Blunt-nosed Burrowing Frog, Blunt-nosed Pyxie, Marbled Bullfrog, Marmorate Pyxie, Moçambique Burrowing Frog, Mozambique Burrowing Frog, Mozambique Dwarf Bullfrog, Mozambique Pyxie, Striped Pyxie
Tomopterna natalensis	Natal Sand Frog	Natalse sandpadda	Natal Burrowing Frog, Natal Pyxie, Natal Bullfrog
Tomopterna tandyi	Tandy's Sand Frog	Tandy se sandpadda	
Tomopterna tuberculosa	Beaded Sand Frog	Skurwesandpadda	Angola Bullfrog, Beaded Burrowing Frog, Beaded Dwarf Bullfrog, Beaded Pyxie, Bearded Pyxie, Rough Sand Frog, Tuberculate Sand Frog, Warty Frog, Gekraalde sandpadda

FAMILY RANIDAE
European Common Frogs (pp.450–455)

Genus Hylarana	Golden-backed Frogs	Gouerugpaddas	
Hylarana darlingi	Darling's Golden-backed Frog	Darling se gouerugpadda	Darling's Frog, Darling's White-lipped Frog, Golden-backed Frog
Hylarana galamensis	Galam Golden-backed Frog	Galam-gouerugpadda	Galam White-lipped Frog, Golden-backed Frog, Lake Galam Frog, Marble-legged Frog, Yellow-striped Frog

FAMILY RHACOPHORIDAE
Foam Nest Frogs (pp.456–459)

Genus Chiromantis	Foam Nest Frogs	Skuimnespadda	
Chiromantis xerampelina	Southern Foam Nest Frog	Grootgrysskuimnespadda	African Gray Treefrog, Foam Nest Frog, Foam Nest Tree Frog, Foam Nest Treefrog, Great African Grey Tree Frog, Grey Foam-nest Frog, Grey Tree Frog, Grey Treefrog, Large Grey Tree Frog, Southern Foam Nest Tree Frog

MORPHOLOGY AND PHYSIOLOGY

Structure and function

The evolution of amphibians from an aquatic to a terrestrial environment and the subsequent exploitation of widely divergent habitats have been achieved through a variety of remarkable physical and functional adaptations.

SKIN

The amphibian skin is a complex organ providing a number of essential functions. It aids in respiration, protects the animal against pathogens, assists with thermoregulation and water balance, provides a cocoon during hibernation and other states of inactivity, changes colour to camouflage the animal and secretes toxic or distasteful fluids to deter predators.

The skin is loosely attached to the body and consists of two layers: the inner dermis and the outer epidermis. The outer surface of the epidermis consists of a layer of cornified keratin cells, the *stratum corneum,* which is replaced by a new layer at intervals of between four and eleven days. On the days prior to moulting, the skin becomes opaque, obscuring colour and pattern. During moulting, some species (especially the toad family) hunch and contort the body to loosen and remove the dead *stratum corneum,* which is then eaten. Other species simply allow fragments of moulting skin to fall away.

There are three types of glands in the inner surface of the epidermis at the interface with the underlying dermal tissue: mucous glands which keep the skin moist, poison glands which exude toxins to deter predators and, in species living in semi-arid environments, wax glands which secrete impermeable fluids that are wiped over the skin to reduce water loss.

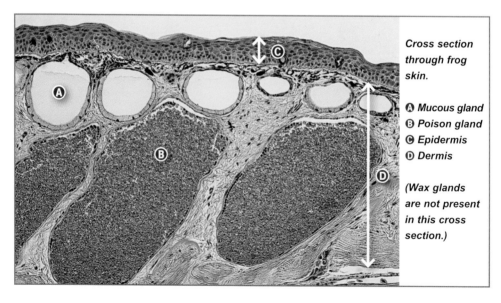

Cross section through frog skin.

Ⓐ *Mucous gland*
Ⓑ *Poison gland*
Ⓒ *Epidermis*
Ⓓ *Dermis*

(Wax glands are not present in this cross section.)

Respiration

An extensive network of blood capillaries runs close to the surface of the skin allowing carbon dioxide to be released through the skin and, to a lesser extent, oxygen to be absorbed. For this to take place the skin must remain moist so that these gases are exchanged in their dissolved state.

Thermoregulation

Amphibians are ectothermic – their body temperature is determined by the temperature of the external environment. Southern African frogs are most active when the surrounding temperature is 20–30°C. Unlike other vertebrates, amphibians are not insulated by a covering of hair, feathers or scales, so at temperatures above 40° and below 3°C they need special mechanisms in order to survive. Most species burrow or withdraw to damp retreats to stabilise body temperature and avoid dehydration during the heat of the day, but in some species, such as the Southern Foam Nest Frog *Chiromantis xerampelina* and some Reed Frogs, the skin becomes almost white in temperatures above 30°C and fluids are secreted to cool the body. These fluids sometimes attract sweat flies.

Water balance

Frogs do not drink water. To regulate moisture levels in their bodies they absorb water by osmosis through their semi-permeable skin when they are submerged in water or sitting on wet surfaces. They release water via the kidneys. Tadpoles and aquatic species, such as the Common Platanna *Xenopus laevis,* constantly need to excrete water and waste in the form of ammonia to compensate for the intake via osmosis. Conversely, terrestrial species reduce

their loss of water by excreting waste as urea. The Southern Foam Nest Frog excretes waste as uric acid, a white paste requiring almost no water to carry it out of the body. It also uses its limbs to spread a waxy glandular secretion over the body to reduce loss of moisture through the skin.

Marius Burger

Foam Nest Frog with feet concealed to reduce water loss.

Most water is lost through the ventral surface of the frog's body where the skin is most permeable. For this reason Tree Frogs and Reed Frogs tuck their feet tightly under their bodies to prevent water loss. Highly terrestrial species such as Sand Frogs and Toads retain water reserves in the bladder and lymph sacs. A sudden discharge of this fluid onto surprised would-be predators serves as a secondary defence mechanism.

When hibernating, some fossorial (burrowing) species retain several layers of the outer epidermis instead of moulting them. This forms an impermeable keratin cocoon that, except for small nostril apertures, completely seals the frog while it remains buried. In this state, metabolism slows, water loss is greatly reduced and hibernation can be sustained throughout the dry winter months – or even for years if the seasons are unsuitable for breeding.

Colour

Many frogs adjust their colour to camouflage themselves or to regulate body temperature. Skin colour is produced by pigments known as chromatophores that are located in branched cells within the dermis. Chromatophores can be withdrawn into a small zone of the cell so that barely any pigment is evident, or they can be distributed throughout the cell to make the colour conspicuous. Controlling the extent of chromatophore dispersal in the cells enables the frog to change colour in response to stimuli such as background colour, temperature, light intensity and even to reflect the emotional state of the animal.

Most amphibians have three types of pigments. Melanophores contain black or brown melanin and are the most deeply imbedded in the skin. Iridiophores contain a silvery light-reflecting pigment and are the next deepest. Uppermost in the skin are xantophores with yellow, orange or red pigments. Light penetrating the skin is reflected back by the iridiophores through the xantophores to produce the bright, conspicuous colours commonly found in tropical frogs.

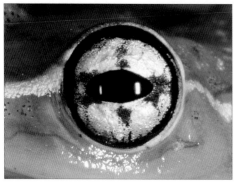

Brightly coloured chromatophores in the eye and skin.

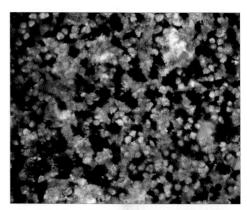

Micrograph of chromatophores in frog skin.

Painted Reed Frog with colour visible (left) and with colour hidden (right).

Camouflage

Polymorphism in two frogs of the same species, Boettger's Caco: polymorphism diminishes vulnerability to predators. Pale specimens are less conspicuous in winter grassland, while striped ones blend in better in summer grassland.

Masked and banded Plain Stream Frog: eye masks and transverse banding on the legs break the outline of the frog.

Mottled specimen of the Tremelo Sand Frog: mottling and coarse texture replicates the gravel substrate.

Striped camouflage in the Rattling Frog: light and dark stripes match the contrasting light patterns in long grass.

Aposematic colours

Red, orange, yellow, white and black often signify toxicity in nature. Predators learn to associate these colours with distasteful or dangerous species and avoid preying on them.

Right: The highly toxic skin secretion of the black and red Banded Rubber Frog is signalled by its colours, and its elevated stance enhances the size of the animal to discourage a predator further.

Flash colours

Some frogs have brightly coloured patches that are concealed when the frog is at rest, but vividly displayed when it moves. It is believed that the striking colours confuse predators as they are visible only intermittently.

Painted Reed Frog at rest (left) and exposing flash colours (right).

SKELETON AND LIMBS

During metamorphosis the boneless tadpole develops a complex skeleton of bone and cartilage comprising spinal column, skull, rib cage and limbs. This gives structure to the body, protects the nervous system and provides attachment points for muscles which allow for effective movement. The evolution of a skeleton strong enough to support the body without the buoyancy of water was a key development that enabled amphibians to develop from their aquatic ancestors.

Adaptation of the limbs reflects the behaviour patterns of different species and is often a useful diagnostic feature. The toes of Tree and Reed Frogs bear adhesive discs for climbing. The more aquatic species have extensive webbing between their toes. Grass Frogs and River Frogs have long and powerful hindlegs with which to leap away from danger. By contrast, the burrowing frogs have short stubby legs with hard, calloused tubercles on their feet which are used to thrust aside soil as they dig.

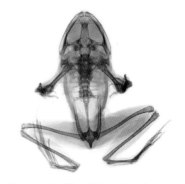

X-ray of a River Frog showing skeletal adaptation for leaping.

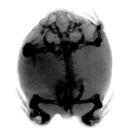

X-ray of a Rain Frog showing skeletal adaptation for burrowing.

BRAIN AND NERVOUS SYSTEM

The frog brain is divided into three parts: the forebrain contains the olfactory centre which is responsible for the highly sensitive sense of smell; the midbrain controls complex integrative activities and includes the optic lobes responsible for sight; and the hindbrain is well developed and plays an important role in maintaining equilibrium and movement.

FROG BRAIN

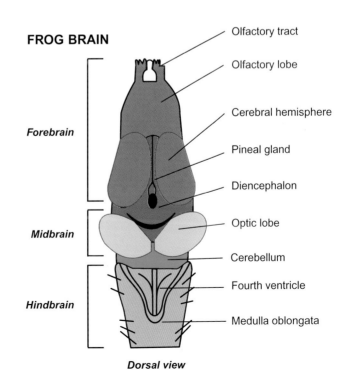

Forebrain

Midbrain

Hindbrain

Olfactory tract

Olfactory lobe

Cerebral hemisphere

Pineal gland

Diencephalon

Optic lobe

Cerebellum

Fourth ventricle

Medulla oblongata

Dorsal view

EYES AND SIGHT

In frogs, vision is critically important for feeding and detecting danger. Except for Platannas, which are largely confined to aquatic habitats, the eyes of frogs need to function on land and under water. They have retractable eyelids and lachrymal glands to lubricate eyes in dry air, and transparent nictitating membranes to protect them under water. Unlike mammals, frogs focus by moving the lens within the eye rather than changing lens shape and focal length. At rest, the eye is focused on a point in the distance. To look at closer objects, the lens moves backwards into the eye.

Species that hunt fast-moving prey after dark have evolved large bulbous eyes with irises that can dilate from narrow slits in daylight to full circles for night vision. Frog eyes are equipped with both rods and cones in the retina and can thus see colours – at least in good light. Because of their large size, eyes can be withdrawn into the skull for protection. A retractable nectitating membrane protects the eye underwater. Prey is usually detected only when it moves.

The shape of the iris in bright light – vertical or horizontal – is a useful diagnostic tool for identification.

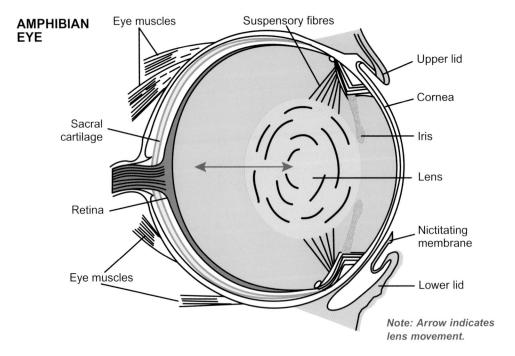

AMPHIBIAN EYE

Eye muscles · Suspensory fibres · Upper lid · Cornea · Iris · Lens · Nictitating membrane · Lower lid · Sacral cartilage · Retina · Eye muscles

Note: Arrow indicates lens movement.

VOICE

Frogs and toads appear to have been the first creatures to develop advanced vocalisation, and the importance of calls and communication is discussed on pages 43–45.

Relative to the size of a frog, the energy and volume of sound produced is prodigious. Calls are produced by inflating the lungs beyond the volume needed for normal breathing. Surplus air is passed rhythmically via the larynx to the buccal or mouth cavity, vibrating the vocal chords as it does so. Unlike most other vocal animals, the mouth is kept closed while calling and sound is amplified by resonance in a thin-walled vocal sac that expands from the base or sides of the buccal cavity.

EARS AND HEARING

The eardrum or tympanum is exposed and visible in most species and is a flat, circular membrane located close to the eye. Behind the tympanum lies the middle ear and a strip of tissue (columella) that transmits sound vibrations from the tympanum to sound sensory organs in the inner ear. A small muscle (opercularis) connects the ear to the shoulder so that the frog can detect ground vibrations via its forelimbs. A blocking mechanism controlled by the columellaris muscle protects the inner ear from particularly loud sounds.

AMPHIBIAN HEARING STRUCTURE

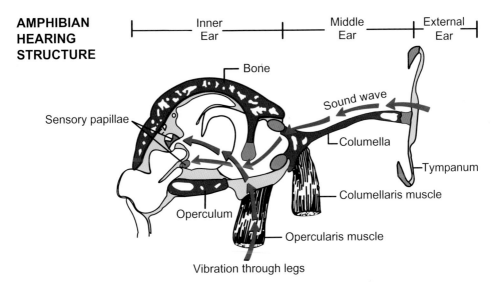

Inner Ear — Middle Ear — External Ear

Bone
Sensory papillae
Sound wave
Columella
Tympanum
Columellaris muscle
Operculum
Opercularis muscle
Vibration through legs

FEEDING, SWALLOWING AND DIGESTION

With the exception of Platannas, southern African species feed on land. Arthropods make up the diet of most frogs, but larger River Frogs and Bullfrogs may take rodents, fledgling birds and other frogs. Cannibalism is a common occurrence, practised especially by newly metamorphosed juveniles which eat one another.

Movement of a prey item generally triggers a feeding response and a frog usually takes whatever appears edible by snapping at it or catching it on its adhesive tongue. Most southern African species have a tongue fastened at the front of the mouth which can be flipped out readily to capture prey. After dirt or indigestible parts, such as wings, have been scraped away with

Giant Bullfrog eating a Red Toad.

Platanna tadpoles in characteristic head-down position.

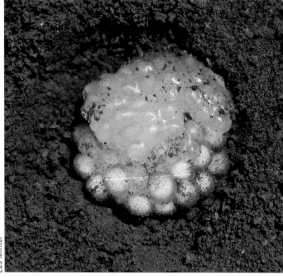

Les Minter

Yoke-filled eggs of a Rain Frog (Breviceps), a genus that lacks a tadpole stage and develops directly into a small frog.

the forelimbs, prey is swallowed whole. If it proves distasteful, the prey is immediately expelled from the mouth. Large prey is sometimes crushed or suffocated before being swallowed. Most species have small recurved teeth to assist with grasping and swallowing. In some species these are restricted to the upper jaw, while in others they may be located in the roof of the mouth (vomerine teeth). After a few gulps, swallowing large items can be assisted by retracting the eyeballs into the buccal cavity so that the food is pressed down the gullet.

Common River Frog tadpole feeding near the bottom of a pond.

Platannas scavenge for detritus (fine debris) underwater. They hover a few centimetres below the surface, waiting for edible fragments to drift their way, and then shovel them into their mouths with their forelimbs. They have neither teeth nor tongue and sometimes rake large food items into manageable pieces with their clawed feet.

Digestive enzymes are secreted in the oesophagus and digestion takes place in the stomach and intestine. Undigested waste is passed through the rectum and out via the cloaca.

Whereas adult frogs are carnivorous, tadpoles are semi-herbivorous, feeding largely on algae and bacteria. Most have sets of keratinised beaks or jaw sheaths (rostrodonts) and scrapers or labial teeth (keratodonts), and these are used to rasp off plant material or bacteria growing on plant material. Food particles are trapped in a filter mechanism when water is pumped into the mouth and out via one or two spiracles at the side of the head. Sticky cells transport the food to the opening of the oesophagus.

Tadpoles of Platannas are filter-feeders. Small shoals hang in a characteristic head-down position in the water while the tip of the tail beats constantly, drawing a flow of water towards the mouth. Microscopic food particles in the water are trapped in filters and ingested in the same manner as other tadpoles.

A number of southern African frogs have no free-living tadpoles. Their eggs are laid in humus or underground and contain sufficient yoke to nourish the developing tadpole until metamorphosis is complete.

HEART AND CIRCULATION

Amphibians have three-chambered hearts with two atria and one ventricle (the muscular pump). Blood from the body enters the right atrium via a receiving chamber known as the *sinus venosus*. From here blood enters the ventricle and is pumped to the lungs where it absorbs oxygen. Oxygenated blood returns to the left atrium from where it is pumped via the ventricle back into the circulatory system of the body. Oxygenated and deoxygenated blood is prevented from mixing in the ventricle by a spiral valve that keeps the blood from the lungs separate.

UROGENITAL ORGANS

The excretory and reproductive systems are closely associated. Primitive kidneys (known as mesonephros) are elongated and situated towards the back, on either side of the aorta. In males, two pale-coloured testes are attached to the kidneys. During the reproductive season they increase in size and sperm gathers in collecting ducts and is transported to the cloaca.

In females, paired ovaries are attached to the kidneys. Each ovary consists of a thin sheet of connective tissue, the ovisac, which encloses the developing ovarian follicles. At the onset of the breeding season the follicles ripen, increase in size, and then pass through coiled oviducts where they are coated with a jelly secretion before reaching the cloaca of a gravid female.

The urinary bladder consists of a smooth epithelium and muscle layers that allow considerable distension of the bladder when filled with urine.

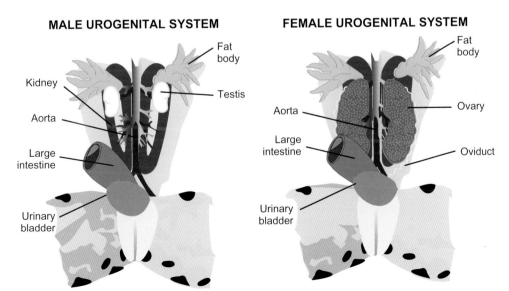

MALE UROGENITAL SYSTEM

Fat body
Kidney
Testis
Aorta
Large intestine
Urinary bladder

FEMALE UROGENITAL SYSTEM

Fat body
Aorta
Ovary
Large intestine
Oviduct
Urinary bladder

RESPIRATION AND VOCALISATION

1: Respiration through buccal cavity and rapid throat oscillation.
1A: Buccal floor muscles (under throat) contract, expelling used air in buccal cavity through nostrils.
1B: Buccal floor muscles relax. Air drawn in through nostrils. Oxygen absorbed through buccal wall.

2: Respiration through lungs.
2A: Larynx closed to prevent air from entering lungs. Buccal floor muscles relax to draw in fresh air.
2B: Larynx opens. Body wall muscles deflate lungs. Used air expelled through open nostrils.
2C: Nostrils closed. Larynx open. Contraction of buccal floor muscles pumps fresh air into lungs.
2D: Nostrils open. Larynx closed. Buccal floor muscles relax drawing fresh air into buccal cavity to be pumped into lungs (2C) or used in buccal cavity and expelled through nostrils (1A).

3: Vocalisation.
Nostrils closed. Body wall muscles deflate lungs, forcing air over vocal chords into extended vocal sac to amplify sound.

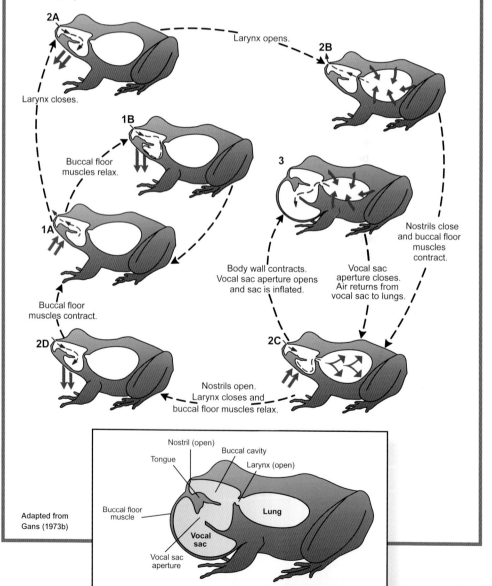

Adapted from
Gans (1973b)

RESPIRATION

Oxygen intake is mainly through the lungs, while carbon dioxide is lost primarily through the skin. Mammals inhale air by contracting the diaphragm. In frogs, however, air is pumped into the lungs by raising and lowering the floor of the mouth. Lowering the mouth floor sucks air through the nostrils into the expanded buccal cavity. The nostrils are then closed and when the floor of the mouth is raised, air is pushed through a valve into the lungs. To expel stale air, the nostrils are closed, air is drawn from the lungs back into the mouth and then expelled through re-opened nostrils. Frogs draw and expel air rapidly in and out of the mouth. After several inhalations they pump air through to the lungs. Oxygen and carbon dioxide are exchanged through the lungs and through the walls of the buccal cavity. The rapid pumping action under the jaw can usually be seen when observing a frog at rest.

Frog lungs are ovoid elastic sacs and the inner surfaces are divided into a network of septa or dividing walls. These are in turn subdivided into smaller compartments, each ending in a blind chamber covered with vascular respiratory surfaces known as alveoli.

Tadpoles have gills for respiration but they also make use of the skin as a respiratory surface. For the first day or so after hatching, tadpoles have external gills but these are soon covered by a membrane so that water can be pumped into the mouth, over the gills and then out through the spiracle. The majority of species have a single spiracle but Platannas have two.

SMELL AND CHEMORECEPTION

Amphibians detect scents in the environment through the olfactory epithelium (cellular tissue) and the epithelium of the Jacobson's organ which is located in the roof of the mouth near the nostrils. It is believed that amphibians use smell for homing orientation and for recognising breeding sites.

ENDOCRINE SYSTEM

Behaviour is to a large extent determined by hormones secreted by ductless glands situated in various parts of the body, most importantly, in the thyroid and pituitary glands.

The main function of the *thyroid gland* is to control metamorphosis in tadpoles through the hormone thyroxin. Production of this hormone is influenced to some extent by water temperature: cold water inhibits thyroid activity, while warm water enhances it. This plays a role in survival in cases where frogs breed in non-permanent water. If the water level drops, a frog's temperature increases, stimulating the thyroid to speed up metamorphosis before the water dries up completely. Conversely, in temperate regions, tadpoles are prevented from metamorphosing as winter approaches so that juveniles are spared the probability of freezing to death.

The *pituitary gland* is situated at the base of the brain and secretes a variety of hormones that control breeding, colour change and water balance in the animal.

AGE, GROWTH AND LONGEVITY

In nature, little is known about the longevity of amphibians. Larger amphibians have the potential to live longer, and records exist of toads living for up to 40 years in captivity. Confirmed ages that have been reported for southern African frogs in captivity are:

30 years for a Common Platanna *Xenopus laevis*
18 years for a Cape Sand Frog *Tomopterna delalandii*
23 years for a Red-legged Kassina *Kassina maculata*
35 years for a Giant Bullfrog *Pyxicephalus adspersus*

REPRODUCTION AND VOCALISATION

Breeding biology and survival

Frog calls are a positive sign of the advent of spring. They are a critical component of the annual reproductive cycle which, although familiar in its simplistic form, is a remarkably complex process linking the aquatic and terrestrial components of the lives of amphibians. Complexity is compounded because different species have adapted the cycle to suit their particular environmental niches.

1. Adult bullfrog ready to breed.

2. Males gather at specific breeding sites and produce calls unique to their species.

3. Females are attracted to the calls, and pairs mate.

BREEDING CYCLE

Giant Bullfrog

8. Juvenile frogs disperse and mature.

4. While mating, females extrude eggs which the males fertilise externally.

7. Tadpoles metamorphose from aquatic to terrestrial form.

6. Eggs develop into tadpoles.

5. Eggs scattered in shallow water.

MATING SEASONS

Although many species have developed ways of reducing their dependence on water, all frogs require some form of moisture in order to breed. In winter rainfall areas of the Western Cape, most species breed at the end of winter when ponds and streams are full and the landscape is saturated. In the interior summer-rainfall areas, breeding usually takes place after the first thunderstorms. Within these broad parameters species will select different mating seasons, stimulated by a combination of day-length, temperature and rainfall.

The duration of a mating season may vary considerably and in warmer and wetter climates, calling and breeding continues for periods of up to nine months of the year. Under these circumstances a female may lay eggs two or more times in a season. In species that breed in cool, permanent water, metamorphosis may take several months.

In regions with erratic rainfall, frogs need to exploit opportunities as they arise and the species that do so are referred to as 'explosive breeders'. Often using temporary water bodies that accumulate after suitable rains, they emerge in large numbers to call, mate and lay eggs in a short period, sometimes in only a single day, although this may be repeated if conditions are favourable. Explosive breeding is typified by vigorous fighting between males competing for females at the breeding site. In particularly dry years these frogs may not breed at all. Metamorphosis is accelerated in temporary water and may take less than four weeks in the warm waters of shallow pools so that tadpoles avoid desiccation as ponds start to dry up (see Endocrine system, page 41). At least one species, the Giant Bullfrog (pages 412–413), shows parental care in protecting tadpoles in these circumstances.

SECONDARY SEX CHARACTERISTICS

As the breeding season approaches the internal reproductive organs in both males and females undergo significant changes. Externally, males develop vocal sacs and nuptial pads. The structure of the vocal sac varies between species, and four broad categories can be identified.

Nuptial pads are rough-surfaced swellings on the fingers and forelimbs that allow the male to clasp the female securely during amplexus. In species that inhabit fast-flowing streams, the nuptial pads may take the form of sharp spines which allow for a more secure grip. Some burrowing species develop adhesive glands that produce substances that glue the pair together during amplexis in order to prevent separation as they dig into the soil.

VOCALISATION

Frogs are more often heard than seen, and calling is a critically important aspect of their survival. Calls serve four purposes and different sounds are produced for each: to attract females to a breeding site, to ensure males keep separated from one another, to signal release from amplexus, and to alarm and discourage predators.

Advertisement calls

The type of call most commonly heard is produced by males to attract females. Males congregate at suitable breeding sites from the start of the breeding season and produce an advertisement call that is unique to each species. Calls are amplified by an expanded vocal sac. The hearing of a female is attuned so that she is responsive only to the sound of a conspecific mate and she homes in on him by cocking her head from side to side to confirm her direction as she approaches. Neither vision nor smell is involved in this approach.

Subgular sac: the elastic membrane expands and resonates as the call is made (Guttural Toad).

Subgular sac with covering disc: the membranous sac is protected by a thick skin when at rest (Painted Reed Frog).

Paired subgular sac: the twin lobes expand only at the instant of the short call (Water Lily Frog).

Paired lateral sac: twin membranous sacs emerge from slits on either side of the jaw (Ornate Frog).

The unique character of the call of each species is known as the 'specific mate recognition system' (SMRS) and it is the principal means by which frogs recognise and mate with conspecific partners and thereby perpetuate the species. Calls can readily be identified by the human ear and they are the most reliable method of identifying species in the field. Sound recordings on the CD that accompanies this field guide and the spectrograms (pages 464–481) are important identification tools.

In species that have extended breeding seasons, females approach the calling males and select one with which to mate. Factors influencing a female's selection may be the volume or frequency of the call or the choice of call site. Occasionally a silent male, referred to as a 'satellite', stations himself close to a robust caller and intercepts the female as she approaches.

In explosive breeders, however, competitiveness at the breeding site and the need to mate urgently drive males to mount approaching females as soon as they are detected. Often other males, frogs of other species and even bits of flotsam on the water are mistaken for females and assaulted.

Males may establish choruses of considerable size, and the sound is orchestrated to enhance their effectiveness. Individuals close to each other tend to call antiphonally – that is, one calls in the brief space between the calls of neighbours so that while their combined and continuous sound is heard from a distance, they still retain their individuality in attracting a mate. Disturbances usually cause the whole group to fall silent simultaneously, after which individuals slowly stimulate reparticipation so that the chorus soon swells again to maximum volume.

Choruses consisting of ten or more different species at one site are not uncommon and the ability of females to negotiate this cacophony and locate the correct mate is assisted by several factors: the zone of the call site is usually consistent within species – for example, certain species prefer emergent vegetation while others call at water level; and some call from mudbanks, while others call from trees. Species also separate themselves with regard to the time of calling – some call only in the early evening while others begin to call only towards midnight.

Spacing and aggressive calls

The selection of a call site by a male determines his ability to attract females. Individuals are known to return constantly to the same site each night and they will defend their positions vigorously. If approached too closely by a potential competitor, the male emits a particular sound to warn the intruder to keep his distance. This spacing call is quite different from the advertisement call. Some species, such as the River Frogs and certain Reed Frogs, produce a dual advertisement and spacing call constantly; the two components – a rattle and a croak in the case of River Frogs – are easily distinguishable. But in most species the spacing call is used only when required and is to be heard more frequently in the early evening while males are establishing their call sites.

If the spacing call fails to deter a challenger, antagonists may resort to punching at each other with distended vocal sacs, kicking or biting one another until one individual is driven off.

Release calls

Females produce short grunting sounds combined with vibrations of the flanks to terminate amplexus once their eggs have been laid. Males give a similar call if inadvertently grasped by other males in the frenzy of the breeding site. Amplexus is quickly terminated in these circumstances – the release call appears to be effective even between different species when accidental mounting occurs.

Distress calls

In some species, such as Rain Frogs, both sexes can give a distress call if molested by potential predators. The call is emitted with the mouth wide open and its purpose is to startle a potential predator into releasing its victim. It has also been suggested that the distress call serves to alert other frogs to danger.

MATING

Fertilisation takes place externally. The male, which in all cases (except Bullfrogs) is smaller than the female, clasps the female from the back with his forelegs and exudes sperm onto the eggs at the moment that she expels them from her cloaca. The system is not always efficient in that sperm and – especially – underwater eggs can be separated before fertilisation takes place. Mating methods that different genera use to improve fertilisation rates are discussed in each generic description.

EGG DEVELOPMENT

The time taken for the development of egg to free-swimming tadpole varies considerably between species and in response to temperature. It can be completed in as little as a day (e.g. African Common Frogs Pyxicephalidae) or it can last several days. The average times given below are for the Guttural Toad *Amietophrynus gutturalis*. Gosner stage refers to the embryological developmental phase of the tadpole.

	Hours	Illustration
Ovum **Outer jelly-like material** • Animal pole. Contains the cells that will divide and give rise to the embryo. Faces upwards to absorb sunlight and is pigmented to shield ultra-violet radiation. Often pigmented to absorb warmth. • Vegetal pole contains yoke as nourishment for the developing tadpole.	0–1	Gosner stage 1
• Ovum starts as a single-cell structure. • Undergoes a series of divisions (known as cleavage) into 2, 4, 8, 16, 32, etc., stages. • Multi-celled stage: the zygote grows around the yolk, which is slowly absorbed as the tadpole develops.	2–3	Gosner stages 2, 4, 8
• A process known as gastrulation leads to the development of the Gastrula stadium with 3 layers of cells, the ecto-, meso- and endoderm from which organs develop during organogenesis. • Ectodermal cells fold in through neurilation to become the brain and nerves. • Mesoderm gives rise to musculature and skeletal elements and vascular system. • Endoderm gives rise to internal organs and inner ear.	3–4	Gosner stages 11, 15, 17

Drawings modified from Anstis, M. (2002) Tadpoles of South-eastern Australia: a guide with keys. New Holland Publishers, Sydney, Australia

TADPOLE DEVELOPMENT AND METAMORPHOSIS

Although the time it takes for tadpoles to develop and metamorphose into juvenile frogs varies from about 3 weeks to more than 2 years (depending on the species), the stages of development are similar for all species.

	Days	Illustration
• External gills develop and start to function. • Tail develops. • Tadpole frees itself from the capsule. • At first, tadpoles adhere to the substrate by means of an oral adhesive structure, but after 1–2 days they swim freely and begin feeding.	1	Gosner stage 20
• External gills are replaced by internal gills. • Keratonised mouthparts develop. • Eyes appear. • Spiracle starts as a slit on the left side.	3	Gosner stage 24
• Hindlegs start growing from a bud. • Tubercles develop on feet. • Forelegs develop inside the gill chamber.	10–14	Gosner stages 26, 38
• Alimentary and other internal organs develop. • Forelimbs break through skin. • Keratinised mouthparts recede and mouth widens for terrestrial feeding.	35–40	Gosner stage 42
• Tail is fully absorbed.	42–70	Gosner stage 46

Drawings modified from Anstis, M. (2002) Tadpoles of South-eastern Australia: a guide with keys. New Holland Publishers, Sydney, Australia

SURVIVAL ADAPTATIONS FOR EGGS AND TADPOLES

Shell-less eggs and tadpoles are constantly vulnerable to disease, aquatic predators such as fish and dragonfly larva, deoxygenated water and desiccation. Many species have evolved special adaptive behaviour to lessen these threats. Jelly surrounds the eggs as protective cushioning against shock and damage, and also to ward off bacterial or fungal attack.

Family and genus	Survival adaptation
ARTHROLEPTIDAE (pp.80–101)	
Arthroleptis Squeakers	Eggs are laid in damp soil or leaf litter away from open water. Tadpoles develop terrestrially from egg to metamorphosis.
Leptopelis Tree Frogs	Eggs are laid in damp soil. Tadpoles are able to survive out of water while they make their way to water to develop.
BREVICIPITIDAE (pp.102–135)	
Breviceps Rain Frogs	Eggs are laid in underground chambers. Tadpoles develop and metamorphose in the chamber, nourished only by the large egg yolk and without contact with open water, so that they are not exposed to aquatic predators or other hazards.
Probreviceps Primitive Rain Frogs	Egg and tadpole development is similar to that of Rain Frogs.
BUFONIDAE (pp.136–195)	
Amietophrynus Typical Toads	Large numbers of eggs (up to 20 000) are laid with the statistical probability that some will survive. Eggs are laid in strings of jelly, making it difficult for predators to take 1 at a time. Tadpoles may be distasteful to predators.
Poyntonophrynus Pygmy Toads	Eggs are laid in strings of jelly making it difficult for predators to take 1 at a time. Tadpoles may be distasteful to predators.
Vandijkophrynus Van Dijk's Toads	Eggs are laid in strings of jelly making it difficult for predators to take 1 at a time. Tadpoles may be distasteful to predators.
Capensibufo Mountain Toadlets	Eggs are laid in strings of jelly making it difficult for predators to take 1 at a time. Tadpoles may be distasteful to predators.
Schismaderma Red Toad	Eggs are laid in strings of jelly around underwater vegetation. Tadpoles form dense swarms that may deter predators. Tadpoles have a specialised respiration flap on the head.
Mertensophryne Forest Toads	Eggs are laid in pools of water trapped in buttressed roots where there are few predators. Tadpoles have a specialised respiration system to survive in stagnant water.
HELEOPHRYNIDAE (pp.196–213)	
Hadromophryne Cascade Frog	Breed in fast-flowing streams. Eggs are laid in shallow water or on damp soil next to water. Tadpoles are strong swimmers and have wide mouths adapted to cling to slippery rocks in strong currents while simultaneously feeding on algal growth.
Heleophryne Ghost Frog	Breed in fast-flowing streams. Eggs are laid in shallow water or on damp soil next to water. Tadpoles are strong swimmers and have wide mouths adapted to cling to slippery rocks in strong currents while simultaneously feeding on algal growth.
HEMISOTIDAE (pp.214–221)	
Hemisus Shovel-nosed Frogs	Eggs are laid in underground nests near water. Adults transport tadpoles to water where they develop further.
HYPEROLIIDAE (pp.222–280)	
Afrixalus Leaf-folding Frogs	Eggs are laid in folded leaf envelopes. Tadpoles dissolve the adhesive binding of the envelope and develop in open water.
Hyperolius Reed Frogs	Eggs are laid by different species in a variety of situations: some sandwich eggs between overlapping leaves, others deposit egg clusters on vegetation or attach them to underwater vegetation.
Kassina Kassinas	Eggs are attached individually to underwater vegetation. Tadpoles are narrow-bodied with deep fins to allow them to swim among thick protective aquatic vegetation. Tadpoles develop bright red tail fins in clear water to scare off predators.

Family and genus	Survival adaptation
Semnodactylus Rattling Frog	Eggs are attached individually to underwater vegetation. Tadpoles are narrow-bodied with deep fins to allow them to swim among thick protective aquatic vegetation.
MICROHYLIDAE (pp.281–289)	
Phrynomantis Rubber Frogs	Tadpoles are filter feeders and swim or drift, motionless, in an orientated school while feeding, but can escape with speed when necessary. They may be distasteful to predators.
PHRYNOBATRACHIDAE (pp.290–299)	
Phrynobatrachus Puddle Frogs	Eggs float in a layer on the surface of the water for warmth and rapid development.
PTYCHADENIDAE (pp.300–327)	
Hildebrandtia Ornate Frogs	Numerous eggs are laid in a large floating mass.
Ptychadena Grass Frogs	Eggs are laid among emergent vegetation and tend to float.
PIPIDAE (pp.328–337)	
Xenopus Platannas	Large numbers of eggs are laid. Eggs develop rapidly. Tadpoles tend to form loosely orientated schools and filter feed while suspended in the water.
PYXICEPHALIDAE (pp.338–449)	
Anhydrophryne Chirping Frogs	Eggs are laid among damp decaying organic matter, in moss or in an underground chamber on the forest floor. Tadpoles develop and metamorphose on land, nourished only by the egg yolk and without contact with open water.
Arthroleptella Moss Frogs	Eggs are laid among damp vegetation or in mud. Tadpoles develop and metamorphose on moist ground.
Cacosternum Cacos	Eggs are attached individually to underwater vegetation and develop rapidly.
Microbatrachella Micro Frog	Eggs are attached in clusters to underwater vegetation.
Natalobatrachus Kloof Frog	Eggs are laid in jelly cakes on rocks or vegetation overhanging water. Tadpoles slip into water as they hatch.
Poyntonia Marsh Frog	Breed in shallow seepage areas with few predators.
Amietia River Frogs	Eggs are scattered on the bottom and soon become covered in debris which adheres to the eggs.
Pyxicephalus Bullfrogs	Eggs are laid in shallow pans at vigorously defended sites. Tadpoles form dense swarms in shallow water and are protected by adult males. Development is accelerated in shallow warm water.
Strongylopus Stream Frogs	Eggs are laid on moist banks or on moss where eggs develop. A rise in water level and the consequent covering of eggs by water will stimulate tadpoles to break free.
Tomopterna Sand Frogs	Large numbers of eggs are laid in shallow warm water.
RANIDAE (pp.450–455)	
Hylarana Golden-backed Frogs	Eggs are laid among vegetation and tend to float.
RHACOPHORIDAE (pp.456–459)	
Chiromantis Foam Nest Frogs	Eggs are laid in foam nests overhanging water. Tadpoles fall from the nest to develop in water below.

FROGS IN THE ENVIRONMENT
Habitats, threats and conservation

The rich amphibian fauna of southern Africa is attributable to the diversity of the region's topography, climate and habitats. Frogs have adapted to almost every type of environment on the subcontinent and many species are highly specialised to suit conditions in a particular locality. Specialisation can, however, leave a species vulnerable when a habitat itself degrades or changes, while conversely, a decline in a frog population may be an early indicator of habitat destruction.

Understanding why and where frogs are distributed can be a useful tool when identifying frogs. It also provides insight into broader environmental issues.

DISTRIBUTION

Frogs are unevenly distributed in southern Africa both in terms of species diversity and in population numbers. The three main determinants of distribution patterns are climate, centres of origin and range restriction:

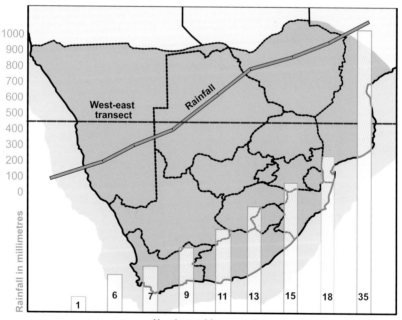

Cross section of southern Africa showing correlation between rainfall and species diversity: all measurements were taken along the red line that transsects southern Africa from west to east. The green diagonal line reflects increasing rainfall from west to east, as shown in millimetres along the left-hand axis. The bars along the bottom axis represent the corresponding rise in the number of frog species from west to east.

Climate

In spite of some remarkable adaptations to cope with changing environmental conditions, all amphibians remain physiologically dependent on moisture and temperature. Thus a larger number of species will be found in areas that are warm and wet. The number of species found at any locality increases along a transect drawn from the arid west to the better-watered east of the subcontinent.

Centres of origin

Most southern African species fall into two broad categories. The first comprises species with evolutionary origins centred in the southern provinces or high altitude areas of the interior. The second comprises species with tropical origins distributed in the northeast.

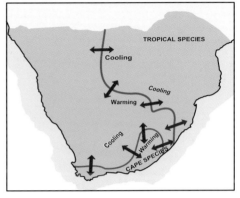

During past periods of climatic warming, the distribution of tropical species expanded southwards, while those already inhabiting the south retreated. During periods of climate cooling this process was reversed. At the interface between these two faunal groups, some populations became isolated and evolved into independent allopatric species. There is an increase in species diversity northwards along the coast from the Western Cape towards northern KwaZulu-Natal, and an increase of endemicity southwards. In general, the interior of the region has a lower level of species diversity and endemicity.

Periods of climate change have left isolated endemic species in the south while species diversity increases in the moist northeast and declines in the dry northwest.

Range restriction

Several southern African species have distribution ranges of less than 20 000 km^2, confined to isolated topographical areas. Most of these species are found on or below the Cape and KwaZulu-Natal escarpments where mountains and deeply incised river valleys offer a variety of different habitats with barriers to movement between them.

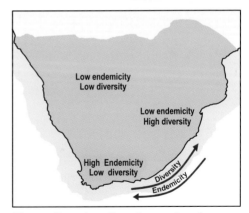

The southwestern Cape is a centre of high endemicity.

HABITATS

Suitable environmental conditions, especially breeding sites, are critically important to frogs and most species tend to be located only in very specific habitats. These, and the distribution ranges of each species, are useful tools in helping to identify species.

In determining habitat types it is useful to categorise localities at three levels: macro-habitats, micro-habitats and activity sites such as call sites or foraging areas.

MACRO-HABITATS

These conform to the nine principal biomes of southern Africa. Although they are botanically defined, they are useful in delineating underlying ecological conditions that prevail in each.

Coastal bush Dense, evergreen vegetation with thick undergrowth and some tall trees growing in sandy soils in a narrow strip along the east and south coasts.

Forest Dense woodland with large trees forming a closed canopy, occurring in patches in high rainfall areas along the south coast and eastern escarpment at various altitudes.

Desert Dry region on the Namibian seaboard, ranging from sand dune to mountain and characterised by very sparse, highly specialised plant and animal life. The only regular source of moisture is derived from coastal fog.

Grassland Open, undulating country with a few indigenous trees, but copses of introduced species are becoming common: stretches across the central highveld region and mountain slopes.

Karoo (semi-desert) Arid stony areas with low, flat-topped koppies and sparse scrub vegetation in the south-central and west-central areas.

Fynbos A unique and strikingly diverse floral kingdom in the winter-rainfall area of the southern and western Cape; includes mountains and coastal lowlands.

Mangroves Isolated pockets of specialised communities of estuarine and intertidal fauna and flora on the northeast and east coasts.

Moist savanna A predominance of broad-leafed, often deciduous, trees in the northeastern, higher rainfall areas. Trees spaced sufficiently apart so that there is an understorey of grass and no closed canopy.

Arid savanna Dominated by acacia species and generally more open in the northwestern parts. Trees spaced sufficiently apart so that there is an understorey of grass and no closed canopy.

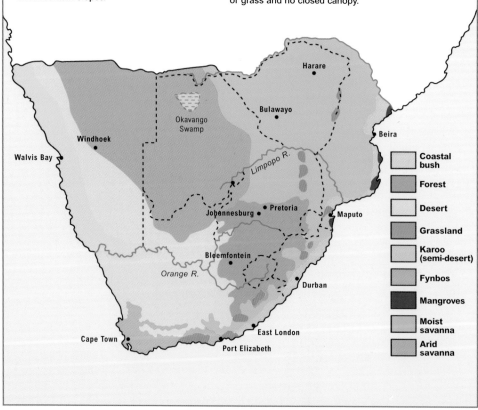

Legend:
- Coastal bush
- Forest
- Desert
- Grassland
- Karoo (semi-desert)
- Fynbos
- Mangroves
- Moist savanna
- Arid savanna

MICRO-HABITATS

Within each macro-habitat, a number of micro-habitats can be identified. Most, but not all, are types of wetland and definitions have been adapted from the *South African National Wetland Inventory* (Ewart-Smith *et al.* 1998) to describe different frog habitats. The use of a micro-habitat by a particular species is determined by the biophysical structures present, such as vegetation (reed beds, trees, moss) and physical substrate (mud banks, sand, rocks).

Endorheic systems Depressions filled by rainwater or seepage and depleted by evaporation or absorption into the substrate; they are neither fed nor drained by a watercourse.	**Pan:** Varies in size from many hectares to a few square metres. It may hold rainwater for some time, but it is seldom permanent and it has widely fluctuating water levels. Hydrophytes can be found in or at the edges of the water. The banks may include open mud, inundated grass, reed beds or copses of overhanging trees – each of which attract different species of frogs.	
	Pool: A small, sometimes manmade, depression such as a ditch or vehicle track filled with rainwater. Water is retained only for a short period, but successive rains may keep a pool filled for several months, thus allowing frogs to breed – especially explosive breeders. Plants growing in, or associated with, pools are generally not specialised hydrophytes. Animal life (and hence predators) in the pool is limited.	
	Pond: A small, usually ornamental, permanent body of standing water, such as a garden fishpond.	John Leyden
Riverine systems Watercourses contained within a channel except in times of flooding.	**Permanent river:** A flow of water in a natural channel.	
	Dry river bed: Natural channel during seasons without water flow.	Leon Meyer
	Floodplain: A flat or depressed area along a riverbank that is periodically inundated and may retain floodwater after the river recedes.	
	Temporary stream: A seasonal flow of water in a natural channel.	
	Perennial stream: A flow of water in a natural channel throughout all seasons.	
	Mountain torrent: A rapid flow of water in a steep natural channel.	

Lacustrine systems Bodies of water greater than 8 ha situated in topographic depressions or dammed river channels and with more than 70% of the water surface open and without emergent vegetation.	**Dam:** A manmade impediment to the flow of a watercourse. Most dams are used for irrigation or watering of livestock, and can support hydrophytes and aquatic animal life. Frogs usually breed in the headwaters of a dam or along shallow parts of the bank. A distinction is drawn between dams and large irrigation schemes such as the Gariep Dam or Hartbeespoort Dam. The latter do not attract many frogs because of wave action and the presence of predators.	
	Lake: A large, natural body of fresh water such as Lake Chrissie or Lake Sibaya. Lakes support relatively few breeding populations of frogs because of wave action and the presence of predators.	
Palustrine systems Shallow marshland areas (less than 2 m deep) with more than 30% of the surface dominated by emergent hydrophytic vegetation.	**Vlei:** Part of a watercourse which spreads out over a flat valley forming a marshy wetland with inundated grass, sedges, reeds and other specialised water-based vegetation. Vleis usually dry up partly or entirely during the dry season. They are the breeding grounds for many different species. In the Western Cape, the word 'vlei' is used for water bodies called 'pans' or 'lakes' elsewhere, e.g., Rondevlei.	
	Hill slope seepage (perched wetland): Subterranean water flow suspended in soils between the surface and an impervious lower substrate.	Leon Meyer
	Inundated grass: Temporarily flooded open grassland.	
Terrestrial systems Ecological systems with no conspicuous standing or flowing water bodies.	**Forest floor:** Ground below closed canopy woodland, usually comprising heavy deposits of humus and leaf litter.	
	Rock outcrop: Exposed assembly of bare rock above soil deposits.	Leon Meyer
	Sand dunes: Elevated deposits of loose sand.	
	Open fynbos: Maccia floral kingdom: an assembly of ericas, proteas and restios endemic to the Western Cape and Southern Cape.	
	Open grassveld: Hills and plains in central southern Africa covered by mixed grass species and an absence of woodland.	

AMPHIBIANS IN DECLINE

In recent decades frogs on several continents have suffered sudden, high mortality rates, resulting in various species becoming extinct and many others undergoing massive population reductions. Globally, amphibians are now the most threatened class of vertebrate. Amphibian population fluctuations are not unusual under natural conditions, but recent declines have been excessively severe and populations have failed to recover. Because of the ecological importance of frog populations in both terrestrial and aquatic ecosystems, these losses may bring about complex and far-reaching consequences.

The global decline in amphibian numbers is one of the most vexing conservation issues of recent times. A current report from the IUCN's Global Amphibian Assessment (www.globalamphibians.org) shows that as many as a third of amphibian species have suffered severe declines worldwide and more than 7% are listed as Critically Endangered, many on the brink of extinction (IUCN *Red List of Threatened Species* www.iucnredlist. org). Despite increased scientific awareness of the threat, recent increases in extinctions remain largely unexplained. Some instances occur in virtually undisturbed regions, far from the adverse effects of habitat destruction and pollution.

A number of hypotheses have been presented to explain these enigmatic extinctions and declines, but there has been no scientific consensus on the matter. Synergy between complex factors may be obscuring the root causes of amphibian declines. Some of the environmental hazards that are known to be contributing to these declines are listed below.

Habitat destruction or modification

Annually large areas of natural wetland and vegetation are destroyed for agriculture, forestry and urban development with largescale and permanent loss of amphibian habitat.

Climate change

Meteorological events and the shifting of seasonal patterns are creating macro-climatic changes that have serious implications for amphibian reproduction and survival. Moreover, shifts in climatic conditions may provide more favourable conditions for disease.

Depletion of stratospheric ozone

The breakdown of atmospheric filters that protect against ultraviolet light and subsequent increased UV exposure affects the development of frog eggs and developing tadpoles, especially in species that breed at high elevations and where eggs are deposited near surface water.

Disease

The recent escalation of amphibian die-offs caused by the fungal pathogen *Batrachochytrium dendrobatidis*, or amphibian chytrid, suggests that this may be a major contributor to amphibian declines and extinctions worldwide. Sudden outbreaks of the disease may be linked to global climate change as well as to international trade in amphibians.

A number of southern African species have been found to be infected with *B. dendrobatidis* and sporadic die-offs have been reported, but there is currently no evidence of significant population declines. However, the large number of IUCN Red Listed species in southern Africa, many of which have very restricted distribution ranges, may be at risk in the future from chytrid fungus.

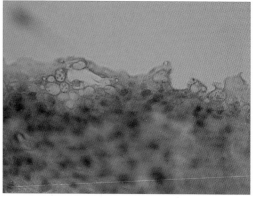

Left: Chytrid-infected Common River Frog. Note that the hindlegs are not tucked in against the body. Right: Amphibian chytrid infection of skin. Compare with healthy skin on p.30.

Chemical pollution

Numerous studies to determine the effects of pesticides and other chemicals on amphibians show that some species are very sensitive to this type of pollution, while others show remarkable resistance. The diversity of amphibians and the variety of pesticides make investigation complicated.

Exploitation in food and pet trade

Human consumption of frogs in southern Africa is confined to a few rural communities but the illegal export of Giant Bullfrogs for food and as pets persists. In places such as Indonesia as many as 200 million frog legs are exported annually to the rest of south Asia.

Frog carcasses for sale in a street market in Malaysia.

Predation

At all stages of their life cycle frogs are an important food resource for a wide range of other animals and, because of their own copious consumption of invertebrates, they are essential links in the natural food web. Eggs and tadpoles are vulnerable to fish and aquatic invertebrates such as spiders, crabs, dragonfly larva and water beetles. The large fishing spider *Thalassius* will also take adult reed frogs, paralysing them and sucking out their fluids.

More usual predators of adult frogs are birds such as kingfishers and herons, snakes, water monitors and small mammals. To avoid the skin toxins secreted by many species, birds often wipe their captive frogs before devouring them while mongooses feed from the underbelly of the frog leaving the glandular dorsal skin untouched. Introduced predators such as trout will also prey on frogs.

Les Minter

Les Minter

Top left: Striped Skaapsteker taking a Bubbling Kassina.
Top right: Fishing Spider eating frog eggs.
Above: Belastromatid Water Bug eating a Foam Nest Frog.
Right: Fishing Spider eating a Water Lily Frog.

PARASITES

Frogs are hosts for all the major animal parasite groups, from microscopic protozoa to large tapeworms. The most common are shown below.

COMMON PARASITES IN FROGS		
Parasite group	**Description**	
Protozoans	Single-celled animals occurring in very large numbers in specific organs. The most common are the opalinid ciliates which live in the intestine of the frog. Pictured right is a ciliate *Trichodina* that lives in the urinary bladder of frogs.	Linda Basson
Monogenetic trematodes	One family, the polystomatids, feeds on blood in the urinary bladder. The life cycle of the parasite is perfectly synchronised with that of the host.	
Digenetic trematodes	Found in organs such as the digestive tract, lungs, gall bladder and urinary bladder. They have complex life cycles that may involve one or several intermediate hosts, such as snails or insects. Others are transmitted to a final mammal or reptile host if it ingests an infected frog.	
Cestodes or tapeworms	Relatively rare in frogs but mature tapeworms are occasionally found in the digestive system while immature encysted forms are found throughout the body of the frog.	
Nematodes or roundworms	Common in amphibians and can vary from microscopic worms in the lymph or the blood, to large worms in the body cavity or digestive system.	
Acantocephalans or spiny-headed worms	Easily distinguished by a proboscis armed with many hooks, but not commonly found in frogs.	
Mites	Frogs are occasionally infested with larval and adult mites. The larval stage of the mite, *Endotrombicula*, burrows into the skin. *Xenopacarus* is adapted to live inside the nostrils of the Platanna *Xenopus laevis*.	
Leeches	Leeches feed opportunistically on frogs. Some are species specific. Note leech on eye of Madagascan Tree Frog.	

AMPHIBIANS AS BIO-INDICATORS

For many reasons, frogs are important and useful indicators of environmental health. Factors that make frogs particularly sensitive to environmental deterioration include:

Absorbent skin surface

Permeable skin readily absorbs water and any solvents that it may contain.

Accessibility

Frogs are a convenient group to monitor, being visually and acoustically conspicuous and widely distributed in most environments.

Food contaminants

Many species of tadpoles feed at the bottom of a water body where they are susceptible to ingesting chlorinated compounds and heavy metals. Adult frogs may also swallow contaminated soil and plant material.

Fragmented distribution

Amphibians usually have specific habitat requirements resulting in a patchy distribution for many species. Habitat losses may isolate surviving populations, putting them under severe risk of becoming extinct in certain areas.

Sequestered tissue contaminants

Exposure to foreign hormones can disrupt the hormone-driven process of metamorphosis and the healthy development of tadpoles.

Temperature

Amphibians are sensitive to extreme environmental temperatures which can adversely affect their biology.

Amphibious lifestyle

Frogs are exposed to the aquatic as well as the terrestrial environment and are thus affected by changes to both.

Trophic level

Amphibians are both voracious predators of invertebrate life and themselves important prey for a wide diversity of predators. In both capacities they influence a wide ecological spectrum.

Healthy wetland landscape: Okavango floodplains in Botswana.

CONSERVATION AND RED DATA LISTED SPECIES

The value of frogs as exceptional representatives of broad ecological systems – and indicators of environmental health – is a persuasive argument for their conservation. Semi-arid southern Africa has an increasing human population and consequent pressure on water resources; it is imperative that we conserve total ecosystems in general, and wetlands in particular.

Assessment of the conservation status of amphibians in the region requires knowledge of their diversity, endemism, habitat requirements, distribution and general biology. That knowledge was consolidated and expanded with the publication of the *Atlas and Red Data Book of the Frogs of South Africa, Lesotho and Swaziland* (Minter, *et al.* 2004) in which the conservation status of many southern African frogs was reviewed: this information is included in the list of Red Data species below. However, the conservation status of frogs beyond the borders of South Africa, Lesotho and Swaziland remains unknown.

RED DATA LISTED SPECIES OF SOUTH AFRICA, LESOTHO AND SWAZILAND

Common name	Scientific name
CRITICALLY ENDANGERED	
Mistbelt Chirping Frog	*Anhydrophryne ngongoniensis*
Hewitt's Ghost Frog	*Heleophryne hewitti*
Table Mountain Ghost Frog	*Heleophryne rosei*
Micro Frog	*Microbatrachella capensis*
ENDANGERED	
Knysna Leaf-folding Frog	*Afrixalus knysnae*
Hogsback Chirping Frog	*Anhydrophryne rattrayi*
Pickersgill's Reed Frog	*Hyperolius pickersgilli*
Long-toed Tree Frog	*Leptopelis xenodactylus*
Kloof Frog	*Natalobatrachus bonebergi*
Western Leopard Toad	*Amietophrynus pantherinus*
Amatola Toad	*Vandijkophrynus amatolicus*
Cape Platanna	*Xenopus gilli*
VULNERABLE	
Natal Leaf-folding Frog	*Afrixalus spinifrons*
Cape Rain Frog	*Breviceps gibbosus*
Desert Rain Frog	*Breviceps macrops*
Northern Forest Rain Frog	*Breviceps sylvestris*
Cape Caco	*Cacosternum capense*
Rose's Mountain Toadlet	*Capensibufo rosei*
Spotted Shovel-nosed Frog	*Hemisus guttatus*
Namaqua Stream Frog	*Strongylopus springbokensis*
NEAR THREATENED	
Landdroskop Moss Frog	*Arthroleptella landdrosia*
Cape Peninsula Moss Frog	*Arthroleptella lightfooti*
Montane Marsh Frog	*Poyntonia paludicola*
Giant Bullfrog	*Pyxicephalus adspersus*
Plain Stream Frog	*Strongylopus wageri*
DATA DEFICIENT	
Van Dijk's River Frog	*Amietia vandijki*
Drewes's Moss Frog	*Arthroleptella drewesii*
Bilbo's Rain Frog	*Breviceps bagginsi*
Whistling Rain Frog	*Breviceps sopranus*
Karoo Caco	*Cacosternum karooicum*
Poynton's Caco	*Cacosternum poyntoni*
Striped Caco	*Cacosternum striatum*

FROGS AND HUMANS
Interactions and aversions

In the past frogs were considered to have very little impact on everyday human life. They are, after all, harmless to humans: they do not bite or sting, they do not damage homes or crops, and they are not carriers of human or animal disease. Yet from earliest recorded times their abundance and their vociferous nightly calling has made humans aware of their presence and in many societies they have featured in myths and legends, in art and in medicine. From infancy, children play with toy frogs and later learn the elements of biology from rearing tadpoles. Almost everyone encounters frogs in literature and learns about them in folklore and custom.

It is only relatively recently that scientific research has led to an understanding of the great ecological importance of frogs in many ecosystems around the world. Our current knowledge of their critical position in the food chain as predators and prey, their bio-indicator status in determining wetland and river health, and their role in keeping down the numbers of insects – many of them vectors of human diseases – continues to grow. It is now thought that frogs are a critically important group of animals to study in connection with issues such as global climate change.

Observing frogs is not only about the frogs themselves. It is about exploring wetlands, listening to the sounds of an African night, conserving the natural world. The study can be scientific or it can be recreational for the whole family. To some it means researching for a postgraduate study; to others it means exciting discoveries on a summer holiday.

Fascination with frogs and tadpoles begins at an early age.

BELIEFS AND LEGENDS

In Ancient Egypt the frogs of the life-giving Nile River, with their thousands of tadpoles and their reappearance each season, symbolised both fertility and resurrection. To ensure the rebirth of the deceased in an afterlife, frogs were carefully folded into the wrappings of mummies. Heqet, the Egyptian goddess of childbirth, took the form of a frog and in hieroglyphics several other Egyptian gods are depicted with the faces or bodies of frogs.

European fairytales and early witchcraft frequently recorded the transformation of people into frogs in different settings, usually as a demotion to a lower life form or as a disguise. Three of the tales that Andrew Lang collected from around the world for inclusion in his popular *Fairy Books* depict a frog being helpful to humans in trouble.

Frogs are associated with magic, mystery and medicine.

European medieval medicine is peppered with references to the power of frogs in potions and poisons. It was suggested that a live frog placed in the mouth would cure inflammation of the throat, and tonsillitis could be prevented by wearing a string from which a frog had been hanged. Even less logically, swallowing a frog was said to prevent incontinence. Presumably it was imagined that the legs of dead frogs dangled around one's neck would cure scrofula because the glandular and warty skin of the frogs could somehow extract the protrusions from human skin.

The large eyes of a frog seemed analogous to some human afflictions. In these cases, ophthalmic trouble could be treated by first licking the eye of a frog and then licking the eye of the patient. Nosebleeds, earache and sprained ankles also had frog-based folk remedies. In *Macbeth*, Shakespeare's witches famously blended 'eye of newt and toe of frog' into their fortune-telling brew, but in *As You Like It* the playwright acknowledged the beauty of a toad's eye, the creature itself 'ugly and venomous, yet wears a jewel in his head'. It is remarkable how the idea that frogs were venomous – so obviously untrue – has survived, and it is possible that it derives from the fact that so many people find frogs physically repugnant, 'slimy' and 'warty', with unattractive nocturnal habits such as inhabiting dark pools and other secret hideouts.

Frog lore appears to be universal and southern African tradition also alludes to the magical and medicinal properties of frogs. There is a strong belief that frogs bring rain – surely based on the observation that many species initiate their breeding behaviour in early spring, shortly before the first summer rains.

Frogs that appear after rain are said to be harbingers of good fortune but, by contrast, some people believe that if a woman brings a frog in with water she has collected, she brings a curse to the family. A froglet, *senqaqane,* and a worm, *kokwana,* are magical ingredients in a Sotho poison that is believed to be able to kill a victim when ingested. In Zulu tradition, burnt frogs are mixed with herbs to treat asthma and chronic oedema. Dried toad skin is administered to treat irregular heart beat and palpitations, and this may have a scientific basis because the cardio-toxins in the parotoid glands of toads may act in the same way that digitalis affects the heart. Giant Bullfrogs are dried and boiled in water to relieve whooping cough, and tadpoles are mixed into a cure for epilepsy.

FROGS AND VENOM

Despite their harmlessness, many people all over the world firmly believe that all frogs are poisonous. Some even think that snakes acquire their venom from frogs that they have eaten, while others believe that if one touches a toad, its glandular secretions will cause warts on the hands. Neither allegation is true.

Many species of frogs do, however, secrete toxins or distasteful fluids from their skins (called bufonin, bufogin or bufotalin) to deter predators. However, these substances can do no harm unless ingested because frogs have no fangs or stings to inject the venom. The best known of the toxic-skinned frogs are the Dendrobatidae, the Poison Arrow Frogs of South America. These are small and brightly coloured terrestrial frogs, generally abundant in the Central and South American forests where the Indian people of tropical America have learnt to isolate and use the poison on their hunting arrows. The frogs are first pierced with a sharp stick, and then heated over a flame causing them to exude droplets of poison which are collected and allowed to ferment. Arrows are dipped into this mixture and dried, and when shot into the bodies of small animals such as monkeys or birds, paralysis is almost instantaneous.

South American Poison Arrow Frogs secrete a toxic fluid that is used by hunters as a poison on their arrow tips.

A number of southern African species also secrete defensive fluids from their skin. Toads release a distasteful whitish secretion when they are molested. It causes dogs to froth at the mouth and drop the frog at once. The secretion is also reputed to be hallucinogenic. Some predators have learnt to avoid the secretion, and some mongooses, for example, have been observed eating toads only from the underside, thus leaving the glandular dorsal skin untouched. The mucous secretion from Platannas is very slippery as well as toxic, providing a double deterrent to predators, but herons and kingfishers can often be seen scraping the surface fluids from Platannas before eating them. Another dual function of toxic skin secretions can be found in Rain Frogs. In this group, the secretions are adhesive and facilitate the amplexus of these plump fogs while also repelling predators. Particularly potent toxins emanate from the glossy skin of the Banded Rubber Frog *Phrynomantis bifasciatus*. However, the aposematic colours of the frog – black, red and white – warn predators of the danger. Handling such a frog can irritate sensitive skin and may even be dangerous if the poison penetrates the skin though an open cut or abrasion. After handling the species, care should be taken not to touch one's eyes.

FROGS AS FOOD

Preparation of a meal of frogs' legs.

Traditionally, France is associated with frog cuisine and frog legs laced with garlic is considered a delicacy. However, the greatest human consumption of frogs takes place in eastern countries such as Malaysia, but even there frogs are more of a luxury than a dietary staple. In southern Africa the Giant Bullfrog *Pyxicephalus adspersus* and the African Bullfrog *P. edulis* are eaten in Mozambique and in Limpopo Province – fried webbing is regarded with particular favour. However, the emergence of these two species is highly seasonal and their value as a dependable food source is thus limited. Farming frogs for their legs (often to be canned) or for the pet market is widely practised in a number of countries but it is uncommon in southern Africa where the trade is rigorously regulated. There is a particular danger in farming frogs and exporting them because of the possibility of spreading parasites and pathogens such as the amphibian chytrid fungus which is now depleting frog populations in many parts of the world.

FROGS AS PETS

Keeping pet frogs is a common practice throughout the world and stimulates a fairly vigorous exchange in captive animals. In general, the rarer the species, the higher the price. Frogs do not make particularly interesting pets and – in contrast to many other pets – are unable to hold one's interest for long because they are secretive and remain dormant and concealed for much of the time. In South Africa permits are required to keep indigenous frogs captive and these are usually not granted by wildlife authorities except for genuine scientific research.

If frogs are kept legally in captivity they have to be cared for responsibly. They need to be housed in a large vivarium that simulates their natural habitat as closely as possible: the perfect combination of terrestrial, aquatic and plant habitat needs to be carefully reconstructed to suit the requirements of each species. Places that serve as retreats must be provided, and frogs must be able to conceal themselves among appropriate plants. Fossorial species need to have a suitable depth of substrate on the floor of the vivarium into which they can burrow. The water supply must be kept fresh and unpolluted and temperature and humidity must be controllable and maintained at optimum levels. In captive conditions, fungal growth can be rapid and lethal in a humid environment and constant vigilance is needed.

Feeding pet frogs can be difficult because most species will take only live prey and this has to be provided regularly. Smaller species, such as Reed Frogs, can be sustained by *Drosophila* fruit flies which are attracted to and can breed in overripe fruit placed in the vivarium. Larger species can survive on mealworms that are bred in containers of bran located outside the vivarium. From time to time other prey items need to be introduced to supplement the diet; crickets are good for this purpose and relatively easy to capture. In addition, sprinkling the crickets with calcium powder (commercially available at most petshops) will further benefit the frog's nutrition.

Breeding frogs in captivity is even more demanding than merely keeping them alive. Every species demands a different suite of conditions in order to reproduce successfully. Requirements include the correct physical environment together with suitable weather conditions, population numbers and sex ratios. Because of the challenges involved, few southern African species have been bred in captivity successfully. The Platanna can usually be bred in large tanks where there is adequate food, while Painted Reed Frogs have been bred in large vivariums under laboratory-like control systems.

Vivarium suitable for keeping certain species of frogs.

John Leyden

Ponds and water features soon attract frogs to the garden.

FROGS IN THE GARDEN

Attracting frogs to one's garden is more rewarding and far less difficult than keeping them as captive pets. In gardens the feeding and breeding of frogs can be appreciated and observed as part of nature. For this to be a success, the correct environment must be created.

First, one should identify the species that occur naturally in the area because these are the ones most likely to come into the garden. Then explore your suburb or district and look out for the characteristics of the natural habitats of local frogs. Take notes from this field guide and from your own observations and identify the species that occur in your area, and where they occur. Reproduce these conditions in your garden – whether they be pond, stream, dense vegetation or hideaway. It is advisable not to create these habitats too close to the house as a chorus of Raucous Toads, for example, can be very loud. For those species that breed in water, the extent, depth and vegetation cover will be critically important. Bear in mind that most species select still, shallow, well-protected breeding sites rather than deep, open or flowing water bodies.

Unlike birds and mammals, frogs are more attracted to an ideal habitat than they are to food. Perhaps an occasional toad will visit a light source that attracts insects, but putting out food will not generally be successful as a lure. Nonetheless, the availability of natural food resources is critically important and the use of insecticides in the garden will almost certainly reduce any possibility of frogs surviving.

Bringing adult frogs from other sites into a garden is seldom successful and it is also illegal in South Africa. As most species are philopatric, translocated adults become disorientated and instinctively try to return to their original breeding ground, with consequent high mortality. Furthermore, translocations increase the probability of transmitting disease and disrupting the natural dispersal processes of genetic material. Collecting tadpoles in your neighbourhood and introducing them into your garden pond may be more successful, but great care must be taken because tadpoles are vulnerable to sudden alterations in water temperature or other environmental conditions.

Once you have established optimum conditions for frogs in your garden, wait for results. The reward will be the sounds of nature on a summer's evening, restoring harmony to what is often a stressful urban environment.

FIELD KEYS
AND DESCRIPTIONS

HOW TO USE A FIELD KEY

A key can be a useful tool to help identify frogs in the field. However, interspecific and intraspecific variations are sometimes considerable and can lead to incorrect classification. Identification based on the key should therefore always be confirmed by other corroborative information provided by species descriptions, illustrations and sound recordings.

When using a key, the specimen should be retained in a small transparent container through which different characters can easily be seen. On occasion it may be necessary to hold the specimen firmly but gently in the hand to observe a particular detail. Consider the two alternatives in the first couplet of the Key to Frog Genera and select the one that applies to the specimen. This will indicate either the genus or the number of the next couplet to be considered. Consider the alternatives in this next couplet and follow the procedure in strict numeric sequence until the genus has been determined. Keys to individual species within the genus are given in the generic descriptions in the pages that follow. In a few instances the key to the genera leads directly to a particular species. In other instances the key may resolve only some of the species (indicated by the word 'part'). The others become resolved later in the key.

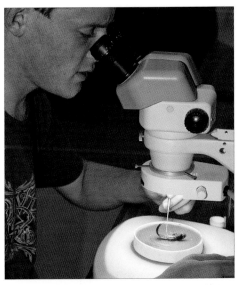

A microscope or good hand lens is needed to examine tadpoles.

Adult frogs can be held in the hand or in a transparent container to study features.

FIELD KEY TO THE GENERA OF ADULT FROGS

The first part of this field key deals with adult frogs (as opposed to tadpoles), and enables identification to the generic level only, except in those instances where the genus contains only one species, which is then named.

KEY TO FROG GENERA

#	a.	b.
1	a. Hard claws on 3 toes of each foot **Platannas** *Xenopus* pp.328–337	b. No hard claws on the toes 2
2	a. Pupil vertically elongated in bright light 3	b. Pupil circular or horizontally elongated in bright light 10
3	a. Adhesive terminal discs on fingers or toes (may be no wider than the toe in some instances) 4	b. No adhesive terminal discs on fingers or toes 8
4	a. Terminal discs on fingers spatulate (squared off at the tip) 5	b. Terminal discs on fingers, not squared off at the tip 6
5	a. Known from the extreme north of the Eastern Cape, KwaZulu-Natal and Mpumalanga **Natal Cascade Frog** *Hadromophryne natalensis* pp.196–199	b. Known from the Western Cape and western part of the Eastern Cape **Ghost Frogs** *Heleophryne* pp.200–213

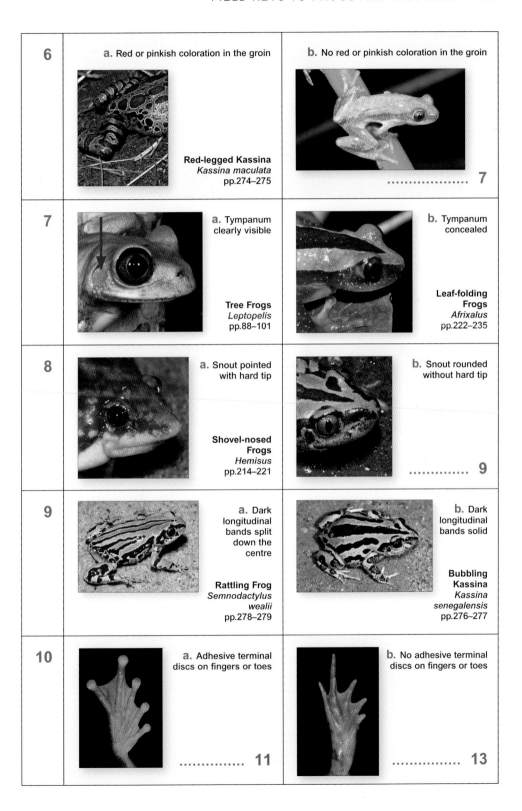

6

a. Red or pinkish coloration in the groin

Red-legged Kassina
Kassina maculata
pp.274–275

b. No red or pinkish coloration in the groin

.... **7**

7

a. Tympanum clearly visible

Tree Frogs
Leptopelis
pp.88–101

b. Tympanum concealed

Leaf-folding Frogs
Afrixalus
pp.222–235

8

a. Snout pointed with hard tip

Shovel-nosed Frogs
Hemisus
pp.214–221

b. Snout rounded without hard tip

.... **9**

9

a. Dark longitudinal bands split down the centre

Rattling Frog
Semnodactylus wealii
pp.278–279

b. Dark longitudinal bands solid

Bubbling Kassina
Kassina senegalensis
pp.276–277

10

a. Adhesive terminal discs on fingers or toes

.... **11**

b. No adhesive terminal discs on fingers or toes

.... **13**

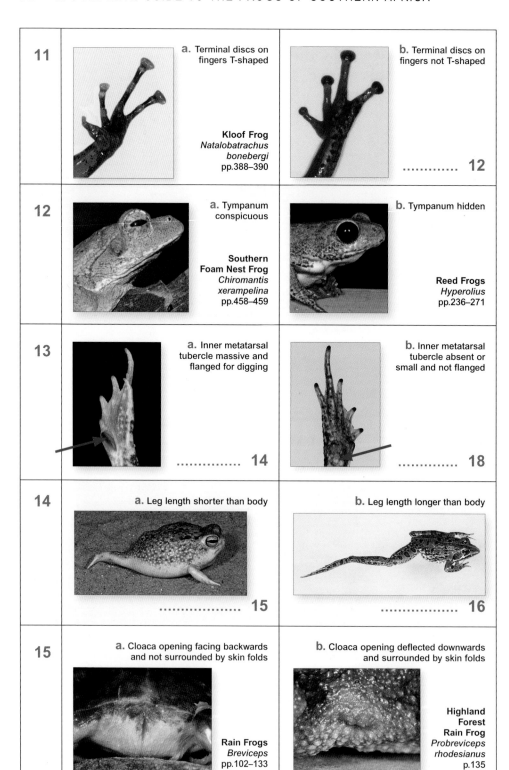

11

a. Terminal discs on fingers T-shaped

Kloof Frog
Natalobatrachus bonebergi
pp.388–390

b. Terminal discs on fingers not T-shaped

.... **12**

12

a. Tympanum conspicuous

Southern Foam Nest Frog
Chiromantis xerampelina
pp.458–459

b. Tympanum hidden

Reed Frogs
Hyperolius
pp.236–271

13

a. Inner metatarsal tubercle massive and flanged for digging

.... **14**

b. Inner metatarsal tubercle absent or small and not flanged

.... **18**

14

a. Leg length shorter than body

.... **15**

b. Leg length longer than body

.... **16**

15

a. Cloaca opening facing backwards and not surrounded by skin folds

Rain Frogs
Breviceps
pp.102–133

b. Cloaca opening deflected downwards and surrounded by skin folds

Highland Forest Rain Frog
Probreviceps rhodesianus
p.135

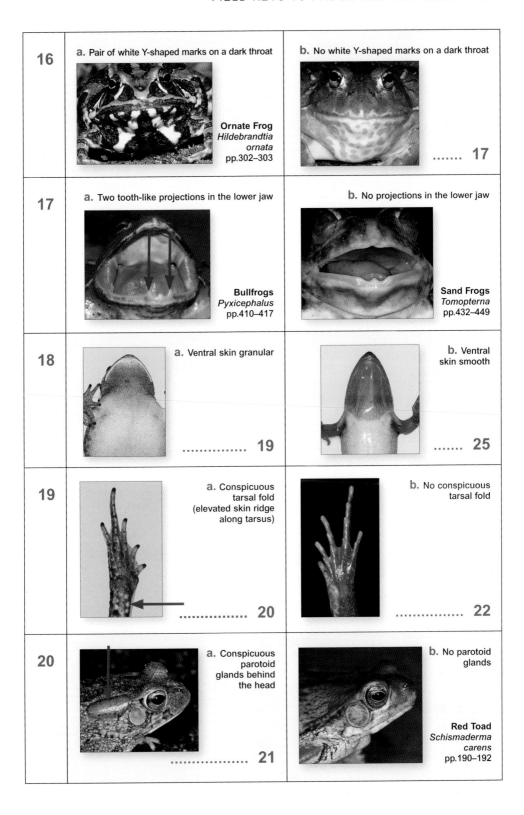

16

a. Pair of white Y-shaped marks on a dark throat

Ornate Frog
Hildebrandtia ornata
pp.302–303

b. No white Y-shaped marks on a dark throat

.... **17**

17

a. Two tooth-like projections in the lower jaw

Bullfrogs
Pyxicephalus
pp.410–417

b. No projections in the lower jaw

Sand Frogs
Tomopterna
pp.432–449

18

a. Ventral skin granular

.... **19**

b. Ventral skin smooth

.... **25**

19

a. Conspicuous tarsal fold (elevated skin ridge along tarsus)

.... **20**

b. No conspicuous tarsal fold

.... **22**

20

a. Conspicuous parotoid glands behind the head

.... **21**

b. No parotoid glands

Red Toad
Schismaderma carens
pp.190–192

21

a. Dark patches arranged in more or less symmetrical pairs on either side of the vertebra

Typical toads *Amietophrynus*
pp.136–155

b. Dark patches randomly distributed over the dorsum

Van Dijk's Toads *Vandijkophrynus*
pp.172–183

22

a. Hourglass dorsal pattern

Squeakers
Arthroleptis
pp.80–87

b. No hourglass pattern on dorsum

.... **23**

23

a. Found only in the southwestern Cape mountains (winter-rainfall area)

Mountain Toadlets
Capensibufo
pp.184–189

b. Found north of the southwestern Cape mountains (summer-rainfall area)

.... **24**

24

a. Parotoid glands prominent and forming a continuous 'platform' with the top of the head

Forest Toads *Mertensophryne*
pp.193–195

b. Parotoid glands not prominent and never forming a continuous 'platform' with the top of the head

Pygmy Toads *Poyntonophrynus*
pp.156–171

25

a. Black or very dark with red or pink markings

Rubber Frogs *Phrynomantis* pp.281–289

b. Coloration not as in **a.**

.... **26**

26

a. No webbing between toes

.... **27**

b. Webbing between toes

.... **29**

27

a. Ventral surface with dark rounded patches, sometimes fused or elongated

Cacos
Cacosternum
pp.362–385

b. Ventral surface immaculate, marbled or speckled

.... **28**

28

a. Found only in the Eastern Cape and KwaZulu-Natal

Chirping Frogs
Anhydrophryne
pp.338–345

b. Found only in the Western Cape

Moss Frogs
Arthroleptella
pp.346–361

29

a. 2 (occasionally 3) pale bars stretching from below eye to upper lip

Montane Marsh Frog
Poyntonia paludicola
pp.391–393

b. No bars as in **a.**

.... **30**

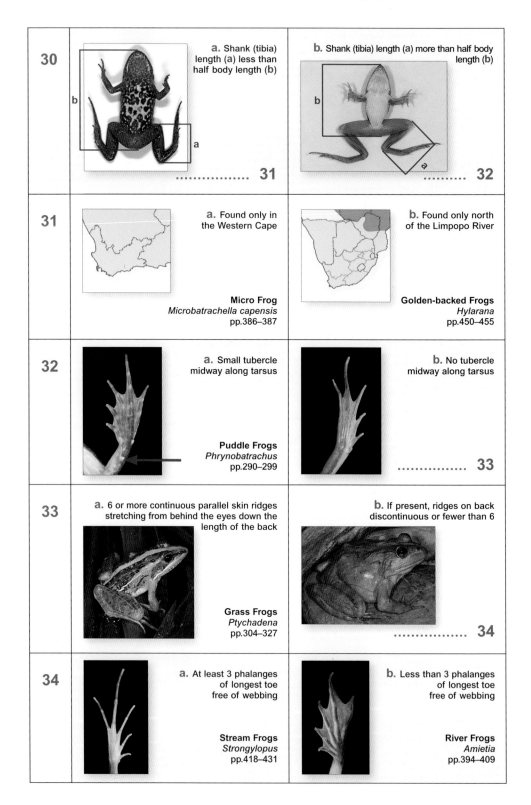

30

a. Shank (tibia) length (a) less than half body length (b) **31**

b. Shank (tibia) length (a) more than half body length (b) **32**

31

a. Found only in the Western Cape

Micro Frog
Microbatrachella capensis
pp.386–387

b. Found only north of the Limpopo River

Golden-backed Frogs
Hylarana
pp.450–455

32

a. Small tubercle midway along tarsus

Puddle Frogs
Phrynobatrachus
pp.290–299

b. No tubercle midway along tarsus **33**

33

a. 6 or more continuous parallel skin ridges stretching from behind the eyes down the length of the back

Grass Frogs
Ptychadena
pp.304–327

b. If present, ridges on back discontinuous or fewer than 6 .... **34**

34

a. At least 3 phalanges of longest toe free of webbing

Stream Frogs
Strongylopus
pp.418–431

b. Less than 3 phalanges of longest toe free of webbing

River Frogs
Amietia
pp.394–409

FIELD KEY TO THE FAMILIES AND GENERA OF TADPOLES

The following field key deals with the tadpole stage of frogs. In some instances, it is possible to determine identification of a specimen to family level only – these are contained in the first part of the tadpole field key. Those tadpoles that can be identified to genus level are covered in the second part of the key.

KEY TO TADPOLE FAMILIES

1	**a.** No jaw sheaths, labial tooth rows or oral papillae **2**	**b.** Oral disc present and usually keratinized jaw sheaths, labial tooth rows and oral papillae present **3**
2	**a.** Mouth with a fold in the lower lip, lacking tentacles and one medial spiracle **Rubber Frogs** Microhylidae *Phrynomantis* p. 282	**b.** Mouth a horizontal slit with tentacles at the sides, and a spiracle at each side **Platannas** Pipidae *Xenopus* p.329
3	**a.** More than 7 lower tooth rows; papillae all around oral disk without gaps; no upper jaw sheath **Cascade Frog and Ghost Frogs** Heleophrynidae p.77	**b.** Less than 8 lower tooth rows; gap in upper jaw papillae; upper jaw sheath present **4**
4	**a.** A broad gap in lower jaw papillae; vent median and marginal **Toads** Bufonidae p.77	**b.** Gap in lower jaw papillae absent or small; vent on right side of fin **5**
5	**a.** Connective tissue extending anteriorly, dorsally and ventrally beyond the tail muscles **Shovel-nosed Frogs** Hemisotidae (part) *Hemisus* p.215	**b.** Tail fin not obscured by connective tissue **6**
6	**a.** Two undivided lower labial tooth rows **7**	**b.** Not as in **a.** **10**

Most drawings by Angelo Lambiris

Most drawings by Angelo Lambiris; drawing of 8a by Jenny Channing

7	a. Vent supramarginal and dextral **Reed Frogs** Hyperoliidae (part) p.78	b. Vent marginal and more or less dextral **8**
8	a. Tadpole with proportionally very long, shallow tail and numerous white-tipped tubercles covering the body and front third of tail; found in seeps on Western Cape mountains **Marsh Frog** Pyxicephalidae (part) *Poyntonia paludicola* pp.392–393	b. Tail not exceptionally long and no white-tipped tubercles covering the body and the front third of the tail; not found in the Western Cape **9**
9	a. Internarial distance > 10x nostril diameter **Puddle Frogs** Phrynobatrachidae *Phrynobatrachus* p.291	b. Internarial distance < 6x nostril diameter **Grass Frogs** Ptychadenidae p.78
10	a. 1 upper labial tooth row present or row absent **Reed Frogs** Hyperoliidae (part) p.78	b. More than 1 upper labial tooth row **11**
11	a. Narrow medial gap in lower jaw papillae; not found in Western Cape **Foam Nest Frogs** Rhacophoridae *Chiromantis* pp.456–459	b. Not as in a. **12**
12	a. Internarial distance > 10x nostril diameter **13**	b. Internarial distance < 6x nostril diameter **14**
13	a. Long finger-like papillae bordering lower jaw; 4 labial tooth rows in lower jaw **Shovel-nosed Frogs** Hemisotidae (part) *Hemisus* p.215	b. Papillae bordering lower jaw not long and finger-like; 3 labial tooth rows in lower jaw **Tree Frogs** Arthroleptidae (part) *Leptopelis* p.89
14	a. Prominent black spots covering body and fins **Golden-backed Frogs** Ranidae *Hylarana* p.451	b. Not as in a. **African Common Frogs** Pyxicephalidae (part) p.78

KEY TO TADPOLE GENERA

BUFONIDAE

1	**a.** Raised horseshoe flap of skin dorsally on the body behind the eyes **Red Toad** *Schismaderma carens* p.192	**b.** No raised flap of skin dorsally on the body **2**

2	**a.** Eyes and nostrils surrounded by doughnut-shaped ring of tissue **Chirinda Toad** *Mertensophryne anotis* pp.193–195
	b. No ring of tissue around eyes and nostrils **3**

3	**a.** Tail more than twice as long as the body **Mountain Toadlets** *Capensibufo* p.185
	b. Tail less than twice as long as the body **4**

4	**a.** Dorsal and ventral fin margins nearly parallel; tail tip bluntly rounded **Van Dijk's Toads** *Vandijkophrynus* (part) p.173
	b. Tail fin with distinct curvature dorsally and ventrally; rounded tip **5**

5	**a.** Eye to nostril distance > eye length **Van Dijk's Toads** *Vandijkophrynus* (part) p.173
	b. Eye to nostril distance < eye length **6**

6	**a.** No pigmentation over the gular region; nostril diameter > half eye length **Pygmy Toads** *Poyntonophrynus* p.157
	b. Pigmentation extends over the gular region, at least posteriorly; nostril diameter < half eye length **Typical toads** *Amietophrynus* p.139

HELEOPHRYNIDAE

1	 **a.** Jaw sheath present in the lower jaw only **Cascade Frog** *Hadromophryne* p.196–199	**b.** Jaw sheaths absent; tail fin not very deep **Ghost Frogs** *Heleophryne* p.201

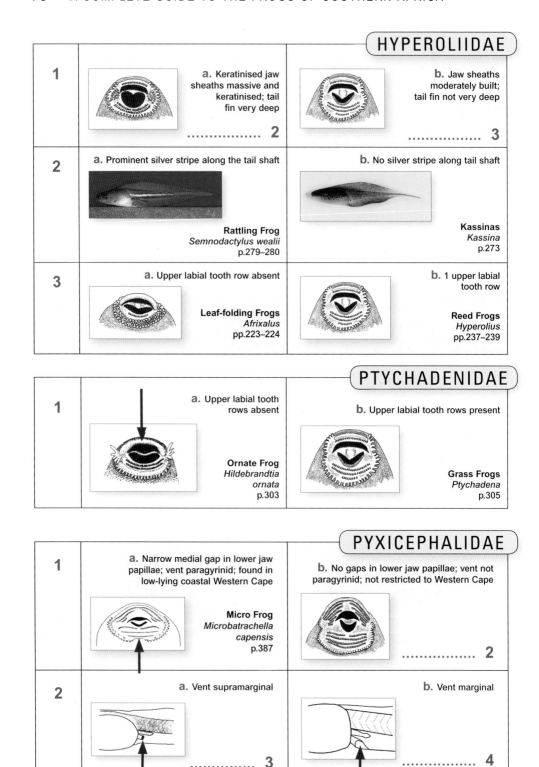

HYPEROLIIDAE

1
a. Keratinised jaw sheaths massive and keratinised; tail fin very deep
.... **2**

b. Jaw sheaths moderately built; tail fin not very deep
.... **3**

2
a. Prominent silver stripe along the tail shaft

Rattling Frog
Semnodactylus wealii
p.279–280

b. No silver stripe along tail shaft

Kassinas
Kassina
p.273

3
a. Upper labial tooth row absent

Leaf-folding Frogs
Afrixalus
pp.223–224

b. 1 upper labial tooth row

Reed Frogs
Hyperolius
pp.237–239

PTYCHADENIDAE

1
a. Upper labial tooth rows absent

Ornate Frog
Hildebrandtia ornata
p.303

b. Upper labial tooth rows present

Grass Frogs
Ptychadena
p.305

PYXICEPHALIDAE

1
a. Narrow medial gap in lower jaw papillae; vent paragyrinid; found in low-lying coastal Western Cape

Micro Frog
Microbatrachella capensis
p.387

b. No gaps in lower jaw papillae; vent not paragyrinid; not restricted to Western Cape
.... **2**

2
a. Vent supramarginal
.... **3**

b. Vent marginal
.... **4**

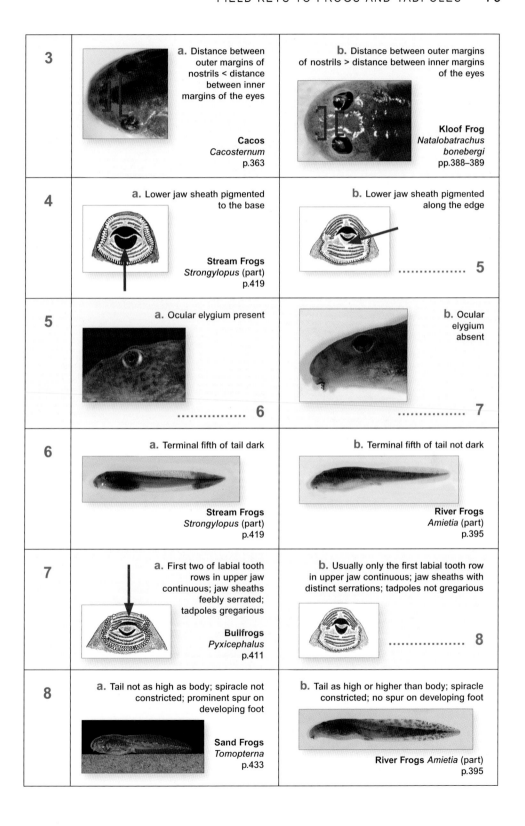

3

a. Distance between outer margins of nostrils < distance between inner margins of the eyes

Cacos
Cacosternum
p.363

b. Distance between outer margins of nostrils > distance between inner margins of the eyes

Kloof Frog
Natalobatrachus bonebergi
pp.388–389

4

a. Lower jaw sheath pigmented to the base

Stream Frogs
Strongylopus (part)
p.419

b. Lower jaw sheath pigmented along the edge

. . . . **5**

5

a. Ocular elygium present

. . . . **6**

b. Ocular elygium absent

. . . . **7**

6

a. Terminal fifth of tail dark

Stream Frogs
Strongylopus (part)
p.419

b. Terminal fifth of tail not dark

River Frogs
Amietia (part)
p.395

7

a. First two of labial tooth rows in upper jaw continuous; jaw sheaths feebly serrated; tadpoles gregarious

Bullfrogs
Pyxicephalus
p.411

b. Usually only the first labial tooth row in upper jaw continuous; jaw sheaths with distinct serrations; tadpoles not gregarious

. . . . **8**

8

a. Tail not as high as body; spiracle not constricted; prominent spur on developing foot

Sand Frogs
Tomopterna
p.433

b. Tail as high or higher than body; spiracle constricted; no spur on developing foot

River Frogs *Amietia* (part)
p.395

SQUEAKERS

KIKKERS

Arthroleptis Smith, 1849

GREEK: *arthron* = joint; *lepto* = slender. Refers to the thin digits that are typical of this genus.

13 species, four in southern Africa

Bush Squeaker: Vernon Crookes Nature Reserve, KwaZulu-Natal.

The southern African species are small – most are less than 30 mm. They are cryptically coloured and usually difficult to locate, even when calling.

With the exception of the Cave Squeaker *A. troglodytes*, they inhabit decaying leaf litter on the forest floor or can be found in adjacent swamps and thickets. The Cave Squeaker was described from caves in eastern Zimbabwe but has not been seen since its initial discovery in 1963.

Species for which the life cycle has been recorded have an extended breeding season beginning with the first summer rains and continuing throughout the season. They call incessantly, particularly during light drizzle or mist, usually from concealed positions among fallen leaves, but occasionally they may scramble onto more exposed elevated call sites.

Clusters of 20 to 40 large unpigmented eggs, each in a stiff jelly capsule, are laid among decaying leaves on the ground. There is no free-swimming tadpole phase; the entire development is completed within the egg capsule, and fully metamorphosed froglets emerge after about four weeks.

DISTINCTIVE CHARACTERS

Dwarf squeaker: Ruo Gorge, Mulanje.

ADULT
- Third finger elongated, particularly so in males
- Diamond-shaped hourglass pattern on dorsum usually present
- Pupil horizontal
- Fingers and toes lack webbing
- Only one metatarsal tubercle – the inner – present

Shovel-footed Squeaker with clear hourglass pattern: St Lucia, KwaZulu-Natal.

TADPOLE
- No free-swimming tadpole phase. Metamorphosis is completed within the egg capsule.

KEY TO SPECIES

ADULT
1 Large inner metatarsal tubercle on the heel .... **Shovel-footed Squeaker** *A. stenodactylus* (p.82)
   Inner metatarsal tubercle inconspicuous or absent **2**
2 Found in KwaZulu-Natal .... **Bush Squeaker** *A. wahlbergii* (p.86)
   Found elsewhere **3**
3 Found in caves and sinkholes in eastern Zimbabwe mountains .... **Cave Squeaker** *A. troglodytes* (p.84)
   Found in woodland or swamps and other non-speleological habitats ....
   .... **Dwarf Squeaker** *A. xenodactyloides* (p.85)

Shovel-footed Squeaker

Graafpootkikker

Arthroleptis stenodactylus Pfeffer, 1893

GREEK: *steno* = narrow; *dactylus* = finger. Refers to the long, thin, third finger of males.

Conservation status: Not threatened.

Shovel-footed Squeaker: Pafuri, Kruger National Park, Limpopo Province.

Identification

Maximum size: 45 mm. **Body:** stocky; larger than other members of genus; head broad and stubby. **Above:** skin smooth; colour varying from light to dark brown; a dark 3-lobed hourglass pattern characteristic of genus and two dark flecks posteriorly; thin pale vertebral line often present; flanks lightly mottled grey; dark facial mask from tip of snout through eye to base of forearm. **Underside:** granular white with grey flecks concentrated over chest. **Forelimbs:** no terminal swellings on fingers. **Hindlimbs:** massive and flange-like inner metatarsal tubercle on foot; soles of feet dark; toes unwebbed and without terminal swelling. **Sexual dimorphism:** third finger of male longer than female; male with dark throat and small spines on legs and dorsum.

Average length

♀

Average length

♂

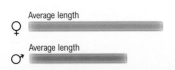

Maximum size: 45 mm

Michael Cunningham

Exceptionally long finger of breeding male: Lujeri Estate, Mulanje, Malawi.

Call

High-pitched metallic *peep-peep* or *wip-wip-wip* chirp. Males call from concealed positions under leaf litter, after rain during the day and at night.

Habitat and habits

Forest floor in dry coastal dune forest and acacia woodland from sea level up to 2 000 m.

KEY ID POINTS

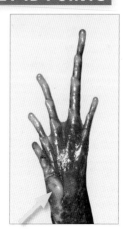

- Exceptionally large inner metatarsal tubercle (distinct from other members of the genus)

Habitat: leaf litter on forest floor.

Cave Squeaker

Grotkikker

Arthroleptis troglodytes Poynton, 1963

LATIN: = *troglodyta*, a hole or cave. Refers to the only known habitat of this species.

Conservation status: Uncertain; limited distribution and habitat. This frog has not been recorded since its initial discovery.

KEY ID POINTS

- Small inner metatarsal tubercle (distinct from *A. stenodactylus*)
- Found only in caves in the eastern highlands of Zimbabwe (distinct from *A. wahlbergi* and *A. xenodactyloides*)

Cave Squeaker: drawn from type specimen, eastern highlands, Zimbabwe.

Angelo Lambiris

Identification

Maximum size: 27 mm. **Body:** small. **Above:** varies from light to dark brown; two- to three-lobed hourglass pattern characteristic of the genus; pale triangular patch on the head present but may be obscured by mottling; snout slightly pointed. **Underside:** granular. **Forelimbs:** tips of the fingers expanded into small bulbs. **Hindlimbs:** inner metatarsal tubercle small; toes unwebbed. **Sexual dimorphism:** fingers of males with spines; third finger of male longer than female; male throat dark.

Call

Unknown.

Habitat and habits

Caves and sinkholes at altitudes above 1 500 m in the eastern highlands of Zimbabwe.

Probable average length
♀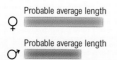

Probable average length
♂

Maximum size: 27 mm

Dwarf Squeaker

Dwergkikker

TRACK
3

Arthroleptis xenodactyloides Hewitt, 1933

GREEK: *xeno* = strange; *dactyloides* = finger. Refers to the unusually long third finger in males of the species.

Conservation status: Limited distribution within the region but not threatened.

Identification
Maximum size: 22 mm. **Body:** slender and small. **Above:** smooth; varies in colour from beige to brown; 3-lobed hourglass pattern characteristic of the genus present in most, but not all, specimens; speckles and mottling may be present; snout slightly pointed. **Underside:** skin texture finely granular and white, with or without dark stippling on the chest. **Forelimbs:** tips of fingers expanded into small bulbs. **Hindlimbs:** inner metatarsal tubercle inconspicuous; toes unwebbed. **Sexual dimorphism:** third finger of male longer than female; male throat dark.

Call
Short high-pitched cricket-like chirp, repeated several times. Males call after rain by day or night from concealed positions under leaf litter.

Habitat and habits
Montane and lowland forests and in high-altitude, dense, swampy grassland.

KEY ID POINTS

- Fingers expanded into bulbs at the tips (distinct from other species except *A. troglodytes*)
- Inconspicuous inner metatarsal tubercle (distinct from *A. stenodactylus*)
- Found in swamps and forest (distinct from *A. troglodytes*)

Dwarf Squeaker: Chimanimani, Malawi.

Average length
♀

Average length
♂

Maximum size: 22 mm

Bush Squeaker

Boskikker

TRACK
2

Arthroleptis wahlbergii Smith, 1849

Named after Swedish naturalist, Johan August Wahlberg, who visited southern Africa in 1839.

Conservation status: Not threatened.

Bush Squeaker: Vernon Crookes Nature Reserve, KwaZulu-Natal.

Identification

Maximum size: 25 mm. **Body:** stocky but small. **Above:** smooth; varies in colour from beige to dark or reddish brown with a 3-lobed hourglass pattern characteristic of the genus and a pale triangular patch on the head; thin, pale vertebral line often present. **Flanks:** flecked. **Head:** snout slightly pointed with

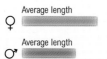

♀ Average length

♂ Average length

Maximum size: 25 mm

a dark facial mask from the tip of the snout through the eye to the base of the forearm. **Underside:** skin granular and white with grey flecks concentrated over the chest. **Forelimbs:** no terminal swellings on fingers. **Hindlimbs:** inner metatarsal tubercle inconspicuous; toes unwebbed, often with slightly swollen tips. **Sexual dimorphism:** third finger of male longer than female; male throat dark; dorsal skin covered with asperities.

Call
High-pitched, drawn-out, metallic *wheep-wheep* or *wheepee-wheepee* chirp, repeated at a rate of one per second in rainy or misty conditions. Males call from concealed positions in the leaf litter both by day and night.

Habitat and habits
Leaf litter in coastal and midland forests and adjacent thickets, and occasionally grassland in KwaZulu-Natal.

KEY ID POINTS

- Prominent hourglass marking on dorsum (generic distinction)
- Found in KwaZulu-Natal coastal and midland forests (distinct from *A. xenodactyloides* and *A. troglodytes*)
- Inconspicuous inner metatarsal tubercle (distinct from *A. stenodactylus*)
- Elongated third finger (generic distinction)

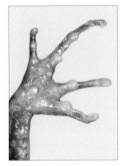

Habitat: forest leaf litter, coastal bush.

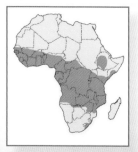

TREE FROGS

BOOMPADDAS

Leptopelis Günther, 1859

GREEK: *lepto* = slender or narrow; *pélis* = pelvis.

47 species, six in southern Africa

Brown-backed Tree Frog with eggs.

Southern African species are medium-sized, with robust bodies and slender limbs. They have large heads with protruding eyes that face slightly forward. The pupil is vertical and surrounded by a distinctively coloured iris.

The genus is widely distributed in areas ranging from dense tropical forests to savanna and open grassland, but each species has a distinct habitat preference. Some species are arboreal, others fossorial; some may be both. Fingers and toes have terminal discs and these are well developed and most conspicuous in the arboreal species. The discs are extremely adhesive, and contact with a single pad to a leaf or branch is sufficient to ensure a safe landing when the frog leaps through vegetation. In burrowing species, the inner metatarsal tubercle is large and flange-like and is used for digging.

Tadpoles are long and streamlined, with powerful, muscular tails.

Advertisement calls are made from prominent, usually elevated, positions. Males defend call sites vigorously, using aggressive territorial calls and physical combat. The vocal sac is internal – only a slight external expansion is visible. Calls are nonetheless loud and audible over long distances.

Those species for which the life cycle is known go into amplexus in trees or on the ground, and then excavate a shallow burrow in mud or decaying leaves close to water. Up to 200 yellowish eggs with a diameter of about 3 mm are laid in a single layered mass in the nest. Tadpoles emerge from the egg capsule after about two weeks, usually after heavy rains. They move towards the water en masse, using wriggling and jumping movements. The instinctive sense of direction is strong and assists them to overcome relatively formidable obstacles. Under dry conditions, egg development may be arrested for several weeks until the next heavy downpour of rain moistens the ground and makes it possible for tadpoles to migrate.

DISTINCTIVE CHARACTERS

ADULT

- Large head with protruding eyes
- Pupil vertical
- Tympanum conspicuous
- Terminal discs on fingers and toes – most prominent in arboreal species
- Inner metatarsal tubercle distinct – most prominent in burrowing species
- Vocal sac internal

TADPOLE

- Vent supramarginal and dextral
- Long, muscular and serpentine

KEY TO SPECIES

ADULT

1 Terminal discs on toes no wider than the width of the digit **2**
   Terminal discs on toes wider than the width of the digit **3**
2 Found east of the KwaZulu-Natal Drakensberg .... **Long-toed Tree Frog** *L. xenodactylus* (p.100)
   Found northwest of the Vaal and Pongola rivers .... **Bocage's Tree Frog** *L. bocagii* (p.90)
3 Dark backwards-pointing triangle on head .... **Broadley's Tree Frog** *L. broadleyi* (p.92)
   Any other pattern **4**
4 Inner metatarsal tubercle smaller than the smallest toe .... **Natal Tree Frog** *L. natalensis* (p.98)
   Inner metatarsal tubercle larger than the smallest toe **5**
5 Fingers with very little or no webbing .... **Brown-backed Tree Frog** *L. mossambicus* (p.96)
   Fingers with moderate webbing, reaching or passing inner tubercle of outer finger ....
   ....**Yellow-spotted Tree Frog** *L. flavomaculatus* (p.94)

TADPOLE

1 Ocular elygium present .... *L. natalensis* (p.98)
   Ocular elygium not present **2**
2 Found through the coastal lowlands along the east coast north of Durban; discs on toe tips visible in
   five-toes stage .... *L. mossambicus* (p.96)
   Found in the foothills of the Natal Drakensberg; no discs on toe tips visible at any stage ....
   .... *L. xenodactylus* (p.100)

TRACK
4

Bocage's Tree Frog

Bocage se boompadda

Leptopelis bocagii (Günther, 1864)

Named after the Portuguese herpetologist, José Vincente
Barboza du Bocage (1823–1907).

Conservation status: Not threatened.

Bocage's Tree Frog: Zimbabwe.

Description

Maximum size: 58 mm. **Body:** toad-like with
short limbs. **Above:** soft and granular; light
pinkish-brown or light brown background, with
a dark horseshoe mark and dark interocular
bar; a thin vertebral line and dark lines along
the flanks sometimes present; juveniles
bright emerald-green above, with a blackish
mask. **Head:** blunt with rounded snout; a
dark facial band from snout through the eye,
over the tympanum to armpit; eyes large and
protruding. **Tympanum:** prominent, at least
half the width of the eye. **Underside:** skin soft
and granular; white with grey mottling on the
throat. **Forelimbs:** fingers not webbed, with
inconspicuous terminal discs. **Hindlimbs:**
inner metatarsal tubercle large and spade-like;
toes moderately webbed, with small terminal

♀ Average length

♂ Average length

Maximum size: 58 mm

Marius Burger

Facial mask extends from snout through eye and over tympanum: northeastern Zimbabwe.

discs no wider than the toe itself.
Sexual dimorphism: male with
pectoral gland on the chest.

Call
Two low-pitched *quacks* spaced
one to three seconds apart.

Habitat and habits
Savanna and open woodland.
Males call at ground level from
concealed sites near the water.

TADPOLE
Streamlined and uniformly
dark green in colour; no
further details available.

KEY ID POINTS

- Interorbital bar without triangle (distinct from *L. broadleyi*)
- Terminal discs small (all species except *L. xenodactylus*)
- Inner metatarsal tubercle large (distinct from *L. natalensis*)
- Webbing limited (distinct from *L. mossambicus* and *L. xenodactylus*)

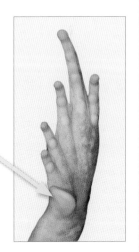

Tadpole: lateral view.

Broadley's Tree Frog

TRACK
5

Broadley se boompadda

Leptopelis broadleyi Poynton 1985

Named after the Zimbabwean herpetologist, Don Broadley.

Conservation status: Not threatened.

Broadley's Tree Frog: Lujeri Estate, Mulanje, Malawi.

Michael Cunningham

Description

Maximum size: 52 mm. **Body:** compact with short limbs. **Above:** smooth; light brown or silver-grey with dark, backwards-pointing triangle between eyes; dark vertebral line usually present; pair of dark lateral bands from behind eyes to vent; dark broken line from snout to eye, continuing behind the eye

♀ Average length
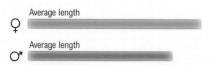

♂ Average length

Maximum size: 52 mm

to groin. **Head:** eyes large – diameter equal to or just less than distance from eye to snout. **Tympanum:** prominent but small – diameter equal to or less than half of eye diameter. **Underside:** skin uniformly cream-coloured with flattened granular texture. **Forelimbs:** fingers unwebbed, with expanded terminal discs. **Hindlimbs:** inner metatarsal tubercle large and spade-like; toes moderately webbed with large terminal discs. **Sexual dimorphism:** no conspicuous differences.

Call

Two or three short croaks and several higher-pitched chirps, not necessarily sequentially.

Habitat and habits

Trees and grass in lightly wooded moist savanna. Males call from dense bushes or tall sedges or grass about 2 m above ground level.

TADPOLE

Unknown.

Habitat: Mimosa dambo, Mulanje, Malawi.

KEY ID POINTS

- Dark, backwards-pointing triangle on head (distinct from other species in the genus)

- Inner metatarsal tubercle large and flanged (distinct from *L. natalensis*)
- Terminal discs on toes large (distinct from *L. xenodactylus* and *L. bocagii*)
- Webbing limited (distinct from *L. mossambicus* and *L. xenodactylus*)

Yellow-spotted Tree Frog

Geelspikkelboompadda

Leptopelis flavomaculatus (Günther, 1864)

LATIN: *flavus* = yellow or gold-coloured; *macula* = a spot. Refers to the yellow spots found on juveniles and some adults of the species.

Conservation status: Not threatened.

Yellow-spotted Tree Frog: Chirinda forest, Zimbabwe.

Description

Maximum size: 70 mm. **Body:** robust with short limbs. **Above:** coarsely granular; light brown with a dark horseshoe mark and a dark interorbital band; juveniles a uniform green with conspicuous small yellow spots which usually persist into adulthood; eyes large and protruding. **Tympanum:** prominent, about half the width of the eye. **Underside:** skin coarsely granular; cream-coloured. **Forelimbs:** fingers not webbed with well-developed terminal discs. **Hindlimbs:** inner metatarsal tubercle prominent; toes

Average length

♀

Average length

♂

Maximum size: 70 mm

extensively webbed with large terminal discs. **Sexual dimorphism:** male with pectoral gland on the chest; in males a dark facial mask sometimes evident.

Call

A series of chirps, sounding further away than they are. Males call from dense vegetation up to 4 m above the ground.

Habitat and habits

Evergreen forests near streams.

Habitat: Chirinda forest, Zimbabwe.

KEY ID POINTS

- Dark interorbital bar and horseshoe mark

Alan Channing

- Small orange or yellow spots cover the dorsum but may fade in older specimens
- Well-developed discs on toes and fingers (distinct from *L. bocagii* and *L. xenodactylus*)
- Webbing moderate

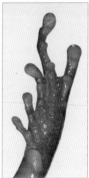

TADPOLE

Length: up to 47 mm. **Shape:** egg-shaped. **Tail:** long and serpentine; well-developed muscles; upper and lower fins of equal depth; tail fin reaches deepest point at about a third of its length; terminates in an acute tip. **Colour:** uniformly brown above; darker pigmentation around the nostrils; scattered dark spots on tail. **Eyes:** dorsolateral. **Nostrils:** small; positioned halfway between eyes and snout tip. **Spiracle:** just below body axis; not free from body; directed backwards at about 20°. **Vent:** marginal; dextral. **Mouth:** anteroventral; two papillae rows; outer row longer; one row laterally at mouth corner with scattered papillae. **Jaw sheaths:** moderate. **LTRF:** 4(2-4)/3.

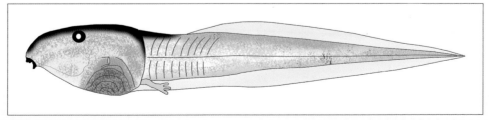

Tadpole: lateral view.

Brown-backed Tree Frog

Bruinrugboompadda

TRACK 7

Leptopelis mossambicus Poynton, 1985

Named after Mozambique where the species is common.

Conservation status: Not threatened.

Brown-backed Tree Frog: Pafuri, Kruger National Park, Limpopo Province.

Description

Maximum size: 63 mm. **Body:** robust with long limbs. **Above:** finely to coarsely granular; tan with a prominent, dark horseshoe mark on the back; dark mask from the snout through the middle of the eye to the arm; subadults plain green; snout blunt, with nostrils closer to the snout tip than to the eyes; eyes large and protruding. **Tympanum:** prominent, more than half the diameter of the eye. **Underside:** skin granular and creamy white with darker stippling on the throat. **Forelimbs:** fingers unwebbed with well-developed terminal discs. **Hindlimbs:** inner metatarsal tubercle large and spade-like; toes with minimal webbing and conspicuous terminal discs; one or two broad, dark crossbands usually present on the upper thigh. **Sexual dimorphism:** male with pectoral gland on the chest.

♀ Average length

♂ Average length

Maximum size: 63 mm

Call

Frequently repeated, loud *kwa-kwa* or *wala* sound. Males call from positions not higher than 1.5 m above the ground in grass, sedges, reeds, shrubs and trees. Dense choruses may develop. Males are territorial and utter an aggressive call if another male comes too close. If the intruder does not retreat, the frogs wrestle with each other to establish dominance.

KEY ID POINTS

- Horseshoe-shaped dark marking on tan background on the back
- Very prominent metatarsal tubercle
- Webbing is minimal (distinct from *L. bocagii*, *L. broadleyi*, *L. natalensis* and *L. flavomaculatus*)
- Found in open savanna woodland (distinct from *L. flavomaculatus*)

Habitat and habits

Variety of vegetation types near water in savanna, sand forest and mangrove swamps. Burrows underground to a depth of 250 mm during dry periods. Amplectant pairs dig a shallow nest in damp or muddy soil or among leaf litter in which the eggs are deposited, generally close to a shallow pan, pool or stream. Emerging tadpoles wriggle themselves into the water.

Pale form: Pafuri, Kruger National Park, Limpopo Province.

Typical subadult coloration: Richards Bay, KwaZulu-Natal.

TADPOLE

Length: up to 60 mm. **Shape:** streamlined; body oval and dorsoventrally flattened. **Tail:** very long; muscular; shallow dorsal and ventral fins; dorsal fin starts well behind body with gentle slope; deepest point midway along the length; terminates in a fine point. **Colour:** body uniform dark brown to grey above; white below; tail muscles and fins densely pigmented to mottled. **Eyes:** near-lateral. **Nostrils:** small; widely spaced; closer to snout than eyes. **Spiracle:** just below body axis; directed backwards at 45°. **Vent:** marginal; dextral. **Mouth:** near-ventral; one papillae row laterally, and two rows posteriorly. **Jaw sheaths:** moderate. **LTRF:** 4(2-4)/3.

Tadpole: lateral view.

Natal Tree Frog

TRACK
8

Natalse boompadda

Leptopelis natalensis (Smith, 1849)

Named after KwaZulu-Natal (formerly Natal) where
the species occurs.

Conservation status: Not threatened.

Natal Tree Frog: Vernon Crookes Nature Reserve, KwaZulu-Natal.

Description

Maximum size: 65 mm. **Body:** compact
with long limbs. **Above:** slightly granular;
colour pattern varies from uniform lime-
green to pale brown or brown, with emerald-
green blotches with a thin black outline.
Head: snout blunt, with nostrils closer to
the snout tip than to the eyes; eyes large
and protruding. **Tympanum:** prominent.
Underside: skin granular and cream-
coloured; underside of the limbs yellowish.
Forelimbs: fingers unwebbed with large
terminal discs. **Hindlimbs:** inner metatarsal
tubercle small; toes extensively webbed
with very large terminal discs. **Sexual
dimorphism:** no conspicuous differences.

Average length
♀

Average length
♂

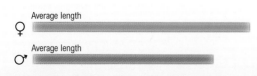

Maximum size: 65 mm

Call

Loud *yack-yack*
sound, usually
preceded by a drawn-
out *eeeeeeee* buzz.
Males call from
exposed positions
in trees and bushes
usually overhanging
or close to water.

Habitat and habits

Coastal forest, sand
forest or coastal
bushveld and
occasionally grassland
in forest and savanna
biomes. Pairs go into
amplexus in trees and
then descend to the
ground where they
excavate a shallow
burrow in which the
eggs are laid.

*Natal Tree Frog: Vernon
Crookes Nature Reserve.*

KEY ID POINTS

- No dark dorsal horseshoe
  pattern (distinct from
  L. mossambicus,
  L. flavomaculatus and
  L. bocagii)

Marius Burger

- Terminal discs on both
  fingers and toes are large
  (distinct from *L. bocagii*
  and *L. xenodactylus*)

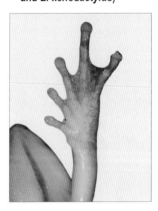

- Inner metatarsal tubercle
  is small
- Extensive webbing (distinct
  from *L. xenodactylus* and
  L. mossambicus)
- Found only in KwaZulu-Natal
  coastal woodland

TADPOLE

Length: up to 50 mm. **Shape:** slender; body elongate
oval; dorsoventrally flattened; upper and lower tail fins
shallow and of equal depth; terminates in sharp tip. **Tail:**
strong and muscular, giving serpentine appearance.
Colour: body and tail muscles dark olive or dark grey;
sometimes with beige reticulation; upper fin and posterior
half of lower fin darkly pigmented. **Eyes:** near lateral;
elygium present. **Nostrils:** small, widely spaced; closer to
snout than to eyes. **Spiracle:** just below body axis; against
body; behind middle of body; directed posteriorly. **Vent:**
marginal; dextral. **Mouth:** one row of papillae at sides; two
rows posteriorly. **Jaw sheaths:** delicate; weakly flexed.
LTRF: 4(2-4)/3, sometimes 4(2-4)/3(1).

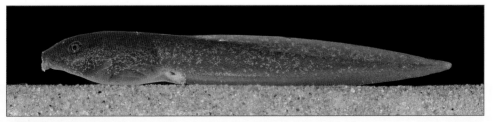

Tadpole: lateral view.

Long-toed Tree Frog

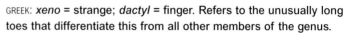

Langtoonboompadda

Leptopelis xenodactylus Poynton, 1963

GREEK: *xeno* = strange; *dactyl* = finger. Refers to the unusually long toes that differentiate this from all other members of the genus.

Conservation status: Endangered. Distribution is limited and habitat is diminishing.

Long-toed Tree Frog: Franklin, KwaZulu-Natal.

Description

Maximum size: 60 mm. **Body:** robust with long limbs and toes. **Above:** granular; uniform lime-green, without dorsal or facial markings. **Head:** snout blunt; eyes large and protruding. **Tympanum:** prominent, but less than half the diameter of the eye. **Underside:** skin granular and creamy white.

Forelimbs: fingers long and narrower than other species in the genus; terminal discs inconspicuous. **Hindlimbs:** inner metatarsal tubercle of moderate size and flanged for digging; toes long and slender with minimal webbing; terminal discs inconspicuous. **Sexual dimorphism:** male with pectoral gland on the chest.

Average length ♀

Average length ♂

Maximum size: 60 mm

Call

One or two brief croaks uttered at long intervals. Males generally call from concealed positions under grass tussocks or from burrows, but occasionally from elevated positions.

Habitat and habits

Wetlands and marshes in moist upland grassland, short mist-belt grassland and northeastern mountain grassland in southern KwaZulu-Natal between 1 000 and 2 800 m above sea level. Not known from the Eastern Cape.

Habitat: marshy ground near Franklin, KwaZulu-Natal.

TADPOLE

Length: up to 50 mm. **Shape:** slender; body ovoid. **Tail:** long, muscular; shallow fins terminating in sharply rounded tip; not as deep as body; dorsal and ventral fins of equal depth; dorsal fin starts well behind body. **Colour:** tadpoles uniformly dark brown to black above, with scattered silver pigments; upper tail fin darkly mottled; anterior two-thirds of lower fin transparent; underside semi-transparent with scattered dark pigment; red gills and yellowish gut show through the ventral skin. **Eyes:** dorsolateral. **Nostrils:** small; widely spaced; closer to snout than to eyes. **Spiracle:** just below body axis; halfway along body; visible from above; directed posteriorly. **Vent:** marginal; dextral. **Mouth:** anteroventral; one row of papillae at mouth corners; two rows below. **Jaw sheaths:** moderate; slightly curved. LTRF: 4(2-4)/3(1).

KEY ID POINTS

- Dorsum uniformly lime-green without markings (distinct from adults of most other species)
- Very long toes and fingers with inconspicuous discs (distinct from other species)
- Webbing moderate

- Grassy wetland habitats, above 1 000 m in KwaZulu-Natal (distinct from other species)

Tadpole: lateral view.

RAIN FROGS

REËNPADDAS

Breviceps Merrem, 1820

LATIN: *brevis* = short; *ceps* = head. Refers to flattened snout.

15 species, 14 in southern Africa

Bushveld Rain Frogs in amplexus.

Globose-bodied frogs with flattened faces and narrow, downturned mouths. They vary in size from about 17 mm to 80 mm. For most species, morphological features vary considerably so that individual features are of limited use in identification – which is therefore dependent on a combination of characters, often including distribution range.

Rain Frogs are endemic to southern Africa where they inhabit a variety of habitats from mountain forest to desert. They are fossorial and generally prefer well-drained sandy or loamy soils. They are cryptic and slow moving, spending most of their time

DISTINCTIVE CHARACTERS

ADULT

- Pupil horizontal
- Globose body with flat face and small, downturned mouth
- Limbs shorter or only slightly longer than body width
- No webbing present, except for *B. macrops* and to a lesser extent *B. namaquensis* which have fleshy webbing
- Inner and outer toes very short
- Cloaca points backwards (not downwards) and is not surrounded by skin folds (distinct from *Probreviceps*)
- Tympanum usually not visible

TADPOLE
- No free-swimming tadpole phase; metamorphosis is completed in underground nest

Les Minter

Stages of development in the nest.

underground. When they do emerge on the surface, they walk or run rather than hop as most other frogs. They burrow backwards using their hindlimbs to shift the soil, slowly rotating as they disappear below the surface. When alarmed, they inflate their bodies into an almost spherical ball and some species produce a milky secretion on the skin.

Rain Frogs occur in both summer- and winter-rainfall areas and breeding takes place at the beginning of the rainy season in both cases. Some species start calling before the rain, apparently responding to changes in atmospheric pressure. Males usually call from the mouth of a burrow or from below leaf litter, but under some circumstances they may scramble up to call from exposed, elevated positions.

The method of amplexus is unique to the genus; the male does not clasp the female but the pair become glued together by adhesive secretions from the male abdomen and female dorsum.

Les Minter

Subterranean egg chamber.

The amplectant pair burrow down and construct a chamber in which the female deposits an egg mass. Egg clutches vary from 20 to 50 eggs, each measuring about 5 mm, and within a 7 to 10 mm jelly capsule. An additional layer of fluid-filled, sterile jelly capsules is usually placed on top of the egg mass and this is thought to break down to a fluid in which the young develop. The female (though sometimes the male) remains in the vicinity of the nest until metamorphosis is complete. Several species are Red Data listed.

KEY TO SPECIES

ADULT

1 Found in the Western and Northern Cape or southern Namibia **2**
   Not found in the Western or Northern Cape or southern Namibia **7**
2 Distinct facial mask from eye to armpit **3**
   Facial mask absent or indistinct **5**
3 Basal subarticular tubercle on hand double .... **Namaqua Rain Frog** B. namaquensis (p.122)
   Basal subarticular tubercle on hand single **4**
4 Found in sandy soils in coastal lowlands of the Western Cape .... **Sand Rain Frog** B. rosei (p.126)
   Found in sandy mountain areas of the Western Cape.. **Cape Mountain Rain Frog** B. montanus (p.118)
5 Fleshy webbing between toes giving foot a paddle-like appearance .... **Desert Rain Frog** B. macrops (p.116)
   Webbing absent **6**
6 Underside plain purplish-brown; dorsum plain grey or brown .... **Plain Rain Frog** B. fuscus (p.112)
   Underside mottled brown and cream; dorsum granular brown with cream patches ....
   .... **Cape Rain Frog** B. gibbosus (p.114)
   Underside plum-coloured with white dots; dorsum reddish or cream with numerous black granules ....
   .... **Strawberry Rain Frog** B. acutirostris (p.106)
7 Underside plain purplish brown; dorsum plain grey or brown; found in coastal bush west of Port
   Elizabeth .... **Plain Rain Frog** B. fuscus (p.112)
   Other than above **8**
8 Tympanum visible .... **Plaintive Rain Frog** B. verrucosus (p.132)
   Tympanum obscured **9**
9 Outer toe longer than its width **10**
   Outer toe equal to, or shorter than, its width **11**
10 Found in Afromontane forest in Limpopo Province ..... **Northern Forest Rain Frog** B. sylvestris (p.130)
   Found in open savanna or grassland .... **Power's Rain Frog** B. poweri (p.124)
                                            or **Mozambique Rain Frog** B. mossambicus (p.120)
                                            Distinguishable only by the call
11 Underside plain white except for gular region and occasional small spots ....
   .... **Bushveld Rain Frog** B. adspersus (p.108)
   Underside stippled or marbled **12**
12 Found in northern KwaZulu-Natal (Zululand) .... **Whistling Rain Frog** B. sopranus (p.128)
   Found in southern KwaZulu-Natal midlands .... **Bilbo's Rain Frog** B. bagginsi (p.110)

Right: Desert Rain Frog showing
characteristic blunt snout and rotund body.

Strawberry Rain Frog
Aarbeireënpadda

TRACK
10

Breviceps acutirostris Poynton, 1963

LATIN: *acuus* = sharp, *rostrum* = snout. Refers to the relatively sharp snout compared with other members of the genus.

Conservation status: Not threatened.

Strawberry Rain Frog: Heidelberg, Western Cape.

Description
Maximum size: 40 mm. **Body:** stout with short legs; snout slightly more pointed than other Rain Frog species; eyes small. **Above:** reddish to creamy white with many elevated black granules which are dense and often fused in the vertebral region. **Tympanum:** not visible. **Underside:** plum-coloured with cream spots; finely granular. **Forelimbs:** palmar tubercles poorly developed; basal subarticular tubercles of the digits single. **Hindlimbs:** no webbing between toes; inner and outer toes longer than wide; inner metatarsal tubercle well developed. **Sexual dimorphism:** granules on the throat heavier in male.

Average length
♀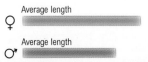

Average length
♂

Maximum size: 40 mm

KEY ID POINTS

- Confined to montane fynbos and Afromontane forest in the southwestern Cape fold mountains
- Dorsum reddish or cream ground colour with dark, closely spaced elevated granules that tend to fuse in vertebral region (distinct from other species)
- Basal subarticular tubercle on hand single (distinct from *B. namaquensis*)
- Facial mask not prominent, or absent (distinct from other species except *B. fuscus*, *B. gibbosus*, *B. sylvestris* and *B. verrucosus*)

- Eyes small (distinct from *B. macrops* and *B. namaquensis*)
- Underside finely granular and plum-coloured with cream spots (distinct from other species)

- Inner and outer toes longer than wide (distinct from

other species, except *B. adspersus*, *B. rosei* and *B. sopranus*)
- Webbing absent

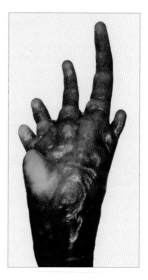

Call

Succession of short, fairly high-pitched whistles produced in rapid succession. Males call during and after rain by day and night, in winter and spring. They call from the soil surface, elevated perches, or from shallow depressions underneath low vegetation or leaf litter.

Habitat and habits

Southwestern ranges of the Cape fold mountains, where they are found in montane fynbos and Afromontane forest. Also occur at sea level where the mountains are close to the coast. Egg clutches consist of about 24 large eggs, measuring 7 mm.

Unusual colour pattern: Jonkershoek, Western Cape.

Groot Watersbos, Western Cape.

Les Minter

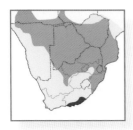

Bushveld Rain Frog

Bosveldreënpadda

TRACK 11

TRACK 12

Breviceps adspersus (Peters, 1882)

Subspecies:
- ■ *B. adspersus adspersus* Peters, 1882 TRACK 11
- ■ *B. adspersus pentheri* Werner, 1899 TRACK 12

LATIN: *adspersus* = scattered. Refers to the white markings on the elevated skin ridges.

Conservation status: Not threatened.

Bushveld Rain Frog, subspecies Breviceps adspersus adspersus: *Polokwane, Limpopo Province.*

Description

Maximum size: 60 mm. **Body:** stout with short legs; head short. **Above:** colour pattern variable but usually includes paired light, yellowish or orange patches on a brown background; dark spots or blotches; pale vertebral line sometimes present; black facial band from eye to the armpit, usually separated from the dark gular patch by a light line; skin granular. **Tympanum:** usually

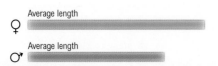

Average length
♀

Average length
♂

Maximum size: 60 mm

KEY ID POINTS

- Facial mask prominent (distinct from *B. acutirostris*, *B. fuscus*, *B. gibbosus* and *B. macrops*)
- Inner and outer toes as long as they are wide (distinct from other species, except *B. acutirostris*, *B. bagginsi*, *B. mossambicus*, *B. sopranus* and *B. rosei*)
- Basal subarticular tubercle on hand single (distinct from *B. namaquensis*)
- Eyes small (distinct from *B. macrops* and *B. namaquensis*)

- Occurs in the savanna biome (distinct from other species, except *B. bagginsi*, *B. mossambicus*, *B. poweri* and *B. sopranus*)
- Underside smooth, white and unmarked

- Webbing absent

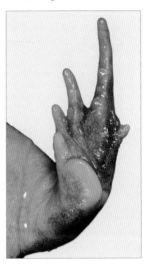

not visible. **Underside:** unmarked, except for a few dark spots occasionally; smooth. **Forelimbs:** palmar tubercles moderately to well developed; basal subarticular tubercles single. **Hindlimbs:** no webbing between toes; inner and outer toes as long as they are wide; inner metatarsal tubercle large and flanged. **Sexual dimorphism:** male throat darkly mottled or uniformly black, often divided in the middle by a white stripe.

Calls

B. a. adspersus emits a series of short, pulsed whistles, usually in groups of three or more. *B. a. pentheri* emits a series of short, high-pitched whistles, singly or occasionally in pairs. Males call after dark or by day after rain. The call site is sometimes a shallow depression about the depth of the frog's body, concealed at the base of vegetation near the burrow; but calling is never from underground within the burrow.

Subspecies Breviceps adspersus pentheri: *Eastern Cape.*

Habitat and habits

Sandy to sandy-loam soils in semi-arid habitats in savanna and grassland, but absent from forests. After the male has become glued to the back of the female, the pair burrows backwards into the ground and creates a chamber in which eggs are laid. Clutches consist of about 45 large eggs, measuring 5 mm, and within 10 mm capsules. A mass of yolkless, fluid-filled capsules is deposited on top of the eggs. The female remains nearby until the froglets are ready to leave the nest.

Marius Burger

Bilbo's Rain Frog

Bilbo se reënpadda

TRACK 13

Breviceps bagginsi Minter, 2003

Named after Bilbo Baggins, the main character in J.R. Tolkien's *The Hobbit*.

Conservation status: Data Deficient. Possibly threatened by habitat degradation.

Marius Burger

Bilbo's Rain Frog: Babanango, KwaZulu-Natal.

Description

Maximum size: 29 mm. **Body:** stout with short legs. **Above:** tan, orange-brown to dark brown with scattered dark speckles on a slightly granular background; pale interorbital band varies from indistinct to prominent; pale paravertebral patches and three dorsolateral patches present; flanks brown with few small white speckles; broad dark facial band runs from eye to base of arm; white stripe runs from eye to angle of mouth and anteriorly along the upper and

Average length ♀

Average length ♂

Maximum size: 29 mm

KEY ID POINTS

- Underside white with dark stippling (distinct from other species, except *B. rosei*, *B. sopranus*, *B. sylvestris* and *B. adspersus pentheri*)

Les Minter

- Restricted to the Melmoth-Babanango and Boston districts of KwaZulu-Natal
- Facial mask prominent (distinct from *B. acutirostris*, *B. fuscus*, *B. gibbosus* and *B. macrops*)
- Length of inner and outer toes equal to their width
- Basal subarticular tubercle on hand single (distinct from *B. namaquensis*)
- Eyes small (distinct from *B. macrops* and *B. namaquensis*)

- Webbing absent

lower lips; moderately granular, with fairly large scattered tubercles; snout extremely abbreviated. **Tympanum:** not visible. **Underside:** white to stippled, or flecked with darker mottling on the throat; smooth to lightly granular. **Forelimbs:** outer (fourth) finger reaches the distal subarticular tubercle of third finger. **Hindlimbs:** no webbing between toes; subarticular tubercles on the third finger undivided; inner and outer metatarsal tubercles separated by a deep cleft. **Sexual dimorphism:** male throat dark.

Call
Series of 7 to 20 short, high-pitched whistles in rapid succession. Males call during the day from exposed positions at the surface or from shallow depressions under vegetation.

Habitat and habits
Known only from grassy verges of roads in exotic plantations in the Melmoth-Babanango and Boston districts of KwaZulu-Natal.

Les Minter

Habitat: road verge near plantation of exotic trees.

Plain Rain Frog

Swartreënpadda

TRACK 14

Breviceps fuscus Hewitt, 1925

LATIN: *fuscus* = dark. Refers to the dark colour of the frog.

Conservation status: Not threatened.

Plain Rain Frog: Keurbooms River, Western Cape.

Description

Maximum size: 51 mm. **Body:** stout with short legs; eyes small and dark. **Above:** uniformly dark brown or black, with no markings; skin, including the face, covered in fairly widely spaced conical tubercles. **Tympanum:** not visible. **Underside:** smooth and purplish-brown, occasionally with indistinct light spots. **Forelimbs:** palmar tubercles moderately to well developed; basal subarticular tubercles single. **Hindlimbs:** no webbing between toes; inner and outer toes longer than wide. **Sexual dimorphism:** throat very dark in male.

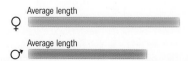

♀ Average length

♂ Average length

Maximum size: 51 mm

KEY ID POINTS

- Confined to forested
- slopes and plateaus of the southern Cape fold mountains
- Underside smooth and purplish-brown (distinct from other species)

- Facial mask absent (distinct from other species, except *B. gibbosus* and *B. macrops* and sometimes *B. acutirostris*)
- Uniform dorsal coloration (see illustration) distinct from other species
- Inner and outer toes longer than they are wide (usually distinct from other species, except *B. acutirostris*, *B. gibbosus*, *B. sylvestris* and *B. verrucosus*, but variation does occur)
- Webbing absent

- Basal subarticular tubercle on hand single (distinct from *B. namaquensis*)
- Eyes small (distinct from *B. macrops* and *B. namaquensis*)

Call

Series of short, pulsed, low-pitched whistles. Males call by day and night from within shallow burrows or from concealed positions on the surface or elevated perches up to 30 cm above the surface.

Habitat and habits

Forested slopes and plateaus of the southern Cape fold mountains. After the male glues himself to the back of the female the pair burrows backwards into the ground and creates a chamber in which the eggs are laid. Clutches consist of about 45 large yellow eggs measuring 5 mm in 8 mm capsules. A mass of sterile, fluid-filled egg capsules is deposited on top of the clutch of eggs.

Habitat: Tsitsikamma Coastal National Park, Western Cape.

Cape Rain Frog

Kaapse reënpadda

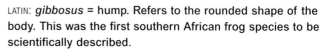

Breviceps gibbosus (Linnaeus, 1758)

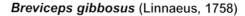

TRACK
15

LATIN: *gibbosus* = hump. Refers to the rounded shape of the body. This was the first southern African frog species to be scientifically described.

Conservation status: Vulnerable, due to habitat loss resulting from urbanisation.

Cape Rain Frog: Rondebosch, Western Cape.

Description

Maximum size: 80 mm. **Body:** stout with short legs; head very short and face flat; eyes small and dark. **Above:** dark brown; a pale band or pale patches in the paravertebral region; a dark patch is present from the eye halfway towards the front leg; coarsely granular especially on the head. **Tympanum:** not visible. **Underside:** mottled brown on cream; coarsely granular especially on the throat. **Forelimbs:** palmar tubercles poorly developed and basal subarticular tubercles single. **Hindlimbs:** no webbing between toes; inner toe of equal length and width, outer toe longer than wide. **Sexual dimorphism:** granulation on throat heavier in male.

Average length

♀

Average length

♂

Maximum size: 80 mm

KEY ID POINTS

- Confined to the southwestern Cape
- Underside very granular and mottled brown on cream (distinct from other species)

- Facial mask absent or indistinct (distinct from other species, except *B. fuscus* and *B. macrops* and sometimes *B. acutirostris*)
- Length and width of inner toe equal, length of outer toe longer than width (usually distinct from other species, except *B. sylvestris*, but variation does occur)
- Dorsum granular and dark with a light paravertebral band or series of light patches

- Basal subarticular tubercle on hand single (distinct from *B. namaquensis*)
- Eyes small (distinct from *B. macrops* and *B. namaquensis*)
- Webbing absent

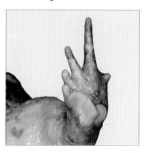

Call

A long, strongly pulsed whistle. Males call during the day and night from exposed positions on the surface or, more usually, from well-concealed shallow depressions under vegetation. Calling begins with the first autumn rains in late April, and continues until spring.

Habitat and habits

Favours well-drained soils on slightly sloping ground in the southwestern Cape. Common in Cape Town gardens. After the male has glued himself to the back of the female, the pair burrows backwards into the ground and creates a chamber where the eggs are laid. Egg clutches consist of about 22 large yellow eggs. A mass of sterile, fluid-filled capsules is deposited on top of the eggs. Until they metamorphose, one of the parents remains with the eggs.

Flat face and inflated body are typical.

Habitat: slopes of Devil's Peak, Cape Town.

Desert Rain Frog

Woestynreënpadda

TRACK
16

Breviceps macrops Boulenger, 1907

GREEK: *macros* = large, *opticos* = sight. Refers to the large eyes.

Conservation status: Vulnerable due to very restricted distribution and loss of habitat as a result of diamond mining.

Desert Rain Frog: Port Nolloth, Northern Cape.

Description

Maximum size: 50 mm. **Body:** stout with short legs; eyes large. **Above:** pale, almost white or yellowish, with chocolate-brown vermiculations which are heavier in the neck region; skin smooth. **Tympanum:** not visible. **Underside:** smooth; white with a transparent vascular window in the central and posterior abdominal area. **Forelimbs:** hands paddle-like; palmar tubercles absent. **Hindlimbs:** feet paddle-like; smooth; digits joined by fleshy webbing; subarticular tubercles absent or poorly developed. **Sexual dimorphism:** gular region deeply wrinkled in male.

Average length
♀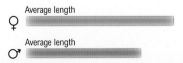

Average length
♂

Maximum size: 50 mm

KEY ID POINTS

- Underside smooth, with a transparent vascular window (distinct from other species, except *B. namaquensis*)

- Confined to a narrow coastal strip in northwest Namaqualand
- Facial mask absent (distinct from other species, except *B. fuscus* and *B. gibbosus* and sometimes *B. acutirostris*)
- Basal subarticular tubercle on hand single (distinct from *B. namaquensis*)
- Eyes large and bulging (distinct from other species, except *B. namaquensis*)

- Feet paddle-like and smooth, with thick fleshy webbing (distinct from other species)

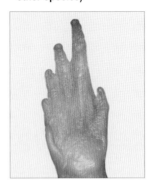

Call

Long, drawn-out rising whistle. Males call from exposed positions or from small excavated depressions during or following periods of onshore fog. Calling and surface activity has been recorded throughout the year.

Habitat and habits

From the highwater mark up to 10 km inland along the Namaqualand coast in strandveld succulent Karoo. Breeding biology not known, but presumably similar to other Rain Frogs.

Les Minter photographing tracks.

Habitat: duneveld at McDougall's Bay, Northern Cape.

Cape Mountain Rain Frog

Kaapse bergreënpadda

TRACK 17

Breviceps montanus Power, 1926

LATIN: *mons* = mountain. Refers to the mountainous habitat of the species.

Conservation status: Not threatened.

Marius Burger

Cape Mountain Rain Frog: Hottentots Holland Reserve, Western Cape.

Description

Maximum size: 31 mm. **Body:** stout with short legs; eyes small to medium. **Above:** dark; large, pale paravertebral patches fused into a scalloped vertebral band with dark, ridged edges; dark markings present in the band; dark facial band from eye to base of arm; skin rough and granular. **Tympanum:** not visible. **Underside:** beige with dark markings concentrated on the throat; slightly to moderately granular; granulation intense on throat. **Forelimbs:** palmar tubercles well developed; basal subarticular tubercles single. **Hindlimbs:** no webbing between toes; length of inner and outer toes less than width. **Sexual dimorphism:** throat darker in male.

♀ Average length
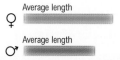

♂ Average length

Maximum size: 31 mm

KEY ID POINTS

- Confined to fynbos on Table Mountain and the Cape fold mountains
- Underside finely granular and beige with dark markings

- Eyes small to medium (distinct from *B. macrops* and *B. namaquensis*)

- Dorsum roughly granular and dark; large pale paravertebral patches fuse into a scalloped vertebral band (distinct from other species, except sometimes *B. rosei*)
- Facial mask prominent (distinct from *B. acutirostris*, *B. fuscus*, *B. gibbosus* and *B. macrops*)
- Inner and outer toes not as long as their width (distinct from other species, except *B. acutirostris*, *B. adspersus*, *B. mossambicus*,

B. sopranus and *B. rosei*)
- Basal subarticular tubercle on hand single (distinct from *B. namaquensis*)
- Webbing absent

Call

Brief whistle. Males call after dark or on overcast days during or after rain from June-November and sporadically up to January. They call from burrows at the base of vegetation, from rock crevices or even while wandering on the surface.

Habitat and habits

Restricted to fynbos from the summit of Table Mountain to the the Cape fold mountains, but also at sea level where mountains reach the coast. Oviposition similar to other Rain Frogs, with eggs being laid in a subterranean chamber.

Typical walking gait of Rain Frog: Caledon, Western Cape.

Mozambique Rain Frog

Mosambiekse reënpadda

TRACK
18

Briceps mossambicus *Peters, 1854*

Breviceps mossambicus Peters, 1854

Named after Mozambique where this species was
first discovered.

Conservation status: Not threatened.

Mozambique Rain Frog: Tembe Reserve, KwaZulu-Natal.

Les Minter

Description

Maximum size: 52 mm. **Body:** stout with short legs; eyes small. **Above:** highly variable and cryptic; background colour varies from light tan or apricot to very dark brown or brick-red; large, pale paravertebral and dorsolateral patches vary from white, light tan or apricot, through to dark brown; dark spots or speckles often form a dark border around dorsolateral patches; pale vertebral stripe and white line from heel to heel often present; dark facial band from eye to armpit; skin granular or

Average length

♀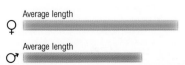

Average length

♂

Maximum size: 52 mm

KEY ID POINTS

- Underside smooth and white to marbled brown (distinct from other species, except *B. bagginsi*, *B. sopranus* and *B. adspersus*)

Les Minter

- Occurs in parts of the bushveld and grassland biomes
- Facial mask conspicuous (distinct from *B. acutirostris*, *B. fuscus*, *B. gibbosus* and *B. macrops*)
- Inner and outer toes not as long as they are wide (distinct from other species except *B. acutirostris*, *B. montanus*, *B. sopranus* and *B. rosei*)
- Basal subarticular tubercle on hand single (distinct from *B. namaquensis*)

- Eyes small (distinct from *B. macrops* and *B. namaquensis*)
- Webbing absent

smooth. **Tympanum:** not visible. **Underside:** white to marbled brown; smooth. **Forelimbs:** palmar tubercles moderately to well developed; basal subarticular tubercles single. **Hindlimbs:** no webbing between toes; inner and outer toes not as long as they are wide. **Sexual dimorphism:** male throat very dark.

Call

A series of two to five short chirps. Calls are emitted singly, or in groups of two to three. Males call from under leaf litter or from a concealed position at ground level. During misty or overcast conditions, males may continue to call for several days and nights.

They may even call until mid morning on clear sunny days.

Habitat and habits

Found in parts of the summer-rainfall savanna and grassland biomes where it prefers shallow, well-drained, humus-rich rocky soils, although occasionally found in deep, sandy, soils. Breeds during spring and early summer after heavy rains. About 20 to 25 eggs are laid in a chamber, often under a stone or log. Females remain in the vicinity of the nest, and metamorphosis is completed after six to eight weeks.

Les Minter

Colour variation: Tembe Reserve.

Les Minter

Specimens from type locality, Mozambique Island (left) and mainland (right).

Namaqua Rain Frog

Namakwareënpadda

TRACK
19

Breviceps namaquensis Power, 1926

Named after the Namaqualand region where this species is found.

Conservation status: Not threatened.

Namaqua Rain Frog: Northwestern Cape.

Marius Burger

Description

Maximum size: 45 mm. **Body:** stout with short legs; eyes large with a pale-coloured iris. **Above:** dark brown with pale paravertebral and dorsolateral patches that tend to fuse, leaving a broad, dark dorsolateral band; short, dark facial band runs from the eye halfway to the armpit; skin granular or smooth. **Tympanum:** not visible. **Underside:** white with translucent patches; smooth except for granules on the throat. **Forelimbs:** palmar tubercles well developed; basal subarticular tubercles double. **Hindlimbs:** fleshy webbing between thick toes; length of

Average length

♀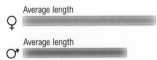

Average length

♂

Maximum size: 45 mm

KEY ID POINTS

- Underside distinct from other species (see description)

- Facial mask conspicuous (distinct from *B. acutirostris*, *B. fuscus*, *B. gibbosus* and *B. macrops*)

- Confined to the Namaqua coast and to the inland mountains in the succulent Karoo
- Inner toe noticeably longer than its width (usually distinct from other species, except *B. bagginsi*, *B. fuscus*, *B. gibbosus*, *B. sylvestris* and *B. verrucosus*, but variation does occur)
- Basal subarticular tubercle on hand double (distinct from other species)
- Eyes large (distinct from other species, except *B. macrops*)

- Fleshy webbing

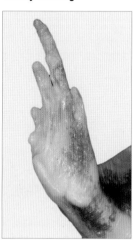

inner toe noticeably longer than width. **Sexual dimorphism:** throat darker in male.

Call

Short low-pitched whistle, repeated at the rate of one per second.

Habitat and habits

Arid sandy habitats from the Namaqua coast to the inland mountains in the succulent Karoo biome. Males call during and after good rains from winter to spring and sporadically during autumn and early summer.

Habitat: Namaqualand coastal region and mountains.

Gerhard Dreyer/IOA

Power's Rain Frog

Power se reënpadda

TRACK 20

Breviceps poweri Parker, 1934

Named after the herpetologist, John Hyacinth Power, director of the McGregor Museum in Kimberley from 1947 to 1958.

Conservation status: Not threatened.

Amplectant pair of Power's Rain Frogs: Napula, Mozambique.

Les Minter

Description
Maximum size: 50 mm. **Body:** stout with short legs; head short; eyes small. **Above:** dark mottling on a tan, brown or brick-red background; pale vertebral line usually present; indistinct paravertebral patches and a series of three to six orange or pale spots usually present along the flanks, tending to fuse into an irregular, light dorsolateral band; characteristic light spot above the

Average length ♀

Average length ♂

Maximum size: 50 mm

vent; pale, light line from this spot along backs of thighs; characteristic short dark band often present between the nostrils and the mouth giving the impression of a moustache; facial band from eye to shoulder; skin smooth or granular. **Tympanum:** not visible. **Underside:** small dark dots on white background; gular region with a marbled or uniformly dark patch, separated from infraorbital patch below the eye by a broad light band running from upper jaw to base of arm; skin smooth. **Hindlimbs:** no webbing between toes; outer toe very small; inner metatarsal tubercle often connected to large, spade-like outer metatarsal tubercle to form a continuous flange. **Sexual dimorphism:** male throat dark.

Dorsolateral view of specimen lacking vertebral line.

Call
Series of short, high-pitched whistles. Males call after dark from the surface or from shallow depressions not far from their burrows.

Habitat and habits
Widely distributed in dry savanna. Breeding behaviour unknown but presumed to be similar to other Rain Frog species.

KEY ID POINTS

- Short dark band often present between the nostrils and the mouth
- Underside distinct from other species (see description)

- Facial mask prominent (distinct from *B. acutirostris, B. fuscus, B. gibbosus* and *B. macrops*)
- Length of inner and outer toes not as long as width (distinct from other species, except *B. acutirostris, B. adspersus, B. montanus, B. mossambicus, B. sopranus* and *B. rosei*)
- Basal subarticular tubercle on hand single (distinct from *B. namaquensis*)
- Light spot above the vent
- Eyes small (distinct from *B. macrops* and *B. namaquensis*)
- Webbing absent
- Short dark band often present between the nostrils and the mouth

Sand Rain Frog

Rose se reënpadda

Breviceps rosei Power, 1926

Subspecies:
■ **B. rosei rosei** Power, 1926 TRACK 21
■ **B. rosei vansoni** FitzSimons, 1946 TRACK 22

Named after the Cape naturalist and herpetologist, Walter Rose (1884-1964).

Conservation status: Not threatened.

Sand Rain Frog, subspecies Breviceps rosei vansoni: *Bontebok National Park, Western Cape. Inset: Subspecies* B. r. rosei, *Cape West Coast.*

Atherton de Villiers

Description
Maximum size: 36 mm. **Body:** stout with short legs; eyes small. **Above:** dark brown with pale paravertebral patches that tend to fuse to form a scalloped band with dark, slightly raised borders; dark dorsolateral patches; *B. r. vansoni* can usually be distinguished by a thin pale vertebral line

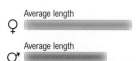

Average length
♀

Average length
♂

Maximum size: 36 mm

KEY ID POINTS

- Occurs in sandy areas in coastal lowlands and on lower slopes of the fynbos and thicket biomes
- Scalloped band and ridges on dorsum distinct from other species
- Facial mask conspicuous (distinct from *B. acutirostris*, *B. fuscus*, *B. gibbosus* and *B. macrops*)
- Inner and outer toes as long as their width (distinct from other species, except *B. acutirostris*, *B. adspersus*, *B. montanus*, *B. mossambicus*, *B. poweri* and *B. sopranus*)

- Underside pale with brown flecks (distinct from other species, except *B. bagginsi*, *B. sopranus*, *B. sylvestris* and *B. verrucosus*)
- Basal subarticular tubercle on hand single (distinct from *B. namaquensis*)

- Eyes small (distinct from *B. macrops* and *B. namaquensis*)
- Broad dark facial band from the eye to the armpit
- Inner and outer toe as long as it is wide
- Webbing absent

and a thin pale line from foot to foot across the vent; short dark facial band from eye to armpit; skin lightly granular. **Tympanum:** not visible. **Underside:** pale with brown flecks; smooth to slightly granular, particularly on the throat but not noticeably heavier on the limbs. **Forelimbs:** palmar tubercles moderate; basal subarticular tubercles single. **Hindlimbs:** no webbing between toes; length of inner and outer toe both equal to their width. **Sexual dimorphism:** male throat dark.

Call

Short, moderately pitched chirp. *B. r. rosei* emits calls rapidly at about three per second; *B. r. vansoni* calls at a slower pace of about one per second. Calling takes place by day or night after rain or in dense fog. Males call from elevated positions of up to 1 m above the ground. When disturbed they will drop to the ground.

Habitat and habits

Well vegetated low-lying sandy areas in coastal lowlands and on lower mountain slopes of the fynbos and thicket biomes. Breeding begins in spring. Eggs are laid in an underground chamber in sandy soil, with the amplexing male assisting the female to dig the burrow.

Subspecies **Breviceps rosei rosei:** *Witsand, Western Cape.*

Whistling Rain Frog

Fluitreënpadda

Briceps sopranus *Breviceps sopranus* Minter, 2003

ITALIAN: *soprano* = high voice. Refers to the clear, high-pitched advertisement call.

Conservation status: Data Deficient.

Les Minter

Whistling Rain Frog: St Lucia, KwaZulu-Natal.

Description

Maximum size: 26 mm. **Body:** stout with short legs; snout extremely blunt; eyes small. **Above:** pale golden to olive or greyish, with light brown to pink patches and small dark speckles or spots; pale interorbital band may be evident; two to four pale dorsolateral patches usually fused; pale vertebral line sometimes present; broad dark facial band from lower margin of eye to base of arm; below dark facial band, a white stripe runs from snout to angle of mouth and along upper and lower lips; skin finely granular. **Tympanum:** not visible. **Underside:** white to stippled or flecked; smooth to lightly granular. **Forelimbs:** subarticular tubercles on the third finger undivided; outer (fourth) finger just reaches the distal subarticular tubercle or just falls short of the third finger in most specimens. **Hindlimbs:** no webbing between toes; inner and outer metatarsal tubercles well developed and separated by a deep cleft. **Sexual dimorphism:** gular patch stippled or dark in male.

Average length
♀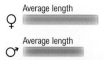

Average length
♂

Maximum size: 26 mm

KEY ID POINTS

- Underside distinct from other species except *B. adspersus*, *B. bagginsi*, *B. mossambicus*, *B. rosei*, *B. sylvestris* and *B. verrucosus*

Les Minter

- Found in forests and woodlands in northern KwaZulu-Natal and Swaziland
- Facial mask prominent (distinct from *B. acutirostris*, *B. fuscus*, *B. gibbosus* and *B. macrops*)
- Length of inner and outer toes as long as their width (distinct from other species, except *B. acutirostris*, *B. adspersus*, *B. montanus*, *B. mossambicus*, *B. poweri* and *B. rosei*)
- Basal subarticular tubercle on hand single (distinct from *B. namaquensis*)

- Eyes small (distinct from *B. macrops* and *B. namaquensis*)
- Webbing absent

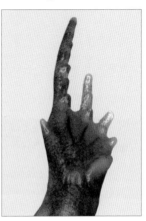

Call

Long, drawn-out, high-pitched whistle, repeated every two to three seconds. Males call during daytime and after dark from leaf litter or elevated positions on fallen branches or herbaceous plants, usually following rain.

Habitat and habits

Found in a variety of vegetation types in forest and savanna biomes including coastal forest and thornveld, riparian forest, Zululand thornveld and grassland. Preferred soil types vary from sandy to clay loam.

Marius Burger

Dark colour variation.

Northern Forest Rain Frog

Transvaal woudreënpadda

TRACK 24

TRACK 25

Breviceps sylvestris FitzSimons, 1930

Subspecies:
- ***B. sylvestris sylvestris*** FitzSimons, 1930 TRACK 24
- ***B. sylvestris taeniatus*** Poynton, 1963 TRACK 25

LATIN: *sylva* = a wood or forest. Refers to the forest habitat of the species.

Conservation status: Vulnerable.

Northern Forest Rain Frog, subspecies Breviceps sylvestris sylvestris: *Magoebaskloof, Limpopo Province. Inset: Subspecies* B. s. taeniatus: *Hanglip, Soutpansberg, Limpopo Province.*

Description

Maximum size: 53 mm. **Body:** stout with short legs, eyes small. **Above:** uniform light tan to black, or tan to dark brown with light brown patches and dark markings that may fuse into bands in *B. s. taeniatus*; dark facial band from eye to armpit and bordered on both sides by a white line; mouth edged with a broad light border; skin with pitted granules; paravertebral skin

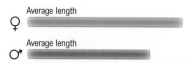

Average length
♀

Average length
♂

Maximum size: 53 mm

ridges on the back. **Tympanum:** usually not visible. **Underside:** mottled brown on white; slightly granular. **Forelimbs:** palmar tubercles well developed and basal subarticular tubercles single. **Hindlimbs:** no webbing between toes; inner toe as long as it is wide, but outer toe is twice as long as its width. **Sexual dimorphism:** throat uniformly dark or darkly mottled on a yellow background in male.

Les Minter

Characteristic clown face.

Call

B. s sylvestris emits a series of short, evenly spaced, pulsed chirps at less than one per second. *B. s. taeniatus* emits a short, soft whistle at about one per second. Large calling aggregations form in wet, misty conditions and may continue uninterrupted for several days and nights. During the day they call from concealed sites, but move to more exposed and sometimes elevated positions after dark.

Habitat and habits

Afromontane forest and northeastern mountain grassland in Limpopo Province. Breed from the first spring rains (September to October) until early December. They construct a network of shallow horizontal subterranean tunnels and chambers. About 50 eggs are laid in a chamber.

KEY ID POINTS

- Confined to the Afromontane forest and northeastern mountain grassland in Limpopo Province
- Underside distinct from other species, except *B. bagginsi*, *B. rosei*, *B. sopranus* and *B. verrucosus*

- Facial mask prominent, giving a clown-like face (distinct from *B. acutirostris*, *B. fuscus*, *B. gibbosus* and *B. macrops*)
- Length of inner toe as long as it is wide, but outer toe twice as long as its width (usually distinct from other species, except *B. bagginsi*, *B. fuscus*, *B. gibbosus*, *B. namaquensis* and *B. verrucosus*, but variation does occur)

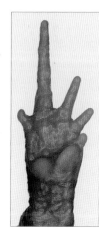

- Basal subarticular tubercle on hand single (distinct from *B. namaquensis*)
- Eyes small (distinct from *B. macrops* and *B. namaquensis*)
- Webbing absent

Plaintive Rain Frog

Klareënpadda

Breviceps verrucosus Rapp, 1842

LATIN: *verruca* = wart. Refers to the coarse skin.

Conservation status: Not threatened.

Plaintive Rain Frog: Port Elizabeth, Eastern Cape.

Description

Maximum size: 53 mm. **Body:** stout with short legs; eyes small. **Above:** uniform tan to dark brown with black markings; pale vertebral line sometimes present; dark facial band from eye to armpit sometimes present, but not as prominent as in most other Rain Frog species; skin with pitted granules; paravertebral skin ridges on the back. **Tympanum:** usually visible but sometimes partially obscured by warts. **Underside:** off-white and often mottled or speckled; densely granular. **Forelimbs:** palmar tubercles moderately developed; basal subarticular tubercles single. **Hindlimbs:** no webbing between toes; inner and outer toes

Average length
♀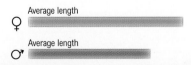

Average length
♂

Maximum size: 53 mm

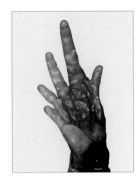

KEY ID POINTS

- Widely distributed in forest and adjacent grassland along the eastern escarpment
- Dorsal pattern distinct from other species
- Facial mask not always prominent
- Inner and outer toes longer than their width (usually distinct from other species, except *B. bagginsi*, *B. fuscus*, *B. gibbosus*, *B. namaquensis* and *B. verrucosus*, but variation does occur)

- Underside distinct from other species (except *B. bagginsi*, *B. rosei*, *B. sopranus* and *B. sylvestris*)

- Basal subarticular tubercle on hand single (distinct from *B. namaquensis*)
- Eyes small (distinct from *B. macrops* and *B. namaquensis*)
- Webbing absent

noticeably longer than their width. **Sexual dimorphism:** throat darker in male.

Call
Protracted, moderately pitched, mournful whistle. Large choruses form during rain or misty conditions and persist by day and night as long as wet conditions prevail. Males call from well-concealed shallow depressions under dense vegetation or from an elevated position on vegetation, a log or rock.

Habitat and habits
Breed in forest and adjacent grassland along the eastern escarpment, but may also be found in suburban gardens and fields adjacent to these habitats. Also found in coastal forest at sea level in southern KwaZulu-Natal. Breeding season is short, from first spring rains in August or early September until early November but may call sporadically until March.

Plain colour variation.

Dark colour variation.

FOREST RAIN FROGS

WOUDREËNPADDA

Probreviceps Parker, 1931

GREEK: *pro* = before; LATIN: *brevis* = short; *ceps* = head. The name means preceding (or more primitive than) the genus *Breviceps*.

Six species, one in southern Africa

DISTINCTIVE CHARACTERS

ADULT	TADPOLE
• Pupils horizontal • Skin texture rough • Tympanum visible • Cloacal opening directed downwards (distinct from Rain Frogs)	• No free-swimming tadpole phase • Metamorphosis is completed within the egg capsule

Found in montane forests in Tanzania and Zimbabwe. The southern African species is a forest form restricted to the eastern Zimbabwe Highlands.

Highland Forest Rain Frogs are very similar to Rain Frogs, *Breviceps*. The most distinctive differences are a conspicuous tympanum which is seldom visible in Rain Frogs; the digging tubercle which is not flanged to form a 'spade' as is the case in Rain Frogs; and the unusual downward-pointing vent. When the frog is at rest, the upper parts of the short limbs are hidden within the body skin.

Clusters of about 20 eggs are laid in a burrow, in humus under a layer of dead leaves on the forest floor. There is no free-swimming tadpole phase and the entire development is completed within the egg capsule. Breeding activity has been observed during November but may occur over a longer period.

Highland Forest Rain Frog with eggs.

Keith Palgrave

Highland Forest Rain Frog

Hoëveldse woudreënpadda

Probreviceps rhodesianus Poynton & Broadley, 1967

Named after Rhodesia, today called Zimbabwe, where the species occurs.

Conservation status: Endangered. It occurs in an area smaller than 5 000 km², its distribution is very fragmented, and the quality and extent of its habitat is declining.

Description

Maximum size: 49 mm. **Body:** rounded with a flat face. **Above:** very granular and without ridges or large warts; colour varies from orange to pale brown to grey with dark purple spots; flanks slightly darker than the back; area behind the eye darker, but not forming a distinct facial band, sometimes extending onto the sides of the body. **Underside:** heavily freckled to marbled purple-brown to cream, sometimes with orange infusions; cloacal openings in both sexes deflected downwards and surrounded by prominent skin folds. **Hindlimbs:** short but powerfully built; toes unwebbed; subarticular tubercles and metatarsal tubercles well developed; inner and outer metatarsal tubercles both massive but not elevated into a spade-like structure as in Rain Frogs. **Sexual dimorphism:** loose skin of the collapsed vocal sac is visible under the male throat; tympanum larger in male.

Call

Advertisement call is unknown. The frog emits a scream if molested.

Habitat and habits

Found under leaf litter or rotting logs on the slopes of evergreen mountain forests on the Zimbabwe-Mozambique border. Around 20 eggs are laid in a burrow in humus beneath a layer of dead leaves.

KEY ID POINTS

- Skin very rough
- Purple spots on an orange to pale brown colour on the back
- Inner and outer metatarsal tubercles are massive
- Downward-pointing vent

Habitat: forest slopes in eastern Zimbabwe.

Average length
♀

Average length
♂

Maximum size: 49 mm

TYPICAL TOADS

GEWONE-SKURWEPADDAS

Amietophrynus Frost et al. 2006

Named after the West African herpetologist, J-L. Amiet.
GREEK: *phrynos* = toad.

38 species, eight in southern Africa

Western Leopard Toad: note prominent parotoid glands behind eyes.

Southern African Typical Toads generally occur in grassland and fynbos, breeding in open water bodies and foraging some distance from the water. They move by hopping and walking and they are not capable of the long leaps of other grassland frogs.

The genus varies little in overall appearance. They are all typical members of the Bufonid (toad) family having squat, robust bodies and slender legs. Skin texture is generally rough and dry, with wart-like protuberances. Colour patterns generally take the form of more-or-less symmetrically placed irregular dark shapes on a neutral background. Prominent parotoid glands are located behind the eyes and exude a sticky, toxic fluid if the toad is molested. Although this is usually a successful deterrent, some predators have learnt to avoid contact with the dorsal glands and attack and eat only the ventral area.

Breeding generally takes place July to October in the winter-rainfall areas and September to January in the summer-rainfall areas. Calling males assemble at breeding sites several weeks ahead of the females and establish loud choruses. Calling is often accompanied by vigorous excitement in anticipation of the arrival of females. As soon as females arrive, mating pairs couple and frequently wander about in amplexus before they enter the water to lay eggs. Single males try to displace amplectant pairs forming knots of several frenzied males gyrating around a female. Between 10 000 and 25 000 eggs are laid underwater in double gelatinous strings, generally wound around submerged vegetation in order to keep the eggs suspended and well aerated. Tadpoles are dark-coloured. Eggs and tadpoles are heavily preyed upon by aquatic predators such as fish, terrapins and dragonfly larvae.

DISTINCTIVE CHARACTERS

ADULT

- Pupils horizontal
- Dark, usually symmetrical, dorsal pattern
- Skin rough with rounded, wart-like elevations on the back
- Distinct parotoid glands
- Underside granular
- Webbing present but restricted

TADPOLE

- Small (seldom exceeding 25 mm)
- Bottom-dwelling
- Broad upper and lower gap in the oral papillae
- Pigmentation extends over the gular region, at least posteriorly
- Nostril diameter less than half eye-length
- Tail muscle lighter in colour below
- Fin terminates in a rounded tip

Tadpole: lateral view.

Mouthparts.

Marius Burger

Left: Male Guttural Toads clasping a gravid female.

Below: Calling male Olive Toad. Extended vocal sac amplifies the sound.

Opposite below: Egg strings typical of the toad family.

KEY TO SPECIES

ADULT

1 Red infusions on upper legs **2**

   No red infusion on legs **5**

2 Pairs of dark markings on snout and between eyes leave a pale cross-shape on head ....
   ....**Guttural Toad** *A. gutturalis* (p.142)

   No pattern as above **3**

3 Snout sharply pointed; elongated parotoid glands extending dorsolaterally ... **Lemaire's Toad** *A. lemairii* (p.144)

   Body shape not as above **4**

4 Foot longer than 40% of body length .... **Eastern Olive Toad** *A. garmani* (p.140)

   Foot shorter than 40% of body length .... **Western Olive Toad** *A. poweri* (p.152)

5 Dark markings on eyelids fused into a bar between eyes .... **Raucous Toad** *A. rangeri* (p.154)

   Dark markings do not form a bar between eyes **6**

6 Found north of the Orange and Tugela rivers; parotoid glands flat and inconspicuous ....
   ....**Flat-backed Toad** *A. maculatus* (p.146)

   Found south of the Orange and Tugela rivers; parotoid glands conspicuous **7**

7 Found in the Western Cape .... **Western Leopard Toad** *A. pantherinus* (p.148)

   Found in the Eastern Cape .... **Eastern Leopard Toad** *A. pardalis* (p.150)

TADPOLE

   A. lemairii – tadpole is unknown.

1 Pigmentation over anterior part of tail covers upper two-thirds **2**

   Pigmentation over anterior part of tail covers more than three-quarters **4**

2 Lower part of tail muscle unpigmented at least for the anterior three-quarters .... *A. rangeri* (p.154)

   Lower part of tail muscle only unpigmented for the anterior two-thirds **3**

3 Tadpole from the Western Cape coastal region, west of Cape Agulhas .... *A. pantherinus* (p.148)

   Tadpole from the Eastern Cape coastal region, east of Knysna .... *A. pardalis* (p.150)

4 Pigmentation extends over posterior region of throat; oral disc not full width of head .... *A. gutturalis* (p.142)

   Pigmentation extends over throat, posteriorly and anteriorly; oral disc full width of head **5**

5 Four labial tooth rows in lower jaw .... *A. maculatus* (p.146)

   Three labial tooth rows in lower jaw; third row shorter .... *A. poweri* (p.152) or *A. garmani* (p.140)

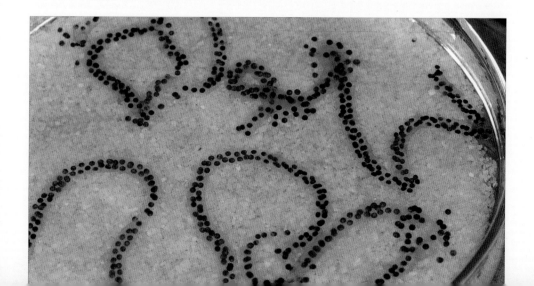

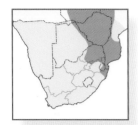

Eastern Olive Toad

Olyfskurwepadda

TRACK
27

Amietophrynus garmani (Meek, 1897)

Named after the ichthyologist, S.W. Garman (1843-1927), of Harvard University, USA.

Conservation status: Not threatened.

Eastern Olive Toad: Berg-en-dal, Kruger National Park, Mpumalanga.

Description

Maximum size: 115 mm. **Body:** thickset; robust; snout blunt; eyes large. **Above:** pairs of dark chocolate or reddish-brown paravertebral patches on yellow-brown to olive-green background; patches behind eyes not fused to form band; no dark patches on snout; back sometimes very dark with blotches barely detectable; skin rough, covered with warts, each having a black tip; prominent parotoid glands on neck behind each eye. **Underside:** dirty white, granular, leathery. **Forelimbs:** glands under forearm form a row of pale tubercles. **Hindlimbs:** thighs infused with red pigmentation, the degree of which

Average length

♀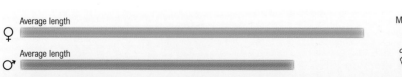

Average length

♂

Maximum size: 115 mm

KEY ID POINTS

- Almost indistinguishable from *A. poweri* in areas where the distribution ranges overlap, but can be identified by slight differences in call and length of the foot
- Foot 40–45% of length of body (distinct from *A. poweri*)
- No dark patches on snout (distinct from other species except *A. poweri* and *A. rangeri*)
- Dark patches not fused into a bar behind eyes (distinct from *A. rangeri*)
- Red infusion on legs (distinct from other species except *A. gutturalis*, *A. poweri* and *A. lemairii*)

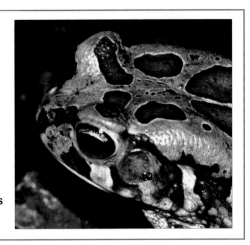

varies considerably; toes with scant fleshy webbing at base. **Sexual dimorphism:** male throat grey to almost black; blackish nuptial pads on outer fingers.

Call

Loud, braying *kwââ-kwââ* often antiphonally. Males call from exposed or semi-concealed sites close to water, forming small choruses and often returning to the same call-site.

Habitat and habits

Vleis and pans in bushveld savanna where there is relatively high rainfall (above 600 mm per annum). The species also adapts to suburban gardens but less readily than the Guttural Toad *A. gutturalis*.

TADPOLE

Length: up to 36 mm. **Shape:** body ovoid; plump. **Tail:** fin shallow, curved, ending bluntly; deepest point in middle of tail; fin tapering gradually to end in rounded tip. **Colour:** lighter and darker colouring to match substrate; fins transparent; dense pigmentation covering more than three-quarters of caudal muscles; sparse pigmentation extending almost to ventral margin of caudal muscles; dense pigmentation extending uniformly over abdomen; less dense across anterior throat region. **Eyes:** dorsolateral; eye to nostril distance less than diameter of eye. **Nostrils:** narrowly spaced; diameter less than half the length of eye, slightly bigger than eye lens; periphery elevated. **Spiracle:** just below body axis. **Vent:** median. **Mouth:** near-ventral; few large papillae confined to mouth corners; broad medial gap in papillae bordering lower jaw. **Jaw sheaths:** moderate. **LTRF:** 2(2)/3. **Development:** free-swimming after 24 hours; metamorphosis complete after 64 to 91 days.

Tadpole: lateral view.

Ventral view.

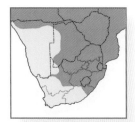

Guttural Toad

TRACK
O
28

Gorrelskurwepadda

Amietophrynus gutturalis (Power, 1927)

LATIN: *guttur* = throat. Refers to the deep, throaty call of the species.

Conservation status: Not threatened.

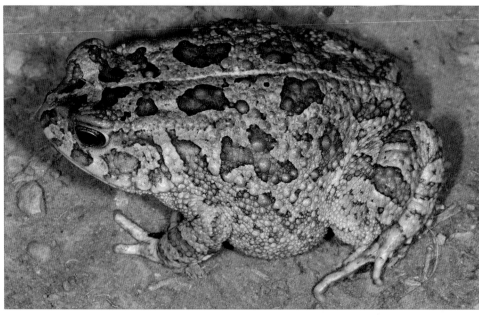

Guttural Toad: Vredefort Dome, North West Province.

Description
Maximum size: 120 mm. **Body:** thickset; robust; snout blunt; eyes large. **Above:** light to dark brown with pairs of dark paravertebral patches; smaller scattered yellow to orange spots sometimes present between larger patches; occasionally a thin brown vertebral line, especially in subadults; pairs of dark patches on snout and behind eyes leave a pale cross on head; skin rough, covered with wart-like elevations; prominent parotoid glands on neck behind each eye. **Underside:** dirty white, granular, leathery. **Forelimbs:** glands under forearm form row of pale tubercles. **Hindlimbs:** thighs with infusion of red pigmentation; toes with scant, fleshy webbing at base. **Sexual dimorphism:** male throat dark, sometimes with tint of yellow along jaw; blackish nuptial pads on outer fingers.

Call
Deep, guttural, pulsed snoring sound with accelerating pulse rate, resembling the last bounces of a dropped ping-pong ball. Males

Average length

♀

Average length

♂

Maximum size: 120 mm

KEY ID POINTS

- Dark patches on snout and behind each eye leave a pale cross on head (distinct from other species except *A. maculatus*)

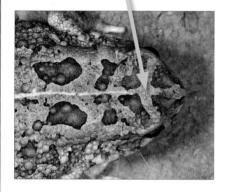

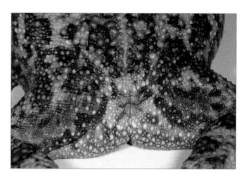

- Red infusion on legs (distinct from other species except *A. garmani*, *A. poweri* and *A. lemairii*)
- Dark patches not fused into a bar behind eyes (distinct from *A. rangeri*)

congregate in large choruses from early spring to late summer and call from exposed or partially concealed sites close to water. When in close proximity to one another they generally call antiphonally.

Habitat and habits

Around open pools, dams, vleis and other semi-permanent or permanent bodies of water in grassland, thicket and savanna. Common in suburban gardens and farmland.

TADPOLE

Length: up to 25 mm. **Shape:** small with plump, ovoid body; rounded snout. **Tail:** fin moderately curved, ending in blunt point; deepest point in middle of tail. **Colour:** body and tail shaft black with iridescent spots; ventral quarter of tail shaft white; fins transparent; sparse or no pigmentation over anterior throat region; belly midline sparsely pigmented. **Eyes:** dorsolateral; eye to nostril distance less than eye length. **Nostrils:** narrowly spaced; nostril diameter less than half diameter of eye – similar in size to eye lens. **Spiracle:** just below body axis; directed backwards at 25°. **Vent:** median. **Mouth:** single row of papillae at mouth corners. **Jaw sheaths:** moderate. LTRF: 2(2)/3. **Development:** free-swimming after two to three days; metamorphosis complete after five to six weeks.

Tadpole: lateral view.

Ventral view.

Lemaire's Toad

Lemaire se skurwepadda

Amietophrynus lemairii (Boulenger, 1901)

Named after the Lemaire expedition to what is today called the Democratic Republic of Congo.

Conservation status: Not threatened.

Alan Channing

Lemaire's Toad: Caprivi, Namibia.

Description

Maximum size: 70 mm. **Body:** large; similar in shape to River Frogs; head narrow and pointed. **Above:** greenish to reddish, often with pale vertebral line; pair of dark patches over back of the eyes separated by a pale bar; pair of dark patches on snout, sometimes extending onto upper eyelids; markings tend to fade in adult specimens; elevated glandular ridge from angle of mouth to base of arm;

♀ Average length

♂ Average length

Maximum size: 70 mm

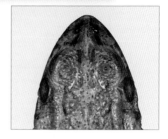

Habitat: savanna floodplain.

elongated parotoid gland prominent, extending back as granular ridge to sacral region. **Tympanum:** very distinct; as large as the eye. **Hindlimbs:** long; inner thighs with infusion of red pigmentation; toes long; feet moderately webbed; single tubercles under fingers. **Sexual dimorphism:** males in breeding condition are uniform bright yellow, throat dark.

Call
Short croak. Males call from flooded grassland.

Habitat and habits
Always near permanent water, primarily occurring on floodplains.

TADPOLE
Unknown.

KEY ID POINTS

- Narrow pointed head (distinct from other species)
- Elongated parotoid glands extending dorsolaterally (distinct from other species)
- Long, moderately webbed toes (distinct from other species)

- Red infusion on legs (distinct from other species except *A. garmani*, *A. poweri* and *A. gutturalis*)
- Dark patches not fused into a bar behind eyes (distinct from *A. rangeri*)

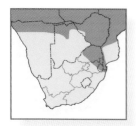

Flat-backed Toad

Gestreepte skurwepadda

**TRACK
29**

Amietophrynus maculatus (Hallowell, 1854)

LATIN: *maculata* = spot. Refers to the spots on the back of
the species.

Conservation status: Not threatened.

Flat-backed Toad: Nelspruit, Mpumalanga.

Description

Maximum size: 80 mm. **Body:** moderate
build; eyes large. **Above:** light to dark
brown with pairs of dark, paravertebral
patches; usually a thin, pale vertebral
line; pairs of dark patches on snout and
behind eyes leave a pale cross on head;
skin rough, covered with warts ending in
sharp, dark tip; parotoid glands flattened
and indistinct; sometimes obscured by
smaller dark-tipped warts. **Underside:**
granular, off-white with dark grey speckles.
Forelimbs: distinct row of pale tubercles
under forearm. **Hindlimbs:** fold of skin

Average length

♀

Average length

♂

Maximum size: 80 mm

along tarsus; thighs without infusion of red pigmentation; toes with scant fleshy webbing at base. **Sexual dimorphism:** male throat dark greenish-black with some yellow pigmentation.

Call

Raucous and rapid *quork-quork-quack-quork*. Males form large choruses on riverine sandbanks and edges of dams. Males generally remain well spaced from one another and call antiphonally.

Habitat and habits

Appears to favour shallow, static or slow-moving water in rivers, weirs and dams in a variety of vegetation types in lowveld grassland and savanna.

TADPOLE

Length: up to 17 mm. **Shape:** small; plump, ovoid body. **Tail:** fin moderately curved; ends in blunt tip. **Colour:** body and tail shaft black with iridescent spots; ventral quarter of tail shaft white; fins hyaline; sparse or no pigmentation over anterior throat region; belly midline sparsely pigmented. **Eyes:** dorsolateral. **Nostrils:** kidney-shaped; larger than eye lens; internarial distance smaller than interorbital distance; closer to snout than to eyes. **Spiracle:** below body axis; directed backwards at 20°. **Vent:** median. **Mouth:** anteroventral; oral disc wider than head; one row of papillae at mouth corners. **Jaw sheaths:** moderate to small. **LTRF:** 2(2)/3. **Development:** metamorphosis complete after two weeks.

KEY ID POINTS

- Parotoid glands flattened and barely elevated above dorsum (distinct from other species)
- No red infusions on legs (distinct from *A. gutturalis*, *A. garmani*, *A. poweri* and *A. lemairii*)

- Dark patches on snout and behind each eye leave a pale cross on head (distinct from other species except *A. gutturalis*)
- Dark patches not fused into a bar behind eyes (distinct from *A. rangeri*)

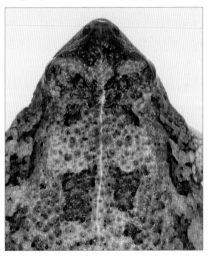

Tadpole: lateral view.

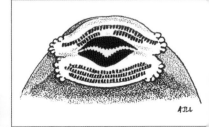

Mouthparts.

Western Leopard Toad

Westelike luiperdskurwepadda

TRACK
30

Amietophrynus pantherinus (Smith, 1828)

LATIN: *pantherinus* = like a leopard or panther. The markings on the back resemble those of a leopard.

Conservation status: Endangered. Much of its habitat has been lost and is diminishing through increased urbanisation. Guttural Toads compete with Leopard Toads for breeding space.

Western Leopard Toad: Tokai, Western Cape.

Description

Maximum size: 140 mm. **Body:** large; thickset; robust; eyes large. **Above:** striking, symmetrical, dark red-brown markings edged in black and yellow; usually a yellow vertebral line; skin rough, covered with wart-like elevations; prominent parotoid glands usually russet-coloured; top of snout free of dark markings except for an occasional asymmetrical dot; dark interorbital patches not fused into a bar. **Tympanum:** prominent. **Underside:** granular; whitish. **Forelimbs:** glands under forearm inconspicuous. **Hindlimbs:** no red infusion on thighs; toes with conspicuous margin of webbing along edges. **Sexual dimorphism:** male throat dark.

Average length

♀

Average length

♂

Maximum size: 140 mm

KEY ID POINTS

- Morphologically difficult to distinguish from *A. pardalis*, but the ranges of the two species are widely separated
- Distinctive symmetrical red and yellow dorsal markings (distinct from other species except *A. pardalis*)
- No red infusions on legs (distinct from *A. garmani*, *A. poweri* and *A. lemairii*)
- Dark patches not fused into a bar behind eyes (distinct from *A. rangeri*)
- No markings on snout except for an occasional asymmetrical dot
- Confined to the southwestern Cape

Call

Long drawn-out snore on overcast days, in early evenings and at night. In spring, males establish large choruses at breeding sites and call from semi-concealed positions in the early evenings; later at night they call while floating on water's surface, legs outstretched.

Habitat and habits

Pans, vleis and dams with relatively deep water in fynbos and thickets, on Cape Peninsula, Cape Flats and Augulhas Plain. Not restricted to pristine natural habitats, and often colonises dams in farmland and suburbs where breeding sites still exist.

TADPOLE

Length: up to 26 mm. **Shape:** body plump; ovoid. **Tail:** upper and lower tail fin with distinctly curved margins; deepest point in middle of tail. **Colour:** body dark; dark pigmentation on tail muscles anteriorly confined to upper two-thirds, and posteriorly covering muscles completely; abdomen dark; no pigmentation directly behind mouth; sparse pigmentation over posterior gular region. **Eyes:** dorsolateral; eye to nostril distance less than the diameter of eye. **Nostrils:** narrowly spaced; big, about same size as eye lens. **Spiracle:** below body axis; directed backwards at 20°. **Vent:** median. **Mouth:** anteroventral; no papillae inside oral disc at mouth corners. **Jaw sheaths:** moderate. **LTRF:** 2(2)/3. **Development:** metamorphosis complete after more than 10 weeks.

Conservation initiative in Noordhoek, Western Cape.

Tadpole: lateral view.

Eastern Leopard Toad

Oostelike luiperdskurwepadda

TRACK
31

Amietophrynus pardalis (Hewitt, 1935)

LATIN: *pardalis* = female leopard. Refers to the leopard-like markings on the back.

Conservation status: Not listed as Threatened, but there are concerns about its conservation status because of the fragmentation of habitat and high road mortalities.

Marius Burger

Eastern Leopard Toad: Thomas Baines Nature Reserve, Eastern Cape.

Description

Maximum size: 147 mm. **Body:** large; thickset; robust; eyes large. **Above:** symmetrical, red-brown markings edged in black and yellow; yellow vertebral line usually present; skin rough, covered with wart-like elevations; prominent parotoid glands; top of snout free of dark markings except for an occasional asymmetrical dot; dark interorbital patches sometimes fused into a

♀ Average length

♂ Average length

Maximum size:147 mm

KEY ID POINTS

- Morphologically difficult to distinguish from *A. pantherinus*, but ranges of the two species are widely separated
- Distinctive symmetrical red and yellow dorsal markings (distinct from other species except *A. pantherinus*)
- No red infusions on legs (distinct from *A. garmani*, *A. poweri* and *A. lemairii*)
- Dark patches sometimes fused into a bar behind eyes (distinct from other species except *A. rangeri*)
- No markings on snout except for an occasional asymmetrical dot
- Confined to Eastern Cape

bar; very prominent but flattened parotoid glands, usually yellowish. **Tympanum:** prominent. **Underside:** granular; creamy-white. **Forelimbs:** glands under forearm inconspicuous; subarticular tubercles single. **Hindlimbs:** no red infusion on thighs; toes with conspicuous margin of webbing along edges. **Sexual dimorphism:** male throat dark.

Call
Long, very deep-pitched drawn-out snore. Males call antiphonally while floating in deep water or on the banks of pans and dams.

Habitat and habits
Thornveld and open savanna in the Eastern Cape.

TADPOLE

Length: up to 25 mm. **Shape:** body plump; ovoid. **Tail:** upper and lower fin with distinctly curved margins; deepest point in middle of tail. **Colour:** pigmentation on tail muscles anteriorly confined to upper two-thirds, posteriorly covering muscles completely; abdomen and posterior area of throat darkly pigmented. **Eyes:** dorsolateral; eye to nostril distance less than diameter of eye. **Nostrils:** narrowly spaced; internarial distance significantly smaller than interorbital distance; slightly closer to snout than eyes. **Spiracle:** just below body axis; terminating in pronounced tube, directed backwards at 40°. **Vent:** median. **Mouth:** no papillae inside oral disc at mouth corners; sometimes single papilla. **Jaw sheaths:** moderate. **LTRF:** 2(2)/3. **Development:** metamorphosis complete after more than 10 weeks.

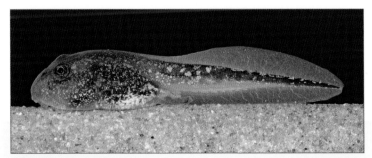

Tadpole: lateral view.

Ventral view.

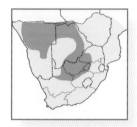

Western Olive Toad

Power se skurwepadda

TRACK 32

Amietophrynus poweri (Hewitt, 1935)

Named after the herpetologist, John Hyacinth Power, director of the McGregor Museum in Kimberley from 1947 to 1958.

Conservation status: Not threatened.

Western Olive Toad: dark colour form from Potchefstroom, North West Province. Inset: Light coloration, also from Potchefstroom.

Description

Maximum size: 100 mm. **Body:** thickset; robust; snout blunt; eyes large. **Above:** pairs of dark-edged chocolate or reddish-brown patches on yellow-brown to olive-green background; patches may be symmetrically placed or randomly scattered; patches behind eyes not fused to form band; no dark patches on snout; skin rough and covered with warts, each having a black tip; prominent parotoid glands on neck behind each eye. **Underside:** dirty white, granular, leathery. **Forelimbs:** glands under forearm form row of pale tubercles. **Hindlimbs:** thighs infused with red pigmentation; toes with scant fleshy webbing at base. **Sexual dimorphism:** male throat grey to almost black; blackish nuptial pads on outer fingers.

♀ Average length

♂ Average length

Maximum size: 100 mm

Call

Loud *kwââ-kwââ*. Males form small choruses and call from exposed or semi-concealed sites.

Habitat and habits

Occurs around vleis and pans in thornveld savanna where rainfall is relatively low, generally less than 600 mm per annum.

TADPOLE

Length: up to 36 mm. **Shape:** body plump; ovoid. **Tail:** fin shallow, rising gently to reach highest point about third of the way along tail; tip of tail ends bluntly. **Colour:** usually black but may have lighter and darker colouring to match substrate; fins hyaline; dense pigmentation covers more than three-quarters of caudal muscles; sparse pigmentation extends almost to ventral margin; dense pigmentation extends more or less uniformly over abdomen and across anterior throat region. **Eyes:** dorsolateral; eye to nostril distance less than eye length. **Nostrils:** round, with inner rim slightly elevated; narrowly spaced; internarial distance significantly smaller than interorbital distance. **Spiracle:** below body axis; short tube; directed backwards at 30°. **Vent:** median. **Mouth:** near-ventral; oral papillae irregular and in single row confined to mouth corners. **Jaw sheaths:** moderate. **LTRF:** 2(2)/3. **Development:** free-swimming after 24 hours; development complete after 73 days (recorded in captivity).

KEY ID POINTS

- Almost indistinguishable from *A. garmani* in areas where the distribution ranges overlap, but can be identified from slight differences in call and length of foot
- Foot 35-40% of length of body (distinct from *A. garmani*)
- No dark patches on snout (distinct from other species except *A. garmani* and *A. rangeri*)

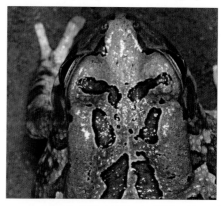

- Dark patches not fused into a bar behind eyes (distinct from *A. rangeri*)
- Red infusion on legs (distinct from other species except *A. gutturalis*, *A. garmani* and *A. lemairii*)

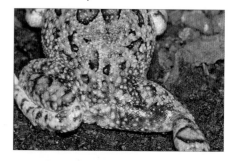

Tadpole: lateral view.

Ventral view.

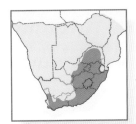

Raucous Toad

Lawaaiskurwepadda

Amietophrynus rangeri (Hewitt, 1935)

Named after the Eastern Cape naturalist, Gordon A. Ranger.

Conservation status: Not threatened.

Raucous Toad: Bloemfontein, Free State.

Description

Maximum size: 115 mm. **Body:** thickset and robust; snout blunt. **Above:** Olive-grey to brown with pairs of irregularly shaped dark paravertebral patches; skin rough and covered with wart-like elevations. Prominent parotoid glands on neck behind each eye; dark patches absent from snout and fused into single interorbital bar across the head. **Underside:** dirty white, granular and leathery. **Hindlimbs:** Distinctive fold of skin along the tarsus; no red infusions on thighs; toes with fleshy webbing at the base.

Average length

♀

Average length

♂

Maximum size: 115 mm

Call

Rasping *kwââ-kwââ* quacks, resembling those of a duck, repeated incessantly. Males call vigorously in groups from exposed positions at the water's edge. In summer-rainfall areas, calling begins early in spring and continues from September to January; in winter-rainfall areas the calling season is slightly later, from November to February.

Habitat and habits

Rivers and streams in grassland and fynbos. This species frequently inhabits gardens and farmland where it appears to favour running water sources, such as ornamental fountains.

TADPOLE

Length: up to 25 mm. **Shape:** body plump; ovoid. **Tail:** fin distinctly convex but shallow; ends bluntly; deepest point just anterior to middle of tail. **Colour:** body dark, sometimes with golden stipples; dark pigment over tail muscles, characteristically confined to upper two-thirds along full length of tail, leaving bright white band below; fins hyaline. **Eyes:** dorsolateral; eye to nostril distance less than eye length. **Nostrils:** small and narrowly spaced. **Spiracle:** below body axis; directed backwards at 20°. **Vent:** median. **Mouth:** single row of large papillae, confined to mouth corners; broad gap above and below. **Jaw sheaths:** moderate. **LTRF:** 2(2)/3. **Development:** free-swimming after 24 hours; development complete after 64 to 91 days.

KEY ID POINTS

- No red infusion on legs (distinct from *A.garmani*, *A. poweri* and *A. lemairii*)

- No dark patches on snout (distinct from other species except *A. poweri*, *A. garmani*, *A. pantherinus* and *A. pardalis*)

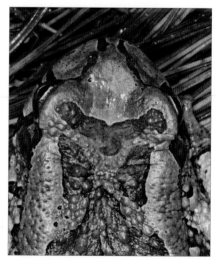

- Dark patches fused into a bar behind eyes (distinct from all other species except, occasionally, *A. pardalis*)

Tadpole: lateral view.

PYGMY TOADS

DWERGSKURWEPADDAS

Poyntonophrynus Frost et al., 2006

Named after the South African herpetologist J.C. Poynton.
GREEK: *phrynos* = toad.

10 species, seven in southern Africa

Southern Pygmy Toad: Bloemfontein, Free State.

Pygmy toads belong to the Bufonid (toad) family. They are small and flattened in shape, with inconspicuous parotoid glands and lacking tarsal folds. Found in open country and often in arid areas. They usually spend daylight hours hiding under rocks, in burrows or in rock crevices.

They are terrestrial frogs that breed in standing or slow-flowing water. Breeding occurs opportunistically after a heavy downpour. Gelatinous strings of eggs are complete. Little is known about the breeding biology of most species in this genus, nor about many of the tadpoles.

DISTINCTIVE CHARACTERS

ADULT

- Pupil horizontal
- Small, flattened shape
- Pale scapular patch with pale bands extending to the upper eyelids
- Parotoid glands present but flattened and often barely discernible
- Vertebral line sometimes present
- Tarsal fold absent

TADPOLE

- Broad central gap on lower jaw papillae
- Tail fin distinctly curved and with rounded tip
- Eye to nostril distance less than eye length
- Lacks pigmentation over gular region
- Nostril diameter more than half length of eye
- Tail muscles uniform in colour

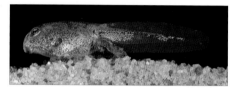

Marius Burger

Amplectant pair.

Marius Burger

Flattened extended vocal sac.

KEY TO SPECIES

ADULT

1 Underside with prominent black blotches that tend to fuse ... **Southern Pygmy Toad** *P. vertebralis* (p.170)
  Underside pale or with small black spots that do not fuse **2**
2 Confined to low-lying eastern parts of Mozambique .... **Beira Pygmy Toad** *P. beiranus* (p.158)
  Not found in low-lying eastern parts of Mozambique **3**
3 Confined to central and northwestern parts of Namibia **4**
  Not found in central and northwestern parts of Namibia **6**
4 Surface of snout granular .... **Damaraland Pygmy Toad** *P. damaranus* (p.160)
  Surface of snout smooth **5**
5 Tympanum distinct .... **Dombe Pygmy Toad** *P. dombensis* (p.162)
  Tympanum obscured .... **Hoesch's Pygmy Toad** *P. hoeschi* (p.166)
6 Tympanum distinct .... **Northern Pygmy Toad** *P. fenoulheti* (p.164)
  Tympanum obscured .... **Kavango Pygmy Toad** *P. kavangensis* (p.168)

TADPOLE

Unknown for most species.

Beira Pygmy Toad

Beira-dwergskurwepadda

TRACK
34

Poyntonophrynus beiranus (Loveridge, 1932)

Named after Beira in Mozambique, the type locality of the species.

Conservation status: Not threatened.

Beira Pygmy Toad: Rio Savanne, Mozambique. Note granular swellings obscuring tympanum.

Dominic Rollinson

Description

Maximum size: 28 mm. Body: small, with short pointed snout. **Above:** dark, usually with a pale vertebral line; pale scapular patch, usually with extensions to dorsal eyelid; skin leathery, with slightly raised warts; top of head with spines and either no or only slightly raised warts; parotoid gland inconspicuous to hardly discernible, often in the form of two or three isolated

Average length
♀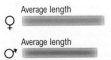

Average length
♂

Maximum size: 28 mm

KEY ID POINTS

- Confined to the Zambezi River area in Mozambique (distinct from other species)
- Underside pale and without markings (distinct from *P. vertebralis*)

- Tympanum inconspicuous (distinct from *P. dombensis* and *P. fenoulheti*)
- Skin on snout smooth (distinct from *P. fenoulheti* and *P. damaranus*)
- Inner and outer metatarsal tubercles equally small (distinct from *P. fenoulheti*)

granular swellings. **Tympanum:** not visible or only faintly discernible through warty skin. **Underside:** lightly to heavily flecked in grey; skin very granular, each wart ending in a small spine. **Hindlimbs:** two or three segments of the longest toe free of webbing; no tarsal fold; subarticular tubercles usually double; small inner and outer metatarsal tubercles. **Sexual dimorphism:** throat of breeding male chrome yellow.

Call

High-pitched insect-like buzz. Males congregate in very large numbers in shallow water but are difficult to capture because they submerge themselves at the slightest disturbance.

Habitat and habits

Found in grassy areas that are flooded during heavy rains.

Dominic Rollinson

Dorsal view showing pale vertebral line and scapular patch.

TADPOLE

Unknown.

Damaraland Pygmy Toad

Damara-dwergskurwepadda

Poyntonophrynus damaranus (Mertens, 1954)

Named after the Damaraland region of Namibia where the species is found.

Conservation status: Unknown (Data Deficient).

Wulf Haacke

Damaraland Pygmy Toad: Damaraland, Namibia.

Description

Maximum size: 37 mm. **Body:** flattened; head broader than long and with pointed snout. **Above:** olive-brown with symmetrical to irregular dark blotches often edged in black; largest blotches in the shoulder region; dark interorbital band; dark vertebral line sometimes present; dorsum and thighs densely covered in warts; small spines on head;

Average length

♀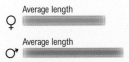

Average length

♂

Maximum size: 37 mm

KEY ID POINTS

- Confined to the Kaokoveld and Waterberg areas of northern and northwestern Namibia (distinct from other species except *P. dombensis* and *P. hoeschi*)
- Underside immaculate (distinct from *P. vertebralis*)
- Tympanum partially obscured (distinct from *P. dombensis* and *P. fenoulheti*)
- Skin on snout granular (distinct from other species except *P. fenoulheti*)

Wulf Haacke

parotoid glands conspicuous, with well-defined edges, but flattened. **Tympanum:** partially obscured by wart-like skin elevations. **Underside:** yellowish-white; granular. **Forelimbs:** first and second fingers of equal length. **Hindlimbs:** subarticular tubercles well defined and sometimes double; inner metatarsal tubercle slightly bigger than outer; no tarsal fold; webbing moderately well developed, with 3 to 3½ phalanges of the longest toe free of web. **Sexual dimorphism:** male throat yellow.

Call
Unknown.

Habitat and habits
Seasonal waterbodies in Damaraland.

TADPOLE
Unknown.

Alan Channing

Habitat: Damaraland, Namibia.

Dombe Pygmy Toad

Dombe-dwergskurwepadda

Poyntonophrynus dombensis (Bocage, 1895)

Named after Dombe in Angola, the type locality of the species.

Conservation status: Not threatened.

TRACK
35

Alan Channing

Dombe Pygmy Toad: Damaraland, Namibia.

Description

Maximum size: 40 mm. **Body:** flattened and slender. **Above:** light to dark brown, with small, dark blotches; pale scapular patch usually present; pale vertebral line and pale patch lower down on the back sometimes present; skin on the back leathery with well-spaced warts except on the smooth snout; parotoid gland flattened; row of glands between base of arm and upper jaw. **Tympanum:** well developed. **Underside:** immaculate; smooth to slightly granular

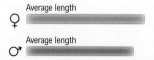

Average length
♀

Average length
♂

Maximum size: 40 mm

and leathery. **Hindlimbs:** subarticular tubercles usually double; webbing scanty and only reaches base of the fourth toe; tarsal fold absent. **Sexual dimorphism:** male throat yellow.

Call
Series of short bleats. Males commence calling only around midnight.

Habitat and habits
Grassland close to rock outcrops in coastal lowlands of northwest Namibia. Breeds in rocky pools with gravel substrate.

Sesriem, Namibia.

Habitat: rocky pool.

KEY ID POINTS

- Confined to northwestern Namibia from sea level to 1 500 m (distinct from other species except *P. damaranus* and *P. hoeschi*)
- Underside immaculate (distinct from *P. vertebralis*)

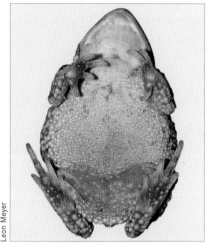

- Tympanum prominent (distinct from other species except *P. fenoulheti*)
- Skin on snout smooth (distinct from *P. fenoulheti* and *P. damaranus*)

TADPOLE
Length: up to 24 mm. **Shape:** plump; body flattened. **Tail:** fin shallow; only slightly higher than body. **Colour:** brown above; body stippled black; tail muscles lightly pigmented with light brown to bronze markings, except for thin line along bottom margin; dorsal fin slightly mottled; ventral fin transparent; abdomen whitish and lightly stippled with clear midventral band. **Eyes:** dorsolateral. **Nostrils:** narrowly spaced; large; oval, with pale raised margin. **Vent:** median. **Mouth:** broad gap in papillae above and below. **Jaw sheaths:** delicate. **LTRF:** 2(2)/3(1).

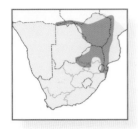

Northern Pygmy Toad

Noordelike dwergskurwepadda

Poyntonophrynus fenoulheti (Hewitt & Methuen, 1913)

Named after the specimen collector, J.P. Fenoulhet.

Conservation status: Not threatened.

Northern Pygmy Toad: Machiya, Kruger National Park, Limpopo Province.

Description

Maximum size: 43 mm. **Body:** flattened. **Above:** grey to brown overall, with dark blotches; pale markings sometimes present; pale scapular patch usually present; sometimes one or two pale patches on lower back; skin on back leathery, with well-spaced warts, each with a central spine; few warts on top of head; parotoid glands present, but flattened and inconspicuous. **Tympanum:** distinct; periphery elevated. **Underside:** immaculate, occasionally with black blotches or spots; leathery smooth to slightly granular with flattened warts; throat smooth. **Forelimbs:** nuptial pads on the first two fingers. **Hindlimbs:** toes scantily webbed; tarsal fold absent; subarticular tubercles on hands and feet usually double; inner metatarsal tubercle three times bigger than outer. **Sexual dimorphism:** male throat yellow to deep orange with dark gular sac.

♀ Average length

♂ Average length

Maximum size: 43 mm

KEY ID POINTS

- Confined to the northeastern parts of South Africa, eastern Swaziland, western Mozambique, most of Zimbabwe and Caprivi (distinct from other species except *P. kavangensis* and *P. beiranus*)
- Underside immaculate with a few sporadic small dots but never blotches (distinct from *P. vertebralis*)

- Tympanum prominent (distinct from other species except *P. dombensis*)
- Skin on snout granular (distinct from other species except *P. damaranus*)

Call

Long, high-pitched creaking sound, emitted in rapid succession. Males call antiphonally from semi-concealed positions or from grass stems up to 150 mm above the water.

Habitat and habits

Variety of bushveld vegetation in the savanna biome and occasionally in adjacent grassland. Strongly associated with rocky outcrops.

Marius Burger

Vocal sac extends beyond snout.

TADPOLE

Length: up to 23 mm. **Shape:** body elongated; oval. **Tail:** fin margins convexly curved; tapers to sharply rounded tip. **Colour:** body and tail shaft black with scattered golden spots; dorsal tail fin mottled; ventral fin clear; ventral quarter of tail muscles sparsely pigmented; pigmentation does not cover gular region. **Eyes:** dorsolateral. **Nostrils:** small and narrowly spaced; closer to snout than to eyes; diameter of nostril greater than half the length of eye. **Spiracle:** below body axis. **Vent:** median. **Mouth:** broad median gap in papillae of upper jaw; smaller gap in lower jaw; papillae at mouth corners and on sides below. **Jaw sheaths:** delicate and lightly flexed. **LTRF:** 2(2)/3; third row in the lower jaw much shorter. **Development:** metamorphosis complete after 19 days.

Tadpole: lateral view.

Hoesch's Pygmy Toad

Hoesch se dwergskurwepadda

Poyntonophrynus hoeschi (Ahl, 1934)

Named after the Namibian herpetologist, W. Hoesch.

Conservation status: Not threatened.

Hoesch's Pygmy Toad: Windhoek, Namibia.

Alan Channing

Description

Maximum size: 37 mm. **Body:** flattened.
Above: brown to reddish-brown with light
and dark markings; prominent light-coloured
scapular patch with pale projections to each
upper eyelid; pale vertebral line or band
sometimes present; skin scattered with
small warts; snout smooth; parotoid gland
distinct to completely flattened. **Tympanum:**
concealed. **Underside:** immaculate; smooth
to slightly granular and leathery; throat not
heavily granular. **Hindlimbs:** tarsal fold
absent; toes with distinct margin of webbing.
Sexual dimorphism: male throat yellow.

Call

Short chirp. Males call from the edge of rock
pools only for a few nights after the first
heavy rains of the season.

Habitat and habits

Occurs in very dry areas; associated with rock
outcrops where it breeds in sandy-bottomed
temporary pools.

Average length
♀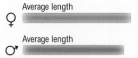

Average length
♂

Maximum size: 37 mm

KEY ID POINTS

- Confined to the central and western parts of Namibia (distinct from other species except *P. damaranus* and *P. dombensis*)
- Underside immaculate (distinct from *P. vertebralis*)

- Tympanum inconspicuous (distinct from *P. dombensis* and *P. fenoulheti*)
- Skin on snout smooth (distinct from *P. fenoulheti* and *P. damaranus*)

Hardap Dam, Namibia.

Habitat: temporary pool in outcrop.

TADPOLE

Length: up to 20 mm. **Shape:** body oval. **Tail:** fin distinctly curved convexly, ending in rounded tip. **Colour:** body and tail muscles heavily pigmented; thin ventral strip of tail muscle more sparsely pigmented; no pigmentation over anterior throat region. **Eyes:** dorsolateral. **Nostrils:** fairly widely spaced; small; same size as eye lens; midway between eyes and snout. **Spiracle:** below body axis; directed backwards at 45°. **Vent:** median. **Mouth:** near-ventral. **Jaw sheaths:** Delicate. **LTRF:** 2(2)/3. **Development:** less than 24 days to complete metamorphosis. **Behaviour:** bottom-dwelling and solitary; developing tadpoles can withstand high water temperature – reportedly as high as 36°C.

Tadpole: lateral view.

Kavango Pygmy Toad

Kavango-dwergskurwepadda

Poyntonophrynus kavangensis
(Poynton & Broadley, 1988)

Named after the Kavango River where this species is found.

Conservation status: Not threatened.

Kavango Pygmy Toad: Caprivi, Namibia.

Description

Maximum size: 33 mm. **Body:** flattened.
Above: usually three pairs of dark patches
with dark interorbital band; light-coloured
scapular patch, with pale projections to
each upper eyelid sometimes present;
pale vertebral line; skin leathery with well-
spaced warts except on the smooth snout;
parotoid glands present but inconspicuous;
of constant width, with outer edge

Average length
♀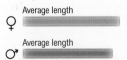

Average length
♂

Maximum size: 33 mm

KEY ID POINTS

- Confined to northeastern Namibia, northern Botswana and western Zimbabwe (distinct from other species except *P. fenoulheti*)
- Underside without dark blotches (distinct from *P. vertebralis*)
- Tympanum not prominent (distinct from *P. fenoulheti* and *P. damaranus*)

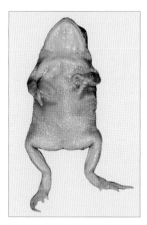

Alan Channing

- Skin on snout smooth (distinct from *P. fenoulheti* and *P. damaranus*)

straight and not extending below level of pupil. **Tympanum:** faintly to moderately discernible. **Underside:** cream-coloured; no dark blotches; pavement of flattened warts. **Forelimbs:** light and dark bands; subarticular tubercles usually double; two enlarged palmar tubercles. **Hindlimbs:** toes short and stumpy; scantily webbed with serrated margin; broad web between toes three and four, metatarsal tubercles oval; tarsal fold absent. **Sexual dimorphism:** male throat yellow with dark gular sac; abdominal warts more prominent in male.

Call

Series of short buzzes. Males call in flooded grassland while clinging to grass stems 100 mm above the water.

Habitat and habits

Uses ephemeral pools that form after rains on Kalahari sand, in grassland areas of northern Namibia, northern Botswana and northwestern Zimbabwe.

TADPOLE

Unknown.

Habitat: Caprivi savanna grassland.

Southern Pygmy Toad

TRACK
38

Suidelike dwergskurwepadda

Poyntonophrynus vertebralis (Smith, 1848)

LATIN: *vertebralis* = spinal joints. Refers to the pale vertebral line or other markings along the back.

Conservation status: Not threatened.

Southern Pygmy Toad: Mountain Zebra National Park, Eastern Cape.

Description

Maximum size: 36 mm. Above: grey to brown with more or less symmetrical patterns; orange and reddish markings common; vertebral line sometimes present; light-coloured scapular patch usually present; single or a pair of light patches on the lower back; leathery with well-spaced warts each having a central spine; snout granular but smoother than dorsum; parotoid glands flattened and inconspicuous. **Tympanum:** inconspicuous; surrounded by glandular skin elevations. **Underside:** white, leathery and slightly granular, with clearly delineated black spots that tend to fuse; throat smooth. **Hindlimbs:** toes scantily webbed; no tarsal fold; inner metatarsal tubercle three times larger than the outer.

Average length
♀
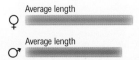

Average length
♂

Maximum size: 36 mm

Sexual dimorphism: breeding male with nuptial pads on the first two fingers; vocal sac in male often bright yellow, flattened and extending beyond snout when inflated.

Call

Long, sustained, cricket-like chirping. Males call from concealed positions close to the water's edge.

Habitat and habits

Found around temporary rain pools in dry rocky areas. Favours brackish soil and gravel in the Nama Karoo and dry savanna and grassland biomes.

Colour variation.

KEY ID POINTS

- Confined to the dry central region of South Africa, south of 27°30' latitude (distinct from other species except *P. fenoulheti*)
- Tympanum inconspicuous (distinct from *P. dombensis* and *P. fenoulheti*)
- Skin on snout smooth (distinct from *P. fenoulheti* and *P. damaranus*)

- Underside with distinct black blotches that tend to fuse (distinct from other species)

TADPOLE

Length: up to 20 mm. **Shape:** body oval; snout very short; body deeper than tail. **Tail:** fin shallow, moderately curved, ending in a rounded tip. **Colour:** body and tail shaft black with scattered to dense golden spots; fins transparent; no pigmentation over anterior throat region. **Eyes:** dorsolateral. **Nostrils:** big and widely spaced; same size as eye-lens. **Spiracle:** below body axis; directed backwards at 60°. **Vent:** median. **Mouth:** near-ventral; single row of papillae laterally and ventro-laterally. **Jaw sheaths:** delicate and moderately curved. **LTRF:** 2(2)/3. **Development:** complete metamorphosis in 16 to 20 days.

Tadpole: lateral view.

VAN DIJK'S TOADS

VAN DIJK SE SKURWEPADDAS

Vandijkophrynus Frost et al., 2006

Named after the South African herpetologist, D.E. van Dijk.
GREEK: *phrynos* = toad.

Five species, all in southern Africa

Cape Sand Toad males contesting a female.

Marius Burger

The genus is confined to southern Africa where all but one of the species have small, distinctly separate distribution ranges. The genus belongs to the Bufonid (toad) family, and has the typical squat, robust form of most toads, the prominent parotoid glands giving the head a square appearance. As a genus, Van Dijk's Toads are not easily distinguishable from other toads, but each species has its own distinctive characters.

DISTINCTIVE CHARACTERS

- Pupil horizontal
- Dark, usually with an asymmetrical dorsal pattern
- Skin rough with rounded wart-like elevations on the back
- Underside granular
- Parotoid glands distinct
- Webbing either absent or restricted to a slight fleshy web at the base of the toes; extending as a fringe around toes of one species

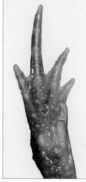

TADPOLE
- Small, seldom exceeding 25 mm
- Benthic dwelling
- Broad upper and lower gap in the oral papillae
- Upper and lower margins of the tail fin parallel
- Fin terminates in a rounded tip

Breeding is triggered by rainfall. Thus in winter-rainfall areas, calling and breeding takes place March to October. In summer-rainfall areas, where climatic conditions may be more erratic, breeding occurs opportunistically after heavy downpours. Females lay gelatinous strings of 2 000 to 3 000 eggs in shallow, often temporary, water.

KEY TO SPECIES

ADULT

1 Found north of the Limpopo River .... **Inyanga Toad** *V. inyangae* (p.180)
   Found south of the Limpopo River **2**
2 Yellow coloration on the upper side of feet .... **Cape Sand Toad** *V. angusticeps* (p.176)
   No yellow coloration on the upper side of feet **3**
3 Found in Namaqualand west of 20ºW and north of 32ºS **4**
   Found elsewhere **5**
4 Dorsal pattern russet-red with green blotches .... **Paradise Toad** *V. robinsoni* (p.182)
   Dorsal pattern not as above **5**
5 Tarsal fold massive .... **Karoo Toad** *V. gariepensis* (p.178)
   Tarsal fold flat or slightly ridged .... **Amatola Toad** *V. amatolicus* (p.174)

TADPOLE

1 Known only from the Amatola Mountains .... *V. amatolicus* (p.174)
   Found elsewhere **2**
2 Known only from the Inyanga Mountains between Zimbabwe and Mozambique .... *V. inyangae* (p.180)
   Found elsewhere **3**
3 Nostrils smaller than eye lens; about 20% of lower jaw sheath deeply pigmented ....
   .... *V. angusticeps* (p.176)
   Nostrils larger than eye lens; more than 25% of lower jaw sheath deeply pigmented **4**
4 Nostril diameter one-third of eye length; abdomen sparsely pigmented .... *V. gariepensis* (p.178)
   Nostril diameter half of eye length; abdomen darkly pigmented .... *V. robinsoni* (p.182)

Amatola Toad

Amatola-skurwepadda

Vandijkophrynus amatolicus (Hewitt, 1925)

Named after the Amatola Mountains in the Eastern Cape, the habitat of this species.

Conservation status: Endangered. Exotic tree plantations are replacing grassland habitat in the limited range of the species.

Amatola Toad: Hogsback, Eastern Cape.

Description

Maximum size: 37 mm. **Body:** compact. **Above:** usually uniformly dark grey to olive, with a light vertebral line, but occasionally with irregular dark markings; many conspicuous flattened warts; parotoid glands elevated and prominent. **Head:** top of head smooth and without markings. **Tympanum:** small and inconspicuous. **Underside:** granular with flattened warts; throat smooth and off-white with occasional bright white spots. **Limbs:** fingers and toes lack a fringe of webbing; tarsal fold flattened or slightly ridged. **Sexual dimorphism:** male throat dark.

Average length

♀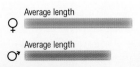

Average length

♂

Maximum size: 37 mm

Call

Brief nasal squawks. Males call from concealed positions. Large choruses may form at breeding sites after heavy rains.

Habitat and habits

Temporary rain pools and seepage in high-altitude, moist, upland grassland in the Winterhoek and Amatola Mountains in the Eastern Cape.

KEY ID POINTS

- Dorsum uniformly dark grey to olive with a light vertebral line (distinct from other species except *V. gariepensis*)
- Head without markings (distinct from *V. angusticeps*)
- Tarsal fold flat or only slightly ridged (distinct from *V. gariepensis* and *V. angusticeps*)
- Toes lack fringe of webbing (distinct from *V. angusticeps*)

Dorsal view showing light vertebral line.

TADPOLE

Length: up to 20 mm. **Shape:** body ovoid; plump. **Tail:** upper and lower tail fin distinctly curved and with rounded tip. **Colour:** body and tail fins brown. **Eyes:** diameter less than distance from eye to nostril. **Nostrils:** widely spaced; nostril bigger than eye lens – smaller than half eye diameter. **Spiracle:** above body axis; directed backwards at 30°. **Vent:** median. **Mouth:** near-ventral; single row of large papillae confined to mouth corners. **Jaw sheaths:** delicate; moderately curved. **LTRF:** 2(2)/3.

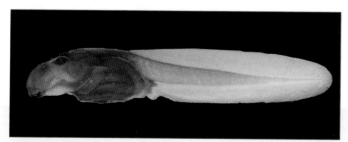

Tadpole: lateral view.

Dorsal view.

Cape Sand Toad

Sandskurwepadda

TRACK
40

Vandijkophrynus angusticeps (Smith, 1848)

LATIN: *angustus* = narrow; *ceps* = head. Refers to the narrow head that is characteristic of this species.

Conservation status: Not threatened.

Cape Sand Toad: Rondebosch, Western Cape.

Description

Maximum size: 58 mm. **Body**: compact. **Above**: rough-skinned and covered with wart-like elevations; parotoid glands prominent; a series of more or less symmetrically placed rectangular dark blotches on a light grey to dark brown background; thin, pale vertebral line often present; pair of dark patches on either side of the snout. **Pupil**: horizontal, with an umbraculum present. **Tympanum**: small but clearly visible. **Underside**: roughly granular; dirty white. **Limbs**: upper surfaces of feet are bright yellow with darker markings; toes with slight interdigital webbing and a narrow margin of web around fingers and toes; tarsal fold elevated and distinct. **Sexual dimorphism**: male throat dark.

Average length

♀

Average length

♂

Maximum size: 58 mm

KEY ID POINTS

- Upper feet yellow in colour (distinct from other species)
- Umbraculum around the eye (distinct from other species except *V. inyangae*)
- Head with dark markings (distinct from *V. amatolicus*)
- Tarsal fold elevated (distinct from *V. amatolicus*)
- Toes have webbing fringe (distinct from *V. amatolicus*)

Marius Burger

Betty's Bay, Western Cape. Note yellow feet.

Call
High-pitched bray emitted singly at long intervals.

Habitat and habits
Temporary rain-filled depressions in sandy soils in the Western Cape.

TADPOLE
Length: up to 27 mm. **Shape:** body ovoid; plump. **Tail:** more or less uniformly deep along its length, terminating in blunt tip. **Colour:** body black; fin opaque white; abdomen dark. **Eyes:** dorsolateral. **Nostrils:** smaller than eye lens; margin projecting slightly; midway between eyes and snout. **Spiracle:** above body axis; directed backwards at $30°$. **Vent:** median. **Mouth:** near-ventral; single row of large papillae confined to mouth corners. **Jaw sheaths:** moderately curved; only medial fifth of lower jaw deeply edged with pigment. **LTRF:** 2(2)/3(1). **Development:** eight weeks.

Tadpole: lateral view.

Dorsal view.

Karoo Toad

Karooskurwepadda

Vandijkophrynus gariepensis (Smith, 1848)

Subspecies:
- **V. gariepensis gariepensis** (Smith, 1848)
- **V. gariepensis nubicolus** (Hewitt, 1927)

Named after the Orange River where this species is found.

Conservation status: Not threatened.

Karoo Toad, subspecies
Vandijkophrynus g. gariepensis:
Mountain Zebra National Park,
Eastern Cape.
Inset: subspecies V. g. nubicolus:
Mont-aux-Sources, KwaZulu-Natal.

Description

Maximum size: 95 mm. **Body:** robust; larger than other species. **Above:** skin rough and covered with rounded elevations; parotoid glands massive in specimens from south of the range, less so from the north; colour variable – usually uniformly khaki to olive-brown in the southwest of the range, asymmetrical dark patches on a tan ground colour typical in the central part, and dark blotches merging to cover most of the dorsum leaving patches of light ground colour in the northeast. **Tympanum:** small and inconspicuous. **Underside:** dirty white, frequently covered with small dark spots, especially in subadults. **Limbs:** fingers and toes with no fringe of webbing; toes with very little interdigital webbing; tarsal fold massive except in northern specimens. **Sexual dimorphism:** male throat dark.

Average length ♀

Average length ♂

Maximum size: 95 mm

KEY ID POINTS

- Dorsum pattern variable and unreliable for identification
- Parotoid gland large and conspicuous (distinct from *V. robinsoni*)
- Tarsal fold massive in southern specimens (distinct from *V. amatolica* and *V. robinsoni*)
- Toes lack fringe of webbing (distinct from *V. angusticeps*)
- Black blotches on underside of subadults (distinct from other small members of the genus)

Subadult: ventral view.

Adult: ventral view.

Dorsal colour variation.

Call

Series of rasping squawks repeated at long intervals. Calling usually starts during daylight hours, especially on overcast days. When close to one another, males tend to call antiphonally and choruses congregate at the edges of pans and temporary or permanent water bodies.

Habitat and habits

Dry thornbush areas in the catchment of the Orange River; arid Karoo scrub, fynbos and grassland occurring up to high altitudes. The species is well adapted to the arid and cold conditions of the central hinterland in both winter- and summer-rainfall regions.

TADPOLE

Length: up to 23 mm. **Shape:** body ovoid; plump. **Tail:** fin shallow with upper and lower margins parallel; ends bluntly. **Colour:** body and tail overall black; tail fins transparent. **Eyes:** dorsolateral; often green. **Nostrils:** diameter considerably larger than eye lens, about a third of eye length; medial margin of nostrils elevated. **Spiracle:** just below body axis; directed backwards at 30°. **Vent:** marginal. **Mouth:** near-ventral; single row of large papillae confined to mouth corners. **Jaw sheaths:** slender and moderately curved with edge; moderately deeply edged with pigment. **LTRF:** 2(2)/3. **Development:** Metamorphosis after 20 days.

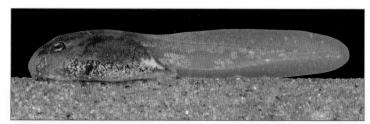
Tadpole: lateral view.

Dorsal view.

Inyanga Toad

Inyanga-skurwepadda

Vandijkophrynus inyangae (Poynton 1963)

Named after the Inyanga District in the eastern highlands of Zimbabwe where this species is found.

Conservation status: Not threatened. Although limited in extent, the habitat is not under particular threat.

Inyanga Toad: Inyanga, Zimbabwe.

Description

Maximum size: 47 mm. **Body:** slender, with thin limbs. **Above:** skin rough and covered with small wart-like elevations, anterior elevations having small black spines; parotoid glands prominent; dark brown reticulated markings with symmetrical elongated blotches on a pale or greenish background.

Pupil: horizontal with an umbraculum. **Tympanum:** small but distinct. **Underside:** slightly granular, off-white, sometimes with grey flecks or fine reticulations. **Limbs:** fingers and toes with no fringe of webbing; toes with very little interdigital webbing; tarsal fold poorly developed. **Sexual dimorphism:** male throat dark.

Average length
♀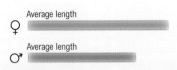

Average length
♂

Maximum size: 47 mm

Call
Unknown.

Habitat and habits
Known only from the mountains and granite outcrops on the Zimbabwe-Mozambique border in the Inyanga area.

KEY ID POINTS

- Dark reticulated dorsal markings (distinct from other species except *V. gariepensis*)
- Tarsal fold inconspicuous (distinct from other species except *V. amatolicus*)
- Toes lack fringe of webbing (distinct from *V. angusticeps*)

Richard Boycott

Colour variation.

Habitat: granite outcrops in eastern Zimbabwe.

TADPOLE
Length: up to 23 mm. **Shape:** distinctly downturned snout in profile; **Tail:** long and narrow with dorsal and ventral margins parallel; tip rounded. **Colour:** dark. **Mouth:** near-ventral; single row of large papillae confined to mouth corners. **Jaw sheaths:** strong; strongly flexed. **LTRF:** 2(2)/3. **Behaviour:** tadpoles disperse between pools by squirming across wet rocks.

Tadpole: lateral view.

Paradise Toad

Paradyskloof-skurwepadda

TRACK
42

Vandijkophrynus robinsoni (Branch and Braack, 1996)

Named after G.A. Robinson, former director of the National
Parks Board of Trustees (today South African National Parks).

Conservation status: Not threatened; however, the
distribution range is restricted.

Paradise Toad: Richtersveld National Park, Northern Cape.

Description

Maximum size: 57 mm. **Body:** compact.
Above: covered with flattened wart-like
elevations on the back; top of head smooth;
parotoid glands prominent but smooth;
green-coloured spots and blotches on a
russet background. **Tympanum:** small but
clearly visible. **Underside:** granular; dirty
white and may be speckled in subadults.
Limbs: green bands around legs; toes
without a narrow margin of web; tarsal fold
indistinct. **Sexual dimorphism:** male is more
vividly coloured than female; male throat
dark.

Call

Subdued and protracted mewing, quite unlike
any other toad species. Males call from the
edges of springs and constantly chivvy and
grapple with one another at call sites.

Average length
♀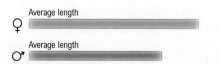

Average length
♂

Maximum size: 57 mm

Light colour variation.

Habitat and habits
Natural springs and
waterholes in the arid
areas of the Richtersveld
and Gordonia in the
Northern Cape.

KEY ID POINTS

- Green markings on a russet background (distinct from other species)
- Toes without margin of webbing around the digits (distinct from *V. angusticeps*)

TADPOLE

Length: up to 28 mm. **Shape:** body ovoid; plump. **Tail:** dorsal and ventral margins parallel; tip rounded. **Colour:** upper and ventral surface solidly pigmented; ventral surface dark; fins usually unpigmented. **Eyes:** dorsolateral. **Nostrils:** large and nearly half width of the eye. **Spiracle:** just below body axis; directed backwards at 30°. **Vent:** marginal. **Mouth:** near-ventral. **Jaw sheaths:** delicate; moderately flexed. **LTRF:** 2(2)/3. **Behaviour:** tadpoles tend to form schools as water bodies dry up.

Tadpole: lateral view.

Dorsal view: note large nostrils.

MOUNTAIN TOADLETS

BERGSKURWEPADDAS

Capensibufo Grandison, 1980

LATIN: *capensis* = of the Cape (of Good Hope); *bufo* = toad.
Named after the Western Cape where this species is found.

Two species, both in southern Africa

The Tradouw Mountain Toadlet breeds in mountain swamps and small ponds of the Western Cape.

The genus is confined to the Western Cape where the 2 species have allopatric ranges. They occur predominantly at high altitudes in the mountains although occasionally they may be found on lower plateaus.

They are small members of the Bufonid (toad) family. Both species have a general toad-like appearance, but they have more elongated bodies than most other toads and the skin is smooth with blister-like elevations rather than warts. Both species deviate uniquely from other toads. Rose's Mountain Toadlet *C. rosei* is voiceless, unlike any

DISTINCTIVE CHARACTERS

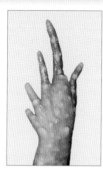

ADULT
- Pupil horizontal
- Body elongated
- Adults less than 40 mm
- Skin smooth, with blister-like elevations and ridges on the back
- Underside coarsely granular, especially posteriorly
- Pear-shaped parotoid glands, usually with orange coloration
- No webbing on fingers and toes

TADPOLE
- Dark with very long, muscular tails

other southern African amphibian, while the Tradouw Mountain Toadlet *C. tradouwi* lays its eggs in clusters and not in strings. Skeletal and other internal morphological differences separate this genus from other toadlets.

Tadpoles are dark, with a long narrow tail. They are benthic, feeding on dead animal detritus and, in the case of the Tradouw Mountain Toadlet, forming dense masses in shallow water.

Breeding is triggered by rainfall from late July until early October. Rose's Mountain Toadlet does not call, but during this time large aggregations of mating pairs (about 80 per m²) congregate at pools of water in montane fynbos. Each female lays about 100 large eggs in a single gelatinous string that resembles a beaded necklace.

The male Tradouw Mountain Toadlet begins calling in August and September in the western part of its range, and as late as November in the eastern part of its range where the climate is transitional (between summer and winter rainfall). Males call from concealed positions around slow-moving water, such as shallow pools, vleis and seepage areas in the mountains. Clusters of up to 60 eggs are laid at a time.

KEY TO SPECIES

ADULT

Tympanum present .... **Tradouw Mountain Toadlet** *C. tradouwi* (p.188)

Tympanum absent .... **Rose's Mountain Toadlet** *C. rosei* (p.186)

TADPOLE

1 Known from Cape Peninsula and mountains southwest of the Breede River Valley .... *C. rosei* (p.186)

   Known from mountains north and east of the Berg and Breede River Valleys .... *C. tradouwi* (p.188)

Rose's Mountain Toadlet

Rose se bergskurwepadda

Capensibufo rosei (Hewitt, 1926)

Named after the Cape naturalist and herpetologist,
Walter Rose (1884-1964).

Conservation status: Vulnerable. The habitat is restricted
and subject to increasing disturbance.

Rose's Mountain Toadlet: Muizenberg, Western Cape.

Identification

Maximum size: 39 mm. **Body:** slightly more
elongated than most toadlets; head narrow.
Above: soft and smooth, with scattered,
blister-like elevations; colour varies from
shades of grey to dark brown, with scattered
dark spots and occasional red or orange
patches; a light vertebral stripe and a pair of
dorsolateral bands is usually present; pale
interorbital bar; parotoid glands prominent,
pear-shaped and usually orange to red in
colour. **Pupil:** an umbraculum is visible on the
upper edge. **Tympanum:** absent. **Underside:**
granular; white with variable light and dark
grey markings; bright pink oval patch below
the vent in both sexes in breeding season.

Average length

♀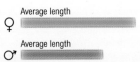

Average length

♂

Maximum size: 39 mm

KEY ID POINTS

- Vent pointed downwards in male (distinct from *C. tradouwi*)
- No tympanum (distinct from *C. tradouwi*)
- The distribution range differs from that of *C. tradouwi* (see distribution maps)

Hindlimbs: toes unwebbed; no tarsal fold.
Sexual dimorphism: male with nuptial pads on the first two fingers during the breeding season; male with distinct swelling in the cloacal region; male vent opens downwards.

Habitat and habits

Restricted to undisturbed montane fynbos in the winter-rainfall areas of the Western Cape. Usually confined to high mountain areas, but occasionally found at lower elevations.

Habitat: pool in mountain fynbos.

Call

This is the only voiceless species known in southern Africa. The tympanum and middle ear elements are absent.

TADPOLE

Length: up to 21 mm. **Shape:** small but long and slender. **Tail:** more than twice body length; tail fin shallow and upper and lower tail fin margins nearly parallel; ends in rounded tip. **Colour:** dark. **Eyes:** dorsolateral. **Nostrils:** small; widely spaced with internarial distance equal to interorbital distance; closer to eyes than snout. **Spiracle:** well below body axis. **Vent:** median and huge. **Mouth:** ventral; single row of papillae at mouth corners. **Jaw sheaths:** moderate. **LTRF:** 2(2)/3. **Development:** metamorphose after six weeks; tadpoles are benthic and have been observed to feed on egg capsules and dead toadlets.

Tadpole: lateral view.

Tradouw Mountain Toadlet

TRACK
43

Tradouw-bergskurwepadda

Capensibufo tradouwi (Hewitt, 1926)

Named after the Tradouw Mountain Pass where the species was first collected.

Conservation status: Not threatened.

Atherton de Villiers

Tradouw Mountain Toadlet: Matroosberg, Western Cape.

Identification

Maximum size: 48 mm. **Body:** slightly more elongated than most toadlets; head narrow. **Above:** soft and smooth with scattered, blister-like elevations; colour varies from shades of grey to dark brown or black, with scattered dark spots and blotches; a light vertebral stripe usually present; a pair of dorsolateral light bands may occur; snout dark with a pale interorbital bar; parotoid glands prominent, pear-shaped and usually orange to red in colour; a row of reddish

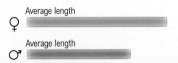

Average length

♀

Average length

♂

Maximum size: 48 mm

Habitat: rock pools in the Matroosberg, Western Cape.

warts from the parotoid glands along the flanks. **Pupil:** horizontal; elygium sometimes visible on the upper edge. **Tympanum:** visible. **Underside:** white with grey markings varying from specks to extensive marbling; throat smooth, abdomen granular with posterior section very coarsely granular. **Hindlimbs:** toes unwebbed; no tarsal fold. **Sexual dimorphism:** male with nuptial pads on the first two fingers during the breeding season; male with distinct swelling in the cloacal region; male vent opens to the rear (compare Rose's Mountain Toadlet).

Habitat and habits
Occurs in high altitude fynbos in the inland areas of the Cape folded mountains.

Call
A creaking chirrup.

KEY ID POINTS

- Vent pointed backwards in male (distinct from *C. rosei*)
- No tympanum (distinct from *C. rosei*)
- Distribution range differs from that of *C. rosei* (see distribution maps)

TADPOLE
Length: up to 19 mm. **Shape:** long and slender; streamlined; snout rounded. **Tail:** more than twice the length of body; tail fin shallow; upper and lower tail fin margins nearly parallel, ending in rounded tip. **Colour:** dark. **Eyes:** dorsolateral to dorsal. **Nostrils:** small and widely spaced. **Spiracle:** well below body axis; directed backwards at 25°. **Vent:** median; very large. **Mouth:** ventral; single row of papillae at the corners. **Jaw sheaths:** moderate. LTRF: 2(2)/3.

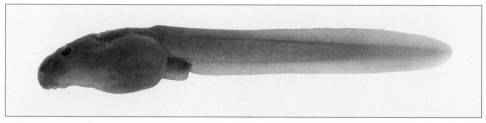

Tadpole: lateral view.

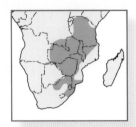

RED TOAD
ROOISKURWEPADDA

Schismaderma (Smith, 1848)

LATIN: *schisma* = cleft or division; GREEK: *derma* = skin. Refers to the ridge that separates the reddish dorsal surface from the contrasting flanks.

Only one species in the genus

Red Toad
Rooiskurwepadda

TRACK
44

Schismaderma carens (Smith, 1848)

LATIN: *careo* = to be without, thus noting the absence of parotoid glands.

Conservation status: Not threatened.

Red Toad: Vredefort Dome, North West Province.

Description

Maximum size: 92 mm. **Body:** leathery, lacking the parotoid glands or large skin elevations in other toads. **Above:** brick-red to light brown with a pair of small dark spots on the lower back and a pair of

♀ Average length

♂ Average length

Maximum size: 92 mm

larger markings on the shoulder region; flanks sharply delineated by a conspicuous and dark glandular ridge stretching from above the tympanum to the hindleg; eyes large. **Pupil:** horizontal. **Tympanum:** as large as the eye. **Underside:** whitish and usually speckled with grey. **Hindlimbs:** toes webbed at the base and fringed with webbing around the digits; tarsal fold present. **Sexual dimorphism:** Nuptial pads on first three fingers of breeding males.

Call

Long, low, repetitive *whoob*. Large choruses of males call at night and on overcast days. They congregate around emergent vegetation and call either while floating in the water or on the water's edge.

Habitat and habits

Widespread in savanna and woodland, and readily adapts to human habitation. Breeds in fairly deep water bodies, but wanders to forage. Hibernates at a considerable distance from water. Moderately competent at climbing and may hide under the bark of tree trunks, under the eaves of houses or in similar retreats.

KEY ID POINTS

* Pupil horizontal
* Lacks parotoid glands
* Tympanum large and distinct
* Prominent dorsolateral skin ridge
* Pair of dark markings low down on the dorsum
* Dorsum leathery and granular, without large wart-like skin protuberances
* Toes moderately webbed

Light colour variation, but lateral skin ridges and dark sacral spots are characteristic.

Marius Burger

Calling from floating position. Males often call in the daytime.

Egg strings.

Tadpole schools in deep water.

Red Toads are both diurnal and nocturnal and they are commonly encountered within their distribution range. They share the general squat, robust form of other toads but are easily recognised by the absence of parotoid glands and by the presence of a dorsolateral ridge separating the dorsum from the flanks. Despite the absence of parotoid glands, they defend themselves as other toads do by secreting a toxic fluid from the dorsal skin when molested.

Breeding is stimulated by rainfall, and calling males congregate at suitable breeding sites after the first summer rains. Calling persists by day and night, especially if the weather is overcast. The low-frequency sound carries over long distances. As each protracted call is emitted, the vocal sac distends from the whole gular and chest area, enveloping the upper arms. Males chivvy each other when females approach, and a male often continues to call for a while after coupling with a female. Amplectant pairs deposit double gelatinous strings of about 20 000 eggs, threading them among underwater vegetation. Calling and breeding takes place intermittently from September to March, but Red Toads forage and actively seek out retreats until May.

TADPOLE

Length: up to 49 mm. **Shape:** body ovoid; peculiar horseshoe-shape skin flap extends from eyes to middle of body, probably functioning as respiratory organ. **Tail:** fin fairly deep; ends bluntly. **Colour:** uniformly black; pigmentation over abdomen sparse to dense. **Eyes:** dorsolateral. **Nostrils:** narrowly spaced; smaller than eye lens. **Spiracle:** below body axis; directed posteriorly and slightly upwards. **Vent:** median. **Mouth:** anteroventral; single row of large papillae, confined to mouth corners. **Jaw sheaths:** delicate. **LTRF:** 2/3. **Behaviour:** tadpoles form dense spherical schools moving up and down in deeper water, with a column of individuals periodically trafficking to and from the surface. **Development:** 37 to 52 days to complete metamorphosis.

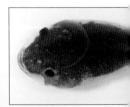

Above: Tadpole in lateral view – note headflap. Right: Mouthparts.

Dorsal view: note headflap.

FOREST TOADS

WOUDSKURWEPADDAS

Mertensophryne Tihen, 1960

Named after German herpetologist, Robert Mertens.
LATIN: *phryne* = toad.

14 species, one in southern Africa

Chirinda Toad, one of the Forest Toads: Chirinda Forest, Zimbabwe.

This is a forest frog that has a highly specialised breeding habitat. The pale-coloured, flat back is distinctive when compared with other toads.

    The genus is found only in forests on the Zimbabwe-Mozambique border. It lays strings of approximately 100 eggs in pools of water that form in the buttress roots of large trees. Species such as the Fluted Milkwood *Chrysophyllum gorongosum* are favoured, and the water bodies need only be very small – a few cm^2 in size. The head of the tadpole bears a circular crown of spongy vascular tissue surrounding the eyes and nostrils. While the tadpole feeds on the living walls of the pool, the crown rests on the surface and absorbs oxygen from the air through a network of blood vessels, thus avoiding dependence on the deoxygenated water in the small pool.

DISTINCTIVE CHARACTERS

• See species account

Tadpole head; note circular spongy tissue around mouthparts.

Chirinda Toad

Chirinda-woudskurwepadda

Mertensophryne anotis (Boulenger, 1907)

GREEK: *an* = without; *otic* = ear. Refers to the hidden tympanum.

Conservation status: Not threatened. The distribution range is limited, but the habitat is not under threat.

Chirinda Toad: Chirinda Forest, Zimbabwe. Note flat back.

Description
Maximum size: 46 mm. **Body:** dorsum flattened and squared off laterally, giving the body a box-like shape. **Above:** granular; top of back and head brown with a few small, dark spots; sides darker; a light scapular patch extends onto the head; parotoid glands broad and flattened. **Tympanum:** not visible. **Below:** off-white with yellow extending from belly onto the hindlegs; often with irregular grey-brown infusions. **Hindlimbs:** tarsal fold is absent; webbing moderate.

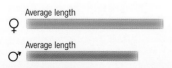

Maximum size: 46 mm

KEY ID POINTS

- Flat back
- Head with squared-off sides
- Light-coloured back and shoulders
- Parotoid glands broad and flattened
- Tympanum not visible

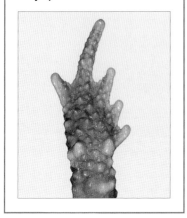

Richard Boycott

Call
Plaintive, medium-pitched chirp.

Habitat and habits
Leaf litter on the floor in the Chirinda Forest in Zimbabwe and adjacent forests in Mozambique.

Habitat: Chirinda Forest, Zimbabwe. Breeds in pools of water trapped in buttress roots of forest trees.

TADPOLE

Length: up to 19 mm. **Shape:** body oval; ring of tissue around eyes and nostrils. **Tail:** fin starts off low, reaching deepest point in middle of tail; terminates in blunt tip. **Colour:** dark; fins transparent. **Eyes:** dorsal. **Nostrils:** narrowly spaced; small with prominent light and elevated margin; about same size as eye lens. **Spiracle:** below and directed backwards. **Mouth:** branched papillae in mouth corners; single row of papillae posteriorly. **Jaw sheaths:** Upper, keratinised jaw sheath heavy and gently curved; lower sheath thin and U-shaped. **LTRF:** 2(2)/2.

Tadpole: lateral view.

CASCADE FROG

SNELSTROOMPADDA

Hadromophryne Van Dijk, 2008

GREEK: *hadrus* = stout; *omus* = humerus; *phrynos* = toad – hence 'strong-armed frog'.

Only one species in the genus

Natal Cascade Frog

Natalse snelstroompadda

TRACK
45

Hadromophryne natalensis (Hewitt, 1913)

Named after the province of Natal (now KwaZulu-Natal) from where this species was first described.

Conservation status: Not Red Listed but threatened by introduced trout and habitat destruction.

Cascade Frog: Vernon Crookes Nature Reserve, KwaZulu-Natal.

Average length
♀

Average length
♂

Maximum size: 65 mm

DISTINCTIVE CHARACTERS

ADULT
- Restricted to perennial forest streams along the Natal monocline and Drakensberg escarpment
- Pupil vertical, with horizontal dark line in the eye (distinct from other genera, except some ghost frogs)
- Body flattened
- Tympanum hidden
- Extensive webbing
- Glandular fold present behind the eye
- Spatulate fingertips and toe tips

TADPOLE
- Large, flattened head (distinct from other tadpoles, except those of Ghost Frog genus)
- Jaw sheath present in the lower jaw only

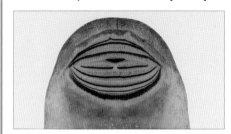

Description

Size: 65 mm. **Body:** flattened; eyes large and protruding; vertical and horizontal line through eye. **Above:** green or yellow reticulated markings on dark brown, purple-brown or black background; alternating broad dark and thin pale bars on thigh; granular. **Underside:** dirty white; light brown marbling under throat; limbs dark chocolate-brown; skin smooth. **Forelimbs:** fingertips spatulate. **Hindlimbs:** discs on fingertips slightly wider than finger; webbing between

Plain colour form: Karkloof, KwaZulu-Natal.

Les Minter

Characteristic flattened posture.

Habitat: fast-flowing forest stream.

toes extensive. **Sexual dimorphism:** Male smaller than female; cloaca directed ventrally in male, posteriorly in female; breeding male has loose dorsal skin, swollen forearms, and spines on chest and inner fingers.

Call
High-pitched, bell-like *ting*, repeated about twice per second; sometimes prefaced by *currick* as though winding up. Males call from under boulders, from deep crevices in rocky ledges or from nearby vegetation in the spray zone of waterfalls and rapids.

Habitat and habits
At low and high altitudes in cold, clear, swiftly flowing, densely vegetated mountain streams, in kloofs, forest and grassland. Sometimes found quite far from water, under vegetation or rocks.

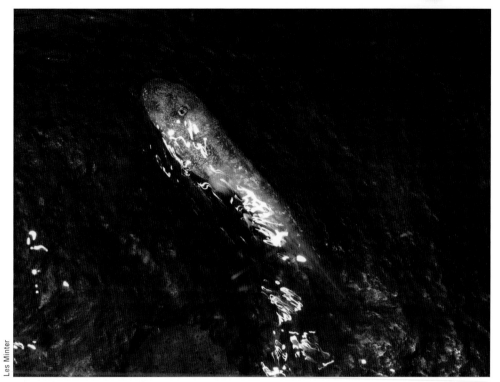

Les Minter

Tadpole climbing waterfall.

TADPOLE

Length: up to 85 mm. **Shape:** streamlined body; huge oral disc acting as sucker. **Tail:** muscular; tail fin only starts in middle of tadpole and after initial shallow stretch, it rises sharply to reach deepest point behind middle of tail; no tail fin in first third of tail. **Colour:** body often mottled to blend with substrate; fin slightly mottled; terminates in rounded tip which is sometimes black; semi-transparent below; red gills and dark intestine evident. **Eyes:** dorsolateral; directed laterally; pupil vertical. **Nostrils:** narrowly spaced; small; directed anterolaterally; closer to snout than to eyes. **Spiracle:** well below body axis; thin, free tube; directed posteriorly. **Mouth:** Large, sucker-shaped, completely circled by two rows of papillae above; four rows below. **Jaw sheaths:** upper jaw sheath absent; lower sheath small. **LTRF:** 4/14 to 4/17. **Development:** Slow; up to two years to complete metamorphosis. **Behaviour:** scrapes algae from rocks leaving clear tracks; has been observed feeding outside water, working its way forward by means of movements of rows of labial teeth; may even climb vertical rock faces; when disturbed, escapes by detaching and drifting downstream.

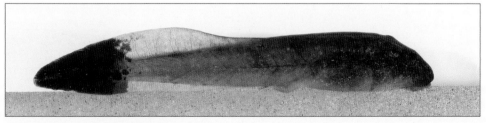

Tadpole: lateral view showing black tail tip.

GHOST FROGS

SPOOKPADDAS

Heleophryne Sclater, 1898

GREEK: *hélos* = marsh; *phrynos* = toad, hence 'marsh-toad'. However, this name is inappropriate because Ghost Frogs are not found in marshes, nor are they toads. The common name 'Ghost Frog' originates from the locality of *H. rosei*, namely, Skeleton Gorge on Table Mountain, which is a rather ghostly, dark gorge.

Six species, all restricted to southern Africa

Eastern Ghost Frog: Tradouw Pass, near Barrydale, Western Cape.

Heleophryne is endemic to South Africa with all six species restricted to the Western and Eastern Cape.

Ghost Frogs are restricted to swiftly flowing, permanent mountain streams. Extremely well adapted to this environment, they are dorsoventrally flattened so that they can hide in deep crevices; extensive webbing on the feet makes them excellent swimmers; well-developed discs on the toes ensure a firm grip on rocks in fast-flowing water; limbs are long and fingertips and toe tips are expanded to improve their grip on wet rocks. Tadpoles have huge sucker mouths to adhere to rocks so that they are not swept away in the torrent.

Mature individuals develop external sexual characteristics before the breeding season. These include asperities on the fingers, arms, chest, head, body and around the cloaca. Amplexus is probably inguinal with the male holding the female around the waist.

Developing eggs.

Eggs in shallow water.

DISTINCTIVE CHARACTERS

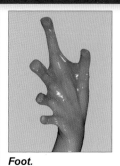

Foot.

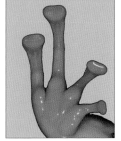

Hand.

ADULT
- Pupil vertical, many with horizontal dark line in the eye
- Body flattened
- Tympanum hidden
- Extensive webbing on foot
- Glandular fold present behind the eye
- Spatulate fingertips and toe tips

TADPOLE
- Sucker mouths extremely large with multiple rows of keratinised labial teeth
- Jaw sheaths absent
- Long muscular tails, making them strong swimmers
- Feed by scraping algae off rock faces, sometimes leaving trails
- May leave water to feed on wet rocks
- Can climb vertical rockfaces

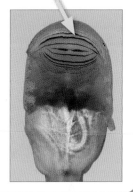

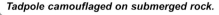

Tadpole camouflaged on submerged rock.

As many as 200 large yellow eggs are laid under rocks or, in the case of some species, beyond the water in damp areas. Males call from above or below the water surface. The call is high pitched, enabling females to hear it above the noise of fast-flowing water.

Two species, *H. hewitti* and *H. rosei*, are listed as 'critically endangered' owing to the degradation and/or loss of suitable habitats as a result of commercial afforestation.

KEY TO SPECIES

ADULT AND TADPOLE

Known only from Table Mountain .... **Table Mountain Ghost Frog** *H. rosei* (p.212)

Known from the Elandsberg range near Port Elizabeth .... **Hewitt's Ghost Frog** *H. hewitti* (p.204)

Known from the Robertson Pass in the east to the Kareedouw Mountains in the west ....
.... **Southern Ghost Frog** *H. regis* (p.210)

Known from the area east of Montagu along the Langeberg to the Gouritz River ....
.... **Eastern Ghost Frog** *H. orientalis* (p.206)

Known from the Cederberg range, south and east of the Breede and Berg rivers ....
.... **Cape Ghost Frog** *H. purcelli* (p.208)

Known from the Cederberg range, north and west of the Breede and Berg rivers ....
.... **Cederberg Ghost Frog** *H. depressa* (p.202)

Cederberg Ghost Frog

Sederbergspookpadda

TRACK
46

Heleophryne depressa FitzSimons, 1946

LATIN: *depressare* = to flatten or force down. Refers to the flattened head.

Conservation status: Not threatened.

Cederberg Ghost Frog: Keeromsberg, Worcester, Western Cape.

Description

Size: 44.5 mm. **Body:** snout very depressed; depth of snout in front of eyes shallower than diameter of eye; interorbital space narrow, less than upper eyelid or internarial distance. **Above:** light to dark olive; large, irregular, purplish-brown to maroon blotches; scattered pale specks on limbs and back; dorsum granular and covered in flattened warts, each with a conical asperity,

Average length

♀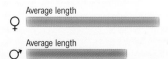

Average length

♂

Maximum size: 44.5 mm

Atherton de Villiers

more pronounced in males; horizontal line through eye gives impression of a cross. **Underside:** creamy white to yellowish; thighs yellowish to orange; granular. **Forelimbs:** outer metacarpal tubercle elliptical; fingertips spatulate. **Hindlimbs:** dark crossbars on thighs narrower than pale spaces between bars; fingers and toes terminate in broadly expanded discs; extensive webbing between toes. **Sexual dimorphism:** male smaller than female; cloaca directed ventrally in male, posteriorly in female; breeding male has loose dorsal skin, swollen forearms, spines on chest and inner fingers.

KEY ID POINTS

- Restricted to the Cederberg range to the north and west of the Breede and Berg rivers (distinct from other species)
- Lacks thumb-like metacarpal tubercle on first finger (distinct from *H. rosei*)
- Horizontal line through eye (distinct from *H. rosei*)
- Webbing reaches last phalanges of fifth toe (distinct from *H. rosei*)

Call

Two to four very soft, bell-like *pings*.

Habitat and habits

Clear mountain streams in the Cederberg range to north and west of the Breede and Berg rivers. Often found stationary and well camouflaged among river-bed stones.

Andrew Turner

Flat posture enables the frog to retreat into narrow fissures.

TADPOLE

Length: up to 60 mm. **Shape:** streamlined body; well adapted for life in fast-flowing mountain streams with huge oral disc acting as sucker. **Tail:** muscular; dorsal fin deeper than ventral; deepest point middle of tail; tip of tail bluntly rounded and often dark. **Colour:** body mottled dark grey to brown; closely matches dark rocks of habitat; tail opaque but tip with dark blotches. **Eyes:** dorsal-facing; near-lateral. **Nostrils:** narrowly spaced; closer to eyes than to snout. **Spiracle:** tube slightly separated from body; well below body axis; directed backwards at about 40°. **Vent:** median. **Mouth:** large; sucker-like; ventral; multiple rows of papillae around oral disc. **Jaw sheaths:** absent. **LTRF:** 4/14 to 4/17. **Development:** slow; may take two years to complete metamorphosis. **Behaviour:** attaches itself under rocks with sucker in fast-flowing currents; scrapes algae from rocks, leaving clear tracks; when disturbed, escapes by detaching and drifting downstream.

Tadpole: lateral view.

Hewitt's Ghost Frog

TRACK
47

Hewitt se spookpadda

Heleophryne hewitti Boycott, 1988

Named after herpetologist, John Hewitt (1880-1961), director
of the Albany Museum, Grahamstown, from 1910 to 1958.

Conservation status: Critically Endangered owing to habitat
degradation and/or loss through commercial afforestation.

Richard Boycott

Hewitt's Ghost Frog: Geelhoutboom River, Elandsberg, Eastern Cape.

Description

Size: 50 mm. **Body:** eyes large. **Above:**
dark maroon-brown spots with pale margin;
pale beige to olive-brown background; thin
vertical line through eye gives impression
of a cross. **Underside:** dirty white; skin
granular. **Forelimbs:** fingertips spatulate.
Hindlimbs: distinctive dark bands present
on legs; fingers and toes terminate in
prominent spatulas; thumb-like metacarpal
tubercle present; webbing between toes
extensive. **Sexual dimorphism:** male smaller
than female; cloaca directed ventrally in
male, posteriorly in female; breeding male
has loose dorsal skin, swollen forearms,
spines on chest and inner fingers.

Call

Sequence of short, soft whistles. During
the day males call from under partially
submerged rocks, at night from the edges
of shallow, fast-flowing waters.

Average length
♀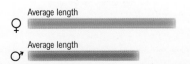

Average length
♂

Maximum size: 50 mm

KEY ID POINTS

- Restricted to the Elandsberg range (distinct from other species)
- Lacks thumb-like metacarpal tubercle on first finger (distinct from *H. rosei*)
- Horizontal line through eye (distinct from *H. rosei*)
- Webbing reaches last phalanges of fifth toe (distinct from *H. rosei*)

Habitat: Geelhoutboom River, Eastern Cape.

Habitat and habits

Adults and tadpoles found under rocks in upper reaches of clear, fast-flowing, perennial, mountain streams near grassy fynbos. Distribution limited to the Elandsberg range and only four rivers: the Geelhoutboom, Martin's, Klein and Diepkloof.

TADPOLE

Length: up to 62 mm. **Shape:** body flattened; wide; streamlined. **Tail:** muscular; a little longer than body; dorsal and ventral tail fin of equal depth; deepest point middle of tail; tip bluntly rounded. **Colour:** light golden-brown. **Eyes:** dorsolateral, facing near-lateral. **Nostrils:** narrowly spaced. **Spiracle:** tube slightly separated from body; well below body axis; pointing 40° posterodorsally. **Vent:** median. **Mouth:** large; sucker-like; ventral; multiple rows of papillae around oral disc. **Jaw sheaths:** absent. **LTRF:** 4/14 to 4/17. **Behaviour:** attaches itself to rocks by means of the sucker and feeds off algae.

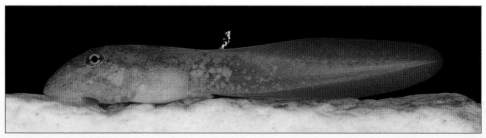

Tadpole: lateral view.

Eastern Ghost Frog

Oostelike spookpadda

TRACK
○
48

Heleophryne orientalis FitzSimons, 1946

Orient means 'the east', and perhaps refers to an easterly
distribution of this species.

Conservation status: Not threatened.

Eastern Ghost Frog: Swellendam, Western Cape.

Description

Size: 46 mm. **Body:** flattened; eyes
large, protruding; vertical and horizontal
lines through eye give impression of a
cross. **Above:** pattern varies; usually
dark spots or blotches on pale beige-
olive background; interocular bar usually
present; skin granular. **Underside:** white;
limbs fleshy-orange; skin granular.
Forelimbs: fingertips spatulate. **Hindlimbs:**
distinct transverse bands present;
triangular discs on fingertips slightly

Average length
♀

Average length
♂

Maximum size: 46 mm

wider than finger; webbing between toes extensive. **Sexual dimorphism:** male smaller than female; cloaca directed ventrally in male, posteriorly in female; breeding male has loose dorsal skin, swollen forearms, and spines on chest and inner fingers.

Call

High-pitched, clear ringing *ik* note, repeated at intervals of about two seconds. Unlike other Ghost Frogs, males of this species tend to form breeding aggregations.

Habitat and habits

Cold, clear, slow- to swift-flowing perennial mountain streams in forested ravines and gorges. Confined to Afromontane forest surrounded by Mesic montane fynbos. Unlike other Ghost Frog species, Eastern Ghost Frogs do not lay their eggs in the water, but on a moist surface under moss-covered rocks or boulders either close to water or slightly submerged. Partially submerged egg clutches have been reported.

KEY ID POINTS

- Restricted to the Langeberg range from Montagu to Kogman's Kloof (distinct from other species)
- Horizontal line through eye (distinct from *H. rosei*)
- Lacks thumb-like metacarpal tubercle on first finger (distinct from *H. rosei*)

- Webbing reaches last phalanges of fifth toe (distinct from *H. rosei*)

TADPOLE

Length: up to 60 mm. **Shape:** huge oral disc acting as sucker; streamlined body. **Tail:** muscular; dorsal and ventral tail fin of equal height; deepest point slightly behind middle of tail; tip of tail bluntly rounded. **Colour:** body and tail mottled dark grey to brown; closely matches dark rocks of habitat. **Eyes:** dorsal facing; near-lateral. **Nostrils:** narrowly spaced. **Spiracle:** tube slightly separated from body; well below body axis; pointing $40°$ posterodorsally. **Vent:** median. **Mouth:** large; sucker-like; ventral; multiple rows of papillae around oral disc; in early stages of development prominent fang-like teeth drop out as labial tooth rows develop. **Jaw sheaths:** absent. **LTRF:** 4/14 to 4/17. **Development:** slow; may take two years to complete. **Behaviour:** attaches itself under rocks in fast-flowing currents by means of the sucker; scrapes algae from rocks, leaving clear tracks; when disturbed escapes by detaching and drifting downstream.

Tadpole: lateral view.

Cape Ghost Frog

Kaapse spookpadda

TRACK
49

Heleophryne purcelli Sclater, 1898

Refers R.F. Purcell who discovered the species in November 1896.

Conservation status: Not threatened.

Cape Ghost Frog: Du Toit's Kloof, Western Cape.

Description
Size: 56 mm. **Body:** flattened; eyes large and protruding. **Above:** varies from yellowish-brown to bright green with reddish-brown dots or blotches; interocular bar usually present; skin granular; horizontal line through eye gives impression of a cross. **Underside:** white; limbs fleshy-orange; granular.
Forelimbs: fingertips spatulate. **Hindlimbs:** distinct transverse bands; triangular discs on fingertips prominent, twice as wide as finger; webbing between toes extensive; webbing to tip of fifth toe. **Sexual dimorphism:** male smaller than female; cloaca directed ventrally in male, posteriorly in female; breeding male has loose dorsal skin, swollen forearms, spines on chest and inner fingers.

Call
High-pitched, clear ringing *ik* note repeated at intervals of about two per second. Males also utter a higher-pitched call to guide receptive females towards them. Calling is intense at dusk and becomes more sporadic after dark. Males call from cracks and crevices in rocks close to waterfalls and cascades.

Average length

♀

Average length

♂

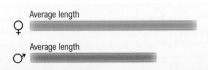

Maximum size: 56 mm

KEY ID POINTS

- Restricted to the Cederberg range south and east of the Breede and Berg rivers (distinct from other species)
- Lacks thumb-like metacarpal tubercle on first finger (distinct from *H. rosei*)
- Horizontal line through eye (distinct from *H. rosei*)
- Webbing reaches last phalanges of the fifth toe (distinct from *H. rosei*)

Plain colour form.

Habitat and habits

Cold, clear, slow- to swift-flowing perennial mountain streams in montane fynbos that receive midday sunlight.

TADPOLE

Length: up to 60 mm. **Shape:** huge oral disc acting as sucker; streamlined body. **Tail:** muscular; dorsal and ventral tail fin of equal height; deepest point in middle of tail; tip of tail bluntly rounded. **Colour:** body and tail mottled dark grey to brown; closely matching dark rocks of habitat; tail muscles dark grey-brown; fins opaque. **Eyes:** dorsolateral. **Nostrils:** narrowly spaced; closer to eyes than to snout. **Spiracle:** tube slightly separated from body; well below body axis; pointing 60° posterodorsally. **Vent:** median. **Mouth:** large; sucker-like; ventral; two rows of papillae around oral disc. **Jaw sheaths:** absent. **LTRF:** 4/16. **Development:** slow; may take two years to complete. **Behaviour:** in fast-flowing currents attaches itself under rocks with suckers; scrapes algae off rocks, leaving clear tracks; when disturbed escapes by detaching and drifting downstream.

Andrew Turner

Habitat: mossy bank.

Tadpole: lateral view.

Southern Ghost Frog

Suidelike spookpadda

Heleophryne regis Hewitt, 1909

LATIN: *regius* = royal. Name refers to timber merchant, George Rex, who lived in the Knysna area in the early 1800s.

Conservation status: Not threatened. Numbers abundant.

Southern Ghost Frog: Diepwalle, Knysna, Western Cape.

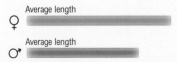

♀ Average length

♂ Average length

Maximum size: 49 mm

KEY ID POINTS

- Restricted to the area from the Robertson Pass in the east to the Kareedouw Mountains in the west (distinct from other species)
- Lacks thumb-like metacarpal tubercle on first finger (distinct from *H. rosei*)
- Horizontal line through eye (distinct from *H. rosei*)
- Webbing reaches last phalanges of fifth toe (distinct from *H. rosei*)

Description

Size: 49 mm. **Body:** flattened; eyes large and protruding; horizontal and vertical line through eye. **Above:** usually conspicuously marked with dark spots or patches on brown to greenish to purple background; occasionally dark markings absent; skin smooth; few asperities confined to mouth region and anterior surface of arms. **Underside:** white; limbs a pale flesh-colour; skin granular. **Forelimbs:** fingertips spatulate. **Hindlimbs:** transverse bands may be present; triangular discs on fingertips prominent, twice as wide as finger; webbing between toes variable and in some specimens may reach tip of fifth toe. **Sexual dimorphism:** male smaller than female; cloaca directed ventrally with a fleshy anal flap in male, posteriorly in female; breeding male has loose dorsal skin, swollen forearms, and spines on chest and inner fingers.

Call

Harsh, low-pitched, creaking sound, about two per second. Calling is most intense at dusk, becoming sporadic after dark. Males form breeding aggregations and call from positions such as rocky cracks and crevices that are close to waterfalls and cascades, or from under spongy moss and in overhanging vegetation.

Habitat and habits

Cold, clear, slow- to swift-flowing mountain streams in moist, forested montane fynbos with Afromontane plant communities. After a complex courtship of gentle touching, between 120 to 200 large-yolked yellow eggs are laid under rocks in quiet backwaters of pools.

TADPOLE

Length: up to 60 mm. **Shape:** wide, flattened, steamlined body; huge oral disc acts as a sucker. **Tail:** muscular; dorsal and ventral tail fin of equal depth; deepest point in middle of tail; tip of tail bluntly rounded. **Colour:** body and tail grey-brown; often with black and golden blotches; underside transparent over gill region; silvery-white over abdomen. **Eyes:** dorsal; facing near-lateral. **Nostrils:** narrowly spaced. **Spiracle:** tube slightly separated from body; well below body axis; pointing 45° posterodorsally. **Vent:** median. **Mouth:** large; sucker-like; ventral; multiple rows of papillae around oral disc. **Jaw sheaths:** absent. **LTRF:** 4/14 to 4/17.

Tadpole: lateral view.

Table Mountain Ghost Frog

Tafelberg-spookpadda

TRACK
51

Heleophryne rosei Hewitt, 1925

Named after Cape herpetologist and naturalist,
Walter Rose (1884–1964).

Conservation status: Critically Endangered; restricted
to only a few streams on Table Mountain.

Atherton de Villiers

Table Mountain Ghost Frog: Skeleton Gorge, Table Mountain, Western Cape.

Description

Size: 63 mm. **Body:** flattened; eyes
large and protruding; no horizontal line
through eye. **Above:** striking pale green
background; brown to purple blotches,
granular. **Underside:** white; limbs pink; skin
granular; throat smooth. **Forelimbs:** inner
metacarpal tubercle on hand enlarged and
thumb-like; fingertips spatulate. **Hindlimbs:**
prominent triangular discs on fingertips;
webbing between toes moderate. **Sexual
dimorphism:** male smaller than female;

Average length
♀

Average length
♂

Maximum size: 63 mm

KEY ID POINTS

- Restricted to Table Mountain (distinct from other species)
- Prominent thumb-like metacarpal tubercle on inner finger (distinct from other species)
- No horizontal line through eye (distinct from other species)
- Webbing does not reach last phalanx of fifth toe

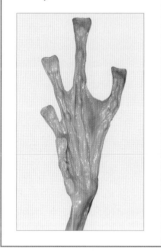

cloaca directed ventrally in male, posteriorly in female; breeding male has loose dorsal skin, swollen forearms, spines on chest and inner fingers.

Call
Percussive ringing note, repeated about four times per second. Males call from concealed and exposed positions.

Habitat and habits
Known only from perennial streams on eastern and southern slopes of Table Mountain; in Afromontane forested gorges and valleys; in montane fynbos on more exposed slopes. Frequents rocky streams, swift-flowing for most of the year, with numerous pools and moss-covered rockfaces. The species has also been collected in caves on Table Mountain.

Atherton de Villiers

Habitat: stream on Table Mountain.

TADPOLE

Length: up to 50 mm. **Shape:** streamlined body; huge oral disc acts as sucker. **Tail:** muscular; dorsal fin starts behind body in gentle slope to reach deepest point about two-thirds along tail. **Colour:** yellowish-brown with varying amounts of pigmentation; transparent, showing red gills and black intestine. **Eyes:** dorsal; facing near laterally. **Nostrils:** small; narrowly spaced; closer to eyes than to snout. **Spiracle:** well below body axis; directed backwards at $30°$ upwards. **Mouth:** completely circled by two rows of papillae above and four rows below. **Jaw sheaths:** absent. **LTRF:** 4/14 to 4/16. **Development:** slow; may take 12 months to complete. **Behaviour:** leaves tracks on rocks after scraping off algae; when disturbed detaches itself and drifts downstream.

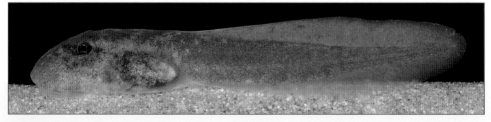

Tadpole: lateral view.

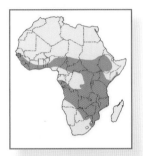

SHOVEL-NOSED FROGS

GRAAFNEUSPADDAS

Hemisus Günther, 1859

GREEK: *hemi* = half; *ous* = ear. Possibly refers to the concealed tympanum.

Nine species, three in southern Africa

Mottled Shovel-nosed Frog. Inset: Female with eggs.

Les Minter

The characteristic spherical body shape and sharp-pointed head with hardened snout distinguishes this from other burrowing genera such as Rain Frogs (Breviceps) and Sand Frogs (Tomopterna). South of the Tropic of Capricorn, Shovel-nosed Frogs can easily be differentiated from each other by differences in dorsal pattern. In the tropics, however, positive identification is sometimes not possible.

Shovel-nosed Frogs spend most of the time underground, close to water. Unlike other burrowing frogs, they tunnel head-first, using the hardened tip of the snout as a shovel. The frog pushes itself into the ground with its hindlimbs, while displaced soil is thrust aside by the powerful forelimbs. The small eyes, narrow pointed head and receding jaw-line are adaptations to this mode of burrowing.

Breeding takes place during the rainy season. Unlike Rain Frogs, amplexus is inguinal. The clutch of large, unpigmented eggs in large jelly capsules is laid in an underground chamber in damp soil, close to the edge of a pan or vlei. The female remains with the eggs until they hatch, when she digs a tunnel or canal to open water and carries the tadpoles out of the nest on her back to complete their metamorphosis in the water. The tadpoles have a highly developed blood system on the skin surface, facilitating respiration through the skin.

DISTINCTIVE CHARACTERS

- Almost spherical body with bloated appearance
- Narrow head, with pointed, chisel-shaped snout
- Transverse skinfold across top of the head
- Tympanum concealed
- Lower jaw recedes under snout
- Pupil vertical and eyes small
- Snout hardened for digging

TADPOLE
- Connective tissue extending anteriorly, dorsally and ventrally beyond the tail muscles

KEY TO SPECIES

ADULT

1 Found south of Limpopo Province **2**

  Found in Limpopo Province and north of the Limpopo River **3**

2 Dorsum mottled light and dark brown, without distinct yellow spots ....
.... **Mottled Shovel-nosed Frog** *H. marmoratus* (p.220)

  Dorsum with distinct yellow spots on a plain dark background .. **Spotted Shovel-nosed Frog** *H. guttatus* (p.218)

3 Dorsum mottled light and dark brown .... **Mottled Shovel-nosed Frog** *H. marmoratus* (p.220)

  Dorsum dark with small yellow, orange or white spots ..... **Guinea Shovel-nosed Frog** *H. guineensis* (p.216)

Occasionally specimens of *H. guineensis* occur with irregular marbling. These specimens are indistinguishable from *H. marmoratus* in the field.

TADPOLE

1 Six labial tooth rows in upper jaw and three in lower; two rows of papillae bordering lower jaw; posterior half of tail usually dark .... *H. guttatus* (p.218)

2 Five labial tooth rows in upper jaw and four in lower; one row of papillae bordering lower jaw; posterior half of tail not darker .... *H. marmoratus* (p.220) or *H. guineensis* (p.216)

Guinea Shovel-nosed Frog

Guinee-graafneuspadda

Hemisus guineensis Cope, 1865

Named after Guinea on the African West Coast.

Conservation status: Not threatened.

Guinea Shovel-nosed Frog: Moremi Game Reserve, Botswana.

James Harvey

Description

Maximum size: 55 mm. **Body:** rotund with small head and hard, sharply pointed snout; skin fold behind head. **Above:** small yellow or orange dots on dark grey or black background; a pale vertebral line and minute white spots sometimes present, especially in specimens from Mozambique; skin smooth to slightly granular; tympanum hidden. **Pupil:** vertical

Average length

♀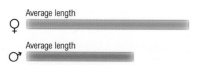

Average length

♂

Maximum size: 55 mm

but difficult to discern because eyes are small.
Underside: uniform greyish-white without mottling;
skin smooth. **Forelimbs:** muscular with thick
fingers. **Hindlimbs:** foot with large inner metatarsal
tubercle; no outer metatarsal tubercle; webbing
reduced, barely reaching base of digits. **Sexual
dimorphism:** male throat dark, male with glandular
areas on upper surface of hand.

Call
Long trill lasting several seconds. Males call from
the entrances of their burrows, close to water.

Habitat and habits
Temporary pans formed during rainy season
in grassland and open bush in Mopane bushveld
in savanna.

Habitat: grassy pan.

KEY ID POINTS

- Found only north of the
  Tropic of Capricorn (distinct
  from *H. guttatus*)
- Back uniformly dark or with
  small yellow or orange spots
  (distinct from *H. marmoratus*)
- Thin, pale vertebral line often
  present (distinct from
  H. guttatus)
- Toes with slight webbing
  (distinct from *H. guttatus*)

TADPOLE
Shape: body oval; anterior end dorsoventrally flattened. **Tail:** dorsal tail fin very deep;
anterior half of tail with connective tissue extending well onto fins. **Colour:** pale grey with
black spots. **Eyes:** near lateral. **Nostrils:** small; widely spaced. **Spiracle:** below body axis.
Vent: marginal; dextral. **Mouth:** anteroventral. **Jaw sheaths:** moderate. **LTRF:** 5(2-5)/4(1).

Tadpole: lateral view.

Spotted Shovel-nosed Frog

Gespikkelde graafneuspadda

Hemisus guttatus (Rapp, 1842)

LATIN: *guttatus* = spotted.

Conservation status: Vulnerable, due to the small area it occupies, as well as habitat fragmentation and degradation.

Marius Burger

Spotted Shovel-nosed Frog: St Lucia, KwaZulu-Natal.

Description

Maximum size: 80 mm. **Body:** rotund with small head and hard, sharply pointed snout used for digging; skin fold behind head. **Above:** skin smooth; bright yellow spots on dark olive to brown background; tympanum hidden. **Pupil:** vertical but difficult to discern because eyes are small. **Underside:** white; skin smooth. **Forelimbs:** muscular with thick fingers. **Hindlimbs:** foot with large, flanged, inner metatarsal tubercle; no outer metatarsal tubercle; webbing absent. **Sexual dimorphism:** male throat dark.

Call

Long high-pitched buzz. Males call from deep burrows.

Average length

♀

Average length

♂

Maximum size: 80 mm

KEY ID POINTS

- Found only in northern KwaZulu-Natal and extreme south of Mpumalanga and Swaziland (distinct from *H. guineensis*)
- Back smooth, dark with bright yellow spots (distinct from other species)
- No vertebral line (distinct from *H. guineensis*)
- Toes lack webbing (distinct from other species)

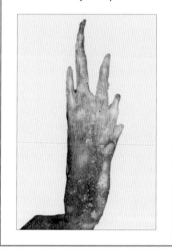

Habitat and habits

Pans and marshy ground in coastal bush and grassland, and in northeastern mountain grassland in central KwaZulu-Natal savanna. Appears to forage over extensive distances and in diverse habitats, and has even been found in forested areas more than 200 m from the closest breeding site.

Characteristic digging snout.

Les Minter

TADPOLE

Length: up to 65 mm. **Shape:** body flattened. **Tail:** about twice as long as body; muscular; front half of tail with connective tissue extending well onto fins; fin moderately deep, reaching deepest point halfway along tail; ending in sharp tip. **Colour:** dark brown; abdomen white; terminal part of tail pigmented; front part mottled grey. **Eyes:** near lateral. **Nostrils:** small; widely spaced; closer to snout than to eyes. **Spiracle:** above body axis; directed backwards at about 70°. **Vent:** marginal; dextral. **Mouth:** anteroventral; few very long papillae on lower jaw. **Jaw sheaths:** moderate; strongly convex. **LTRF:** 6(2-6)/3 or 6(3-6)/3.

Tadpole: lateral view. Note dark tail tip.

Mouthparts.

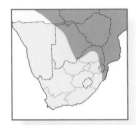

Mottled Shovel-nosed Frog

Marmergraafneuspadda

Hemisus marmoratus (Peters, 1854)

LATIN: *marmoratus* = covered in marble. Refers to the mottled colour pattern on the back.

Conservation status: Not threatened.

Mottled Shovel-nosed Frog: Kruger National Park, Mpumalanga.

Description

Maximum size: 55 mm. **Body:** rotund, with small head and hard, sharply pointed snout; skin fold behind head. **Above:** light grey, yellowish or light brown background with grey or brown marbling; pale vertebral line sometimes present; upper lip yellow; skin smooth to slightly granular; tympanum hidden. **Pupil:** vertical but difficult to discern because eyes are small. **Underside:** smooth; white. **Forelimbs:** muscular with thick fingers. **Hindlimbs:** foot with large inner metatarsal tubercle; no outer metatarsal tubercle; webbing reduced, barely reaching base of digits. **Sexual dimorphism:** male throat dark.

Average length ♀
Average length ♂

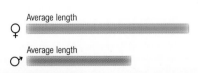

Maximum size: 55 mm

Call

Long, high-pitched-buzz lasting up to five seconds. Males call from underground burrow or concealed under vegetation; may form choruses of five to eight males; do not call antiphonally.

Habitat and habits

Marshy ground and in sandy riverbanks in bushveld savanna throughout subSaharan Africa.

Characteristic yellow upper lip.

KEY ID POINTS

- Back marbled with yellow upper lip and no spots (distinct from *H. guineensis* and *H. guttatus*)
- Thin pale vertebral line sometimes present (distinct from *H. guttatus*)
- Toes with slight webbing (distinct from *H. guttatus*)

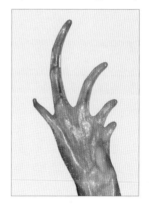

TADPOLE

Length: up to 55 mm. **Shape:** body oval; like other tadpoles in genus, front part of tail with thickened sheath extending onto fins dorsally and ventrally. **Tail:** slopes up from body to reach deepest point in middle of tail. **Colour:** mottled yellow-brown to grey; abdomen white; throat grey. **Eyes:** dorsolateral. **Nostrils:** small and widely spaced; close to snout. **Spiracle:** below body axis; short; directed backwards at about 40°. **Vent:** marginal; dextral. **Mouth:** single row of small papillae above and laterally; double row posteriorly; few very long papillae on lower jaw. **Jaw sheaths:** moderate; weakly flexed; lower jaw sheath only partially keratinised. **LTRF:** 5(2-5)/4(1) to 5(3-5)/4(1). **Development:** tadpoles emerge from jelly capsules in about eight days; female will remain with eggs until they hatch; tadpoles leave brood chamber when it floods; mother may carry eggs to water or dig canal to guide tadpoles to water; in dry periods, egg development may be arrested for up to two months.

Tadpole: lateral view.

Mouthparts.

LEAF-FOLDING FROGS

BLAARVOUPADDAS

Afrixalus Laurent, 1944

GREEK: *Afr* = Africa; *ixalus* = bounding or springing

29 species, six in southern Africa

Leaf-folding Frog: asperities on the body vary between species.

The genus is similar in overall appearance to Reed Frogs (Hyperolius) but it is readily distinguished by the vertical pupil. With the exception of the Greater Leaf-folding Frog *A. fornasinii*, the southern African species are all less than 25 mm in length and they are often difficult to distinguish from one another. They inhabit marginal or emergent vegetation around palustrine wetland areas in subtropical and tropical regions. During daylight they usually retreat into the axils of large-leafed plants such as bananas and arum lilies, but they also sometimes bask in the sun.

Two species, the Knysna Leaf-folding Frog *A. knysnae* and the Natal Leaf-folding Frog *A. spinifrons*, are endemic to South Africa and both are Red Data listed.

DISTINCTIVE CHARACTERS

ADULT
- Pupil vertical
- Elongated body
- Body covered or partly covered with asperities
- Tympanum concealed
- Fingers and toes with terminal discs
- Underside granular; sometimes dotted with asperities

TADPOLE
- Head dorsoventrally flattened
- Mouth terminal
- Keratinised jaw sheaths slender
- Upper labial tooth rows absent
- At most, a single row of labial tooth rows in the lower jaw

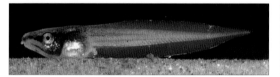

Males call from elevated positions in vegetation up to 2 m above the ground or from water level. They emit two kinds of calls, one to attract females and the other to regulate spacing between callers. Some males remain silent and motionless at the call site, flattening their bodies against the foliage to conceal their presence. As females approach in response to the advertisement calls of the other males, the concealed 'satellite' males ambush them – but with only occasional success.

After coupling, the amplectant pair moves away from the call site. They deposit their eggs in a unique manner: positioning themselves along the axis of a leaf or blade of grass close to, or below, the surface of the water, the two frogs move slowly along the length of the leaf. While doing so, the female deposits between 20 and 50 colourless eggs that the male fertilises as they emerge from her body. With his hindlegs the male then folds the leaf to form a tube that encloses the eggs behind him. The tube is sealed with an adhesive secretion deposited with the eggs. A female may take several different mates in the course of one or two nights, and a new leaf tube is constructed each time. The eggs remain in the safety of the folded leaf nest until the tadpoles emerge to continue their metamorphosis in the water.

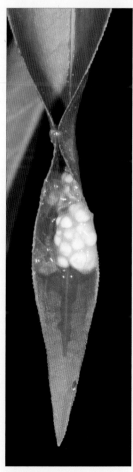

Eggs exposed.

Eggs in folded leaf tube.

KEY TO SPECIES

ADULT

1 Larger than 30 mm with pale upper tibia .... **Greater Leaf-folding Frog** A. fornasinii (p.230)
  Smaller than 30 mm with dark-coloured or patterned tibia **2**
2 Found in the Eastern or Western Cape .... **Knysna Leaf-folding Frog** A. knysnae (p.232)
  Not found in Eastern and Western Cape **3**
3 No dark bands on the tibia .... **Natal Leaf-folding Frog** A. spinifrons (p.234)
  Dark bands, with or without lighter stippling, on the tibia **4**
4 Found north of the Limpopo and Save Rivers **5**
  Found south of the Limpopo and Save Rivers **6**
5 Dark transverse band extending across full width of tibia ..... **Delicate Leaf-folding Frog** A. delicatus (p.228)
  Dark transverse band not extending across full width of tibia ... **Snoring Leaf-folding Frog** A. crotalus (p.224)
6 Underside without spines .... **Golden Leaf-folding Frog** A. aureus (p.226)
  Spines on underside, notably in throat region .... **Delicate Leaf-folding Frog** A. delicatus (p.228)

Because of the close interspecies similarity in this genus and the variation within each species, the outcome from the keying process must be thoroughly checked against other diagnostic factors, including – if possible – the call.

TADPOLE

1 One continuous labial tooth row in the lower jaw .... A. fornasinii (p.230)
  Labial tooth rows absent **2**
2 Known only from the coastal region between Groenvlei (Western Cape) and Covie (Eastern Cape) ....
  .... A. knysnae (p.232)
  Known northwards from Cintsa Bay (in eastern part of the Eastern Cape) **3**
3 Two rows of papillae in lower jaw .... A. spinifrons (p.234)
4 A single row of papillae in lower jaw .... A. aureus (p.226) or A. delicatus (p.228) (not separable)

Snoring Leaf-folding Frog

TRACK
55

Snorkblaarvoupadda

Afrixalus crotalus Pickersgill, 1984

LATIN: *crotalum* = rattle. Refers to the rattling call of this species.

Conservation status: Not threatened.

Identification

Maximum size: 24 mm. **Body:** slender and elongated, with pointed snout. **Above:** pale yellow, usually with a faint brown vertebral line and a pair of broken paravertebral lines; no distinct patches on lower back; dark band with

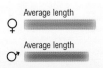

♀ Average length

♂ Average length

Maximum size: 24 mm

Snoring Leaf-folding Frog: Mulanje, Malawi.

small white speckles along the flanks; minute spines only on the head; all dark markings may be very faint or absent. **Underside:** small spines present on throat; chest and belly smooth. **Hindlimbs:** broad transverse band does not encircle the entire tibia; divided subarticular tubercles on outer two fingers. **Sexual dimorphism:** male has a yellow gular disc with scattered spines and convex posterior edge.

Call
Series of indistinct clicks and rattles.

Habitat and habits
Palustrine wetlands in dry grassland.

TADPOLE
Unknown.

KEY ID POINTS

- Vertebral line, if present, never broad or well defined (distinct from *A. fornasinii*)
- Dark band on leg does not encompass the full width of the tibia (distinct from *A. aureus* and *A. delicatus*)
- Subarticular tubercles on outer two fingers divided (distinct from other species)
- Very small spines only on the head (distinct from *A. aureus* and *A. delicatus*)
- Spines on underside confined to throat (distinct from *A. aureus* and *A. delicatus*)
- Distributed north of the Limpopo River in South Africa and north of the Save River in Mozambique (distinct from *A. aureus*, *A. spinifrons* and *A. knysnae*)

The close similarity between species requires careful examination of all the above characters.

Golden Leaf-folding Frog

Goueblaarvoupadda

TRACK 54

Afrixalus aureus Pickersgill, 1984

LATIN: *aureus* = golden. Refers to the golden colour of this species.

Conservation status: Not threatened.

Golden Leaf-folding Frog: Kruger National Park, Mpumalanga.

Identification

Maximum size: 24 mm. **Body:** shape delicate and elongated; snout pointed. **Above:** light brown to intense golden-yellow; dark paravertebral patches on the lower back coincide with a darker patch on the lower leg when in seated position; poorly defined vertebral line may be present; darker band, at times lightly speckled on the flanks, extends from snout to groin overlapping with the upper eyelid; dark colour patterning may be indistinct or absent, leaving a uniform golden colour; head and snout covered with many tiny spines that are most prominent in the breeding season. **Underside:** white and smooth; hidden areas of limbs and

♀ Average length

♂ Average length

Maximum size: 24 mm

KEY ID POINTS

- Vertebral line, if present, is never broad or well defined (distinct from *A. fornasinii*)
- Broad oblique band across full width of the tibia (distinct from *A. crotalus*)
- Dorsal spines distributed more or less evenly over the back (not concentrated on head as in *A. spinifrons* and *A. crotalus*)
- Underside without spines except occasionally a few on the gular region (distinct from other species)
- Very little webbing between fingers (distinct from *A. fornasinii*)
- Male gular disc covers full area of throat (distinct from *A. delicatus*)

- Distributed north of 29°S except for rare isolated occurrences (distinct from *A. spinifrons* and *A. knysnae*)

toes yellow. **Forelimbs:** very little webbing between fingers. **Hindlimbs:** tibia with dark, broad oblique band; moderate webbing between toes. **Sexual dimorphism:** male with bright orange gular pouch covering entire gular region and back covered in widely spaced spines.

Call
Short, repeated buzz.

Habitat and habits
Lowland coastal bushveld and grassland from sea level to about 300 m. Also found in mixed Lowveld bushveld.

TADPOLE

Length: up to 35 mm. **Shape:** long; streamlined; shark-like; head is dorsoventrally flattened. **Tail:** dorsal fin slightly shallower than ventral fin; tapers gradually to fine tip. **Colour:** golden-brown above; white below; grey line runs from snout along head to eyes; ventrally opaque. **Eyes:** lateral. **Nostrils:** small; widely spaced; close to tip of snout. **Spiracle:** below body axis; directed backwards at angle of 15°. **Vent:** supramarginal; dextral. **Mouth:** anterior; double row of small, widely spaced papillae. **Jaw sheaths:** moderate. **LTRF:** no labial teeth.

Tadpole: lateral view.

Mouthparts.

Delicate Leaf-folding Frog

Delikate blaarvoupadda

TRACK
56

Afrixalus delicatus Pickersgill, 1984

LATIN: *delicatus* = dainty. Refers to the delicate build of frogs of this species.

Conservation status: Not threatened.

Delicate Leaf-folding Frog: KwaMbonambi, KwaZulu-Natal.

Identification

Maximum size: 22 mm. **Body:** shape delicate and elongated; snout pointed. **Above:** dorsal colour varies but predominant colour is yellow; brown band on flank from snout to groin and other dark dorsolateral markings not always strongly defined; small spines scattered sparsely over the dorsum; not concentrated on the head. **Underside:** varies from white to yellow; slightly granular with scattered spines more prominent on centre of abdomen. **Forelimbs:** very little webbing between fingers. **Hindlimbs:** tibia with irregular transverse stripe or band, but not always distinct; moderate webbing between toes. **Sexual dimorphism:** male with orange or yellow gular disc not covering entire throat region.

Average length
♀

Average length
♂

Maximum size: 22 mm

Call
High-pitched *zick* on a rising note, interspersed with a sustained trill or buzzing. Males call in small groups on low vegetation.

Habitat and habits
Tropical and subtropical coastal bush and grassland, including marshes and swamp forests east of the Lebombo Mountains and the Zimbabwe escarpment.

Calling male with distended vocal sac.

Colour variation.

KEY ID POINTS

- Vertebral line, if present, never broad or well defined (distinct from *A. fornasinii*)
- Broad band across full width of the tibia but sometimes indistinct (distinct from *A. crotalus*)
- Dorsal spines distributed more or less evenly over the back (not concentrated on head as in *A. s. spinifrons* and *A. crotalus*)
- Underside with spines concentrated in the centre of the abdomen (distinct from other species)
- Very little webbing between fingers (distinct from *A. fornasinii*)
- Male gular disc does not cover full area of throat (distinct from *A. aureus*)
- Distributed north of 29°S except for rare isolated occurrences (distinct from *A. spinifrons* and *A. knysnae*. Note: *A. delicatus* overlaps with *A. spinifrons* between 28–30°S)

TADPOLE
Length: up to 38 mm. **Shape:** long, streamlined, shark-like; head flattened. **Tail:** dorsal fin shallower than ventral fin; tail tapering to sharp tip. **Colour:** light brown to transparent; tail fin slightly mottled; abdomen white; transparent towards front. **Eyes:** lateral. **Nostrils:** small; widely spaced, close to tip of snout. **Spiracle:** below body axis; directed backwards at about 20°. **Vent:** supramarginal; dextral. **Mouth:** anterior; single row of medium-sized papillae laterally and ventrally; ventrally a second row of weakly developed papillae closer to mouth. **Jaw sheaths:** delicate. **LTRF:** labial tooth rows absent. **Development:** complete after six weeks.

Tadpole: lateral view.

Mouthparts.

Greater Leaf-folding Frog

Grootblaarvoupadda

Afrixalus fornasinii (Bianconi, 1849)

Named after Carlo Fornasini.

Conservation status: Not threatened.

TRACK 57

Greater Leaf-folding Frog: Mtunzini, KwaZulu-Natal.

Marius Burger

Identification

Maximum size: 40 mm. **Body:** elongated; snout pointed; larger and more robust than other *Afrixalus* species. **Above:** bold, dark vertebral band beginning from a point between the eyes continuing to the vent; dark, lateral band extending from snout to groin; colour varies from cream to grey-brown, sometimes becoming indistinguishable from vertebral band; back covered in small spines, each on a small white speckle. **Underside:** granular, creamy white. **Forelimbs:** fingers conspicuously webbed. **Hindlimbs:** exposed part of

Average length
♀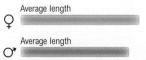

Average length
♂

Maximum size: 40 mm

KEY ID POINTS

- Larger than other species
- Prominent broad, dark brown, vertebral band terminating in a point between eyes (distinct from other species)
- Spines situated on small white speckles (distinct from other species)
- Tibia pale on exposed surface (distinct from other species)
- Underside without spines (distinct from other species)
- Webbing between fingers (distinct from other species except *A. knysnae* and *A. spinifrons*)

tibia light-coloured. **Sexual dimorphism:** male has yellow gular disc on the throat.

Call
Burst of loud, rapidly repeated *clack* sounds preceded by a short, soft buzz. Males, often in small groups, call from elevated positions on emergent vegetation.

Habitat and habits
Wide variety of densely vegetated habitats in coastal swamps, streams and dams in bushveld and grassland from sea level to 300 m.

Yellow gular disc on the throat of the male.

TADPOLE
Length: up to 65 mm. **Shape:** long, streamlined, shark-like; head dorsoventrally flattened. **Tail:** tapering to acute tip; dorsal and ventral fins of equal depth; tail fin transparent. **Colour:** olive to dark brown above; mottled; shiny white below, with area behind mouth transparent. **Eyes:** lateral. **Nostrils:** small; widely spaced; close to tip of snout. **Spiracle:** about two-thirds along length of body; opens directly posteriorly. **Vent:** supramarginal; dextral. **Mouth:** single row of medium-sized papillae laterally; triple row below. **Jaw sheaths:** delicate. **LTRF:** no upper labial tooth row; single short labial tooth row below; formula 0/1. **Development:** complete after three months.

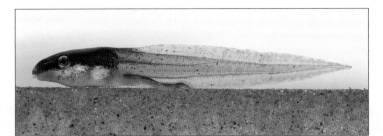

Tadpole: lateral view.

Mouthparts.

Knysna Leaf-folding Frog

Knysna-blaarvoupadda

TRACK 58

Afrixalus knysnae (Loveridge, 1954)

Named after the coastal town of Knysna, in the southeastern Cape.

Conservation status: Endangered. The distribution range is limited and suitable habitat is diminishing as a result of coastal and urban development.

Knysna Leaf-folding Frog: Covie, Eastern Cape.

Identification

Maximum size: 25 mm. **Body:** small but robust; head broad. **Above:** background yellow to brown with a darker vertebral band; plain dark stripe from nostril through eye to groin; dark broken paravertebral stripes on back in most specimens; prominent spines uniformly scattered over head and back. **Underside:** granular, creamy white; gular disc smooth. **Forelimbs:** slight webbing between fingers; subarticular tubercles of outer two fingers conspicuous and not divided. **Hindlimbs:** no dark transverse band on tibia;

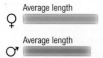

♀ Average length

♂ Average length

Maximum size: 25 mm

KEY ID POINTS

- Dark band on flanks without white speckles and asperities (distinct from all species except *A. spinifrons*)
- No transverse band across tibia (distinct from *A. aureus*, *A. delicatus* and *A. crotalus*)
- Dorsal spines distributed more or less evenly over the back (not concentrated on head as in *A. spinifrons* and *A. crotalus*)
- Underside without spines (distinct from *A. delicatus*)
- Slight webbing between fingers (distinct from other species except *A. spinifrons* and *A. fornasinii*)
- Distributed only on southern Cape coast from Groenvlei in the west to Covie in the east (distinct from other species)

moderate webbing between toes. **Sexual dimorphism**: male with yellow gular disc on throat.

Call
Soft, insect-like trill, lasting for one or two seconds, and occasionally followed by a sharp *zip*.

Habitat and habits
Marshy areas in the coastal mosaic of montane fynbos and Afromontane forest on the border between the Eastern and Western Cape.

TADPOLE
Length: up to 38 mm. **Shape:** oval body; head flattened. **Tail:** streamlined; twice as long as body; tapering to sharp tip; tail fin nearly transparent. **Colour:** brown above, shiny white below. **Eyes:** lateral. **Nostrils:** small; widely spaced; close to tip of snout. **Spiracle:** below body axis. **Vent:** supramarginal; dextral. **Mouth:** anterior; single row of medium-sized papillae laterally and below; second row of poorly developed papillae below this. **Jaw sheaths:** delicate. **LTRF:** lacks labial tooth rows. **Development:** complete after six weeks.

Habitat: pond at Covie, Eastern Cape

Tadpole: lateral view.

Natal Leaf-folding Frog

Natalse blaarvoupadda

TRACK 59

Afrixalus spinifrons (Cope, 1862)

Subspecies:
- *A. spinifrons spinifrons* Pickersgill, 1996
- *A. spinifrons intermedius* Pickersgill, 1996

LATIN: *spine* = thorn; *frons* = forehead. Refers to the spines on the head of this species.

Conservation Status: Vulnerable. Farming and urban development is reducing the suitable habitat in the restricted distribution range.

Adam Shuttleworth

Natal Leaf-folding Frog, subspecies Afrixalus spinifrons spinifrons: KwaMbonambi, KwaZulu-Natal. Inset: Subspecies A. s. intermedius: KwaZulu-Natal midlands.

Identification

Maximum size: 25 mm. **Body:** small; snout rounded. In *A. s. spinifrons,* snout is swollen and bulbous and densely covered with small black spines; in *A. s. intermedius,* snout is not bulbous and spines are distributed evenly over back. **Above:** colour varies from ivory to golden-yellow with wide brown vertebral band narrowing at tip of snout, broadening towards rear and split by light-coloured

Average length
♀

Average length
♂

Maximum size: 25 mm

KEY ID POINTS

- Vertebral line, if present, never broad or well defined (distinct from *A. fornasinii*)
- No dark lateral band on flanks or tibia (distinct from other species)
- Dorsal spines concentrated on bulbous snout in *A. s. spinifrons* (distinct from other species and *A. s. intermedius*)
- Underside without spines except on throat (distinct from other species)
- Slight webbing between fingers (distinct from other species except *A. knysnae* and *A. fornasinii*)
- Distributed north of the Bashee River in the Eastern Cape and south of 29°S in KwaZulu-Natal – except for rare, isolated occurrences up to 28°S (distinct from *A. crotalus*, and *A. knysnae*)

wedge above cloaca of *A. s. spinifrons.* In *A. s. intermedius,* dorsal markings are either absent or confined to posterior part of back. **Underside:** creamy white with spines confined to the gular area. **Forelimbs:** some webbing at the base of fingers. **Hindlimbs:** dark lateral bands and bands on thighs absent. **Sexual dimorphism:** male with yellow gular disc (with spines) on the throat.

Call
Short *zip*, followed by a longer trill of about five seconds. Males call in small choruses of 4 to 20 frogs.

Habitat and habits
Wide variety of habitats in coastal bushveld grassland and moist upland grassland. *A. s. intermedius* occurs at higher altitudes in KwaZulu-Natal midlands.

Tadpole
Length: up to 32 mm. **Shape:** streamlined, shark-like, head flattened. **Tail:** tapering to sharp tip. **Colour:** body brown with dark markings on head, tail transparent or slightly mottled. **Eyes:** lateral. **Nostrils:** small, widely spaced. **Spiracle:** below body axis. **Vent:** supramarginal; dextral. **Mouth:** anterior; single row of medium-sized papillae laterally and below; second poorly developed row below this. **Jaw sheaths:** delicate. **LTRF:** labial tooth rows absent. **Development:** complete after six weeks.

Tadpole: lateral view.

REED FROGS

RIETPADDAS

Hyperolius Rapp, 1842

GREEK: *hyper* = above; eleios = *smooth*. Refers to the smooth back of frogs in this genus.

130 species in Africa, 16 in southern Africa
Assignment of species, subspecies or clines in this genus is not definitively resolved and may differ slightly from that used in some other publications.

Painted Reed Frog: Durban, KwaZulu-Natal. Colour patterns are variable and often striking.

This is a large and complex genus of often strikingly coloured climbing frogs. Colour patterns and morphology are extremely variable and may differ between sexes in some species or alter with age or become more vibrant at night. A distinctively patterned population in one geographic area may gradually merge with a totally different pattern in another area with no clear boundary, and divisions between species, subspecies or clines (see p.14) are often indistinct.

Reed Frogs are most common in well-vegetated habitats in warmer, high-rainfall areas. Males usually call from well-defended positions on emergent vegetation, retreating into trees and foliage away from the water during daylight and returning to the

DISTINCTIVE CHARACTERS

ADULT
- Pupil horizontal
- Dorsal colour pattern distinctive and colourful
- Webbing on toes extensive
- Fingers and toes with terminal discs
- Tympanum concealed

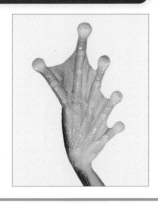

TADPOLE
- Vent supramarginal and dextral
- Single upper labial tooth row
- Bottom dwelling

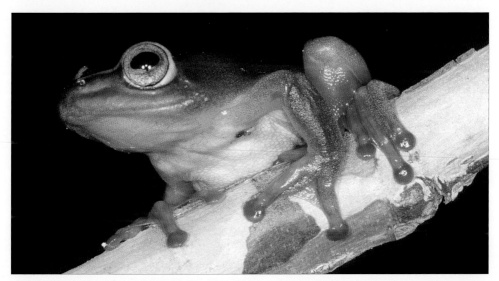

Female Argus Reed Frog: St Lucia, KwaZulu-Natal.

same call sites every night. Females approach males by leaping through reeds, cocking their heads from side to side to ascertain the direction of the call.

Because they occur largely in humid and warm conditions, most species have extended breeding seasons. Some form large choruses, the noise of which can be deafening. Calling activity peaks during warm nights following rain. Territorial calls and fighting between males are common. Eggs are usually attached to submerged or emergent plants, each species having a particular mode of attaching eggs to vegetation.

Note yellow protective disc on the vocal sac.

KEY TO SPECIES

ADULT

1 Body elongated, snout pointed and projecting well beyond lower jaw **2**

Body not elongated, snout not pointed nor projecting well beyond lower jaw **4**

2 Usually two pairs of light longitudinal lines on dorsum ....
.... **Bocage's Sharp-nosed Reed Frog** *H. benguellensis* (p.244)

Mid-dorsal line of spots and one pair of light longitudinal lines usually on dorsum **3**

3 Occurs west of 25° latitude (northern Botswana and northern Namibia) ... **Long Reed Frog** *H. nasutus* (p.254)

Occurs east of 25° latitude (Zimbabwe, northern Mozambique and coastal KwaZulu-Natal) ....
.... **Power's Long Reed Frog** *H. poweri* (p.240)

4 Confined to central, northern or western Zimbabwe, northern Botswana and northern Namibia **5**

Confined to eastern Zimbabwe and coastal and lowland Mozambique and South Africa **6**

5 Green to brown; dark brown to black dorsolateral band; confined to central and northern Zimbabwe ....
.... **Marginated Reed Frog** *H. marginatus* (p.248)

Red or brown bold vermiculations to uniform red; confined to northern Botswana and Caprivi Strip ....
.... **Angolan Reed Frog** *H. parallelus* (p.256)

Lime-green spots on bright green or yellow background; confined to western Zimbabwe ....
.... **Laurent's Reed Frog** *H. rhodesianus* (p.264)

6 Males green or grey; yellow lateral band from snout to flanks; female purple-brown; yellow horseshoe
mark on snout continues into dorsolateral dots or band; snout rounded; lowlands of KwaZulu-Natal and
Mozambique .... **Argus Reed Frog** *H. argus* (p.242)

Ivory to light brown; pale dorsolateral band; confined to coastal Western Cape ....
.... **Arum Lily Frog** *H. horstockii* (p.246)

Black, white, red and yellow longitudinal stripes; northern KwaZulu-Natal, Swaziland, Mpumalanga,
Limpopo Province and southern Mozambique; feral population around Cape Town ....
.... **Painted Reed Frog** *H. marmoratus taeniatus* (p.250)

Irregular mottled patterns of yellows, browns, orange and black; coastal KwaZulu-Natal from Port
Edward to St Lucia .... **Painted Reed Frog** *H. marmoratus marmoratus* (p.250)

Pale spots on a dark background; KwaZulu-Natal south coast to Tsitsikamma ....
.... **Painted Reed Frog** *H. marmoratus verrucosus* (p.250)

Brown with prominent white dorsolateral bands edged in black; lowland Mozambique north of Beira ....
.... **Mitchell's Reed Frog** *H. mitchelli* (p.252)

Translucent green; white dorsolateral band; coastal Mozambique north of Beira ....
.... **Parker's Reed Frog** *H. parkeri* (p.258)

Males brown with dark-edged light dorsolateral stripe; female brilliant yellowish-green; coastal
KwaZulu-Natal lowlands from Kingsburgh to St Lucia ...... **Pickersgill's Reed Frog** *H. pickersgilli* (p.260)

Translucent green, with small black spots; small; lowlands from Cebe in Eastern Cape northwards ....
.... **Water Lily Frog** *H. pusillus* (p.262)

Green or olive-brown; yellow dorsolateral band; Port Elizabeth northwards to southern Mozambique and
inland to Nelspruit .... **Yellow-striped Reed Frog** *H. semidiscus* (p.266)

Pale beige-yellow with dark, dense reticulations fusing to form a uniform black; confined to forest-
savanna of eastern Zimbabwe and central west Mozambique ....
.... **Swynnerton's Reed Frog** *H. swynnertoni* (p.268)

Uniform lime-green or yellow; translucent green; lowlands from Port Edward northwards ....
.... **Tinker Reed Frog** *H. tuberilinguis* (p.270)

TADPOLE

1 Outermost labial tooth row in lower jaw, more than half as long as adjacent row **2**

   Outermost labial tooth row in lower jaw, less than half as long as adjacent row **3**

2 Posterior fifth of tail dark grey or black; black pigment along dorsal and ventral limits of tail muscles ....
   .... *H. pusillus* (p.262)

   Not as above .... *H. poweri* (p.240)

3 Posterior region of tail dark grey or black .... *H. marmoratus* (p.250)

   Posterior region of tail not darker than rest of tail **4**

4 Longitudinal axis of tail and margin of upper and lower fins dark with dense pigmentation, forming broad
   stripes; known from coastal KwaZulu-Natal and Mozambique .... *H. tuberilinguis* (p.270)

   Broad stripe on middle of tail muscles with thin black line along uppermost and lowermost margin of tail
   muscle; known from coastal southern and Western Cape .... *H. horstockii* (p.246)

Tadpole identification not possible through key for: *H. argus, H. benguellensis, H. marginatus,
H. mitchelli, H. nasutus, H. parallelus, H. parkeri, H. pickersgilli, H. rhodesianus, H. semidiscus* and
H. swynnertoni

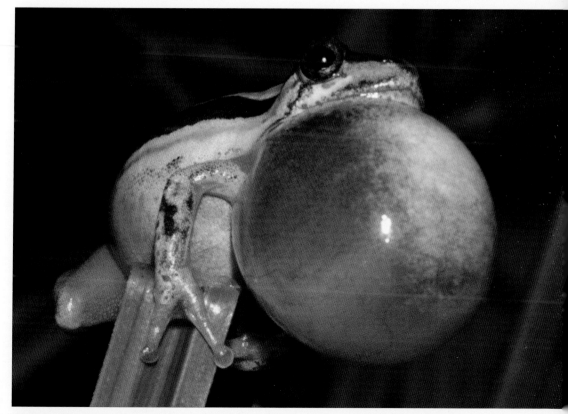

*Typical posture of calling male Painted Reed Frog, allowing space for the large vocal sac:
Mkuzi, KwaZulu-Natal.*

Power's Long Reed frog

Power se skerpneusrietpadda

Hyperolius poweri Loveridge, 1938

Named after the herpetologist, John Hyacinth Power, director of the McGregor Museum in Kimberley from 1947 to 1958.

Conservation status: Not threatened but rare and localised.

Werner Conradie

Power's Long Reed Frog: Mkambati, Eastern Cape.

Description
Maximum size: 22 mm. **Body:** narrow; pointed snout, protruding beyond lower jaw. **Above:** green to brown; variations include lines of small dots; overall stippling of dark specks. **Underside:** smooth, translucent silvery-white. **Hindlimbs:** concealed translucent green surfaces of limbs; webbing and digits green or yellow; small black spots under feet and hands; webbing moderately extensive; toes with discs. **Sexual dimorphism:** breeding male has yellow throat and prominent white dorsolateral stripes through the eye to the tip of snout.

Average length
♀

Average length
♂

Maximum size: 22 mm

KEY ID POINTS

- Colour pattern distinguishes this from other species; distinctive colour pattern dorsally and ventrally (except *H. nasutus* and some *H. benguellensis*)
- Body elongated and snout acutely pointed (distinct from other species, except *H. nasutus*, *H. benguellensis* and *H. parkeri*)
- Concealed translucent green or yellow surfaces of body (distinct from other species, except *H. nasutus*, *H. benguellensis*, *H. parkeri*, *H. pickersgilli* and *H. pusillus*)
- Distribution extends from southern Mozambique along KwaZulu-Natal coast of South Africa and entering the Eastern Cape (distinct from *H. nasutus* and *H. benguellensis*)

Jeanne Tarrant

Call

Harsh insect-like *dzeee-dzeee* chirp. Males call from elevated positions on vegetation. They often engage in territorial disputes.

Habitat and habits

At or near sea level in coastal bushveld and grassland. Approximately 290 eggs are laid in clutches of 2 to 20, submerged and attached to vegetation. The eggs are white with a greenish-grey dorsal pole.

Colour form without lateral stripe: Richards Bay, KwaZulu-Natal.

TADPOLE

Length: up to 32 mm. **Shape:** body rounded to ovoid. **Tail:** more than twice as long as body; deepest point in middle of tail; acutely pointed. **Colour:** overall light brown with dark spots; tail shaft usually has dark line to tip; does not have light and dark markings, unlike *H. pusillus;* fin slightly mottled with tip grey-brown; whitish below. **Eyes:** near lateral. **Nostrils:** small; widely spaced; close to tip of snout. **Spiracle:** below body axis; directed backwards. **Vent:** supramarginal; dextral. **Mouth:** double row of small papillae at sides and below; outer row with slightly longer papillae. **Jaw sheaths:** moderate; weakly flexed. **LTRF:** 1/3 with third row in lower jaw only half the length of first row.

Werner Conradie

Tadpole: lateral view.

Argus Reed Frog

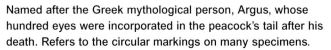

Argus-rietpadda

Hyperolius argus Peters, 1854

Named after the Greek mythological person, Argus, whose hundred eyes were incorporated in the peacock's tail after his death. Refers to the circular markings on many specimens.

Conservation status: Not threatened.

Argus Reed Frog – female colour pattern showing prominent markings on snout: St Lucia, KwaZulu-Natal.

Description

Maximum size: 34 mm. **Body:** more heavily built than other Reed Frogs. **Above:** males green or grey; small brown dots on back; yellow lateral band edged with a broad black line from snout to flanks; female light to dark purple-brown; horseshoe-shaped yellow to orange band edged in black from eye to eye over snout; may continue as a dorsolateral band; often broken into a few asymmetrical dots low on back. **Underside:** white or yellow; skin granular. **Hindlimbs:** concealed orange or brown surfaces of limbs, toes and fingers; 1 to 1½ phalanges of longest toe free of webbing; toes with well-developed discs. **Sexual dimorphism:** dorsal patterns differ (see above); throat of breeding male yellow; granular.

Average length
♀

Average length
♂

Maximum size: 34 mm

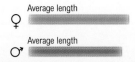

KEY ID POINTS

- Dorsal colour pattern distinct from other species
- Body stocky, snout rounded (distinct from *H. nasutus*, *H. benguellensis* and *H. parkeri*)
- Concealed orange to brown surfaces of body (distinct from other species, except *H. mitchelli*, *H. semidiscus* and *H. tuberilinguis*)

Call

Rapidly repeated cluck. Males call from elevated positions on emergent or floating vegetation.

Habitat and habits

Coastal bushveld grassland, at or close to sea level. Breeds in temporary, shallow water-filled depressions or coastal pans, favouring those with emergent or floating vegetation.

Male lacks prominent marks on snout: Richards Bay, KwaZulu-Natal.

TADPOLE

Length: up to 48 mm. **Shape:** body oval. **Tail:** fins deep; moderately curved. **Colour:** brown; pale underside; mottled fins; terminal tip sometimes black. **Eyes:** lateral. **Nostrils:** small, widely spaced on snout edge. **Spiracle:** below; directed backwards at $20°$. **Vent:** supramarginal; dextral. **Mouth:** near-ventral; single row of small papillae at mouth corners. **Jaw sheaths:** delicate. **LTRF:** 1/3(1); third row in lower jaw very short.

Pale colour form – female: St Lucia, KwaZulu-Natal.

Tadpole: lateral view.

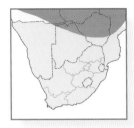

Bocage's Sharp-nosed Reed Frog

Bocage se skerpneusrietpadda

Hyperolius benguellensis Bocage, 1893

Named after the town of Benguela on the west coast of Angola.

Conservation status: Not threatened.

Bocage's Sharp-nosed Reed Frog; four dorsal bands are characteristic of the species: Mazambuka, Zambia.

Description

Maximum size: 21 mm. **Body:** narrow; sides of head straight; snout elongated and pointed, projecting beyond mouth and giving it a shark-like appearance. **Above:** prominent pairs of light paravertebral and dorsolateral bands, especially in younger individuals; bands are formed by absence of dark pigment in these areas rather than by white pigment; juveniles reddish-brown, unlike closely related *H. nasutus.* **Underside:** belly transparent; whitish. **Forelimbs:** hands green, with well-developed palmar tubercles. **Hindlimbs:** tibia more than half body length;

Average length

♀

Average length

♂

Maximum size: 21 mm

KEY ID POINTS

- Distinctive colour pattern dorsally and ventrally (except occasionally *H. nasutus* and *H. poweri*)
- Body elongated and snout acutely pointed (distinct from other species, except *H. nasutus*, *H. poweri* and *H. parkeri*)
- Concealed translucent green surfaces of body (distinct from other species except *H. nasutus*, *H. benguellensis*, *H. parkeri*, *H. pickersgilli* and *H. pusillus*)
- Distribution in southern Africa distinct from *H. nasutus* and *H. poweri*

Martin Pickersgill

- Two pairs of dorsolateral lines usually present (distinct from *H. nasutus* and *H. poweri*)

hidden surfaces of the body green; small inner and outer metatarsal tubercles; well-developed subarticular tubercles; terminal discs on toes distinct; webbing moderate to reduced, reaching middle tubercle of fourth toe, leaving two phalanges free of web. **Sexual dimorphism:** male gular disc bright yellow.

Call
High-pitched piercing chirp or rasping creak, similar to that of *H. nasutus*. Males call through the night, from inundated grass, sedges or reeds.

Habitat and habits
Emergent vegetation at margins of a variety of vegetation types in savanna and grassland, including swamps, rivers and lakes, but breeds in deep, permanent water. Occurs at higher altitudes than *H. nasutus*.

TADPOLE
Unknown.

Unusual colour variation lacking dorsolateral lines: Rundu, Namibia.

Arum Lily Frog

Aronskelkrietpadda

TRACK 63

Hyperolius horstockii (Schlegal, 1837)

Named after Hubertus B. van Horstock, who practised medicine in the Cape Colony from 1826 to 1834.

Conservation status: Not threatened.

Arum Lily Frog: Cape Flats, Western Cape.

Atherton de Villiers

Description

Maximum size: 43 mm. **Body:** elongated and robust. **Above:** ivory to pale yellow to light brown; small dark spots on back; prominent pale band from snout along flanks to groin, bordered by delicate thin line of small black spots. **Underside:** creamy white; skin granular. **Hindlimbs:** webbing moderately extensive, reaching last tubercle of longest toe on one side only; concealed bright red surfaces of limbs; toes with discs. **Sexual dimorphism:** throat of breeding male bright ochre.

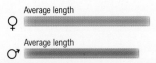

♀ Average length

♂ Average length

Maximum size: 43 mm

Call

Harsh *quee-quee* bleat. Males call from elevated positions on emergent or floating vegetation. Advertisement calls sometimes interspersed with territorial croaks.

Habitat and habits

Large or small pans, dams, vleis and slow-flowing streams in coastal fynbos. Eggs are cream with a brown dorsal pole and are laid in clutches of 10 to 30 attached to submerged vegetation.

Typical retreat in Arum Lily flower.

KEY ID POINTS

- Colour pattern is distinct from other species but may be confused with the brown form of *H. marmoratus*
- Stocky body; snout rounded (distinct from *H. nasutus*, *H. benguellensis* and *H. parkeri*)
- Concealed bright red surfaces of body (distinct for all other species, except *H. marginatus*, *H. marmoratus*, *H. parallelus*, *H. rhodesianus* and *H. swynnertoni*)

TADPOLE

Length: Up to 40 mm. **Shape:** body pear-shaped. **Tail:** moderately curved; terminating in sharp tip. **Colour:** overall brown; terminal part of tail not dark; broad dark axial stripe and narrow dark stripes along upper and lower limits of tail muscles. **Eyes:** lateral. **Nostrils:** small; widely spaced; on snout edge. **Spiracle:** just below body axis. **Vent:** supramarginal; dextral. **Mouth:** near-ventral; single row of papillae at sides; double row below; outer row with slightly larger papillae. **Jaw sheaths:** delicate. **LTRF:** 1/3; third row in lower jaw only half the length of first row.

Marius Burger

Tadpole: lateral view.

Marginated Reed Frog

Rooiflankrietpadda

__Hyperolius marginatus__ Peters, 1854

Refers to the distinctive dark dorsolateral marginal band.

Conservation status: Not threatened.

Marginated Reed Frog: North Luangwa, Zambia.

Description

Maximum size: 33 mm. **Body:** snout truncate; pug-like. **Above:** dorsum and upper surfaces of limbs green to brown; distinct dark brown to black dorsolateral band from tip of snout usually present through eyes to vent; flanks pale-coloured, heavily stippled with red, sometimes appearing uniformly red; occasional black speckling present; dark spots may be present on

Average length

♀

Average length

♂

Maximum size: 33 mm

KEY ID POINTS

- Dorsal colour pattern distinct from other species
- Stocky body with truncate snout (distinct from *H. nasutus*, *H. poweri*, *H. benguellensis* and *H. parkeri*)
- Concealed dark red surfaces of body (distinct from other species, except *H. horstockii*, *H. marmoratus*, *H. parallelus*, *H. rhodesianus* and *H. swynnertoni*)

Johan Marais

back; juveniles with well-defined hourglass mark with elongated patches low down on the back; some individuals may be whitish or yellowish-white above; flanks granular. **Underside:** crimson. **Forelimbs:** well-developed discs on fingertips. **Hindlimbs:** feet red; concealed red surfaces of limbs; no inner and small outer metatarsal tubercles; webbing extensive with 1 to 1½ phalanges of longest toe free of web. **Sexual dimorphism:** gular sac distinct in male.

Call
Short, high-pitched, explosive whistles, repeated frequently. Tall vegetation, such as reeds and sedges, favoured as call sites.

Habitat and habits
Emergent vegetation at margins of swamps, rivers and lakes in all types of savanna, grassland and bushveld; also in many modified habitats in cultivated land, towns and gardens. The species rapidly colonises newly created water bodies.

TADPOLE
Unknown.

North Luangwa, Zambia.

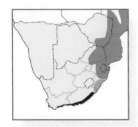

Painted Reed Frog

Skilderbontrietpadda

TRACK 65

Hyperolius marmoratus Rapp, 1842

Subspecies: ■ *H. marmoratus marmoratus* Rapp, 1842
■ *H. marmoratus taeniatus* Peters, 1854
■ *H. marmoratus verrucosus* Smith, 1849

LATIN: *marmoratus* = covered in marble. Refers to the mottled colour pattern of the species.

Conservation status: Not threatened.

Above: Painted Reed Frog, subspecies Hyperolius marmoratus marmoratus: *KwaMbonambi, KwaZulu-Natal. Top right: Subspecies* H. m. taeniatus: *Sodwana Bay, KwaZulu-Natal. Above right: Subspecies* H. m. verrucosus: *Jeffrey's Bay, Eastern Cape.*

Description

Maximum size: 33 mm. **Body:** snout rounded; slightly concave at the sides. **Above:** colour and pattern extremely variable; three subspecies with different coloration are recognised in southern Africa and colour patterns correlate with geographic distribution (see map); *H. m. taeniatus* has black, white, red and yellow longitudinal stripes; *H. m. marmoratus* has irregular mottled patterns of yellow, brown, orange and black; *H. m. verrucosus* has pale spots on a dark background; intermediate colour patterns

Average length
♀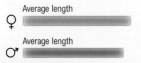

Average length
♂

Maximum size: 33 mm

occur at the interface between subspecific distribution ranges; a brown and tan variation is common in all subspecies. **Underside:** white or pink; skin granular. **Forelimbs:** terminal discs well developed. **Hindlimbs:** concealed red surfaces of limbs, toes and fingers; webbing moderately extensive reaching last tubercle of longest toe; toes with well-developed discs. **Sexual dimorphism:** Breeding male has grey gular disc, often with orange spots.

Call

Short, high-pitched, explosive *whipp-whipp* whistles; repeated about once every second; often in large choruses. At dusk, breeding adults descend to the breeding site and call from reeds and sedges. Individual males return to the same site every evening.

Habitat and habits

Reeds and other vegetation types around the edges of a wide variety of waterbodies in savanna, grassland and forest; occasionally in fynbos. During daylight they retreat into tall reeds, sedges and trees where they often shelter in the axils of leaves. They also occasionally lie exposed in the sunlight with the skin pigmentation reduced to pale grey, and vulnerable surfaces (such as feet) tucked underneath.

KEY ID POINTS

- Dorsal colour patterns of subspecies distinct from other species and from each other
- Snout rounded (distinct from *H. poweri, H. nasutus, H. benguellensis* and *H. parkeri*)
- Concealed dark red surfaces of body (distinct for other species, except *H. horstockii, H. marmoratus, H. parallelus, H. rhodesianus* and *H. swynnertoni*)

Juvenile pattern.

TADPOLE

Length: up to 44 mm. **Shape:** body horseshoe-shaped. **Tail:** tapers to sharp tip. **Colour:** brown with pale underside and speckled fins; last 25% of tail often jet-black; underside of body often glistens gold and silver; area below mouth transparent. **Eyes:** lateral. **Nostrils:** small; widely spaced; on snout edge. **Spiracle:** just below body axis; directed backwards at about 10°. **Vent:** supramarginal; dextral. **Mouth:** anteroventral; single row of small papillae at sides; double row below, of which outer row is slightly bigger. **Jaw sheaths:** heavy. **LTRF:** 1/3; third row in lower jaw short. **Development:** metamorphosis completed after six to eight weeks.

Tadpole: lateral view.

Mitchell's Reed Frog

Mitchell se rietpadda

TRACK
66

Hyperolius mitchelli Loveridge, 1953

Named after B.L. Mitchell, an official in the Nyasaland (now Malawi) Department of Game, Fish and Tsetse.

Conservation status: Not threatened.

Mitchell's Reed Frog: Amani, Tanzania.

Alan Channing

Description

Maximum size: 27 mm. **Body:** stocky; head width about a third of body length; snout pointed. **Above:** yellowish-brown to dark brown with prominent bright white dorsolateral bands edged with a thin, yellow line; bands extending through the eye and to the tip of the snout as a pale line; white bands surrounded by black dots often fusing into a striking black band contrasting with the white and yellow; prominent white heel spot edged in black usually present;

♀ Average length

♂ Average length

Maximum size: 27 mm

KEY ID POINTS

- Dorsal colour pattern distinct from other species
- Body stocky, snout rounded (distinct from *H. nasutus, H. poweri, H. benguellensis* and *H. parkeri*)

- Concealed dark yellow to orange surfaces of body (distinct from other species, except *H. argus, H. marmoratus, H. semidiscus, H. tuberilinguis* and *H. swynnertoni*)

dark spots often present on arms and legs. **Underside:** yellowish. **Forelimbs:** webbing reduced. **Hindlimbs:** concealed yellow to orange surfaces of limbs, toes and fingers; webbing moderately extensive, reaching last tubercle of longest toe; toes with well-developed discs. **Sexual dimorphism:** underside yellow in male; orange in female.

Call
Short chirp.

Habitat and habits
Dry forest, including degraded former forest and farmland. Breeds in permanent and temporary ponds in open woodland and bush.

TADPOLE
Length: up to 36 mm. **Shape:** body oval. **Tail:** deeper than body; tapers to sharp tip. **Colour:** lightly stippled over body and tail; fins and tail mottled; **Eyes:** dorsolateral to lateral. **Nostrils:** small; widely spaced; closer to snout than to eyes. **Spiracle:** just below body axis; constricted; directed backwards at about 20°. **Vent:** supramarginal; dextral. **Mouth:** anteroventral; 70% of head with double row of oral papillae; inner row forms a cluster of about seven papillae at the oral angle; an effective filter is formed by a series of striking papillae in front of upper jaw sheath; a complex of papillae present just inside the mouth. **Jaw sheaths:** moderate. **LTRF:** 2(2)/2 or 3(2-3)/2.

Alan Channing

Colour variation with dark outline to white lateral band: Ifakara, Tanzania.

Long Reed Frog

Langneusrietpadda

TRACK
67

Hyperolius nasutus Günther, 1864

LATIN: *nasutus* = prominent nose. Refers to the long and pointed snout.

Conservation status: Not threatened.

Long Reed Frog: Okavango, Botswana.

Description

Maximum size: 25 mm. **Body:** narrow; snout elongated and acutely pointed, projecting beyond mouth. **Above:** uniform translucent green to brown; pale to bright white dorsolateral bands often present; may have small dark spots that tend to form longitudinal lines. **Underside:** silvery-white to transparent, showing internal organs sheathed in white. **Hindlimbs:** concealed translucent yellowish-green surfaces of legs; webbing moderately extensive. **Sexual dimorphism:** gular disc in male bright yellow.

Call

High-pitched piercing chirp or rasping creak. Males may call late in the afternoon, but calling reaches full strength after dark. Call sites are among inundated grass, sedges or reeds.

Average length

♀

Average length

♂

Maximum size: 25 mm

The shark-like snout is characteristic: Okavango, Botswana.

KEY ID POINTS

- Dorsal colour pattern distinct from other species (except occasionally *H. poweri* and *H. benguellensis*)
- Body elongated and snout acutely pointed (distinct from other species, except *H. poweri*, *H. benguellensis* and *H. parkeri*)
- Concealed translucent green or yellow surfaces of body (distinct from other species, except *H. poweri*, *H. benguellensis*, *H. parkeri*, *H. pickersgilli* and *H. pusillus*)
- Distribution in southern Africa distinguishes this species from *H. poweri* and *H. parkeri*

Habitat and habits

Emergent vegetation at margins of a variety of aquatic sites in savanna and grassland; includes pools, swamps, shallow plans, streams and large rivers. About 200 eggs are laid in clusters of four or five and attached to submerged vegetation.

TADPOLE

Length: up to 32 mm. **Shape:** body rounded to ovoid. **Tail:** tail more than twice as long as body; deepest point in middle of tail; acutely pointed. **Colour:** overall colour is light brown with dark spots; tail shaft dark, especially towards the tip; whitish below. **Eyes:** near lateral. **Nostrils:** small; widely spaced; close to tip of snout. **Spiracle:** below body axis; directed backwards at $15°$. **Vent:** supramarginal; dextral. **Mouth:** double row of small papillae at sides and below; outer row with slightly longer papillae. **Jaw sheaths:** moderate; weakly flexed. **LTRF:** 1/3 with third row in lower jaw only half the length of first row.

Tadpole: lateral view.

Angolan Reed Frog

Angolese rietpadda

TRACK
68

Hyperolius parallelus Günther, 1858
Also known as *Hyperolius parallelus angolensis*

LATIN: *parallelus* = adjacent to another. Origin of name not recorded, but possibly used by Günther if this species occurred sympatrically with another.

Conservation status: Not threatened.

Angolan Reed Frog – one of many colour variations: Okavango, Botswana.

Description

Maximum size: 35 mm. **Body:** elongated; snout rounded. **Above:** distinctive; bold red or brown vermiculations; often with black on cream background; markings occasionally blend into a uniform red dorsum; blotches and spots often interlinked; vermiculated pattern also commonly found. **Underside:** white; skin granular. **Hindlimbs:** fingers, toes and inner legs brilliant red; webbing extensive with 1 to 1½ phalanges of the longest toe free of webbing. **Sexual dimorphism:** male vocal sac white with red stippling along margin.

Call

Brief chirp; chorus resembles tinkling of many drinking glasses. Males begin calling early in the evening from vegetation overhanging water.

Habitat and habits

Rivers and streams in savanna. Breeds in deep bodies of water.

Average length
♀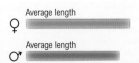

Average length
♂

Maximum size: 35 mm

KEY ID POINTS

- Snout rounded (distinct from
  H. poweri, H. nasutus, H. benguellensis
  and *H. parkeri*)
- Concealed dark red surfaces of body
  (distinct for all other species, except
  H. horstockii, H. marmoratus,
  H. mitchelli, H. rhodesianus and
  H. swynnertoni)

Marietjie Brown

Angolan Reed Frog swallowing Long Reed
Frog: Okavango, Botswana.

Spotted colour variation.

Habitat: Okavango Delta, Botswana.

TADPOLE

Length: up to 65 mm. **Shape:** body robust. **Tail:** muscular; deepest point in middle of
tail; terminates in fine tip. **Colour:** brown; anterior part of tail reddish; fins mottled. **Eyes:**
lateral. **Nostrils:** small; widely spaced; closer to snout than eyes. **Spiracle:** below body axis;
directed backwards at $0°$. **Vent:** supramarginal; dextral. **Mouth:** anteroventral; single row of
papillae laterally; double row below. **Jaw sheaths:** delicate to moderate. **LTRF:** 1/3 with third
row in lower jaw very short.

Tadpole: lateral view.

Parker's Reed Frog

Parker se rietpadda

Hyperolius parkeri Loveridge, 1933

Named after herpetologist, H.W. Parker, who was based at
the Natural History Museum in London from 1923 to 1957.

Conservation status: Not threatened.

TRACK
69

Parker's Reed Frog: Zambezia Province, Mozambique.

Bob Drewes

Average length

♀

Average length

♂

Maximum size: 24 mm

KEY ID POINTS

- Dorsal colour pattern distinct from other species
- Body elongated and snout acutely pointed (distinct from other species except *H. poweri, H. benguellensis* and *H. nasutus*)
- Concealed green to whitish surfaces of body (distinct from other species except *H. poweri, H. benguellensis, H. nasutus, H. pickersgilli* and *H. pusillus*)

Description

Maximum size: 24 mm. **Body:** snout elongated; pointed; projecting beyond mouth. **Above:** translucent green, yellow or brown; white dorsolateral band extends over the eye to tip of snout; a row of dark spots along upper and lower margins of the dorsolateral band usually edged in black; scattered small dark spots on back. **Underside:** whitish. **Forelimbs:** no webbing on hands; fingers with prominent discs. **Hindlimbs:** webbing extensive; toes with distinct discs; concealed green to whitish surfaces. **Underside:** whitish; smooth. **Sexual dimorphism:** male larger than female; dark spines under feet and body of breeding male.

Call

Long, loud trill. Males call from peripheral vegetation along forest streams or from vegetation in pools.

Habitat and habits

Streams in forests, pools and marshes in coastal lowlands and humid savanna woodland; also scrubby coastal forest; previously degraded forested land at medium altitudes. About 36 to 110 white eggs are attached to the underside of leaves or to sedges, just above the water level.

TADPOLE

Unknown.

James Vonesh

Note lateral band bordered with spots.

Pickersgill's Reed Frog

TRACK 70

Pickersgill se rietpadda

Hyperolius pickersgilli Raw, 1982

Named after the herpetologist Martin Pickersgill, who discovered the species.

Conservation status: Endangered because it occurs in a small area where there is considerable habitat degradation.

Pickersgill's Reed Frog. Male colour pattern with white dorsolateral bands: Mtunzini, KwaZulu-Natal.

Description
Maximum size: 29 mm.
Body: snout slightly pointed; barely extends beyond nostrils. **Above:** males brown; dark-edged white to silver stripe from tip of snout over eye extending as dorsolateral band to groin; band often bordered by thin black line; pale heel spot sometimes present; female brilliant yellowish-green; no dorsolateral bands; dark stripe may be present on side of snout; flanks off-white to brownish white; skin granular. **Underside:** yellowish to white; smooth. **Hindlimbs:** concealed surface of limbs not brightly coloured; toes and fingers lack pigmentation; webbing well developed; toes with well-developed discs. **Sexual dimorphism:** male and female colour patterns distinct (see above).

Call
Soft, insect-like chirp.

Average length
♀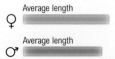

Average length
♂

Maximum size: 29 mm

Marius Burger

Brown male pattern: Kingsburgh, KwaZulu-Natal.

Green female pattern: Durban, KwaZulu-Natal.

Habitat and habits

Densely vegetated marshy areas in coastal bushveld and grassland. Breeding sites are well concealed in thick emergent vegetation.

KEY ID POINTS

- Dorsal colour pattern distinct from other species
- Concealed surfaces of body lack pigmentation (distinct from other species, except *H. poweri*, *H. benguellensis*, *H. nasutus*, *H. pickersgilli* and *H. pusillus*)

TADPOLE

Length: up to 40 mm. **Shape:** body deep; sides parallel in dorsal view; snout bluntly rounded. **Tail:** muscular; slightly deeper than body; dorsal fin rises gently reaching deepest point a third of the way along tail; terminating in fine tip. **Colour:** body dark brown above; tail muscles and fins mottled dark grey; terminal quarter usually dark; silver speckles along dorsal and ventral fin margins. **Eyes:** lateral. **Nostrils:** small; widely spaced; closer to snout than eyes. **Spiracle:** well below; directed posteriorly at 0°. **Vent:** supramarginal; dextral. **Mouth:** anteroventral; single row of papillae bordering oral disc; two prominent swollen but short papillae at oral angle between jaw sheaths and outer ring of papillae. **Jaw sheaths:** moderate; lower sheath V-shaped. **LTRF:** 1/3(1); third row in lower jaw one-third as long as the second row.

Tadpole: lateral view.   *Right: Dorsal view showing rounded snout.*

Water Lily Frog

Waterleliepadda

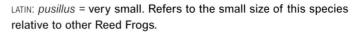

TRACK
71

Hyperolius pusillus (Cope, 1862)

LATIN: *pusillus* = very small. Refers to the small size of this species relative to other Reed Frogs.

Conservation status: Not threatened.

Water Lily Frog: Vernon Crookes Nature Reserve, KwaZulu-Natal. Note eggs under semi-transparent skin of female. Inset: Speckled variation: KwaMbonambi, KwaZulu-Natal.

Description

Maximum size: 25 mm. **Body:** flat; head broad; snout blunt with slightly rounded edges. **Above:** translucent green; sometimes with small black spots or faint dorsolateral stripes. **Underside:** translucent green; often internal organs are visible through ventral body wall. **Hindlimbs:** concealed green or yellowish surfaces of limbs, toes and fingers; webbing moderately extensive; toes with well-developed discs. **Sexual dimorphism:** breeding male has white gular sac with two subsidiary lobes when fully distended.

Call

Series of blurred, high-pitched *chick-chick* clicks. Breeding males call from exposed positions on floating or emergent vegetation

Average length
♀

Average length
♂

Maximum size: 25 mm

at water level. Dense choruses often form after rain. Fighting is common among males, including butting one another with inflated vocal sacs.

Habitat and habits

Open grassy pans, ponds, vleis and dams in open savanna and grassland; often found sitting on floating vegetation, such as water-lily leaves. Breeding activity takes place from early evening and males only leave the breeding site in the early hours of the morning to ascend to higher surrounding trees or other vegetation. About 300 small, light green eggs are laid in clutches of 20 to 120 in a single layer between overlapping lily leaves on the water's surface or in clusters around aquatic vegetation.

Characteristic green eggs on vegetation.

KEY ID POINTS

- Dorsal colour pattern distinct from other species but may be confused with *H. poweri*, *H. benguellensis* and *H. nasutus*
- Snout bluntly rounded (distinct from *H. poweri*, *H. benguellensis*, *H. nasutus* and *H. parkeri*)
- Concealed translucent green or yellow surfaces of body (distinct from other species except *H. poweri*, *H. benguellensis*, *H. parkeri*, *H. pickersgilli* and *H. nasutus*)

TADPOLE

Length: up to 35 mm. **Shape:** body ovoid. **Tail:** shallow fins tapering to sharp tip. **Colour:** greenish-brown; white below; area immediately behind mouth usually transparent; as tadpoles develop they become more green; pale dorsolateral line often present in older tadpoles; tail fin slightly mottled with silvery blotches; tail shaft with black line along upper and lower edge leaving pale stripe in middle; last 30% of tail is often jet-black. **Eyes:** lateral. **Nostrils:** small; widely spaced. **Spiracle:** below; directed 30°. **Vent:** supramarginal; dextral. **Mouth:** anteroventral; single row of small papillae at sides; double row below; all equally sized. **Jaw sheaths:** delicate. **LTRF:** 1/3; third row in lower jaw 75% the length of the first row. **Development:** metamorphosis completed after five to six weeks.

Tadpole: lateral view.

Laurent's Reed Frog

Laurent se rietpadda

Hyperolius rhodesianus Laurent, 1948

Named after Rhodesia, the former name of Zimbabwe.

Conservation status: Not threatened.

Laurent's Reed Frog: Matetse River Bridge, Zimbabwe.

Arné Schiøtz

♀ Average length
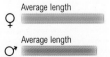

♂ Average length

Maximum size: 28 mm

KEY ID POINTS

- Dorsal colour pattern distinct from other species
- Body stocky and snout rounded (distinct from *H. nasutus, H. poweri, H. benguellensis* and *H. parkeri*)

- Concealed dark red surfaces of body (distinct from other species, except *H. horstockii, H. marmoratus, H. parallelus, H. marginatus* and *H. swynnertoni*)

Description
Maximum size: 28 mm. **Body:** snout truncate; pug-like. **Above:** striking lime-green spots about half the diameter of eye on bright green or yellow background; green spots sometimes with grey centres; flanks granular. **Underside:** white, sometimes infused with strong red vermiculation. **Forelimbs:** hands with small subarticular but no palmar tubercles; webbing moderately extensive. **Hindlimbs:** concealed surfaces of limbs, toes and fingers reddish; webbing extensive; 1 to 1½ phalanges of longest toes free of web; toes with well-developed discs; inner metatarsal tubercle present; outer lacking; subarticular tubercles. **Sexual dimorphism:** gular disc visible in male.

Call
Short, high-pitched *whipp-whipp* whistle; repeated rapidly.

Habitat and habits
Emergent vegetation along margins of swamps, rivers and lakes in all types of savanna, grassland and bush at low altitudes. As an opportunistic species, its breeding habitat varies from temporary to permanent ponds which may be small or large.

TADPOLE
Unknown.

Habitat: Hwange National Park, Zimbabwe.

Roger de la Harpe/IOA

Yellow-striped Reed Frog

Geelstreeprietpadda

TRACK
72

Hyperolius semidiscus Hewitt, 1927

LATIN: *semi* = half; *discus* = disc. Refers to the semicircular gular disc in males.

Conservation status: Not threatened.

Yellow-striped Reed Frog: Port Alfred, Eastern Cape.

Description
Maximum size: 35 mm. **Body:** snout blunt; rounded; sides curved. **Above:** uniform green or olive-brown; conspicuous yellow band edged with a thin black line, from eye or tip of snout over eye, and along flanks; band sometimes broken into rows of spots on flanks. **Underside:** cream or yellow; slightly granular. **Hindlimbs:** small yellow spots nearly always present on legs; concealed yellow to orange-red surfaces of limbs, toes and fingers; webbing reduced, reaching second tubercle of longest finger; toes with well-developed discs. **Sexual dimorphism:** breeding male has dark yellow semicircular gular disc.

Average length
♀

Average length
♂

Maximum size: 35 mm

Call

Harsh croak followed by a short creak. Breeding males call from floating vegetation, such as water-lilies, or from elevated positions on emergent vegetation or trees beside the water.

Habitat and habits

Low-lying areas of east-coast savanna. Breeds in rivers, pans, pools and dams, in moderately deep water with dense reed beds and emergent vegetation along the banks. About 200 eggs are laid in clutches of about 30, loosely attached to vegetation just below the surface of the water.

Note blunt, rounded snout: Kowie River, Eastern Cape.

KEY ID POINTS

- Concealed dark yellow to orange-red surfaces of body (distinct from all other species, except *H. argus*, *H. marmoratus*, *H. mitchelli*, *H. tuberilinguis* and *H. swynnertoni*)
- Dorsal colour pattern distinct from other species
- Body stocky and snout rounded (distinct from *H. nasutus*, *H. acuticeps*, *H. benguellensis* and *H. parkeri*)

TADPOLE

Length: Up to 48 mm. **Shape:** body ovoid. **Tail:** fin deep; tapers to sharp tip. **Colour:** light brown; white below; tail fin uniformly mottled without stripes or dark terminal tip. **Eyes:** lateral. **Nostrils:** small; widely spaced; on snout edge. **Spiracle:** just below body axis; directed backwards at about $10°$. **Vent:** supramarginal, dextral. **Mouth:** anteroventral; single row of small papillae at sides; double row below, with small gap in middle. **Jaw sheaths:** Moderate. **LTRF:** 1/3; third row in lower jaw very short.

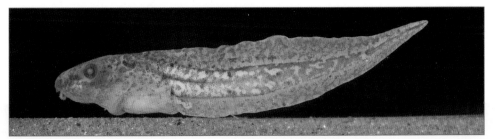

Tadpole: lateral view.

Swynnerton's Reed Frog

TRACK
73

Swynnerton se rietpadda

Hyperolius swynnertoni FitzSimons, 1941

■ *'Swynnertoni' form*
■ *'Broadleyi' form*

This is an unresolved species and currently comprises two forms referred to as the *'broadleyi'* form and the *'swynnertoni'* form. They will probably be treated as separate species in future.

Named after R.J.M. Swynnerton, director of agriculture in Kenya in the 1930s.

Conservation status: Not threatened.

Swynnerton's Reed Frog, 'swynnertoni' form: Chimanimani, Zimbabwe.

♀ Average length
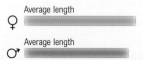

♂ Average length

Maximum size: 38 mm

Description

Maximum size: 38 mm. **Body:** snout rounded. *'Broadleyi'* form: Broad dark paravertebral bands and lateral bands leaving pale vertebral and dorsolateral bands, each with a thin red line in the centre. Dark bands may break up into blotches that tends to fuse. *'Swynnertoni'* form: Pale beige or off-white; dark rather dense reticulations often fusing to form a uniform black background, or dark or light speckling. **Underside:** off-white; granular. **Forelimbs:** subarticular tubercles on hands moderately developed; no palmar tubercles; webbing moderate to extensive. **Hindlimbs:** concealed reddish surfaces of limbs, toes and fingers; webbing extensive; only 1 to 1½ phalanges of longest toes free of web; toes with well-developed discs; inner and small outer metatarsal tubercle present; subarticular tubercles well developed. **Sexual dimorphism:** gular disc in male; some males uniformly brown, usually have a paravertebral band with thin yellow vertebral line and a pale broken dorsolateral line extending from eye.

KEY ID POINTS

- Dorsal colour pattern distinct from other species
- Body stocky and snout rounded (distinct from *H. nasutus*, *H. poweri*, *H. benguellensis* and *H. parkeri*)
- Concealed dark red surfaces of body (distinct from other species, except *H. horstockii*, *H. marmoratus*, *H. parallelus*, *H. marginatus* and *H. rhodesianus*)

Call

Short, sharp whistles about a second apart.

Habitat and habits

Emergent vegetation at margins of swamps, rivers and lakes in all types of savanna, grassland and forest as well as in human-modified habitats, such as cultivated lands and gardens.

TADPOLE

Unknown.

Above left: **'swynnertoni'** *form: Chimanimani, Zimbabwe.*
Above right: **'broadleyi'** *form: Chirinda Forest, Zimbabwe.*

Tinker Reed Frog

Groenrietpadda

TRACK
74

Hyperolius tuberilinguis Smith, 1849

LATIN: *tuber* = swelling; *lingua* = tongue. Refers to a papilla
that is present on the tongue.

Conservation status: Not threatened.

Tinker Reed Frog; yellow colour pattern: Tshaneni, Swaziland.

Description

Maximum size: 36 mm. **Body:** snout pointed
with straight sides. **Above:** uniform lime-
green or yellow; pale-coloured backwards-
pointing triangle may be present between
eyes; juveniles brown or mottled green with
geometric pattern. **Underside:** cream; granular.
Hindlimbs: concealed yellow or orange
surfaces of limbs, toes and fingers; webbing
reaching middle tubercle of longest toe; toes
with well-developed discs. **Sexual dimorphism:**
breeding male has yellow gular sac.

Average length
♀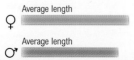

Average length
♂

Maximum size: 36 mm

Call

Two or three sharp staccato taps with long intervening silences. The advertisement call may be preceded by growl-like croak when other calling males venture too close. Large numbers of males call from emergent vegetation just above water level, diving into the water if disturbed. Calling lasts from early evening until early hours of the morning.

Males call low down in vegetation.

Egg mass above water level.

KEY ID POINTS

- Dorsal colour pattern distinct from other species
- Body stocky and snout rounded (distinct from *H. nasutus*, *H. poweri*, *H. benguellensis* and *H. parkeri*)
- Concealed dark yellow to orange surfaces of body (distinct from other species, except *H. argus*, *H. marmoratus*, *H. mitchelli*, *H. semidiscus* and *H. swynnertoni*)

Habitat and habits

Breeds in moderately deep waters with dense vegetation along rivers or in pans, pools and dams in low-lying areas of savanna; especially in coastal bushveld and grassveld. Readily occupies artificial ponds and garden water features. About 300–400 sticky white eggs are laid in a cluster, attached to vegetation just above the water level.

TADPOLE

Length: up to 46 mm. **Shape:** body ovoid; anteriorly dorsoventrally flattened. **Tail:** fins deep; curved; deepest in middle of tail; tapers to sharp tip. **Colour:** mottled brown; stippled below; tail shaft dark with middle third very dark; outer tail fin margin heavily mottled to form dark stripe along margins. **Eyes:** two or three rows of small papillae at sides and below; several long, finger-like papillae below. **Nostrils:** small; widely spaced; on snout edge. **Spiracle:** just below body axis, directed at $10°$. **Vent:** supramarginal; dextral. **Mouth:** ventral. **Jaw sheaths:** heavy; weakly curved. **LTRF:** 1/3; third row in lower jaw about 30% of the length of first row.

Tadpole: lateral view.

KASSINAS

VLEIPADDAS

Kassina Girard, 1853

Named after John Cassin (1813-1869), a prominent naturalist at the Academy of Natural Sciences in Philadelphia, USA.

16 species, two in southern Africa

Bubbling Kassina, showing bullet-shaped body.

The southern African species are easily distinguished from one other. However, the Bubbling Kassina *K. senegalensis* is similar to the Rattling Frog *Semnodactylus wealii*. The latter can be distinguished by its longitudinally divided dorsal stripes and yellow feet.The Red-legged Kassina *K. maculata* may be confused with some of the Tree Frog species *Leptopelis* but the dark dorsal spots on the Kassina have a pale outline that is absent from the markings on Tree Frogs.

DISTINCTIVE CHARACTERS

ADULT
- Pupil vertical
- Body bullet-shaped with smoothly rounded snout
- Toes slightly webbed
- Tympanum hidden
- Inner metatarsal tubercle absent or poorly developed
- Angle approximately the same between all fingers
- Tends to run rather than hop
- Smooth, rounded snout

TADPOLE
- Tail very deep and often bright red
- Keratinised jaw sheaths massive and pigmented to the base
- Vent supramarginal and dextral

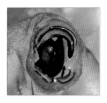

Kassinas occur in the moister regions within the summer-rainfall areas of southern Africa. *K. senegalensis* is very widespread in both tropical and temperate regions and its call is a familiar evening sound. *K. maculata* is confined to humid tropical areas.

Calling and breeding occurs from when the rains begin until late in February. Breeding habitats include any temporary or permanent water bodies. Both species start calling in the late afternoon and continue into the evening; initially *K. senegalensis* calls from concealed sites well away from the water. Female *K. senegalensis* approach calling males on dry terrain and the amplecting pair then makes its way towards the water in which 100 to 500 eggs are deposited. The pair dives well beneath the water surface, and while the female clasps onto vegetation, she releases her eggs singly or in groups of up to 20 and they either drop to the bottom of the pond or they may become attached to vegetation. *K. maculata* favours deeper, more permanent sites than does *K. senegalensis* and generally calls from emergent vegetation well away from the banks. Mating takes place in water and up to 600 eggs are attached to submerged vegetation.

Kassina tadpoles have characteristically deep fins with a high upper fin that is often infused with bright yellow or red. Keratinised jaw sheaths are heavy and deep. The tadpoles are ferocious feeders on plant material.

KEY TO SPECIES

ADULT
1 Bold, dark longitudinal vertebral and paravertebral bands .... **Bubbling Kassina** *K. senegalensis* (p.276)
  Large circular spots with pale borders .... **Red-legged Kassina** *K. maculata* (p.274)

TADPOLE
1 Two interrupted labial tooth rows in the lower jaw; no gap below in row or oral papillae; dorsal fin starts off gradually on top of the head from a position behind the eye .... *K. senegalensis* (p.276)
  Two interrupted labial tooth rows, plus a very short third labial tooth row in the lower jaw; dorsal fin starts out with a steep angle on top of the head from the level of the eye .... *K. maculata* (p.274)

Red-legged Kassina

Rooibeenvleipadda

TRACK
75

Kassina maculata (Duméril, 1853)

LATIN: *maculata* = spot. Refers to the spotted dorsal colour pattern.

Conservation status: Not threatened.

Red-legged Kassina: Sodwana Bay, KwaZulu-Natal.

Description
Maximum size: 68 mm. **Body**: robust; bullet-shaped with protruding eyes; skin texture smooth to slightly granular; if handled, its skin secretion leaves a characteristic smell on the hands. **Above**: beige to grey background with large dark brown spots bordered by a thin pale line; skin smooth.

Underside: white and granular. **Limbs**: groin and armpits infused with scarlet; small terminal bulbous discs on fingers and toes. **Sexual dimorphism**: male gular disc laterally oval and grey-brown in colour; folds of the vocal sac visible from the side; female vent pointing downwards and surrounded by lobes covered in small spines.

Average length
♀

Average length
♂

Maximum size: 68 mm

KEY ID POINTS

- Large dark spots with pale outline on beige background (distinct from *K. senegalensis*)
- Groin and armpits infused with red (distinct from *K. senegalensis*)
- Bulbous discs on fingers and toes (distinct from *K. senegalensis*)
- Underside granular and white (distinct from *K. senegalensis*)

Call

Short sharp *quack* or *wêp* repeated at short intervals. Choruses begin in the late afternoon and build up as evening draws on. At first, males call from well-concealed positions in dense emergent vegetation in deep water, but as the nightly chorus intensifies, they climb up to more elevated sites.

Note red infusions on legs.

Habitat and habits

Densely vegetated permanent or semi-permanent water bodies in tropical, low-lying areas of coastal bush and savanna. By day takes refuge in the axils of large-leafed plants. Breeds in moderately deep waters in which there is dense vegetation. Eggs may be laid singly or in groups of four to five; they are submerged and attached to vegetation.

TADPOLE

Length: up to 130 mm. **Shape:** body is ovoid and deep. **Tail:** anterior very muscular; upper tail fin very high, starting at back of head and rising sharply to reach deepest point about thirdway along tail; tapers gradually to acute tip. **Colour:** mottled brown; fin is usually darkly mottled but may be bright red; underside immaculate. **Eyes:** lateral. **Nostrils:** small; widely spaced; close to tip of snout. **Spiracle:** below body axis; directed posteriorly at $20°$. **Vent:** supramarginal; dextral. **Mouth:** anterior; gap in middle of lower jaw papillae. **Jaw sheaths:** massive; additional accessory plates on each side of lower jaw sheath. **LTRF:** 1/3; third row in lower jaw about 30% of the length of first row. **Development:** may take two to three months.

Tadpole: lateral view.

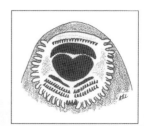

Mouthparts showing massive jaw sheath.

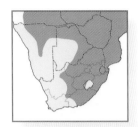

Bubbling Kassina

Borrelvleipadda

TRACK
76

Kassina senegalensis (Duméril & Bibron, 1841)

Named after Senegal, the West African country in which this species was first found and scientifically described.

Conservation status: Not threatened.

Bubbling Kassina: Suikerbosrand, Gauteng.

Description
Maximum size: 49 mm. **Body:** bullet-shaped and smooth-skinned; eyes large and protruding. **Above:** solid, bold black vertebral band and a pair of broken paravertebral bands on a yellow, olive or silver-beige background; skin smooth. **Underside:** off-white; smooth anteriorly and granular posteriorly. **Limbs:** toes slightly webbed and whitish; toes and fingers lack terminal discs or bulbs. **Sexual dimorphism:** male with a grey-brown, longitudinally elliptical gular disc with dark lateral folds; female vent surrounded by two pairs of lobes covered in small spines.

Call
Short, ventriloquial *boip*, on a rising note with long intervals between calls. Males begin their calling in late afternoon, well away from water. As darkness descends they move closer to water until eventually they occupy semi-concealed positions at the water's edge. When a male calls, he triggers calls from his neighbours with the result that choruses have a rippling or bubbling effect.

Average length

♀

Average length

♂

Maximum size: 49 mm

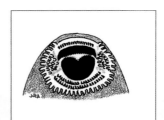
KEY ID POINTS

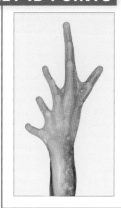

- Solid (undivided) vertebral and paravertebral bands down centre of body (distinct from *Semnodactylus wealii*)
- Toes without terminal discs or bulbs (distinct from *K. maculata*)
- Hands and feet whitish (distinct from *S. wealii*)
- Underside smooth anteriorly and granular posteriorly (distinct from *K. maculata*)

- Gular disc of the male is longitudinally oval (distinct from *K. maculata*)

Habitat and habits

Grassland around vleis and pans. Breeds in temporary and permanent water bodies, including vleis, marshes, pans, ponds and dams. Females approach calling males on dry terrain and the amplecting pair then makes its way towards the water in which 100 to 500 eggs are deposited. The pair dives well beneath the water surface, and while the female clasps vegetation, she releases her eggs singly or in groups of up to 20; and they either drop to the bottom of the pond or they may become attached to vegetation.

Unusual colour pattern: Bloemfontein, Free State.

TADPOLE

Length: up to 80 mm. **Shape:** large; body ovoid and deep. **Tail:** tail deep and keel-like; arises from level of eyes to reach deepest point about thirdway along the length; tapers to acute tip. **Colour:** mottled brown to dark olive; fin slightly mottled and usually bright red; underside immaculate. **Eyes:** lateral. **Nostrils:** small; widely spaced; close to tip of snout. **Spiracle:** below body axis; directed posteriorly at angle of 20°. **Vent:** supramarginal; dextral. **Mouth:** anterior; gap in middle of lower jaw papillae. **Jaw sheaths:** massive; deep; pigmented to base; hardened plate on each side. **LTRF:** 1/2(1). **Development:** slow; metamorphosis may take two to three months. **Behaviour:** in the middle of the day they feed close to the surface in midwater; voracious feeders consuming large amounts of plant material.

Tadpole: lateral view.

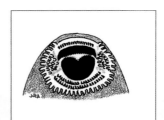

Mouthparts showing massive jaw sheath.

RATTLING FROG

RATELPADDA

Semnodactylus Hoffman, 1939

GREEK: *semnos* = mysterious; *dactylos* = finger. Refers to the zygodactylous hand, where the angle between the third and fourth finger is small and the angle between the second and third large.

Only one species in the genus

Rattling Frog

Ratelpadda

TRACK
77

Semnodactylus wealii (Boulenger, 1882)

Named after F.P.M. Weale, resident of the Kaffraria region of the Eastern Cape.

Conservation status: Not threatened.

Rattling Frog: Ladybrand, Free State. Note divided dorsal and lateral bands and yellow feet.

Average length
♀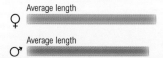

Average length
♂

Maximum size: 44 mm

DISTINCTIVE CHARACTERS

ADULT
- Pupil vertical
- Centrally divided dark vertebral and paravertebral bands (distinct from *Kassina senegalensis*)
- Hands and feet yellow (distinct from *K. senegalensis*)
- Underside coarsely granular throughout (distinct from *K. senegalensis*)
- Large angle between second and third fingers but very small between third and fourth (distinct from all other species)

TADPOLE
- Silver stripe along tail shaft

Description

Maximum size: 44 mm. **Body:** bears a superficial resemblance to the Bubbling Kassina *K. sengalensis* but can be distinguished by its longitudinally divided dorsal stripes; bullet-shaped and smooth-skinned with large protruding eyes. **Above:** yellow, olive or silver-beige background with a dark vertebral band from between the eyes to vent, split along its length; dark paravertebral bands along the posterior two-thirds of the back, divided longitudinally; flanks with broken or irregular dark bands. **Pupil:** vertical. **Tympanum:** concealed. **Underside:** off-white and granular, often with a dark network between granulations. **Hindlimbs:** arms and legs long and slender; hands and feet bright yellow, as are concealed parts of the hindlegs; fingers and toes long, lacking terminal discs or bulbs. **Sexual dimorphism:** male vocal sac transversely oval and darkly pigmented.

Call

Short, coarse rattle. Initially males usually call from concealed positions under tufts of grass, but as the number of callers increases, they climb to more elevated sites on grass stems or piles of exposed soil.

Defensive posture shamming death.

Habitat and habits

Summer- and winter-rainfall areas. Inhabit well-vegetated areas around pans and vleis in grassland or in fynbos heath in the south of its range. Fingers are arranged into partially opposing pairs and this probably enables the frog to climb grass stems. Tends to walk or run rather than hop and, if disturbed, feigns death by curling up and remaining motionless with feet tucked under the body.

Breeds in temporary or permanent water bodies, especially well-vegetated vleis, pans and marshy land. The male rattling call can be heard in explosive bursts in the late afternoon or on overcast days. Males and females meet some distance away from water and amplectant pairs walk to it. In southern Africa Rattling Frogs breed from September to the end of February, depositing 100 to 300 individual eggs onto submerged vegetation in shallow water.

Rattling Frogs tend to climb and cling to vegetation: Ladybrand, Free State.

TADPOLE

Length: up to 58 mm. **Shape:** body ovoid and deep. **Tail:** muscular; fin begins on top of head, reaching deepest point not more than thirdway along the tail; tapers gradually to fine tip. **Colour:** brown to dark olive-brown above; characteristic and very prominent silver stripe along middle of tail shaft. **Eyes:** lateral. **Nostrils:** small; widely spaced; closer to snout than to eyes. **Spiracle:** well below body axis; directed posteriorly. **Vent:** supramarginal; dextral. **Mouth:** anterior; three rows of papillae at mouth corners; double row below without gaps. **Jaw sheaths:** massive; pigmented to base; hardened plate on each side of jaw sheath. **LTRF:** 1/3; third row in lower jaw very short. **Development:** about eight weeks; developing legs are yellow. **Behaviour:** voracious feeders, consuming large amounts of plant material.

Tadpole: lateral view showing prominent silver stripe.

Mouthparts.

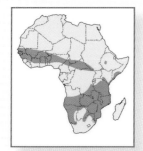

RUBBER FROGS

RUBBERPADDAS

Phrynomantis Peters, 1867

GREEK: *phryne* = toad; *mantis* = leaf (foliage). It is not clear why
Peters ascribed this name to the genus.

Five species, three in southern Africa

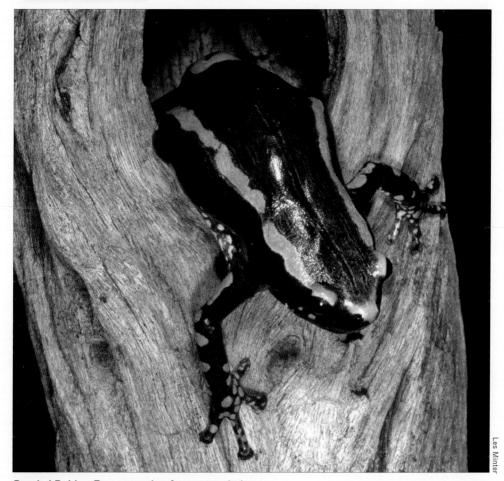

Banded Rubber Frog emerging from a tree hole.

In overall appearance there is little variation within the genus. The head is narrow and
the long neck allows Rubber Frogs to move their heads to some extent from side to side.
They have aposematic colouring with cream, orange and red to brick-red markings on
a dark grey to black background. The skin is rubbery and contains high concentrations
of cardiotoxins that may kill other frogs if they are placed in the same container as
Rubber Frogs. Fingertips are usually slightly expanded (not in *P. affinis*). The pupil is

circular. Webbing between fingers and between toes is reduced or absent. Limbs are long and slender.

Habitats range from the edges of gallery forests to arid and barren environments.

Rubber Frogs tend to walk rather than hop. They can inflate and arch the body, most likely so as to appear large and menacing in order to scare off predators. Although most species have toe discs, they generally remain at ground level, but they can climb and hide in crevices or in holes in tree trunks. They breed in both temporary and permanent water bodies.

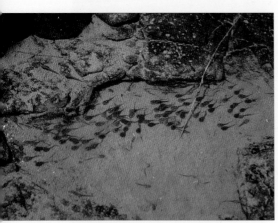

Tadpoles orientated in one direction

DISTINCTIVE CHARACTERS

ADULT
- Skin soft and rubbery
- Neck long and head narrow
- Markings orange to red, background dark to black
- Webbing between toes reduced or absent
- Toxic skin secretions may kill other frogs
- Pupil circular

TADPOLE
- Gregarious, forming dense schools in midwater, individuals orientated in one direction
- Filter feeders
- Keratinised mouthparts absent
- Single mid-ventral spiracle
- Deep fins terminate in acute tip

KEY TO SPECIES

ADULT
1 Two broad paravertebral reddish bands running from snout over eyes to flanks ....
.... **Banded Rubber Frog** *P. bifasciatus* (p.288)

   Reddish spots or blotches on dorsum but no solid bands **2**

2 Asymmetrical irregular patches on dorsum .... **Marbled Rubber Frog** *P. annectens* (p.286)

   Small reddish spots, roughly in two dorsolateral bands .... **Spotted Rubber Frog** *P. affinis* (p.284)

TADPOLE
P. affinis – tadpole is unknown.

1 Spiracle close to posterior end of trunk; dorsum silvery with black vertebral line .... *P. bifasciatus* (p.288)

2 Spiracle about 75% from mouth along the body; dorsum mottled silver and black ... *P. annectens* (p.286)

Marbled Rubber Frog: note flattened vocal sac of calling male.

Amplectant pair of Marbled Rubber Frogs: Karibib, Namibia.

Spotted Rubber Frog

Gespikkelde rubberpadda

Phrynomantis affinis Boulenger, 1901

LATIN: *affinis* = neighbouring. Not dissimilar to *P. bifasciatus* to which it is closely related.

Conservation status: Not threatened.

Spotted Rubber Frog: Namibia.

Mike Griffin

Identification

Maximum size: 65 mm. Body: flattened; elongated; when viewed from above, the head resembles that of the Platanna (*Xenopus*); snout extends over mouth; horizontal diameter of eye about two-thirds of distance between eye and tip of snout. **Above:** back with small orange or red spots, to some extent aligned in dorsolateral bands running from nostril, above eye, to vent; scattering of reddish spots on upper jaw; skin texture slightly

Average length

♀

Average length

♂

Maximum size: 65 mm

KEY ID POINTS

- Small reddish spots more or less in two dorsolateral bands on dark background (distinct from other species)
- Underside colour not known
- Tips of toes lack discs (distinct from other species)
- Toes lack webbing (distinct from other species)

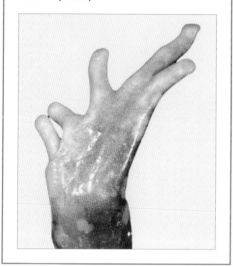

Wulf Haacke

Dark colour variation.

granular. **Underside:** colour not known. **Forelimbs:** arms short; dark brown or black with scattered pale reddish spots extending to fingers; fingertips without discs. **Hindlimbs:** legs short; dark brown or black with scattered pale reddish spots extending to toes; toes without webbing; toe tips without discs.

Call
Unknown.

Habitat and habits
Sandy and rocky country in dry savanna.

TADPOLE

Shape: body broad and deep. **Tail:** fin deep, convex in profile; reaches deepest point in middle of tail; tip tapers to acute tip. **Colour:** dorsally body has dark pigmentation. **Nostrils:** small; very narrowly spaced. **Spiracle:** single spiracle; opening situated mid-ventrally. **Mouth:** anterior; wide with soft borders; no oral papillae; labial tooth rows or jaw sheaths; small skin folds on lower lip; mouth has prominent fold in lower lip. **Jaw sheaths:** absent. **LTRF:** absent.

Angelo Lambiris

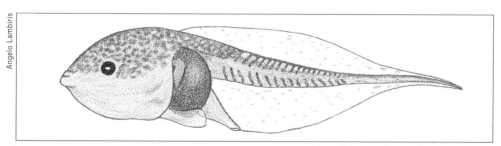

Tadpole: lateral view.

Marbled Rubber Frog

Marmerrubberpadda

TRACK 78

Phrynomantis annectens Werner, 1910

LATIN: *annexum* = to connect. The relevance of the name is not known.

Conservation status: Not threatened.

Marbled Rubber Frog: Augrabies, Northern Cape.

Identification
Maximum size: 40 mm. **Body:** flattened; elongated; eyes small. **Above:** dark brown, black or silver-black; bold irregular red, orange, pink, yellow, silver or golden patches; skin smooth. **Underside:** pinkish-brown; smooth. **Forelimbs:** arms short; fingertips enlarged to form small discs. **Hindlimbs:** legs short, webbing reduced; small discs on toes. **Sexual dimorphism:** male throat dark.

Call
Long, insect-like trill lasting up to 12 seconds;

Average length

♀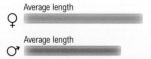

Average length

♂

Maximum size: 40 mm

KEY ID POINTS

- Irregular asymmetrical reddish blotches on dark background (distinct from other species)
- Underside pinkish-brown (distinct from other species)

- Tips of fingers and toes dilated to form small discs (distinct from *P. affinis*)
- Toes slightly webbed (distinct from *P. affinis*)

ventriloquial. Males call from exposed or partially concealed positions under rocks, in crevices, in shallow water, or from the edges of pools, sometimes even metres away from the water. A territorial call consisting of a series of shorter notes is uttered if an intruding male comes too close, in which case the intruder is usually attacked and a brief wrestling bout follows.

Habitat and habits
Arid environments; closely associated with inselbergs and rocky areas.

Tadpoles in rock pool: note orientation.

TADPOLE
Length: up to 50 mm. **Shape:** head broad, dorsoventrally flattened. **Tail:** fin deep; and convex in profile; reaching deepest point in middle of tail; tapering to acute tip. **Colour:** back with dense, dark pigmentation and scattered golden flecks; golden line stretching from body along upper edge of tail muscles; ventrally without pigmentation except for dark abdomen; dorsal and ventral margins of fins with dark pigmentation and scattered red, gold and brown infusions. **Nostrils:** small; narrowly spaced. **Spiracle:** single spiracle; opening mid ventral. **Mouth:** anterior; wide with soft borders; no oral papillae; prominent fold in lower lip. **Jaw sheaths:** absent. **LTRF:** absent. **Development:** completed within eight weeks. **Behaviour:** gregarious, forming dense schools, orientated in same direction, resembling a squadron of fighter planes; feed on suspended algae in mid water.

Tadpole: dorsolateral view. Note gold pigmentation.

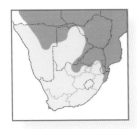

Banded Rubber Frog

TRACK
79

Gebande rubberpadda

Phrynomantis bifasciatus (Smith, 1847)

LATIN: *bi* = two; *fascia* = band. Refers to the two paravertebral red bands on the back.

Conservation status: Not threatened.

Banded Rubber Frog: Manzini, Swaziland.

Description

Maximum size: 65 mm. **Body:** elongated; flattened; pear-shaped with narrow head; eyes small. **Above:** black or dark gold sheen; two broad paravertebral reddish bands running from snout over eyes to flanks; short reddish band low down on back just above cloaca; bands and spots varying from deep crimson to almost white; skin smooth, shiny, rubbery.

Average length

♀

Average length

♂

Maximum size: 65 mm

KEY ID POINTS

- Underside grey with numerous white spots and blotches (distinct from other species)
- Two paravertebral red bands on dark background (distinct from other species)
- Tips of fingers and toes dilated to form discs (distinct from *P. affinis*)
- Toes slightly webbed (distinct from *P. affinis*)

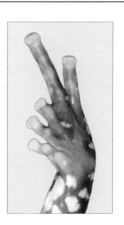

Tympanum: small. **Underside:** greyish with white spots and blotches; spots on throat small or sometimes absent; skin smooth, shiny, rubbery. **Hindlimbs:** arms and legs with reddish spots or blotches; webbing almost absent; small truncated discs on fingers and toes. **Sexual dimorphism:** male throat dark.

Call

Long, high-pitched melodious *pirrrrrrrrrrr* trill lasting up to three seconds. Males call from concealed or semi-concealed positions at the water's edge among vegetation, under rocks or logs or even from depressions in the mud made by the hoofs of animals.

Habitat and habits

Hot semi-arid to subtropical environments; savanna woodland, grassland and wide variety of bushveld vegetation types; also agriculturally developed areas.

TADPOLE

Length: up to 37 mm. **Shape:** flattened; head wide. **Tail:** fin deep; tapering abruptly into long thread-like acute tip. **Colour:** dark; many iridiophores along midline; tail with broad longitudinal dark bands and sometimes a narrow red band; gill region transparent; abdomen white. **Eyes:** lateral. **Nostrils:** small; narrowly spaced. **Spiracle:** single; opening mid ventral. **Mouth:** anterior; wide with soft borders; no oral papillae; prominent fold in lower lip. **Jaw sheaths:** absent. **LTRF:** absent. **Development:** complete in eight weeks or longer. **Behaviour:** usually gregarious, forming dense schools; feed on suspended algae in mid water; swim head-up, unlike the Platanna (*Xenopus*).

Tadpole: lateral view.

Dorsal view: note extended lip.

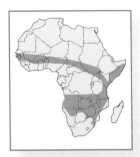

PUDDLE FROGS

MODDERPADDAS

Phrynobatrachus Günther, 1862

GREEK: *phryne* = toad; *batrachos* = frog. Refers to the toad-like appearance of the genus.

76 species, four in southern Africa

Snoring Puddle Frog: note toad-like, warty skin surface.

The southern African species are small – less than 30 mm – and somewhat similar in appearance. They are generally drab except for occasional colourful vertebral bands. A distinctive feature of the genus is the characteristic tarsal tubercle halfway along the tarsus. Positive identification of each species requires careful inspection of all the characters provided.

Puddle Frogs are found in a variety of wetland habitats in the summer rainfall regions of southern Africa where annual rainfall exceeds 600 mm. Breeding takes

DISTINCTIVE CHARACTERS

ADULT
- Body squat, head narrow, snout pointed
- Tarsal tubercle halfway along the tarsus
- Fingers lack webbing
- Pupil horizontal

TADPOLE
- Internarial distance greater than 10 times the nostril width
- Vent marginal and dextral

place in shallow standing water throughout the summer months. Males call at breeding sites from mid afternoon and may persist through most of the night. Eggs are laid underwater or deposited in a single floating layer which remains on the surface for a few hours before gradually sinking and dispersing when disturbed. The small tadpoles metamorphose rapidly in warm shallow water.

Eggs float on water surface.

KEY TO SPECIES

ADULT

1 Webbing prominent – less than 2½ phalanges of longest toe free **2**
   Webbing reduced – more than three phalanges of longest toe free **3**
2 Pair of elongated, usually chevron-shaped, skin ridges in shoulder region ....
   .... **East African Puddle Frog** *P. acridoides* (p.292)
   Warts may be oval but do not form an elongated ridge .... **Snoring Puddle Frog** *P. natalensis* (p.296)
3 Abdomen heavily spotted or speckled, at least posteriorly .... **Small Puddle Frog** *P. parvulus* (p.298)
   Rear half of abdomen immaculate .... **Dwarf Puddle Frog** *P. mababiensis* (p.294)

TADPOLE

1 Single labial tooth row in the upper jaw; jaw sheaths very narrow; a row of widely spaced, very long papillae bordering lower jaw .... *P. mababiensis* (p.294)
   More than one labial tooth row in the upper jaw; jaw sheaths moderate; no extra long papillae bordering lower jaw .... *P. natalensis* (p.296) and *P. acridoides* (p.292) (not separable)
   P. parvulus – tadpole cannot be identified by key .... (p.298)

East African Puddle Frog

Oostelike modderpadda

Phrynobatrachus acridoides (Cope, 1867)

Acrididae are the cricket family. Possibly refers to the cricket-like call.

Conservation status: Not threatened.

East African Puddle Frog: Malawi.

Description

Maximum size: 30 mm. **Body:** chubby; pointed snout. **Above:** grey-brown to tan, sometimes with a few darker blotches; light vertebral line or band usually present; pair of longitudinal ridges (usually chevron-shaped) running from behind eye to shoulder region, often enclosing a greenish, reddish or yellowish band; skin mostly smooth with few scattered warts. **Tympanum:** visible.

Underside: heavily mottled grey, especially on hind part of abdomen and on ventral surface of thighs. **Forelimbs:** hands with distinct subdigital tubercles. **Hindlimbs:** posterior face of thigh with light and dark mottling, sometimes forming longitudinal stripes; webbing variable; two phalanges of longest toe free of webbing; subarticular tubercles distinct and separate from tarsal fold; toe tips expanded into bulbous swellings.

Average length
♀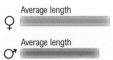

Average length
♂

Maximum size: 30 mm

KEY ID POINTS

- Dorsal skin generally smooth with a pair of longitudinal chevron-shaped ridges from behind the eye over the shoulder region (distinct from other species)
- Toe tips dilated to form terminal bulbs (distinct from other species except occasionally *P. natalensis*)
- At least two phalanges of longest toe free of webbing (distinct from *P. mababiensis*)

- Mottling behind the thigh sometimes forming longitudinal stripes (compare with *P. parvulus*)

- Tarsal tubercle separate from tarsal fold (distinct from *P. mababiensis*)
- No bands on jaw (distinct from *P. mababiensis* and occasionally *P. parvulus*)

Colour variation with broad vertebral band: Kosi Bay, KwaZulu-Natal.

Sexual dimorphism: male with small folds in vocal pouch running parallel to jaw-line; gular pouch dark in male, freckled in female.

Call
Slow, continuous harsh *waak, waak, waak* snore. Males call by day and night from semi-concealed positions in shallow water or among vegetation on the bank.

Habitat and habits
Dry and humid savannas, shrubland, grassland and coastal habitats; tolerates altered habitats. Opportunistic species that breeds in pans, roadside ditches, flooded grassy depressions, puddles, pools, swamps and vleis. Eggs are laid in clumps attached to vegetation just below the water surface.

TADPOLE
Shape: body small, oval, fat. **Tail:** 1½ times as long as body; dorsal fin deepest halfway along length. **Colour:** brown. **Eyes:** large; dorsal. **Nostrils:** small; widely spaced; closer to tip of snout than to eyes. **Spiracle:** small; well below body axis. **Vent:** marginal; dextral. **Mouth:** single row of small papillae laterally; double row dorsolaterally; ventrally an additional characteristic row of long, finger-like papillae. **Jaw sheaths:** delicate; finely pigmented. **LTRF:** 1/2; inner lower row V-shaped.

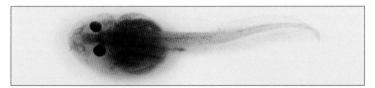
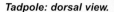

Tadpole: dorsal view.

Mouthparts.

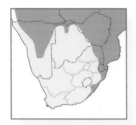

Dwarf Puddle Frog

Dwergmodderpadda

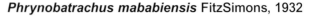

TRACK 81

Phrynobatrachus mababiensis FitzSimons, 1932

Named after the Mababe Depression in Botswana where this species was first collected.

Conservation status: Not threatened.

Dwarf Puddle Frog: Nelspruit, Mpumalanga.

Description

Maximum size: 21 mm. **Body:** small; chubby; snout pointed. **Above:** grey to brown with dark or light markings; green, red or yellow vertebral line or band sometimes present; interorbital triangle pointing backwards; elongated dark patches usually on both sides low down on back; jaws banded, with bands on upper and lower jaws corresponding; skin with many small warts; pair of elongated warts in shoulder region but no skin ridges. **Tympanum:** rarely visible. **Underside:** chest usually speckled grey; rear half of abdomen white, sometimes with yellow infusions in groin; skin smooth. **Forelimbs:** hands with distinct subdigital tubercles; palmar tubercles large. **Hindlimbs:** webbing poorly developed; at least 3¾ phalanges of longest toe free of webbing;

Average length
♀

Average length
♂

Maximum size: 21 mm

KEY ID POINTS

- Dorsal skin with many warts including a conspicuous pair on the shoulders, but not elongated into ridges (distinct from *P. acridoides*)

- Toe tips not expanded into terminal bulbs (distinct from *P. acridoides* and occasionally *P. natalensis*)
- At least 3½ phalanges of longest toe free of webbing (distinct from *P. acridoides* and *P. natalensis*)
- No bands or stripes behind the thigh (distinct from *P. acridoides* and *P. parvulus*)
- Tarsal tubercle fused with tarsal fold (distinct from other species)
- Corresponding bands on upper and lower jaw (distinct from other species and occasionally *P. parvulus*)

tarsal fold present; well-developed inner metatarsal tubercle a continuation of tarsal fold; small outer metatarsal tubercle; toe and fingertips not expanded. **Sexual dimorphism:** male smaller; throat speckled-grey to black with a transverse fold; female throat immaculate.

Call

Insect-like buzz lasting about one second, frequently followed by few clicks. Males call from concealed positions at base of vegetation near or in shallow water. Chorus peaks at dusk, diminishing after nightfall. On overcast days, calling continues all day.

Habitat and habits

Open wooded savanna, sometimes grassland at high and low altitudes; survives in agricultural land. Breeds among emergent vegetation in permanent, semi-permanent and temporary marshy areas, vleis, ponds, slow-flowing streams, the edges of small pans, and shallow stagnant water. Eggs are laid in a dense mass and float on the surface among emergent vegetation.

TADPOLE

Length: up to 18 mm. **Shape:** body oval; snout blunt. **Tail:** fin of moderate depth, reaching deepest point around middle of tail; tapering into fine point. **Colour:** abdomen dark with silver iridiophores; throat and gill region transparent. **Eyes:** dorsolateral. **Nostrils:** small; widely spaced; almost at tip of snout. **Spiracle:** below; directed backwards and slightly upwards. **Vent:** marginal; dextral. **Mouth:** oral disc bordered by single row of small rounded papillae laterally and posteriorly; second row behind mouth corner; posteriorly mouth bordered by additional row of much longer papillae. **Jaw sheaths:** very thin; slightly flexed. **LTRF:** 1/3. **Development:** complete in about five weeks.

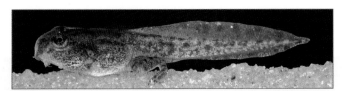

Tadpole: lateral view.

Mouthparts: note delicate structure with long papillae.

Snoring Puddle Frog

TRACK
82

Snorkmodderpadda

Phrynobatrachus natalensis (Smith, 1849)

Named after KwaZulu-Natal (formerly Natal) where the species occurs.

Conservation status: Not threatened.

Above and insets: Snoring Puddle Frog with range of colour variations: De Hoek, Gauteng.

Description

Maximum size: 40 mm. **Body:** chubby with small head and pointed snout; eyes close-set. **Above:** light to dark grey or brown, sometimes greenish-brown; markings variable including small dark or light blotches; sometimes light green or tan vertebral line or band; two large warts in shoulder region but no granular skin ridges; skin varying from almost smooth to distinctly warty; small skin ridge from eye over tympanum to base of arm; small pale wart below tympanum. **Tympanum:** indistinct. **Underside:** cream-coloured with occasional flecks; skin smooth. **Hindlimbs:** three to four dark bars on thighs with faint

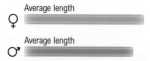

♀ Average length

♂ Average length

Maximum size: 40 mm

KEY ID POINTS

- Dorsal skin with many warts including a conspicuous pair on the shoulders, but not elongated into ridges (distinct from *P. acridoides*)
- Toe tips occasionally expanded into terminal bulbs (distinct from other species except *P. acridoides*)
- At least two phalanges of longest toe free of webbing (distinct from *P. mababiensis*)
- No bands or stripes behind the thigh (distinct from *P. acridoides* and *P. parvulus*)

- Tarsal tubercle not fused with tarsal fold (distinct from *P. mababiensis*)
- No bands on upper and lower jaw (distinct from *P. mababiensis* and *P. parvulus*)

intermediate stripes; webbing moderate; at least two phalanges of the longest toe free of web; tarsal fold present; well-developed inner metatarsal tubercle; small outer metatarsal tubercle; subarticular tubercles fairly well developed; toe and fingertips not expanded into discs but sometimes slightly swollen. **Sexual dimorphism:** male throat dark grey; vocal sac with longitudinal folds parallel to jaw-line.

Call

Slow snore or toad-like vibrant *grrr-ooooo-grrr-ooooo* croak. Males call from semi-concealed to fully exposed positions along edges of vleis and standing pools of water. Chorus starts in the late afternoon and peaks shortly after nightfall. On overcast days calling may continue all day.

Habitat and habits

Along margins of permanent and temporary water bodies including shallow marshes, lakes, rivers, streams and pools; also in semi-desert scrub, arid and humid savanna, agricultural land and occasionally in forest clearings. Open water favoured for breeding.

TADPOLE

Length: up to 35 mm. **Shape:** body rounded. **Tail:** fin of moderate depth; reaching deepest point around middle of tail; tapering into fine point. **Colour:** brown above; white below. **Eyes:** dorsolateral. **Nostrils:** small; narrowly spaced; closer to snout than to eyes; interocular distance double that of internarial distance. **Spiracle:** below body axis. **Vent:** marginal; dextral. **Mouth:** oral disc bordered by single row of small rounded papillae laterally and posteriorly. **Jaw sheaths:** delicate. **LTRF:** 2(2)/2 or 1/2. **Development:** complete in four to six weeks.

Tadpole: lateral view.

Mouthparts.

Small Puddle Frog

Kleinmodderpadda

Phrynobatrachus parvulus (Boulenger, 1905)

LATIN: *parvulus* = very small. Refers to the small size of
this species.

Conservation status: Not threatened. Quite common in its
distribution range, sometimes occurring in large numbers.

Small Puddle Frog: Chimanimani, Zimbabwe.

Description

Maximum size: 25 mm. **Body:** small; snout
stubby. **Above:** light to dark olive-brown;
orange or light brown vertebral line or band
often present; silvery band or series of
spots bordered above and below by dark
lines running from eye under tympanum
to base of arm; upper jaw with silver dots
but usually not barred; skin smooth with
no conspicuous elevations or ridges.
Tympanum: scarcely visible. **Underside:**
heavily spotted, at least posteriorly; lower
jaw uniformly coloured; not barred; skin
smooth. **Forelimbs:** no webbing between
fingers; subarticular tubercles under fingers
small. **Hindlimbs:** pale line or band on
back of thigh running from knee to knee;
webbing reduced with at least 3½ phalanges

Average length

♀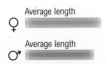

Average length

♂

Maximum size: 25 mm

KEY ID POINTS

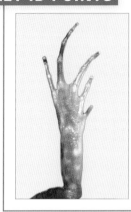

- Dorsal skin smooth without conspicuous elevations or ridges (distinct from other species)
- Toe tips not expanded into terminal bulbs (distinct from other species except *P. acridoides* and occasionally *P. natalensis*)
- At least 3½ phalanges of longest toe free of webbing (distinct from other species except *P. mababiensis*)
- A pale line or band from knee to knee behind the thigh (distinct from other species; compare with *P. acridoides*)
- Tarsal tubercles present and no tarsal fold (distinct from other species)
- Faint band sometimes visible on upper jaw but not lower jaw (distinct from other species; compare with *P. mababiensis*)

of longest toe free of webbing; mid-tarsal tubercle prominent and conical; inner and outer metatarsal tubercles present; no tarsal fold; toe and fingertips not expanded. **Sexual dimorphism:** male vocal sac baggy with transverse fold on gular disc; flattened femoral glands on posterior face of thigh; male throat dark grey to black; throat freckled in female.

Call

Long cricket-like buzz followed by three to four clicks. Males call from semi-concealed to fully exposed positions along edge of water or from vegetation in shallow water. Chorus peaks in the late afternoon to shortly after nightfall, carrying on well into the night. On overcast days males call all day.

Habitat and habits

Moist savanna, penetrating evergreen forests and grassland including montane grassland. Survives well in agricultural land. Breeding peaks in the rainy season but may take place throughout the year if conditions are favourable. Breeds in grassy puddles, ponds, pools, dams, swamps and low streams.

TADPOLE

Length: small. **Shape:** body ovoid. **Tail:** fin of moderate depth; reaching deepest point around middle of tail. **Colour:** brown above; dorsal pigment extends onto head leaving U- or V-shaped mark between nostrils. **Eyes:** dorsolateral. **Nostrils:** small; narrowly spaced. **Spiracle:** small; well below body axis. **Vent:** marginal; dextral. **Mouth:** single row of small papillae laterally; double row dorsolaterally; ventrally an additional row of long, finger-like papillae. **Jaw sheaths:** delicate. **LTRF:** 1/2.

Breda Zimkus

A broad vertebral band is often present.

ORNATE FROGS

SKILDERBONTPADDA

Hildebrandtia Nieden, 1907

Named after nineteenth-century naturalist, J.M. Hildebrandt, who collected amphibians and mammals in East Africa and on Madagascar.

Three species, one in southern Africa

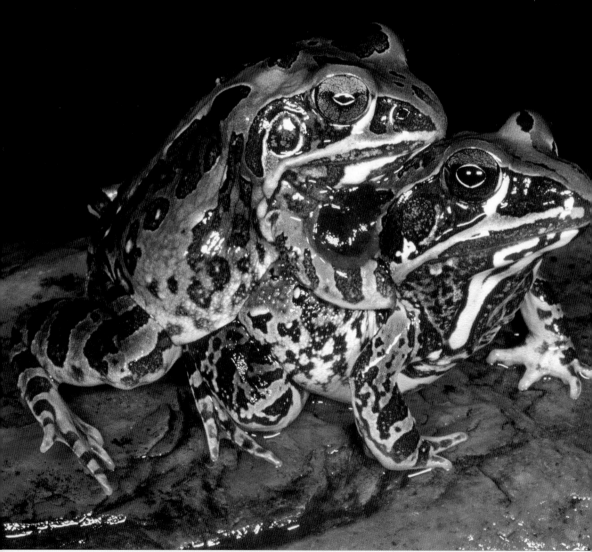

Les Minter

Amplectant pair of Ornate Frogs: Hans Merensky Nature Reserve, Limpopo Province.

DISTINCTIVE CHARACTERS

- See specific description.

A little-studied genus. Widespread in tropical savanna. In general shape and burrowing habits, similar to Sand Frogs (*Tomopterna*) but the southern African Ornate Frog is easily distinguished by its bold colour patterns. Spends much time underground and is seldom observed apart from during the breeding season.

Breeds in early summer after rain, but if rains are late then breeding may be delayed. Uses shallow water at the edge of tropical bushveld pans. The paired vocal sacs of calling males extend until they touch. The raucous call is audible over long distances. Eggs are scattered singly in shallow water. Tadpoles emerge from the jelly capsules after 36 hours.

Les Minter

Ornate Frog showing paired vocal sacs: Hans Merensky Nature Reserve, Limpopo Province.

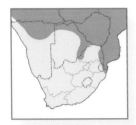

Ornate Frog

Skilderbontpadda

TRACK
83

Hildebrandtia ornata (Peters, 1878)

LATIN: _ornata_ = embellished. Refers to the elaborately coloured pattern on the back.

Conservation status: Not threatened.

Les Minter

Ornate Frog: Skukuza, Kruger National Park, Mpumalanga.

Plain colour variation: Hans Marensky Nature Reserve, Limpopo Province.

Description

Maximum size: 70 mm. **Body:** robust with short legs. **Above:** bold symmetrical pattern of orange, green and golden-brown on a grey or creamy-tan background; markings vary in different specimens; broad golden-brown or green vertebral band usually present from snout to vent; dark brown blotch above each eye and continuous or broken brown paravertebral bands from behind the head to the vent; wedge-shaped pattern of dark patches on flanks; dark mass from the sides of the snout through the nostril and eye; upper lip white with a thin white line from the front of the eye to the mouth; skin slightly granular but lacking warts. **Tympanum:** prominent in adults but barely visible in juveniles. **Underside:** white and smooth; throat dark with two characteristic white Y-shaped markings. **Limbs:** banded green, brown and black with yellow infusions on the posterior surfaces of the thighs; short

Average length

♀

Average length

♂

Maximum size: 70 mm

KEY ID POINTS

- Pupil horizontal
- Throat dark with pair of white Y-shaped markings (distinct from other species)

- Bold symmetrical pattern in golden brown or green (distinct from most other species)
- Males have a pair of lateral vocal sacs (distinct from all species except the genera *Hylarana* and *Ptychadena*)
- Metatarsals fused and not webbed (distinct from *Ptychadena* and *Amietia*)
- Inner metatarsal tubercle is enlarged (distinct from *Ptychadena* and *Amietia*)

stubby fingers with well-developed tubercles; webbing moderate; metatarsals fused and not webbed; inner metatarsal tubercle prominent and flattened. **Sexual dimorphism:** male has twin vocal sacs which emerge from lateral pouches visible below either side of the jaw, in front of the armpit.

Call

Long nasal *kwe-kwe* squawk. Very large choruses may form shortly after rain. Calling begins either at dusk or in the late evening. Males call from shallow water or from semi-concealed positions a few metres from the water's edge.

Habitat and habits

As a burrowing species, found in a variety of savanna types of vegetation; avoids dense woodland and rocky terrain. Hibernates in deep sandy soils, surfacing only during the breeding season.

TADPOLE

Length: up to 95 mm. **Shape:** heavily built. **Tail:** fin starts behind body; shows slightly convex border; tapers to acute whip-like point; ventral section of fin more or less straight. **Colour:** dark brown above and pale below, and with metallic green sheen; as tadpoles reach full size characteristic Y-shaped bands become visible on throat; fin translucent and dark or mottled; colour varies with that of the substrate. **Eyes:** lateral. **Spiracle:** below body axis; directed backwards at $15°$. **Mouth:** anteroventral; single row of large papillae at mouth corners and below; long, four or five, finger-like papillae at mouth corner. **Jaw sheaths:** upper jaw sheath slender and convex; lower jaw sheath massive and broad showing two prominent 'teeth'. **LTRF:** 0/2. **Behaviour:** cannibalistic in captivity, hunting tadpoles of other species (may be a laboratory artefact); also scavenges.

Tadpole: lateral view.

Mouthparts.

GRASS FROGS

GRASPADDAS

Ptychadena Boulenger, 1918

GREEK: *ptyche* = folds; *adenos* = gland. Refers to the ridged skin glands.

49 species, 11 in southern Africa

Dwarf Grass Frog: KwaMbonambi, KwaZulu-Natal.

Mascarene Grass Frog: Okavango, Botswana.

Powerful hindlegs and a streamlined body give Grass Frogs prodigious jumping ability – the Sharp-nosed Grass Frog *Ptychadena oxyrhynchus* holds the world record for the longest frog jump. They are well camouflaged and secretive and easily overlooked until they suddenly escape with one or two giant leaps. They are widespread in savanna bushveld, particularly in low-lying areas, from Egypt south through subSaharan Africa excluding the southwestern parts of southern Africa. They also occur on Madagascar, the Seychelles and the Mascarene Islands. Grass Frogs remain active for most of the year, adopting a sit-and-wait strategy to ambush and feed upon insects. When disturbed, some species tend to dive into the water while others slip quickly into adjacent grass. Most species are explosive breeders. Males form large choruses after rain and the calls of different species peak at different times between dusk and dawn. Males usually call from concealed positions under vegetation but occasionally from exposed positions near the breeding site. Eggs are deposited in small batches in shallow water. During spawning, the cloacae of both sexes are raised above the water. As the eggs emerge, the male uses his feet to funnel sperm over them.

DISTINCTIVE CHARACTERS

ADULT
- Pupil horizontal
- Streamlined with powerful hindlimbs
- Six or more parallel skin ridges on the back
- Paired gular slits in males
- Toes with extensive webbing

TADPOLE
- Two undivided lower labial tooth rows
- Vent marginal and dextral
- Internarial distance less than six times the nostril diameter

KEY TO SPECIES

ADULT

1 Two dark bands on back of thigh continuous and passing below vent; underside usually speckled .... **Speckled-bellied Grass Frog** *P. subpunctata* (p.322)

One dark band on back of thigh continuous and passing below vent; underside not speckled .... **Dwarf Grass Frog** *P. taenioscelis* (p.324)

Dark bands may be present on thigh but not continuous passing below vent; underside usually not speckled **2**

2 Snout paler than rest of body **3**

Snout not paler than rest of body **4**

3 Distance from nostrils to snout tip less than internarial distance .... **Plain Grass Frog** *P. anchietae* (p.306)

Nostrils to snout tip more than internarial distance .... **Sharp-nosed Grass Frog** *P. oxyrhynchus* (p.316)

4 Foot length longer than lower leg (tibia) length **5**

Foot length less than tibia length **6**

5 Outer metatarsal tubercle absent; distance from nostrils to snout tip equal to internarial distance .... **Mascarene Grass Frog** *P. mascareniensis* (p.312)

Outer metatarsal tubercle present; distance from nostrils to snout tip less than internarial distance .... **Guibe's Grass Frog** *P. guibei* (p.308)

6 Internarial distance less than snout-nostril distance .... **Udzungwa Grass Frog** *P. uzungwensis* (p.326)

Internarial distance equal or more than snout-nostril distance **7**

7 Outer metatarsal tubercle absent; webbing extensive, less than two phalanges of longest toe free of web .... **Striped Grass Frog** *P. porosissima* (p.318)

Outer metatarsal tubercle present; webbing reduced with more than two phalanges of longest toe usually free of web **8**

8 Paravertebral folds from head to midback continuous ..... **Broad-banded Grass Frog** *P. mossambica* (p.314)

Paravertebral folds from head to midback interrupted **9**

Pale skin ridge from snout over upper jaw to base of arm continuous .... **Mapacha Grass Frog** *P. mapacha* (p.310)

Pale skin ridge from snout over upper jaw to base of arm broken ... **Schilluk Grass Frog** *P. schillukorum* (p.320)

TADPOLE

1 One labial tooth row in upper jaw; sometimes a very short second row **2**

Two labial tooth rows in upper jaw **3**

2 Two rows of papillae bordering lower jaw; outer row widely spaced, with long papillae; deepest position in fin about 66% from body .... *P. porosissima* (p.318)

One row of papillae bordering lower jaw; deepest position in fin about 40% from body .... *P. anchietae* (p.306)

3 One row of papillae behind the oral angle; area around eyes pigmented .... *P. taenioscelis* (p.324)

Multiple rows of papillae behind the oral angle; area around eyes not pigmented .... *P. oxyrhynchus* (p.316)

Tadpoles not known well enough to be identified by means of a key: *P. guibei, P. mapacha, P. mascareniensis, P. mossambica, P. schillukorum, P. subpunctata* and *P. uzungwensis*

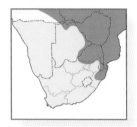

Plain Grass Frog

Rooiruggraspadda

Ptychadena anchietae (Bocage, 1867)

Named after J. d'Anchieta, a Portuguese explorer and naturalist.

Conservation status: Not threatened.

TRACK
84

Plain Grass Frog: Pafuri, Kruger National Park, Limpopo Province.

Description

Maximum size: 62 mm. **Body:** internarial distance equals that between snout and nostril. **Above:** uniform light to darker grey, light brown or reddish-brown; rarely spotted or flecked; pale triangle on snout; dark facial mask stretching from snout through nostril, eye and tympanum to base of arm; occasionally few dark flecks on flanks; no pale vertebral band; skin slightly granular, without warts but finely ridged, some separating into bumps. **Tympanum:** prominent; slightly smaller than eye; edged in white. **Underside:** white, occasional yellowing on belly; grey mottling along jaw; skin smooth. **Hindlimbs:** foot shorter than tibia; no longitudinal line on tibia; dark blotches on back of thighs tending to fuse into longitudinal bands on yellowish background; webbing extensive; 1½ to 2 phalanges of fourth toe and less than one phalanx of fifth toe free of webbing; tarsal fold; small inner but no outer metatarsal tubercle. **Sexual dimorphism:** male with two vocal sacs, tucked into lateral pouches oblique to jaw-line.

Average length

♀

Average length

♂

Maximum size: 62 mm

KEY ID POINTS

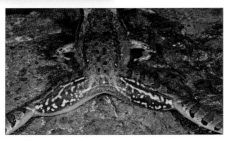

- Black markings on back of thigh tend to fuse to form bands (distinct from *P. oxyrhynchus* and *P. schillukorum*)
- Internarial distance = snout-nostril distance (distinct from other species except *P. mascareniensis* and *P. porosissima*)

- Length of foot less than tibia length (distinct from *P. guibei, P. mascareniensis* and *P. taenioscelis*)
- Pale line on tibia absent (distinct from other species except *P. mossambica, P. oxyrhynchus, P. schillukorum, P. taenioscelis* and *P. uzungwensis*, although sometimes absent also in *P. uzungwensis*)
- Outer metatarsal tubercle absent (distinct from *P. guibei, P. mapacha, P. mossambica* and *P. schillukorum*; sometimes absent also in *P. subpunctata*)
- Snout paler than the rest of the body (distinct from other species except *P. oxyrhynchus, P. schillukorum* and *P. subpunctata*)

Call

Moderately high-pitched *prrrrt-prrrrt* trill, followed by a rapidly repeated *pree-pree-pree*. Males often call from partially concealed positions in shallow water or along water's edge. Sporadic calls may be heard early in the evening; choruses form from early evening and may last until the early hours of the morning.

Habitat and habits

Widely distributed in savanna, open country in woodland, grassland, and agricultural and suburban areas. Often seen sheltering among vegetation close to breeding sites. Active throughout most of the year when moisture or standing water is available. When disturbed, jump away from the water.

TADPOLE

Length: up to 45 mm. **Shape:** body fat, oval. **Tail:** fin reaching highest point in middle of tail with distinct hump; tapering to fine tip. **Colour:** grey to brown above; pale below; bigger tadpoles sometimes with pale triangle on snout, typical of adult frogs; fins opaque with faint grey mottling. **Eyes:** dorsolateral. **Nostrils:** widely spaced; pigmented around edge. **Spiracle:** below body axis; in middle of body; directed backwards and upwards. **Vent:** marginal; dextral. **Mouth:** anteroventral; oral disc bordered by single row of short round papillae laterally; slightly longer papillae posteriorly. **Jaw sheaths:** moderately built; lower jaw sheath V-shaped. **LTRF:** 1/2 or 2(2)/2; where divided, second row of teeth present, which are very short and with broad medial gap. **Development:** embryos emerge from jelly capsules after about 24 hours; metamorphosis complete in about three to four weeks.

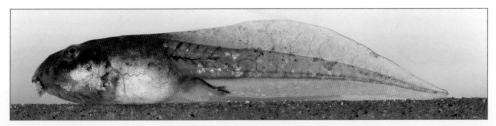

Tadpole: lateral view.

Guibe's Grass Frog

Guibé se graspadda

TRACK
85

Ptychadena guibei Laurent, 1954

Named after J. Guibé, director of the Paris Museum.

Conservation status: Not threatened.

Guibe's Grass Frog: Okavango, Botswana.

Description

Maximum size: 43 mm. **Body:** internarial distance greater than snout-nostril distance. **Above:** dark brown; broad light brown to tan vertebral band running from snout to vent; prominent dark facial band from snout through eye to base of arm; prominent longitudinal skin ridges with dark brown to black spots; paravertebral ridges often broken, not reaching urostyle and alternating with shorter distinct ridges; pale dorsolateral ridge from eye to groin; skin smooth to slightly granular. **Tympanum:** prominent; slightly smaller than eye; white edge. **Underside:** rear and undersides of thighs yellow; skin smooth. **Hindlimbs:** posterior surface of thigh longitudinally banded with yellow and dark grey to black; pale line on tibia; foot as long as or longer than thigh; webbing reduced; 3½ phalanges of fourth toe free of webbing; inner and outer metatarsal tubercles present; row of small tubercles usually present under fourth metatarsal. **Sexual dimorphism:** male with two vocal sacs, tucked into lateral pouches oblique to jaw-line.

Average length

♀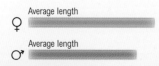

Average length

♂

Maximum size: 43 mm

KEY ID POINTS

- Back of thighs have two dark distinct bands that do not fuse below the vent (distinct from other species)
- Internarial distance greater than snout–nostril distance (distinct from other species except *P. mapacha*, *P. mossambica* and *P. schillukorum*)

- Length of foot greater than tibia length (distinct from other species except *P. mascareniensis*, *P. subpunctata* and *P. taenioscelis*)
- Pale line on tibia present (distinct from *P. anchietae*, *P. oxyrhynchus*, *P. schillukorum* and *P. taenioscelis*)
- Outer metatarsal tubercle present (distinct from other species except *P. mapacha*, *P. mossambica* and *P. schillukorum*, although sometimes absent in *P. subpunctata*)
- Snout not paler than the rest of the body (distinct from *P. anchietae*, *P. oxyrhynchus*, *P. schillukorum* and *P. subpunctata*)

Call
Squeaky *tink-tink*. Males call from concealed positions among grassy vegetation or under debris close to water.

Habitat and habits
Near water in moist grassland or savanna; occasionally common in shallow seasonal wetlands. When disturbed, jumps away from water into grass tussocks.

Habitat: Okavango Delta, Botswana.

TADPOLE
Length: up to 45 mm. **Shape:** body ovoid. **Tail:** deeper than body; gaining deepest point past middle of tail, tapering sharply. **Colour:** body grey-brown with specks of gold, tail fin with specks of green and gold. **Eyes:** dorsolateral. **Nostrils:** narrowly spaced; midway between eyes and snout. **Spiracle:** well below; directed backwards at 40°. **Vent:** marginal; dextral. **Mouth:** anteroventral. **Jaw sheaths:** moderate. **LTRF:** 2(1)/2. **Development:** completed in about nine weeks.

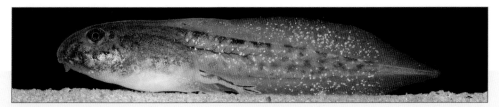

Tadpole: lateral view.

Mapacha Grass Frog

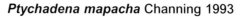

Mapacha-graspadda

Ptychadena mapacha Channing 1993

Named after the Mapacha area near Katima Mulilo in the Caprivi Strip, northern Namibia, where the species is found.

Conservation status: Data Deficient.

Mapacha Grass Frog: Katima Mulilo, Namibia.

Alan Channing

Description

Maximum size: 31 mm. **Body:** internarial distance greater than snout-nostril distance. **Above:** olive-brown with dark spots; reddish-brown infusions behind tympanum and on thighs; vertebral line usually present; snout not paler than rest of dorsum; prominent cream skin ridges on upper lip from snout to base of arm; cream ridge from eye to groin; nine interrupted and indistinct skin ridges present on back; reddish-brown infusions behind the tympanum and on the thighs. **Tympanum:** smaller than eye, with pale edge. **Underside:** immaculate; skin smooth; **Forelimbs:** arms short. **Hindlimbs:** back of thigh mottled, tending to form longitudinal pale line, with a number of small white spots; thin pale line usually present on tibia;

Average length

♀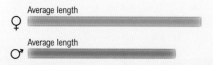

Average length

♂

Maximum size: 31 mm

KEY ID POINTS

- Back of thighs mottled, tending to form longitudinal pale lines (distinct from *P. oxyrhynchus* and *P. schillukorum*)
- Internarial distance greater than snout-nostril distance (distinct from other species except *P. guibei*, *P. mossambica* and *P. schillukoram*)
- Length of foot less than tibia length (distinct from *P. guibei*, *P. mascareniensis* and *P. taenioscelis*)

- Pale line on tibia present (distinct from *P. anchietae*, *P. oxyrhynchus*, *P. schillukorum* and *P. taenloscelis*)
- Outer metatarsal tubercle present (distinct from other species except *P. guibei*, *P. mossambica* and *P. schillukorum*, although sometimes present in *P. subpunctata*)
- Snout not paler than the rest of the body (distinct from *P. anchietae*, *P. oxyrhynchus*, *P. schillukorum* and *P. subpunctata*)

foot shorter than tibia; webbing moderate; $2^2/_3$ to 3 phalanges of fourth toe free of webbing; inner and outer metatarsal tubercles present. **Sexual dimorphism:** male with two vocal sacs, tucked into lateral pouches parallel to jaw-line.

Call
Short chirp repeated rapidly at rate of about six calls per second. Males often call from concealed positions in shallow water.

Habitat and habits
Pans in arid savanna in northern Namibia.

Habitat: pan in Caprivi, Namibia.

TADPOLE
Length: up to 50 mm. **Shape:** body ovoid. **Tail:** deeper than body; deepest just after middle of tail. **Colour:** grey-brown, tail with dark grey blotches and reflecting small spots. **Eyes:** dorsolateral. **Nostrils:** narrowly spaced; equal distance between nostrils and from nostrils to snout. **Spiracle:** well below; directed backwards at 80°. **Vent:** marginal; dextral. **Mouth:** anteroventral. **Jaw sheaths:** moderate. **LTRF:** 2(2)/2.

Tadpole: lateral view.

Mascarene Grass Frog

Maskareense graspadda

TRACK
87

Ptychadena mascareniensis (Duméril & Bibron, 1841)

Named after the Mascarene Islands, east of Madagascar, where the species was first identified. The African mainland form may be a separate species.

Conservation status: Not threatened.

Mascarene Grass Frog: Hluhluwe, KwaZulu-Natal.

Description

Maximum size: 58 mm. Body: internarial distance the same as the distance between nostril and snout and between nostrils and eyes. **Above:** brown or green; rounded green or brown blotches usually present; white, yellow, light tan or green vertebral band usually present; snout not paler than rest of dorsum; six dorsal skin ridges with outer ridges often interrupted; creamy white dorsolateral ridge from eye to groin.**Tympanum:** prominent; slightly smaller than eye. **Underside:** creamy-white to creamy-yellow; colour more intense on throat and groin; skin smooth. **Forelimbs:** distinct tubercles on hands. **Hindlimbs:** foot as long as, or longer than, tibia; pale line on tibia; front of thigh with dark longitudinal band; back of thigh with longitudinal black and yellow stripes; webbing moderately extensive; 2 to 2½ phalanges of fourth toe free of webbing; tarsal fold present; small inner metatarsal tubercle; no outer metatarsal tubercle. **Sexual dimorphism:** gular pouch slits parallel to jaw-line and ending above base of arm; breeding male with swollen nuptial pads on inner three fingers.

Average length

♀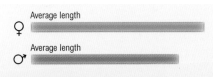

Average length

♂

Maximum size: 58 mm

KEY ID POINTS

- Back of thighs with longitudinal black and yellow stripes (distinct from *P. oxyrhynchus* and *P. schillukorum*)

- Internarial distance is equal to the snout-nostril distance (distinct from other species except *P. anchietae* and *P. porosissima*)
- Length of foot is greater than the tibia length (distinct from other species except *P. guibei*, *P. subpunctata* and *P. taenioscelis*)
- Pale line on tibia present (distinct from *P. anchietae*, *P. oxyrhynchus*, *P. schillukorum* and *P. taenioscelis*)
- Outer metatarsal tubercle absent (distinct from *P. guibei, P. mapacha, P. mossambica* and *P. schillukorum*, although sometimes absent also in *P. subpunctata*)
- Snout not paler than the rest of the body (distinct from *P. anchietae*, *P. oxyrhynchus*, *P. schillukorum* and *P. subpunctata*)

Colour variation: Hluhluwe, KwaZulu-Natal.

Call
Wah-wah-wah nasal quack usually followed by a few clucking sounds. Occasionally other calls may be emitted. Males often call from open to partially concealed positions among vegetation in shallow water or along water's edge.

Habitat and habits
Opportunistic; uses a wide variety of habitats in lowland savanna including irrigation canals, agricultural areas, ricefields, marshy areas, the periphery of large lakes, rivers and other wetland habitats. Although not normally occurring in forests, may occur along roads in forested areas. Active throughout the year at permanent water bodies, in late afternoon and evening. When disturbed the frog often expels a jet of water from the bladder and then dives into the water or into emergent vegetation. When captured, may adopt a rigid posture, secrete foam through the skin, and utter a moaning call to distract predators.

TADPOLE
Length: up to 50 mm. **Shape:** body ovoid. **Tail:** deeper than body; deepest just before middle of tail. **Colour:** grey-brown but pale over the head. **Eyes:** dorsolateral. **Nostrils:** narrowly spaced; midway between eyes and snout. **Spiracle:** below; directed backwards at $70°$. **Vent:** marginal; dextral. **Mouth:** anteroventral. **Jaw sheaths:** moderate. **LTRF:** 2(2)/2. **Development:** completed in about nine weeks.

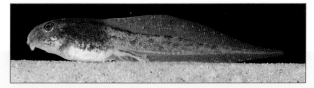

Tadpole: lateral view.

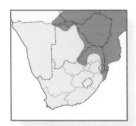

Broad-banded Grass Frog

TRACK
88

Breëbandgraspadda

Ptychadena mossambica (Peters, 1854)

Named after Mozambique where the species was first identified.

Conservation status: Not threatened.

Broad-banded Grass Frog: Tshaneni, Swaziland.

Description
Maximum size: 53 mm. **Body:** internarial distance greater than snout-nostril distance. **Above:** grey-brown to brown or green; broad creamy vertebral band from snout to vent, bordered with elongated blackish spots; snout not paler than rest of body; dorsolateral skin ridges prominent, continuous and creamy-white; dark brown blotches, smaller than eye, between

♀ Average length

♂ Average length

Maximum size: 53 mm

vertebral band and dorsolateral ridges. **Tympanum:** prominent; slightly smaller than eye. **Underside:** white, sometimes with grey mottling along lower jaw and on hind part of abdomen; thighs and groin often yellow; skin smooth. **Forelimbs:** arm comparatively short. **Hindlimbs:** foot shorter than tibia; pale line sometimes present on upper surface of tibia; back of thigh dark grey, with yellow mottling sometimes forming irregular lines; webbing moderate; 2¾ to 3 phalanges of fourth toe and one phalanx of fifth toe free of webbing; tarsal fold present; inner and outer metatarsal tubercles present; row of tubercles under fourth toe. **Sexual dimorphism:** gular slits in male not parallel to jaw-line on lateral view.

Call

Series of *kwe-kwe* clucks. Males call from concealed positions in grass tussocks at the edge of water or even sometimes several metres away from water. Until vegetation establishes itself after winter, males may call along the water's edge in completely exposed sites. Calling peaks after dark till about midnight.

Habitat and habits

Variety of bushveld vegetation types at altitudes of 200 to 1 200 m in dry savanna, thicket and grassland, but also in humid savanna and forested areas. When disturbed, jumps away from water into vegetation, crawls beneath it and is concealed.

TADPOLE

Unknown.

KEY ID POINTS

- Back of thighs with yellow mottling, sometimes forming irregular lines (distinct from *P. subpunctata*, *P. taenioscelis* and *P. guibei*)

- Internarial distance greater than snout-nostril distance (distinct from other species except *P. guibei*, *P. mapacha* and *P. schillukorum*)
- Length of foot less than tibia length (distinct from *P. guibei*, *P. mascareniensis*, *P. subpunctata* and *P. taenioscelis*)
- Pale line on tibia sometimes present (distinct from *P. anchietae*, *P. oxyrhynchus*, *P. schillukorum* and *P. taenioscelis*)
- Outer metatarsal tubercle present (distinct from other species except *P. guibei*, *P. mapacha* and *P. schillukorum*, although sometimes present also in *P. subpunctata*)
- Band extends to snout but snout not paler than the rest of the body (distinct from *P. anchietae*, *P. oxyrhynchus*, *P. schillukorum* and *P. subpunctata*)

Colour variation.

Sharp-nosed Grass Frog

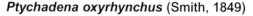

Skerpneusgraspadda

Ptychadena oxyrhynchus (Smith, 1849)

GREEK: *oxyrhynchus* = sharp-snouted. Refers to the pointed snout.

Conservation status: Not threatened.

Sharp-nosed Grass Frog: KwaMbonambi, KwaZulu-Natal.

Description

Maximum size 85 mm. **Body:** one of the largest Grass Frogs with very well developed hindlegs; snout acutely pointed; internarial distance less than snout-nostril distance. **Above:** asymmetrical blotches, equal to or smaller than the size of the eye, on a lighter brown to greenish background; pale triangular patch on top of the snout; thin pale vertebral line sometimes present; dorsal skin ridges well developed, those laterally being less prominent; dark facial mask from the snout through eye and tympanum; prominent cream to yellow skin ridge stretches from under eye to base of arm. **Tympanum:** as large as the eye; with a light border. **Underside:** white with yellowing over the groin; smooth; gular slits parallel to jaw-line. **Hindlimbs:** posterior face of thigh mottled dark brown or grey on a yellow background; no pale line on tibia; length of foot less than tibia length; webbing extensive with only

Average length

♀

Average length

♂

Maximum size: 85 mm

KEY ID POINTS

- Back of thighs mottled, (distinct from *P. schillukorum*)
- Internarial distance less than snout-nostril distance (distinct from other species except *P. subpunctata*, *P. taenioscelis* and *P. uzungwensis*)

- Length of foot less than tibia length (distinct from *P. guibei, P. mascareniensis, P. subpunctata* and *P. taenioscelis*)
- Pale line on tibia absent (distinct from other species except *P. anchietae*, *P. schillukorum*, *P. taenioscelis* and *P. uzungwensis*, although sometimes absent also in *P. mossambica* and *P. uzungwensis*)

- Outer metatarsal tubercle absent (distinct from *P. guibei , P. mapacha, P. mossambica* and *P. schillukorum*, although sometimes absent also in *P. subpunctata*)
- Snout paler than the rest of the body (distinct from other species except *P. anchietae*, *P. schillukorum*, and *P. subpunctata*)

1½ to 2 phalanges of the fourth toe free of webbing; small inner but no outer metatarsal tubercle; no row of tubercles under the fourth metatarsal. **Sexual dimorphism:** breeding male with prominent dark gular slits and nuptial pads on fingers.

Call

Series of moderately high-pitched, penetrating *prrr-prrr* trills. Males often call from partially concealed positions in shallow water or at water's edge, choruses reaching their peak between midnight and predawn. Calls sporadically on overcast days.

Habitat and habits

Moist open savanna and woodland from sea level to about 850 m, where rainfall exceeds 450 mm per annum. Often close to water but will forage far from breeding sites. Renowned for jumping prowess and reported to be able to cover up to 60 times its own body length in a single leap. Holds world record for the longest jump. Breeding begins early in spring, continuing well into summer. Not specific about breeding sites, using pools in rock outcrops, roadside pools, inundated grassland, vleis, pans and pools. Eggs float but will sink if disturbed.

TADPOLE

Length: up to 54 mm. **Shape:** body oval; flattened. **Tail:** fin fairly shallow; clear with mottling; reaches highest point in middle of tail; tapers gently to fine point; fins do not extend onto body. **Colour:** grey-brown; throat with little or no white pigmentation; abdomen immaculate. **Eyes:** dorsolateral. **Nostrils:** small; narrowly spaced; closer to snout than eye. **Spiracle:** below body axis; directed backwards at 40°. **Vent:** marginal; dextral. **Mouth:** oral disc bordered with single row of short papillae above mouth corner; four rows of papillae posteriorly. **Jaw sheaths:** moderate; lower U-shaped. LTRF: 2/2. **Development:** embryos emerge from jelly capsules within two days; complete in about eight weeks.

Tadpole: lateral view.

Striped Grass Frog

Gestreepte graspadda

Ptychadena porosissima (Steindachner, 1867)

LATIN: *poros* = pore, especially of the skin. Refers to the spots on the backs of the thighs, distinctive of the species.

Conservation status: Not threatened.

Striped Grass Frog: KwaMbonambi, KwaZulu-Natal.
Inset: Note tibia line: Sodwana, KwaZulu-Natal.

Description

Maximum size: 49 mm. **Body:** internarial distance equal to that between snout and nostril. **Above:** cream to light brown; scattered brown blotches; yellow vertebral line present; no pale triangular patch on snout; dorsal skin ridges well developed; conspicuous, thickened, pale dorsolateral ridge. **Tympanum:** smaller than eye; sometimes with white central spot. **Underside:** white with yellowing over groin; skin smooth. **Hindlimbs:** tibia slightly longer than foot; prominent thin white line on upper surface of tibia; back of thigh with pale, sometimes indistinct spots separated by dark

Average length
♀

Average length
♂

Maximum size: 49 mm

KEY ID POINTS

Johann du Preez

- Back of thighs with pale spots separated from each other by dark mottling (distinct from other species)
- Internarial distance same as that between snout and nostril (distinct from other species except *P. anchietae* and *P. mascareniensis*)
- Length of foot less than tibia length (distinct from *P. guibei*, *P. mascareniensis*, *P. subpunctata* and *P. taenioscelis*)
- Pale line on tibia present (distinct from *P. anchietae*, *P. oxyrhynchus*, *P. schillukorum* and *P. taenioscelis*)
- Outer metatarsal tubercle absent (distinct from *P. guibei*, *P. mapacha*, *P. mossambica* and *P. schillukorum*, although sometimes absent also in *P. subpunctata*)
- Snout not paler than rest of the body (distinct from *P. anchietae*, *P. oxyrhynchus*, *P. schillukorum* and *P. subpunctata*)

mottling; three phalanges of fourth toe and 1 to 1½ phalanges of fifth toe free of webbing; slight tarsal fold present; small inner and outer metatarsal tubercles present; lacks tubercles under fourth metatarsal. **Sexual dimorphism:** male with two vocal sacs tucked into lateral pouches not parallel to jaw-line.

Call

Three or four short, bird-like *pree-pree* rasping chirps. Males call from concealed positions in shallow water or along the water's edge. Often two or more call antiphonally, beginning in the late afternoon, continuing into the night and peaking between just before midnight and well after.

Habitat and habits

Variety of vegetation types, from sea level to 2 300 m, including subtropical coastal areas, temperate and wooded grassland along the escarpment and on the highveld. Recorded throughout the year in areas with permanent water. Often found close to water but will forage a considerable distance from breeding sites; when disturbed, jumps away from water.

TADPOLE

Length: up to 41 mm. **Shape:** body oval; rather deep. **Tail:** dorsal fin shallow to begin, but rises, gaining deepest point past middle of tail, and finally tapers sharply to end in rounded tip; in fully grown tadpoles vertebral line present. **Colour:** body golden-brown above; yellowish-white below; semi-transparent over gill region; tail fin mottled brown. **Eyes:** dorsolateral. **Nostrils:** small; narrowly spaced. **Spiracle:** above body axis; directed $45°$. **Vent:** marginal; dextral. **Mouth:** oral disc bordered by double row of papillae laterally and posteriorly; lateral and inner posterior rows consisting of small rounded papillae; outer posterior row longer, finger-like and sparser. **Jaw sheaths:** moderately developed; upper jaw sheath gently curved; lower jaw sheath strongly flexed. **LTRF:** 1/2. **Development:** embryos emerge from jelly capsules within two days; complete in about four weeks.

Tadpole: lateral view.

Schilluk Grass Frog

Schilluk-graspadda

Ptychadena schillukorum (Werner, 1908)

Named after the Schilluk people and area of Sudan.

Conservation status: Not threatened.

Schilluk Grass Frog: Beira, Mozambique.

Alan Channing

Description

Maximum size: 49 mm. **Body:** legs short; internarial distance greater than snout-nostril distance; internarial distance greater than interorbital distance. **Above:** grey-brown with dark blotches; snout not paler than rest of dorsum; dark facial band running from snout through eye and tympanum to arm; dark blotch on upper eyelid; six broken dorsal skin ridges; dorsolateral skin ridges continuous, reddish-cream; pale ridge along upper jaw to base of arm; skin along flanks coarsely granular. **Tympanum:** prominent; smaller than eye. **Underside:** immaculate; lower jaw marbled; gular pouch slits end in middle of

Average length

♀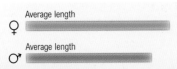

Average length

♂

Maximum size: 49 mm

base of arm; gular slits oblique to jaw-line. **Hindlimbs:** upper surface of tibia without pale line; back of thigh with yellow mottling forming irregular lines; foot length less than tibia length; webbing reduced; two to three phalanges of fourth toe free of webbing; foot length less than tibia length; no tubercles under fourth metatarsal; outer metatarsal tubercle distinct. **Sexual dimorphism:** legs longer and gular slits present in male.

Call
Very rapid bursts of three to six explosive *chuck* sounds. Males call while floating among dense vegetation at the edge of shallow pools.

Habitat and habits
Poorly known; a savanna species associated with large rivers, lakes and permanent swamps.

TADPOLE
Unknown.

KEY ID POINTS

- Back of thighs with fine vermiculations (distinct from other species except *P. oxyrhynchus*)

- Internarial distance less than snout-nostril distance (distinct from *P. guibei* and *P. mapacha*)
- Length of foot less than tibia length (distinct from *P. guibei*, *P. mascareniensis*, *P. subpunctata* and *P. taenioscelis*)
- Pale line on tibia absent (distinct from other species except *P. anchietae*, *P. oxyrhynchus*, *P. taenioscelis* and *P. uzungwensis*, although sometimes absent also in *P. mossambica* and *P. uzungwensis*)
- Outer metatarsal tubercle present (distinct from other species except *P. guibei*, *P. mapacha* and *P. mossambica*, although sometimes present also in *P. subpunctata*)
- Snout not paler than rest of the body (distinct from other species except *P. anchietae*, *P. oxyrhynchus* and *P. subpunctata*)

Habitat: large rivers and lakes in northern Mozambique and Malawi.

Speckled-bellied Grass Frog

Spikkelpens-graspadda

Ptychadena subpunctata (Bocage, 1866)

LATIN: *sub* = beneath; *punctum* = marked with points or dots. Refers to the black speckled markings on the underside of this species.

Conservation status: Not threatened.

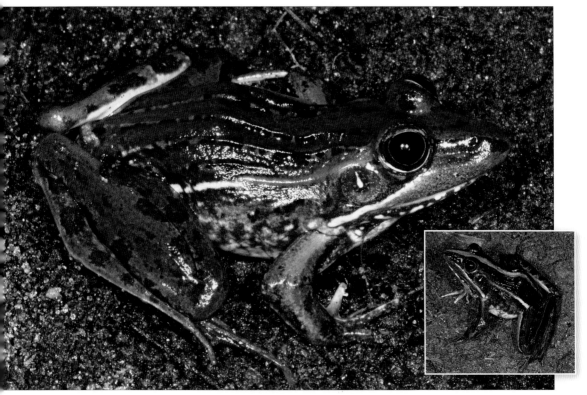

Speckled-bellied Grass Frog: Okavango, Botswana. Inset: Colour variation, with green or orange vertebral band.

Identification

Maximum size: 68 mm. **Body:** internarial distance less than snout-nostril distance. **Above:** light to dark brown; pale triangular patch on snout; sometimes infusions of red behind eyes; broad pale cream or green vertebral band from snout to vent sometimes present; paravertebral skin ridges continuous, swollen; dorsolateral skin ridge from eye to groin prominent,

♀ Average length

♂ Average length

Maximum size: 68 mm

pale; prominent pale skin ridge from under the eye to base of arm. **Tympanum:** prominent; about size of eye. **Underside:** cream; speckled in black; skin smooth; gular slit oblique to jaw-line. **Hindlimbs:** upper surface of tibia usually with longitudinal pale line; back of thigh with two or more longitudinal dark lines running from knee to knee; webbing extensive; 1½ to 2 phalanges of fourth toe free of webbing; no tubercles under fourth metatarsal. **Sexual dimorphism:** male throat dark.

Call

Soft croaks in rapid succession, interspersed with loud clucks, resembling the sound of some *Amietia* species. Males call from the edges of deep pans.

Habitat and habits

When disturbed, dives into water but quickly returns to land. Prefers deep permanent water in savanna, including pools, swamps and river backwaters. Eggs are scattered in shallow water.

TADPOLE

Length: up to 55 mm. **Shape:** body shallow. **Tail:** fin moderately curved; reaches deepest point just past middle of tail. **Colour:** dark, densely marbled. **Eyes:** dorsal to dorsolateral. **Nostrils:** narrowly spaced; facing anterolaterally. **Spiracle:** below body axis; directed backwards at 45°. **Vent:** marginal; dextral. **Mouth:** anteroventral; single row of papillae laterally; double row posteriorly. **Jaw sheaths:** moderate; serrated. LTRF: 2(2)/2.

Tadpole: lateral view.

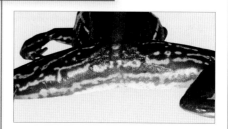

- Back of thighs with two or more longitudinal dark lines running continuously from knee to knee below vent (distinct from other species except *P. taenioscelis*)
- Internarial distance less than snout-nostril distance (distinct from other species except *P. oxyrhynchus*, *P. taenioscelis* and *P. uzungwensis*)
- Length of foot greater than tibia (distinct from other species except *P. mascareniensis*, *P. guibei* and *P. taenioscelis*)
- Pale line present on tibia (distinct from *P. anchietae*, *P. oxyrhynchus*, *P. schillukorum* and *P. taenioscelis*)
- Outer metatarsal tubercle usually present (distinct from other species except *P. guibei*, *P. mapacha*, *P. mossambica* and *P. schillukorum*)
- Snout paler than rest of body (distinct from other species except *P. anchietae*, *P. oxyrhynchus* and *P. schillukorum*)
- Underside speckled (distinct from all other species)

Dwarf Grass Frog

Kleingraspadda

Ptychadena taenioscelis Laurent, 1954

LATIN: *taenia* = band-like. Refers to the parallel lines on the backs of the thighs.

Conservation status: Not threatened.

Dwarf Grass Frog: KwaMbonambi, KwaZulu-Natal.

Description

Maximum size: 40 mm. **Body:** internarial distance less than snout-nostril distance. **Above:** brown; darker brown rectangular markings; pale vertebral line sometimes present; usually dark facial band running from snout through eye; flanks mottled with black; paravertebral skin ridges well developed; pair of ridges extending onto snout; dorsolateral skin ridge eye to arm, swollen, prominent, pale, often with infusions of orange; prominent pale ridge from under eye to base of arm. **Tympanum:** smaller than eye. **Underside:** creamy white to yellow; throat usually spotted; lower jaw marbled; skin smooth; gular slit ends at middle of base of arm. **Hindlimbs:** upper surface of tibia without pale line; dark marking on back of thigh forms two to three parallel lines on a yellow background, one of which is continuous from one thigh to the other below the vent; foot length greater than tibia length; webbing moderate with three phalanges

Average length
♀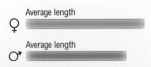

Average length
♂

Maximum size: 40 mm

KEY ID POINTS

- Back of thighs have two to three parallel lines on a yellow background, one of which is continuous from one thigh to the other below the vent (distinct from other species except *P. subpunctata*)
- Internarial distance less than snout-nostril distance (distinct from other species except *P. oxyrhynchus*, *P. subpunctata* and *P. uzungwensis*)

- Length of foot greater than tibia length (distinct from other species except *P. guibei* and *P. mascareniensis*)
- Pale line on tibia absent (distinct from other species except *P. anchietae*, *P. oxyrhynchus*, *P. schillukorum* and *P. uzungwensis*, although sometimes absent also in *P. mossambica* and *P. uzungwensis*)
- Outer metatarsal tubercle absent (distinct from *P. guibei*, *P. mapacha*, *P. mossambica* and *P. schillukorum*, although sometimes absent also in *P. subpunctata*)
- Snout not paler than the rest of the body (distinct from *P. anchietae*, *P. oxyrhynchus*, *P. schillukorum* and *P. subpunctata*)

of fourth toe free of webbing; outer metatarsal tubercle usually absent, no row of tubercles under fourth metatarsal. **Sexual dimorphism**: male with black-lined gular sac; breeding male with swollen nuptial pads on inner three fingers.

Call
Short, nasal bleats emitted at a rate of about one per second. As well as the mating call, there is a harsher growling call that probably functions to separate males. Males often call from wet mud, shallow water or flooded short grass. Calling peaks early to mid evening and may continue to daybreak. Dense breeding aggregations form in summer and between three to eight males congregate in calling units. They call sporadically during drier periods.

Habitat and habits
Savanna woodlands, coastal bushveld and grassland in KwaZulu-Natal, river-valley savanna and open grassland further north in the range. Survives in altered habitats. Amplectant pairs deposit eggs over a three-hour period and may move several metres during the egg-laying process.

TADPOLE
Length: up to 36 mm. **Shape**: body oval. **Tail**: tail fin reaches highest point before middle of tail; tapers to fine point. **Eyes**: dorsolateral. **Nostrils**: small; narrowly spaced; equal distance between eyes and snout. **Spiracle**: directed backwards and upwards; opening slightly constricted. **Vent**: marginal; dextral. **Mouth**: oral disc bordered with single row of short round papillae laterally; slightly longer papillae posteriorly. **Jaw sheaths**: moderately built; lower jaw sheath V-shaped. **LTRF**: 2/2; where divided second row is present, teeth are very short with broad gap.

Udzungwa Grass Frog

Udzungwa-graspadda

TRACK
94

Ptychadena uzungwensis (Loveridge, 1932)

Named after the Udzungwa Mountains in Eastern Tanzania.

Conservation status: Not threatened.

Udzungwa Grass Frog: Serengeti National Park, Tanzania.

Alan Channing

Description

Maximum size: 48 mm. Body: internarial distance less than snout-nostril distance; distance between eyes significantly less than distance between nostrils. **Above:** light brown; dark spots along skin ridges sometimes fusing to obscure ground colour; pale vertebral line present; lower jaw may be distinctly barred; snout not paler than rest of dorsum; dorsal skin ridges well developed; pair of short pale skin ridges running from upper eyelids to snout, continuous with pale paravertebral

♀ Average length
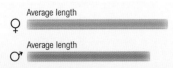

♂ Average length

Maximum size: 48 mm

KEY ID POINTS

- Back of thighs with row of light spots sometimes fusing into pale band (distinct from *P. guibei, P. mascareniensis, P. oxyrhynchus, P. subpunctata* and *P. taenioscelis*)
- Internarial distance less than snout-nostril distance (distinct from other species except *P. oxyrhynchus, P. subpunctata* and *P. taenioscelis*)
- Length of foot less than tibia length (distinct from *P. taenioscelis*)

- Pale line on tibia sometimes present (distinct from *P. anchietae, P. oxyrhynchus, P. schillukorum* and *P. taenioscelis*)
- Outer metatarsal tubercle absent (distinct from *P. guibei, P. mapacha, P. mossambica* and *P. schillukorum*, although sometimes absent also in *P. subpunctata*)
- Snout not paler than the rest of the body (distinct from *P. anchietae, P. oxyrhynchus, P. schillukorum* and *P. subpunctata*)

ridges behind eyes. **Tympanum:** half the diameter of the eye. **Underside:** creamy white, throat yellowish; skin smooth; gular slits oblique to jaw-line. **Hindlimbs:** heavily banded; back of thigh with row of light spots sometimes fusing into pale band; no line on tibia; length of foot equal to or slightly shorter than tibia; webbing moderate; three phalanges of fourth toe free of webbing; outer metatarsal tubercle absent; row of tubercles under the fourth metatarsal. **Sexual dimorphism:** male throat and groin deep yellow.

Call
A repetitive *prrrrp* trill. Males call antiphonally from shallow water.

Habitat and habits
Never far from water in grassy or woodland areas; medium- to high-altitude grassland at 800 to 2 300 m. When disturbed, dives away from water into vegetation. Most active during rains, emerging during the day to feed on insects. When captured, adopts a rigid posture and squeaks.

TADPOLE

Shape: body plump; oval. **Tail:** fin moderately deep. **Colour:** dark grey-brown with dark mottling. **Eyes:** dorsolateral. **Nostrils:** small; narrowly spaced; closer to snout than eyes. **Spiracle:** directed dorsoposteriorly. **Vent:** marginal; dextral. **Jaw sheaths:** unknown. **LTRF:** unknown.

Michael Cunningham

Tadpole: dorsolateral view.

PLATANNAS OR CLAWED FROGS
PLATANNAS

Xenopus Wagler, 1827

GREEK: *xenos* = strange; *pous* = foot. Refers to the strange appearance of the clawed feet. DUTCH: *plat* = flat; *hander* = hands. Refers to the flat hands and feet of the Platanna genus.

17 species, four in southern Africa

Cape Platanna: Betty's Bay, Western Cape.

Platannas are totally aquatic and only emerge from water when migrating in search of fresh bodies of water. They are streamlined in shape with very powerful hindlegs and are remarkably adapted to their environment. Tympanum, tongue and movable eyelids are all lacking – they are of limited use under water. They have a well-developed lateral line system (like fish) that is used to detect vibrations and movement under water.

The genus is truly African, but there are known feral populations of *Xenopus laevis* in many countries, including on Ascension Island, in Chile, the USA, the UK and France, where they were often first introduced for now-outdated pregnancy tests.

Platannas are both predators and scavengers and they use their hands to guide food into their mouths. Food particles that are too large to swallow are held in the mouth and then shredded using the clawed and powerful hindlegs. During the day they tend to hide in deeper water but move to shallow water at night. Although they are able to take up oxygen through the skin, they have to break the water surface in order to breathe. This they do quickly while gulping for air. In hot conditions, surfacing to breathe is often synchronised in a group of frogs.

Platannas call underwater and the method of call production is unique. They have no vocal cords or vocal sacs and their characteristic clicking or popping sounds are produced by the movement of modified laryngeal cartilage elements rubbing against each other.

In the early 1930s two South African scientists discovered that if urine from a pregnant woman was injected subcutaneously into a female Platanna she would spawn. This became the first commercially available pregnancy test and enormous

DISTINCTIVE CHARACTERS

ADULT

- Pupil circular
- Conspicuous system of lateral lines
- Tympanum absent
- Toes fully webbed
- Claws on the inner three toes
- Fingers not webbed
- Tongue absent
- Eyelids immovable
- Skin smooth and slippery
- Amplexus inguinal

TADPOLE

- Nektonic filter-feeding
- Keratinised mouthparts absent
- Semi-transparent
- Head flattened, with sensory tentacles at mouth angles

numbers of platannas were exported to countries around the globe for this purpose. Until more sophisticated chemical methods became available in the 1960s, this was the standard and only available pregnancy test.

In the breeding season the female cloacal folds swell and become reddish, while males develop dense black asperities on hands and inner forearms to assist in amplexus. Tadpoles are nektonic and filter-feed on phytoplankton, typically hanging the head down at an angle of 45° with the tip of the tail vibrating to maintain position. Small tadpoles often hide among aquatic vegetation, while larger tadpoles aggregate in schools and hang in mid water.

The Cape Platanna *Xenopus gilli* is Critically Endangered.

KEY TO SPECIES

ADULT

1 No subocular tentacle .... **Cape Platanna** *X. gilli* (p.330)
Subocular tentacle present **2**

2 Subocular tentacle at least half as long as diameter of eye .... **Müller's Platanna** *X. muelleri* (p.334)
Subocular tentacle shorter than half as long as diameter of eye **3**

3 Underside immaculate or mottled with grey .... **Common Platanna** *X. laevis* (p.332)
Underside dark yellow with dark grey speckles or blotches .... **Peters' Platanna** *X. petersii* (p.336)

TADPOLE

1 Unpigmented band running from each eye, sideways and backwards; oral tentacles shorter than body width .... *X. gilli* (p.330)
No unpigmented band running sideways from eyes, oral tentacles as long as, or longer than, body width. **2**

2 Distance between nostrils less than 1½ times nostril width; oral tentacles twice body width ... *X. muelleri* (p.334)
Distance between nostrils more than 1½ times nostril width; oral tentacles as long as body width **3**

3 Inner margin of nostrils and area between nostrils with dark pigmentation .... *X. laevis* (p.332)
Inner margin of nostrils and area between nostrils not darkly pigmented .... *X. petersii* (p.336)

Cape Platanna

Kaapse platanna

Xenopus gilli Rose & Hewitt, 1927

Named after E.L. (Leonard) Gill (1877–1956) director of the South
African Museum in Cape Town from 1924–1942.

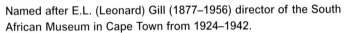

Conservation status: Endangered, owing to habitat loss through urbanisation, but also
because species hybridises with the Common Platanna in disturbed water bodies.

Cape Platanna: Kleinmond, Western Cape.

Identification

Maximum size: 60 mm. **Body:** head more
pointed than other *Xenopus* species; lacks
subocular tentacles; eyes facing slightly
forward. **Above:** beige to yellow-brown; dark
olive-green to dark brown paravertebral
bands extending from between eyes to
three-quarters down back; breaks up into
blotches on lower back and upper surfaces
of thighs; series of dark blotches (which
tend to fuse) form longitudinal bands along
flanks; 20 to 24 lateral line organs along
flanks less conspicuous than in most other
Xenopus species; skin smooth. **Underside:**
pale to dark grey to blackish with chrome-
yellow vermiculations. **Forelimbs:** hands
with four long, thin fingers. **Hindlimbs:** feet
fully webbed; webbing usually grey; inner
three toes with black claws; inner metatarsal
tubercle reduced and barely discernible.

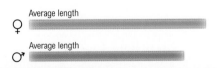

Average length

♀

Average length

♂

Maximum size: 60 mm

KEY ID POINTS

- Snout more pointed and eyes facing more forward than for other Platanna species (distinct from other species)
- Dark blotches on back fuse to form longitudinal bands (distinct from other species)

- Subocular tentacles absent (distinct from other species)
- 20 to 24 lateral line bars (less conspicuous than in other species)
- Restricted to a few localities in low-lying coastal fynbos wetlands between the Cape Peninsula and Cape Agulhas (distinct from *X. muelleri* and *X. petersii*)
- Underside pale to dark grey to blackish with chrome-yellow vermiculations (distinct from other species)

Sexual dimorphism: cloacal folds of female more swollen than those of male; hand palms of male darken in breeding season.

Call

Series of short, rapidly pulsed metallic buzzes produced while frog is fully submerged. During breeding season males call day and night.

Habitat and habits

Endemic to certain blackwater sponges and lakelets in low-lying wetlands in the coastal fynbos, stretching from the Cape Peninsula eastwards towards Cape Agulhas. Preferred water is usually dark, low in nutrients, high in dissolved solids and with a low pH. Cape Platanna tadpoles can develop in water with a pH as low as 3.6.

Habitat: Cape Point Nature Reserve, Western Cape.

TADPOLE

Length: up to 50 mm. **Shape:** body flattened; pair of long, sensory tentacles resembling catfish, about three-quarters of body width. **Tail:** long; terminating in acute tip. **Colour:** grey; not pigmented, clear pale band on each side of head, running backwards from eye; throat without pigmentation. **Eyes:** lateral. **Nostrils:** small; narrowly spaced; close to tip of snout. **Spiracle:** two midventral. **Mouth:** papillae; labial tooth rows; keratinised. **Jaw sheath:** absent.

Tadpole: lateral view.

Dorsal view.

Common Platanna

Gewone platanna

Xenopus laevis (Daudin, 1802)

LATIN: *laevis* = smooth. Refers to the slimy skin surface of the frog.

Conservation status: Not threatened.

TRACK
96

Common Platanna: Johannesburg, Gauteng.

Average length

♀

Average length

♂

Maximum size: 147 mm

KEY ID POINTS

- Underside whitish or mottled with grey (distinct from *X. gilli* and *X. petersii*)
- Snout rounded and eyes face dorsally (distinct from *X. gilli*)
- Brown to grey; irregular dark blotches (distinct from *X. gilli*)

- Subocular tentacles shorter than half the diameter of eye (distinct from *X. gilli* and *X. muelleri*)
- More than 24 lateral line bars (distinct from *X. gilli* and *X. petersii*)
- Distributed throughout southern Africa so not geographically distinguishable

Identification

Maximum size: 147 mm. **Body:** rounded snout; subocular tentacles shorter than half diameter of eye; eyes face upwards. **Above:** dark brown to grey; irregular dark blotches; 24 or more conspicuous lateral line organs; skin smooth. **Underside:** immaculate or mottled with grey. **Forelimbs:** hands with four long thin toes. **Hindlimbs:** large; powerful; feet fully webbed; inner metatarsal tubercle of moderate size. **Sexual dimorphism:** cloacal folds of female more swollen than those of male; hand palms of male darken in breeding season.

Call

Constant, undulating snoring sounds produced while frog is fully submerged. Both males and females call. During breeding season males call day and night.

Habitat and habits

Restricted to aquatic habitats but opportunistic and can be found in any form of wetland whether natural or man-made.

TADPOLE

Length: up to 80 mm. **Shape:** body flattened with pair of long sensory tentacles, resembling a small catfish; tentacles as long as body width. **Tail:** long; high; translucent; terminates in acute tip. **Colour:** translucent; light scattering of dark stipples on body and tail. **Eyes:** lateral. **Nostrils:** small; narrowly spaced close to tip of snout; distance between nostrils more than 1½ times nostril width; inner margin of nostrils darkly pigmented. **Spiracle:** two midventral. **Mouth:** keratinised mouthparts absent.

Tadpole: lateral view.

Müller's Platanna

TRACK
97

Geelpensplatanna

Xenopus muelleri (Peters, 1844)

Named after German anatomist, Johannes Müller (1801–1858).

Conservation status: Not threatened.

Müller's Platanna: Ndumu, KwaZulu-Natal.

Identification

Maximum size: 90 mm. **Body:** snout rounded; subocular tentacles at least half as long as diameter of eye; eyes facing upwards; protective membrane covering half the eye. **Above:** brown to dark grey; irregular dark blotches; 22 to 27 conspicuous lateral line organs along flanks; skin smooth. **Underside:** light grey on pectoral region; blending to deep orange-yellow on belly and underside of thighs; grey spots often present. **Forelimbs:** hands with four long, thin fingers. **Hindlimbs:** large; powerful; feet

Average length

♀

Average length

♂

Maximum size: 90 mm

fully webbed; webbing yellowish; inner metatarsal tubercle small and pointed. **Sexual dimorphism:** cloacal folds of female more swollen than those of male; hand palms of male darken in breeding season.

Call

Series of regular, metallic tapping sounds produced while frog is fully submerged. Both females and males call. During breeding season males call day and night.

Habitat and habits

Occurs widely in subtropical and tropical savanna areas.

TADPOLE

Length: up to 70 mm. **Shape:** body more rounded than *X. laevis*; sensory tentacles very long, twice as long as body width; resembles small catfish; significantly longer than other *Xenopus* species in region. **Tail:** long; high; translucent; terminates in acute tip. **Colour:** dorsal colour varies from transparent to heavily pigmented; ventral abdominal colour creamy white; only area covering viscera semi-transparent. **Eyes:** lateral. **Nostrils:** obliquely elliptical; margins not darker; diameter of nostrils greater than 1½ times internarial distance. **Spiracle:** two midventral. **Mouth:** keratinised mouthparts absent. **Behaviour:** nektonic; filter-feeding on phytoplankton; swim horizontally with tip of tail pointed upwards.

KEY ID POINTS

- Underside light grey on pectoral region, blending to deep orange-yellow on belly and underside of thighs (distinct from other species)
- Snout rounded and eyes face dorsally (distinct from *X. gilli*)
- Brown to grey; irregular dark blotches (distinct from *X. gilli*)
- Subocular tentacles at least half as long as diameter of eye (distinct from other species)

- 22–27 lateral line bars
- Restricted to Zululand, Mozambique, Zimbabwe, northern Botswana and the Caprivi in Namibia (distinct from species beyond this range)

Tadpole: lateral view.

Dorsal view.

Peters's Platanna

Peters se platanna

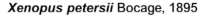

Xenopus petersii Bocage, 1895

Named after the German herpetologist, W.C.H. Peters (1815–1883).

Conservation status: Not threatened.

Alan Channing

Peters's Platanna: Mafia Island, Tanzania.

Identification

Maximum size: 80 mm. **Body:** head bluntly pointed; subocular tentacles short, less than half diameter of eye; internasal distance less than interorbital distance. **Above:** brown to dark grey; irregular dark blotches; 24 (or fewer) lateral line organs along flanks; skin smooth.

Tympanum: not visible. **Underside:** dark yellow with dark grey speckles or blotches. **Forelimbs:** hands with four long, thin fingers. **Hindlimbs:** feet fully webbed; inner metatarsal tubercle raised into narrow ridge. **Sexual dimorphism:** cloacal folds of female more swollen than those of male; hand palms of male darken in breeding season.

♀ Average length

♂ Average length

Maximum size: 80 mm

Call

Series of metallic chirps produced while fully submerged. Both males and females call.

Habitat and habits

Occurs widely in permanent water bodies, including rivers, lakes and wells, in savanna and coastal lowland.

Habitat: Okavango Delta.

KEY ID POINTS

- Snout rounded and eyes face dorsally (distinct from *X. gilli*)
- Brown to grey; irregular dark blotches (distinct from *X. gilli*)
- Subocular tentacles shorter than half diameter of eye (distinct from *X. gilli* and *X. muelleri*)
- 24 or fewer lateral line bars (distinct from *X. laevis* and *X. gilli*)
- Underside dark yellow with dark grey speckles or blotches (distinct from *X. laevis* and *X. gilli*)

- Restricted to northern Botswana, Namibia, southern Angola and south-western Zambia (distinct from species beyond this range)

TADPOLE

Length: up to 80 mm. **Shape:** body flattened; pair of long sensory tentacles; resembles small catfish; length of tentacles about equal to body width. **Tail:** long; high; translucent; terminating in acute tip. **Colour:** light scattering of dark stipples on body and tail; legs often blotched. **Eyes:** lateral. **Nostrils:** small; very narrowly spaced close to tip of snout; distance between nostrils less than 1½ times nostril width; narial periphery pigmented. **Spiracle:** two midventral. **Mouth:** keratinised mouthparts absent.

Tadpole: dorsal view.

CHIRPING FROGS

KWETTERPADDAS

Anhydrophryne Hewitt, 1919

LATIN: *an* = without; *hydro* = water; *phryne* = toad. Refers to full development of tadpoles within the nest rather than in a water body.

Three species, all in southern Africa

Natal Chirping Frog: Nkandla Forest, KwaZulu-Natal.

The three members of the genus are all small, cryptically coloured and difficult to find, even when they are calling. They are confined to the southeastern parts of the Eastern Cape and KwaZulu-Natal, and can be found in damp environments among vegetation or leaf litter in forest or grassland – but never in open bodies of water. Calling is persistent during misty or rainy conditions and the calls of all three species can easily be mistaken for the sounds of insects.

DISTINCTIVE CHARACTERS

ADULT

- Pupil horizontal
- Prominent dark facial mask from snout to axilla
- Poorly developed tubercles on hands and feet
- No webbing on hands and feet
- Metatarsal tubercles poorly developed or absent

TADPOLE

- No free-swimming tadpole phase. Metamorphosis is completed within the terrestrial nest.

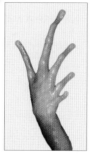

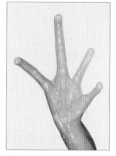

Foot.   *Hand.*

Clutches of about 30 eggs are laid in nests excavated in the mud among decaying leaves. This can be a shallow scoop or, in the case of the Hogsback Chirping Frog *A. rattrayi*, a spherical subterranean chamber. The eggs are unpigmented and about 5 mm in diameter – large for this size of frog. Initially the tadpole is colourless, but the head becomes darker as it develops. Metamorphosis is completed within the nest and the tadpole feeds off the yolk until it emerges as a fully formed frog about 3 mm in length.

Roger de la Harpe/IOA

Chirping Frogs occur in damp forest or grassland in the southeastern provinces of South Africa.

KEY TO SPECIES

ADULT

1 Ventral surface white without markings .... **Mistbelt Chirping Frog** *A. ngongoniensis* (p.342)
   Ventral surface with dark mottling or speckles 2
2 Found in the Eastern Cape west of the Mbhashe River .... **Hogsback Chirping Frog** *A. rattrayi* (p.344)
   Found in KwaZulu-Natal or the Eastern Cape east of the Mbhashe River ....
   ... . **Natal Chirping Frog** *A. hewitti* (p.340)

Natal Chirping Frog

Natalse kwetterpadda

TRACK 99

Anhydrophryne hewitti (FitzSimons, 1947)

Named after herpetologist, John Hewitt (1880–1961), director of the Albany Museum, Grahamstown.

Conservation status: Not threatened.

Natal Chirping Frog: Nkandla Forest, KwaZulu-Natal.

Identification

Maximum size: females seldom exceed 30 mm but specimens of up to 36 mm collected from Nkandla Forest, KwaZulu-Natal. **Above:** ground colour varies from orange-brown, dark brown, slate-grey to almost black; uniform or with dark edging around small skin elevations; sometimes with pale yellowish or reddish vertebral line; often a pale triangle between eyes and snout; prominent dark facial band running from snout through eye and over tympanum to base of arm; white band on upper lip with dark mottling along jaw-line; skin smooth

Average length
♀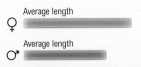

Average length
♂

Maximum size: 30 mm

with some granulated spots. **Tympanum:** small, half the size of the eye. **Underside:** off-white with irregular diffused mottling; throat grey, darker in males; no vocal sac but throat expands when calling. **Forelimbs:** hands with small tubercles. **Hindlimbs:** no webbing; outer metatarsal tubercle absent or weakly developed. **Sexual dimorphism:** male throat dark grey, female throat lighter.

Call

Rapid series of high-pitched *tik-tik* notes repeated at rate of four to six per second. Males may climb to more exposed positions after nightfall to call from mossy areas near clear streams. In overcast conditions males conceal themselves and may call throughout the day.

Habitat and habits

At altitudes of up to 2 700 m, in forested areas, dense natural vegetation alongside streams in the Drakensberg and KwaZulu-Natal midlands; among leaf litter; in mossy embankments near waterfalls and streams or in small pools.

KEY ID POINTS

- Underside off-white with irregular diffused mottling (distinct from *A. ngongoniensis*)
- Found only in KwaZulu-Natal (distinct from *A. rattrayi*)

TADPOLE

No free-swimming tadpole phase. Metamorphosis is completed in the terrestrial nest within about 20 days.

Dark colour form without vertebral line.

Marius Burger

Mistbelt Chirping Frog

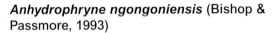

Misbeltkwetterpadda

Anhydrophryne ngongoniensis (Bishop & Passmore, 1993)

Refers to Ngongoni veld, a vegetation type where the species occurs.

Conservation status: Critically Endangered. Restricted to an area smaller than 10 km² which is under severe pressure from commercial afforestation.

Mistbelt Chirping Frog: Ixopo, KwaZulu-Natal.

Identification

Maximum size: 22 mm. **Above:** ground colour sandy to golden-brown with four indistinct dorsal stripes comprising small dark brown spots; dark brown stripe bordered above and below by thin silvery stripe running from snout through eye and tympanum, fading away at base of arm;

Average length
♀

Average length
♂

Maximum size: 22 mm

skin smooth. **Tympanum:** small; half the size of the eye. **Underside:** immaculate white; throat and limbs pale yellow. **Hindlimbs:** webbing absent; small inner but no outer metatarsal tubercle. **Sexual dimorphism:** sexes indistinguishable; male lacks vocal sac.

Call

Soft cricket-like trill consisting of eight to ten pulses, in bouts of up to seven

Marius Burger

Nocturnal calling position on elevated vegetation.

KEY ID POINTS

- Underside immaculate without stippling or marbling (distinct from *A. hewitti* and *A. rattrayi*)
- Found only in the mistbelt area of KwaZulu-Natal (distinct from *A. rattrayi*)

calls, generally at night from elevated positions on grass stems. In misty conditions, males call throughout the day from concealed positions at the base of vegetation.

Habitat and habits

Mistbelt area of KwaZulu-Natal; frequents moist grassland and Afromontane forest where it occurs in dense vegetation on slopes along seepage channels.

TADPOLE

No free-swimming tadpole phase. Metamorphosis is completed in the terrestrial nest within about 27 days.

Habitat: grassland in mistbelt, Franklin, KwaZulu-Natal.

TRACK
101

Hogsback Chirping Frog

Hogsback-kwetterpadda

Anhydrophryne rattrayi Hewitt, 1919

Named after George Rattray, a principal of Selborne College in East London, who first discovered this species in the Hogsback area.

Conservation status: Endangered owing to limited, fragmented distribution. Under favourable conditions, however, it can be abundant and densities of up to 70 individuals per 25 m^2 have been reported.

Hogsback Chirping Frog: Hogsback, Eastern Cape. Inset: Female lacks the hardened snout tip of the male.

Identification

Maximum size: 22 mm. Above: ground colour from light grey to copper to dark brown, occasionally with irregular dark markings; narrow pale vertebral line sometimes present; dark brown facial band running from snout through eye, over tympanum to base of arm; narrow white line bordering lower edge of facial band from between eye and tympanum to base

Average length

♀

Average length

♂

Maximum size: 22 mm

of arm; skin smooth with scattered skin elevations. **Tympanum:** small, half the size of the eye. **Underneath:** white, marbled with dark blotches not extending onto throat. **Hindlimbs:** webbing absent; tubercles on hands and feet poorly developed; outer metatarsal tubercle poorly developed or absent. **Sexual dimorphism:** male with pale hardened flat tip on snout, probably used to dig the nest.

Call

Soft, high-pitched, melodious *ping-ping-ping* repeated rapidly; males call from concealed positions on forest floor near mountain streams by day or night, especially in misty weather.

KEY ID POINTS

- Underside with variable degree of dark mottling on a white background (distinct from *A. ngongoniensis*)

- Found only in the Eastern Cape (distinct from *A. ngongoniensis* and *A. hewitti*)

Habitat and habits

Moist vegetation along mountain streams in the Katberg and Amatola Mountains; also found in the grassland-forest ecotone as well as in small open wetland patches in forested areas.

TADPOLE

No free-swimming tadpole phase. Metamorphosis is completed in the terrestrial nest within about 26 days.

Left: Frogs inhabit damp areas near waterfalls or seepages.
Below: Developmental stages of the Hogsback Chirping Frog.

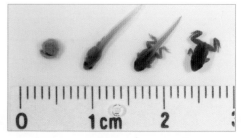

MOSS FROGS
MOSPADDAS

Arthroleptella Hewitt, 1926

GREEK: *arthron* = joint; *lepto* = slender. With the diminutive ending *ella,* refers to the slightness and small size of the species.

Seven species in southern Africa, all restricted to the Western Cape

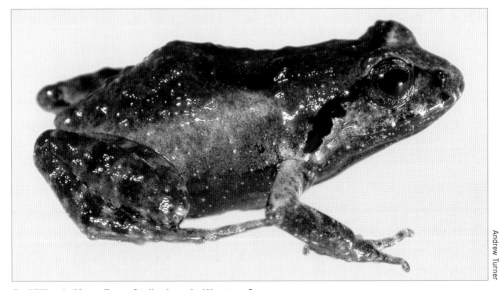

De Villiers's Moss Frog: Stellenbosch, Western Cape.

All species in this genus are small and cryptic. They can be confused with some members of the genus *Cacosternum*, but the ventral coloration differs. They are secretive and remain concealed at the base of dense vegetation. The species within the genus are difficult to identify from morphological characters without the aid of magnification.

The genus is confined to the Western Cape fold mountains where they occur in seepages and other permanently moist areas of fynbos or, occasionally, in forested kloofs, but are not found in open water. Most species have allopatric ranges so the precise locality of each species is a useful method of identification. As with all frogs, the call is also diagnostic.

Moss frogs aestivate during the dry summer months and breeding commences with the winter rains and usually lasts throughout the rainy season until early summer. Males call during the day and occasionally into the night from well-concealed positions under vegetation. Males call in small interactive choruses with one frog stimulating the calls of others. Small clusters of 6 to 12 eggs are laid in moss or at the base of restio tussocks. Here they hatch into tadpoles that squirm about on the damp substrate for 10 to 14 days until they metamorphose into froglets about 4 mm long. Males continue to call near the oviposition site.

DISTINCTIVE CHARACTERS

ADULT
- Pupil horizontal but almost circular
- Ventral surface is smooth and may be marbled but does not have rounded spots
- Females white below in most species
- Dark facial band from the snout through the eye to the armpit
- No webbing on hands or feet
- Tympanum small and inconspicuous
- Legs slender and proportionately shorter than most other species
- Second toe proportionately longer than most other species

Andrew Turner

TADPOLE
- No free-swimming tadpole. Metamorphosis is completed within the terrestrial nest.

Andrew Turner

Habitat: wet, mossy bank.

KEY TO SPECIES

1 Outer metatarsal tubercle well developed 2
   Outer metatarsal tubercle not well developed 3
2 Restricted to Cape Peninsula .... **Cape Peninsula Moss Frog** *A. lightfooti* (p.354)
   Restricted to Klein Swartberg at Caledon .... **Rough Moss Frog** *A. rugosa* (p.356)
   Occurs from Paarl Mountain to Cape Agulhas .... **De Villiers's Moss Frog** *A. villiersi* (p.360)
3 Skin ridge present from angle of mouth to base of arm 4
   No skin ridge present from angle of mouth to base of arm ... **Landdroskop Moss Frog** *A. landdrosia* (p.352)
4 Restricted to Limietberg, Watervalsberg and Slanghoek mountains .. **Bainskloof Moss Frog** *A. bicolor* (p.348)
   Restricted to Groot Winterhoek Mountains .... **Northern Moss Frog** *A. subvoce* (p.358
   Restricted to Kleinriviersberg and Babilonstoring Mountains ... **Drewes's Moss Frog** *A. drewesii* (p.350)

Bainskloof Moss Frog

Bainskloof-mospadda

TRACK
102

Arthroleptella bicolor Hewitt, 1926

LATIN: *bi* = two; *color* = colour. Refers to the contrasting dark upper and white underside of some of the females of this species.

Conservation status: Not threatened.

Bainskloof Moss Frog: Limietberg, Western Cape.

Atherton de Villiers

Description

Maximum size: 22 mm. **Body:** squat with short limbs; head rounded and may be paler than rest of dorsum. **Above:** orange-brown to black with darker blotches and paler spots on the back and legs; thin, pale vertebral stripe sometimes present; dark band running from nostrils to armpit;

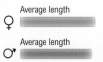
Average length
♀

Average length
♂

Maximum size: 22 mm

smooth with a few slightly raised glands. **Tympanum**: small. **Underside**: See sexual dimorphism. **Forelimbs**: fingers unwebbed with slightly swollen fingertips. **Hindlimbs**: relatively short with slightly raised glands on the dorsal surfaces; webbing absent; well-developed outer metatarsal tubercle; toe tips slightly swollen. **Sexual dimorphism**: male throat dark with a discernible gular sac; rest of ventrum mottled with dark and light spots; female immaculate white to pale grey below, with grey vermiculations.

Call

Irregular series of rapid clicks, more rapid and less regular than calls of other *Arthroleptella* species; calls heard May to December.

Habitat and habits

Permanently moist positions within dense restios and accumulated organic matter in mountain seeps in the Limietberg, Watervalsberg and Slanghoek mountains at altitudes of 500 to 1 500 m. Breeding takes place from first winter rains until seeps dry up in summer; 8 to 10 eggs are laid in damp moss.

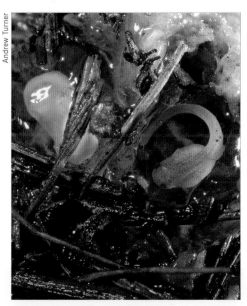

Developing tadpoles in nest.

KEY ID POINTS

- Restricted to Limietberg, Watervalsberg and Slanghoek mountains (distinct from other species)
- Dorsal surface smooth with a few raised glands (distinct from *A. rugosa*)

- Snout rounded (distinct from *A. lightfooti* and *A. villiersi*)

TADPOLE

No free-swimming tadpole phase. Tadpoles develop in damp terrestrial nest.

Drewes's Moss Frog

Drewes se mospadda

Arthroleptella drewesii Channing, Hendricks & Dawood, 1994

Named after R.C. Drewes of the California Academy of Science, USA, who collected the type specimen.

Conservation status: Data Deficient. When a conservation assessment was made in 2004 the distribution range of this species was uncertain. It is still known only from a very limited area.

Drewes's Moss Frog: Babilonstoring Mountain, Western Cape.

Andrew Turner

Description
Maximum size: 18 mm. **Body**: snout rounded in both horizontal and vertical planes; limbs and toes well developed; snout and profile rounded. **Above**: variable from black to red-brown with irregular darker markings; limbs paler with dark brown blotches; an irregular darker band from nostrils to armpit with scattered white spots particularly on lips; broken skin ridge from upper lip to base of arm; eyelids warty; several linear warts present on back, although overall

Average length
♀

Average length
♂

Maximum size: 18 mm

impression is smooth. **Underside:** see sexual dimorphism. **Forelimbs:** fingertips with noticeable round terminal expansion. **Hindlimbs:** well developed; subarticular tubercles under toes rounded; inner metatarsal tubercle prominent; outer tubercle a small ridge; toes slightly expanded at tips. **Sexual dimorphism:** male throat black with remaining underside darkly marked and pale background nearly obscured; underside of female white; male has swollen granular area between thighs.

Call

Series of five to seven unevenly spaced, modulated peeps; noticeable amplitude modulation during the call creates a tune-like effect, especially in longer series; males usually call from concealed positions in thick restios and other vegetation in seeps and on stream sides.

Habitat and habits

Moist, well-vegetated and mossy areas near streams and seepages in riverine forest on

KEY ID POINTS

- Restricted to Kleinrivier and Babilonstoring Mountains near Hermanus (distinct from *A. lightfooti*, *A. bicolor*, *A. rugosa* and *A. subvoce*)
- Dorsal surface smooth with several elongated warts (distinct from *A. rugosa*)
- Snout rounded (distinct from *A. lightfooti* and *A. villiersi*)
- Outer metatarsal tubercle a small ridge (distinct from well-developed tubercle in the sympatric *A. villiersi*)
- Toe tips more expanded than sympatric *A. villiersi*

the Kleinrivier and Babilonstoring Mountains near Hermanus; prefers higher altitudes and steeper slopes than *A. villiersi*. Breeds June to September; eggs are laid in moss or similar vegetation.

TADPOLE

No free-swimming tadpole phase. Tadpoles develop in damp terrestrial nest.

Dark colour form: Hermanus, Western Cape.

Landdroskop Moss Frog

Landdroskop-mospadda

Arthroleptella landdrosia Dawood & Channing, 1994

Named after Landdroskop in the Hottentots Holland Mountains near Gordon's Bay where this species was first collected.

Conservation status: Near Threatened.

TRACK
104

Landdroskop Moss Frog: Swartboskloof, Western Cape.

Andrew Turner

Average length
♀

Average length
♂

Maximum size: 15 mm

KEY ID POINTS

- Restricted to Hottentots Holland, Jonkershoek and Helderberg ranges (distinct from *A. lightfooti*, *A. bicolor*, *A. rugosa* and *A. subvoce*)
- Dorsal surface smoothy glandular (distinct from *A. rugosa*)
- Snout rounded (distinct from *A. lightfooti* and *A. villiersi*)
- Nostrils set slightly wider than sympatric *A. villiersi*
- Toe tips more expanded than sympatric *A. villiersi*

Andrew Turner

Description

Maximum size: 15 mm. **Body:** squat with short limbs; snout rounded; nostrils small and positioned midway between the anterior corner of the eye and tip of the snout. **Above:** colour varies from red-brown to very dark brown; usually with darker dorsolateral markings and dark bands and blotches on the dorsal surfaces of the thighs; thin, pale vertebral line may be present; usually a few white spots on the lips; surface smoothly glandular with no skin ridge from the upper lip to the base of the arm. **Underside:** dark with a few silvery patches on sides and posterior (see also sexual dimorphism). **Forelimbs:** fingertips rounded and flattened; well-developed palmar tubercle. **Hindlimbs:** toe tips slightly swollen; subarticular tubercles single, rounded and smooth; inner metatarsal tubercle well developed and the outer hardly detectable. **Sexual dimorphism:** in male, ventral surface dark; dark grey to black throat with a discernable gular sac; vocal sac black with lateral folds; female paler below.

Call

Series of strident clicks made slightly melodious by amplitude modulation. Males usually call from concealed positions in very dense restios in well-developed seeps throughout the year except in high summer.

Habitat and habits

Near streams in riverine forest and on very steep seepages including cliff faces in the Hottentots Holland, Jonkershoek and Helderberg mountain ranges. Generally prefers higher altitudes and steeper slopes than *A. villiersi*. Breeds from September to February; eggs laid on very moist and dense vegetation in seepages.

TADPOLE

No free-swimming tadpole phase. Tadpoles develop in damp terrestrial nest.

Cape Peninsula Moss Frog

TRACK
105

Skiereilandmospadda

Arthroleptella lightfooti (Boulenger, 1910)

Named after R.M. Lightfoot, an assistant at the South African Museum, Cape Town.

Conservation status: Near Threatened; distribution is restricted and vulnerable due to habitat degradation.

Cape Peninsula Moss Frog: Constantia Nek, Western Cape.

Description

Maximum size: 22 mm. **Body:** long-limbed species with a pointed snout. **Above:** variable from light tan, red-brown to black with the flanks and snout lighter; dark band from nostril, through the eye, to base of arm; white spots on the upper lip; generally smooth with a few, scattered, raised glandular patches; interorbital distance smaller than or equal to the

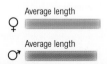

Average length
♀

Average length
♂

Maximum size: 22 mm

breadth of the upper eyelid. **Underside:** lower flanks and hindlimbs with dark marbling on light background. **Hindlimbs:** longer than other species; fingers and toes with slightly swollen tips; outer metatarsal tubercle well developed. **Sexual dimorphism:** male throat black and ventral surface dark; white in female.

Call

High-pitched chirp consisting of three pulses. Males call from concealed positions often near previously laid eggs. Calling generally May to September, but continues as long as wet conditions prevail.

Habitat and habits

Under dense vegetation in montane fynbos and Afromontane forest on Table Mountain and the Cape Peninsula. Its distribution does not overlap with any other described species of Moss Frog. Breeds July to November in wet seepages and streamside vegetation. About 5 to 12 eggs are laid on damp soil in both exposed and concealed situations.

TADPOLE

No free-swimming tadpole phase. Tadpoles develop in damp terrestrial nest.

KEY ID POINTS

- Restricted to Table Mountain and the Cape Peninsula (distinct from all other species)
- Dorsal surface smooth with several elongated warts (distinct from *A. rugosa*)
- Snout pointed (distinct from other species except *A. villiersi*)
- Longer limbed than other species

Atherton de Villiers

Pale colour form: Silvermine, Western Cape.

Rough Moss Frog

TRACK
106

Skurwe-mospadda

Arthroleptella rugosa Turner & Channing, 2008

LATIN: _rugosus_ = wrinkled. Refers to the raised glandular lumps on the dorsum.

Conservation status: Not evaluated; as with other species in this genus, the distribution range may be restricted thus rendering it vulnerable.

Andrew Turner

Rough Moss Frog: Caledon, Western Cape.

Description

Maximum size: 19 mm. **Body:** generally very dark and lumpy unlike other Moss Frogs; snout rounded. **Above:** dark chocolate-brown with slightly paler, indistinct dorsolateral bands; top of snout sometimes slightly paler than the rest of the dorsum; many raised glandular bumps on the dorsum,

Average length
♀

Average length
♂

Maximum size: 19 mm

particularly in males. **Underside:** see sexual dimorphism. **Hindlimbs:** well developed, but not as long as *A. villiersi* or *A. lightfooti*; inner and outer metatarsal tubercles well developed. **Sexual dimorphism:** female larger than male and speckled grey below; male with black throat and much of remaining belly dark; female throat black and much of the ventrum black or covered with dark blotches on a grey background; female mottled dark grey on grey below.

Call
Rough chirp and occasionally a rattling sound. Males call mostly during the morning after rain, May to August and probably beyond these months if sufficient rain has fallen.

Habitat and habits
Mountain seeps on the slopes of the Klein Swartberg near Caledon, in places that are permanently wet and have a dense cover of restio. Breeds mid to late winter.

KEY ID POINTS

- Restricted to the Klein Swartberg near Caledon (distinct from other species)
- Dorsal surface very granular (distinct from other species)
- Snout rounded (distinct from *A. lightfooti* and *A. villiersi*)

TADPOLE
No free-swimming tadpole phase. Tadpoles develop in damp terrestrial nest.

Andrew Turner

Tadpole about to emerge from egg capsule.

Andrew Turner

Dark colour form showing rough skin: Caledon, Western Cape.

Northern Moss Frog

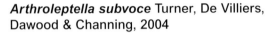

Noordelike mospadda

Arthroleptella subvoce Turner, De Villiers,
Dawood & Channing, 2004

LATIN: *sub* = under; *vox* = voice. Refers to the very subdued
call of this species.

Conservation status: Data Deficient. Further research is needed.

Atherton de Villiers

Northern Moss Frog: Groot Winterhoek Mountains, Western Cape.

Description

Maximum size: 14 mm, making it probably
the smallest frog in southern Africa.
Body: squat, short-limbed; snout round,
more blunt than any other members of
genus. **Above**: pairs of paravertebral
and dorsolateral dark brown bands on a
mottled brown base colour; dark blotches

Average length
♀

Average length
♂

Maximum size: 14 mm

on top of head and on upper surfaces of thighs; solid or blotched dark facial band extending from snout through eye to base of arm; a few scattered white dots on upper lip, sometimes extending to base of arm; skin smooth with pair of slightly elevated glandular ridges from behind the eyes, over the tympanum to base of arm. **Underside:** speckled with dark pigmentation; tends to become paler towards the centre. **Forelimbs:** upper surface of forelimb orange-brown; palms of hands smooth. **Hindlimbs:** upper surface of thighs have irregular dark brown bands; toe tips slightly expanded; subarticular tubercles moderately developed; well developed inner metatarsal tubercle; outer metatarsal tubercle a weakly defined ridge. **Sexual dimorphism:** male gular region is pale with diffuse mottling on pale grey background; vocal sac smooth and barely discernible.

Call

Repertoire of several notes: a chirp of four to six pulses is followed by two to six double clicks, often ending with one or two single-pulse clicks. Males call from concealed positions under dense vegetation.

Habitat and habits

Thickly vegetated seeps on gentle mountain slopes dominated by restio vegetation in montane fynbos in the Groot Winterhoek Mountains. Eggs and gravid females have been observed August to September; 6 to 12 eggs are laid in a single mass in dense restio seeps surrounded by taller vegetation.

TADPOLE

No free-swimming tadpole phase. Tadpoles develop in damp terrestrial nest.

KEY ID POINTS

- Restricted to the Groot Winterhoek Mountains (distinct from other species)
- Dorsal surface smooth with several elongated warts (distinct from *A. rugosa*)
- Snout bluntly rounded (more rounded than other species and distinct from *A. lightfooti* and *A. villiersi*)

Atherton de Villiers

- Underside and in particular the gular region is very pale (distinct from other species)

Atherton de Villiers

TRACK
108

De Villiers's Moss Frog

De Villiers se mospadda

Arthroleptella villiersi Hewitt, 1935

Named after zoologist Con de Villiers, who lectured at Stellenbosch University.

Conservation status: Not threatened.

De Villiers's Moss Frog: Kleinmond, Western Cape.

Description

Maximum size: 22 mm. **Body:** stout; snout bluntly pointed; head less depressed than in *A. lightfooti.* **Above:** variable from beige to black, usually khaki with lighter dorsolateral bands and irregular brown spots; pale vertebral line often present; dark band from nostril through the eye

Average length
♀

Average length
♂

Maximum size: 22 mm

KEY ID POINTS

Andrew Turner

- Found from the Hottentots
  Holland, Kogelberg and Kleinrivier
  mountains to the Bredasdorp
  mountains (distinct from
  A. lightfooti, A. bicolor, A. rugosa
  and *A. subvoce*)
- Dorsal surface smooth with several
  elongated warts (distinct from
  A. rugosa)
- Snout bluntly pointed (distinct from
  other species except *A. lightfooti*)
- A well-defined skin ridge from
  the angle of the mouth to the base
  of the arm (broken to absent in
  other species)

to base of arm; skin smooth with some low skin elevations sometimes forming dorsolateral elongate folds; well-defined skin ridge from the angle of the mouth to the base of the arm. **Underside:** see sexual dimorphism. **Hindlimbs:** posterior part of thigh with conspicuous glandular corrugation on the ventral side and upper surface of the thighs with small, blister-like elevations on the skin; webbing absent; inner metatarsal tubercle of moderate size, the outer much smaller; fingers and toes dark with lighter joints. **Sexual dimorphism:** male throat and underside dark with whitish markings; in female the white markings are often large blotches that tend to fuse.

Call

High-pitched chirp. Males call from concealed positions often close to previously laid eggs. Calling persists throughout most of the year as long as wet conditions prevail.

Habitat and habits

Seepages in montane fynbos along the Hottentots Holland, Kogelberg and Kleinrivier mountains to the Bredasdorp mountains. Parts of the distribution range overlap with those of *A. drewesii* and *A. landdrosia*. Breeds July to November; about 11 eggs are laid in a small jelly mass often on moss on rockfaces.

TADPOLE

No free-swimming tadpole phase. Tadpoles develop in damp terrestrial nest.

Andrew Turner

Egg nest in moss.

CACOS

BLIKSLANERTJIES

Cacosternum Boulenger, 1887

GREEK: *kakos* = bad; *stérnos* = breast. Refers to the reduced pectoral girdle and absence of an ossified omosternum and clavicle.

13 species, 11 in southern Africa

Boettger's Caco: Kubusi State Forest, Stutterheim, Eastern Cape.

Concentrated largely in southern Africa, this is a non-tropical group of frogs of which three species are known from the winter-rainfall areas of the region. Cacos are found in all southern African biomes. Most species prefer open areas with short, grassy vegetation but the Karoo Caco *C. karooicum* and Namaqua Caco *C. namaquense* are found in rocky places where they can shelter in cracks. These small, cryptic frogs are difficult to collect when they hide in tufts of grass.

Cacos are very small frogs with elongated bodies and small heads. The limbs are long and slender and the long digits are not webbed. Males often form very large choruses and may begin calling in the daytime especially after rain. Some 400 eggs are laid in individual clusters of 8–50. Tadpoles may develop either quickly or very slowly.

In terms of conservation status *C. karooicum*, *C. poyntoni*, and *C. striatum* are listed as 'Data Deficient' and *C. capense* as 'Vulnerable'.

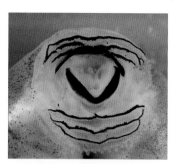

DISTINCTIVE CHARACTERS

ADULT
- Pupil horizontal
- No webbing on fingers and toes

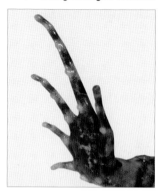

TADPOLE
- Small and benthic
- Develop rapidly to complete metamorphosis in as few as 17 days
- Vent supramarginal and dextral

- Dark spots on otherwise smooth white underside

KEY TO SPECIES

ADULT

TADPOLE
A key to the tadpoles in this genus cannot be resolved because of variation and complexity.

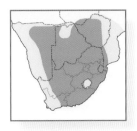

Boettger's Caco

Gewone blikslanertjie

Cacosternum boettgeri (Boulenger, 1882)

Named after herpetologist Oscar Boettger (1844–1910) of the Senckenberg Museum, Germany.

Taxonomy

The species currently named *C. boettgeri* may comprise more than one species, the precise status of which have not been determined. This field guide separates *Cacosternum* sp. A, formerly included with *C. boettgeri*.

Conservation status: Not threatened.

Bloemfontein, Free State.

Boettger's Caco: Mosdene, Limpopo Province.

Bloemfontein, Free State.

Description

Maximum size: 23 mm. **Body:** head narrow; neck long. **Above:** varies from emerald-green to light to dark brown; spots or stripes or uniform colour; upper lip with pale line from below nostril to base of arm; dark band bordered above by skin ridge running from eye to base of arm; skin smooth to slightly granular; soft; few small scattered warts. **Tympanum:** small; indistinct. **Underside:** smooth with discrete small grey to black spots; vocal sac of males often orange-brown and without spots. **Forelimbs:** thin; fingers without webbing; subarticular tubercles small. **Hindlimbs:** thin; toes without webbing; subarticular tubercles small; inner metatarsal tubercle small and rounded to conical; outer metatarsal tubercle absent to well developed. **Sexual dimorphism:** throat dark orange-brown in male.

Average length
♀

Average length
♂

Maximum size: 23 mm

Call

Rapid series of high-pitched clicks. Males call from concealed positions among vegetation at water level. In the early part of the season males call both day and night after rain. Very large choruses form in breeding season when they call until around midnight.

Habitat and habits

Variety of habitats in Nama Karoo, succulent Karoo, grassland and thicket; favouring open areas and especially abundant in grassland areas; may be found in forest clearings but usually absent from dense forest. During dry season they aestivate in cracks, under logs and stones and in animal burrows or unused termitaria.

TADPOLE

Length: up to 28 mm. **Shape:** body ovoid; slightly flattened. **Tail:** fin reaches deepest point in middle of tail; tapers to fine rounded tip. **Colour:** body moderately pigmented; varies in colour from cream to brown, can even be greenish but is rarely grey; fin opaque with fine stippling, sometimes with colourful reflections. **Eyes:** dorsolateral. **Nostrils:** small; narrowly spaced with lateral margins of nostrils smaller than interorbital distance. **Spiracle:** below body axis; directed 15°. **Vent:** supramarginal; dextral. **Mouth:** near-ventral. **Jaw sheaths:** delicate to moderate; moderately curved. **LTRF:** 4(2-4)/3 to 4(2-4)/4 to 3(2-3)/3(1); variation may represent different species within species complex. **Development:** eggs hatch within two days; development is rapid; tadpoles complete metamorphosis in about three weeks.

Tadpole: lateral view.

KEY ID POINTS

- Distributed very widely throughout southern Africa but absent from Namaqualand, Lesotho highlands, summit of the Zoutpansberg and most of the Mpumalanga escarpment, central Botswana and the Mozambique floodplains (distinct from *C. namaquense*)
- Dorsum smooth to slightly granular (distinct from *C. capense*)

- Underside with discrete small grey to black spots except on the throat (distinct from other species except *C. platys*, *C. striatum*, *C.* sp. A and *C.* sp. B)

- Subarticular tubercles on hands present, but small (distinct from *C. nanum*, *C. poyntoni*, *C.* sp. A and *C.* sp. B)
- Outer metatarsal tubercle absent to distinct
- Tympanum not visible (distinct from *C.* sp. A and sometimes *C. nanum*)

Cape Caco

Kaapse blikslanertjie

TRACK
110

Cacosternum capense Hewitt, 1925

LATIN: *capensis* = of the Cape (of Good Hope). Refers to the area in which this species is found.

Conservation status: Vulnerable. The range is restricted and the habitat is fragmented through agricultural development.

Cape Caco: Durbanville, Western Cape.

Description

Maximum size: 39 mm. **Body:** head narrow; body wide. **Dorsal skin:** colour varies from cream to grey to light brown with orange, dark brown or green flecks; upper lip has pale line from below nostril to base of arm; dark band bordered above by a skin ridge runs from eye to base of arm; granular with pair of huge blister-like glands low down on the back; second pair laterally in middle of back; smaller glands scattered over body. **Tympanum:** obscured. **Underside:** creamy white with distinct irregular dark olive to black patches which tend to fuse and become smaller peripherally; smooth. **Forelimbs:** subarticular tubercles on hands present but small; no webbing on fingers. **Hindlimbs:** no webbing; inner metatarsal tubercle flattened and flange-like; outer metatarsal tubercle absent. **Sexual dimorphism:** male throat dark.

Call

Harsh creak repeated at a rate of about two per second. Males occasionally call during

Average length
♀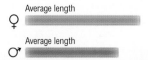

Average length
♂

Maximum size: 39 mm

the day but mainly at night, when they sit partially submerged in shallow water. Calling males are usually scattered and do not form dense choruses.

Habitat and habits
Restricted to low-lying flat or gently undulating areas with poorly drained clay or loamy soils. Breeds in shallow, temporary rain-filled depressions, pans or cultivated land June to August.

Atherton de Villiers

Habitat: pan in Swartland, Western Cape.

TADPOLE
Length: Up to 27 mm. **Shape:** body oval. **Tail:** deepest part of fin just behind middle; fin tapering to blunt tip. **Colour:** grey-brown with speckles of emerald-green. **Eyes:** dorsal to dorsolateral. **Nostrils:** distance between outer margins of nostrils smaller than interorbital distance. **Spiracle:** just below body axis. **Vent:** supramarginal; dextral. **Mouth:** single row of small papillae bordering laterally and behind; up to three rows postero-laterally. **Jaw sheaths:** moderate. **LTRF:** 2(2)/3(1) or 3(2-3)/3(1); outermost row in lower jaw half as long as other rows. **Development:** complete metamorphosis in about three months.

KEY ID POINTS

- Confined to the low-lying parts of the Western Cape west of the Cape fold mountains (distinct from other species except *C. platys* and *C. karooicum*)
- Dorsum with huge, blister-like warts low down (distinct from other species)
- Underside with prominent, large, irregularly shaped dark patches that become smaller peripherally (distinct from other species except *C. karooicum* and *C. namaquense*)

- Subarticular tubercles on hands present but small (distinct from *C. nanum*, *C. poyntoni*, *C.* sp. A and *C.* sp. B)
- Outer metatarsal tubercle absent (distinct from other species except *C. poyntoni*, *C. striatum* and sometimes *C. boettgeri* and *C. namaquense*)
- Tympanum not visible (distinct from *C.* sp. A and sometimes *C. nanum*)

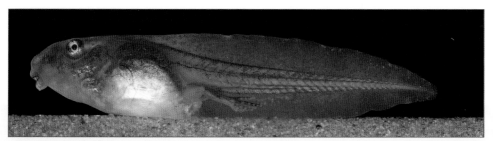

Tadpole: lateral view.

Karoo Caco

Karooblikslanertjie

TRACK
111

Cacosternum karooicum Boycott, De Villiers & Scott, 2002

Named after the Karoo, the region in which this species occurs.

Conservation status: Data Deficient. There is very little information about the distribution or ecology of this species.

Atherton de Villiers

Karoo Caco: Vrolijkheid Nature Reserve, Western Cape.

Description

Maximum size: 31 mm. **Body:** flattened; head narrow; body wide. **Above:** uniform olive-brown to khaki-brown, sometimes with tinge of orange or red; skin slightly granular with small warts. **Tympanum:** not visible. **Underside:** smooth; bold dark blotches bigger in middle and tending to fuse; throat of males dirty mustard-yellow. **Forelimbs:** fingers lack webbing, subarticular tubercles prominent. **Hindlimbs:** toes unwebbed; fifth toe short, extending to just before second subarticular tubercle of fourth toe; inner and outer metatarsal tubercles present. **Sexual dimorphism:** throat dirty mustard-yellow in male; small dark patches on white background in female; white velvety nuptial pads on upper surfaces of first and second fingers of breeding male.

Average length

♀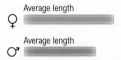

Average length

♂

Maximum size: 31 mm

KEY ID POINTS

- Confined to Karoo areas south of Grootdrif near Vanrhynsdorp and west of Beaufort West (distinct from other species except *C. boettgeri*)
- Dorsum slightly granular (distinct from *C. capense*)
- Underside with prominent dark blotches that tend to fuse (distinct from other species)

- Subarticular tubercles on hands present but small (distinct from *C. nanum, C. poyntoni, C.* sp. A and *C.* sp. B)
- Outer metatarsal tubercle absent (distinct from other species except *C. poyntoni, C. striatum* and sometimes *C. boettgeri* and *C. namaquense*)
- Tympanum not visible (distinct from *C.* sp. A and sometimes *C. nanum*)

Call

Prolonged coarse rattle; territorial call a short, loud croak. Males call occasionally during the day after rain but mainly at night from concealed to partially exposed sites under grass tufts or under rocks. Males often call sitting in water with only head, vocal sac and forelimbs protruding above water. Males maintain a territory and are usually spaced about 1 m apart. When another male intrudes, the dominant male will utter a territorial call.

Habitat and habits

Restricted to arid Karoo regions of the Western and Northern Cape. At present known only from a few widely separated localities – full distribution unknown.

TADPOLE

Length: up to 41 mm. **Shape:** body oval, flattened. **Tail:** long; fin shallow; deepest point of tail halfway along tail; rounded tip. **Colour:** body dark brown to grey; tail light brown; underside pigmented laterally. **Eyes:** dorsolateral. **Nostrils:** small; widely spaced. **Spiracle:** midway along body; constricted; directed backwards at 40°. **Vent:** supramarginal; dextral. **Mouth:** large; ventral; single row of papillae laterally and ventrally; double row at mouth corner. **Jaw sheaths:** moderate; strong; flexed with lateral inflections; slightly serrated margin. **LTRF:** 4(2-4)/3(1). **Development:** completed in about four weeks.

Atherton de Villiers

Habitat: Vrolijkheid Nature Reserve, Western Cape.

Tadpole: lateral view.

Namaqua Caco

Namakwa-blikslanertjie

TRACK
112

Cacosternum namaquense Werner, 1910

Named after Namaqualand where this species was first discovered.

Conservation status: Not threatened.

Namaqua Caco: Kamieskroon, Northern Cape.

Description

Maximum size: 25 mm. **Body:** head narrow; body wide. **Above:** cryptic coloration with blotches of beige and brown and stippled markings; distinct pale triangle on the head; skin granular. **Nostrils:** small. **Tympanum:** small and often obscured. **Underside:** smooth and light coloured with distinct dark patches that tend to become smaller peripherally; mottling on the throat. **Forelimbs:** subarticular tubercles present and variable in size; no webbing. **Hindlimbs:** toes lack webbing; inner metatarsal tubercle is distinct but narrow; outer metatarsal tubercle reduced or absent. **Sexual dimorphism:** male throat dark.

Average length
♀

Average length
♂

Maximum size: 25 mm

Call

Harsh creak with a slightly rising note. Males call from concealed positions among vegetation, from under rocks or in cracks or exposed sites alongside or in the water. Males also emit a clicking territorial call and fight off intruding males.

Habitat and habits

Occurs mainly in upland succulent Karoo vegetation. Breeds opportunistically during rainy weather, at any time July to April, in temporary rain-filled rock pools, river beds, permanent pools, seeps and springs and also in dams, quarries and borrow-pits.

Habitat: dam in Kamieskroon area.

KEY ID POINTS

- Distributed throughout Namaqualand from Vanrhynsdorp northwards to southern Namibia (distinct from species beyond this range)
- Dorsum granular and with distinct pale triangle between eyes and snout (distinct from other species)
- Underside with bold, dark, irregular blotches (distinct from other species except *C. karooicum* and *C. capense*)

- Subarticular tubercles on hands present and variable
- Outer metatarsal tubercle reduced or absent (distinct from *C. karooicum*)
- Tympanum not visible (distinct from *C.* sp. A and sometimes *C. nanum*)

TADPOLE

Length: up to 50 mm. **Shape:** body large; oval. **Tail:** shallow; reaching deepest point in middle of tail; tip bluntly rounded. **Colour:** overall brown; underside sparsely pigmented. **Eyes:** dorsolateral. **Nostrils:** small; narrowly spaced; smaller than eye lens; positioned closer to snout than eyes. **Spiracle:** below body axis; directed postero-dorsally at $45°$ angle. **Vent:** supramarginal; dextral. **Mouth:** anteroventral; single row of papillae below; three rows laterally around mouth corner. **Jaw sheaths:** moderate to extremely large. **LTRF:** 4(2-4)/3.

Tadpole: lateral view.

Bronze Caco

Bronsblikslanertjie

Cacosternum nanum Boulenger, 1887

LATIN: *nanus* = dwarf. Refers to the very small size of this species.

Conservation status: Not threatened.

TRACK
113

Bronze Caco: Drakensberg Gardens, KwaZulu-Natal.

Description

Maximum size: 23 mm. **Above:** grey or brown, usually with bronze tinge; darker flecks on warts; pale vertebral line often present; dark facial line running from snout through eye almost to base of arm; skin granular; slightly elevated granular skin ridge running from behind eye, over tympanum to base of arm. **Tympanum:** partially obscured to not detectable.
Underside: varying amount of grey or black spotting, especially towards front and sides; smooth; gular sac collapses into two lateral folds. **Forelimbs:** subarticular tubercles prominent; palmar tubercles smaller than subarticular tubercles. **Hindlimbs:** usually with prominent dark transverse bands on thigh; webbing rudimentary or absent; inner metatarsal tubercle small; outer tubercle small to well developed. **Sexual dimorphism:** throat of male with dense dark spots leaving a pale reticulation.

Average length
♀

Average length
♂

Maximum size: 23 mm

KEY ID POINTS

- Distributed widely through the southern and eastern parts of South Africa (distinct from *C. capense*, *C. karooicum*, *C. namaquense* and *C. platys*)
- Dorsum granular (distinct from *C. capense*)
- Subarticular tubercles on hands well developed (distinct from other species except *C. poyntoni*, *C.* sp. A and *C.* sp. B)
- Outer metatarsal tubercle small to well developed (distinct from *C. capense*, *C. poyntoni*, *C. striatum* and sometimes *C. namaquense*)
- Tympanum sometimes visible (distinct from other species except *C.* sp. A

- Underside white with dense black spots concentrated anteriorly (distinct from other species except *C. parvum*)

Call

Metallic *che-che-she* followed by a very rapidly repeated series of clicks. Males call from concealed positions among vegetation close to water. Calling peaks at night; may call on overcast days following rain.

Note large vocal sac.

Habitat and habits

Areas with relatively high rainfall in a variety of vegetation types: fynbos, savanna, grassland, thicket and forest. Breeds mostly in small ponds, dams, vleis, streams, roadside pools or flooded grassland.

TADPOLE

Length: up to 28 mm. **Shape:** body flat; oval. **Tail:** dorsal fin slightly deeper than lower fin; tail deepest about two-fifths from front; ends in sharp tip. **Colour:** dark grey; fins mostly transparent with darker grey mottling especially on tail shaft; head semi-transparent; three dark stripes running backwards; dark stripe from snout to each eye. **Eyes:** dorsolateral; well spaced. **Nostrils:** narrowly spaced; distance between outer margins of nostrils smaller than interorbital distance. **Spiracle:** about halfway along flank; directed posteriorly at 60°. **Vent:** supramarginal; dextral. **Mouth:** anteroventral; single row of papillae laterally and behind; double row at mouth corner. **Jaw sheaths:** delicate to moderate. **LTRF:** 3(2-3)/3; sometimes proximal row in lower jaw has small medial gap. **Development:** complete in 17 days.

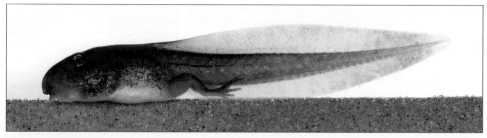

Tadpole: lateral view.

Mountain Caco

Bergbliklslanertjie

Cacosternum parvum Poynton, 1963

LATIN: *parvus* = small. Refers to the extremely small size of this species.

Conservation status: Not threatened.

TRACK
114

Mountain Caco: Dragon's Peak, KwaZulu-Natal.

Description

Maximum size: 16 mm. **Body:** eye large; eye diameter exceeding eye-nostril distance. **Above:** olive-brown to dark brown to blackish; often with faint orange vertebral line; darker markings centred on elevated skin glands; upper lip black with white speckles; skin slightly granular; warts on head elongated almost to middle of back. **Tympanum:** not visible. **Underside:** white with intense black spotting on chest and throat, leaving faint grey network; isolated black spots over abdomen; very dense, dark spots on thighs; smooth. **Forelimbs:** subarticular tubercles well developed. **Hindlimbs:** single broad transverse band on thigh; toes lack webbing; inner metatarsal tubercle small and rounded; outer metatarsal tubercle minute. **Sexual dimorphism:** male throat dark.

Average length

♀

Average length

♂

Maximum size: 16 mm

Call

Brisk chirp emitted at long intervals; the territorial call consists of rapidly repeated clicks. Males call from concealed positions under grass at edges of shallow puddles.

Habitat and habits

High altitudes on Drakensberg escarpment and parts of Mpumalanga and Swaziland. Breeds in grassy ponds, marshes, streams and undulated grassland.

TADPOLE

Not described, but probably very similar to *C. nanum*.

KEY ID POINTS

- Seepage wetlands on the lower slopes of the Drakensberg escarpment and parts of Mpumalanga and Swaziland (distinct from other species except *C. boettgeri* and *C. nanum*)
- Dorsum smooth to slightly granular (distinct from *C. capense*)
- Underside white with dense black spots concentrated anteriorly (distinct from other species except *C. nanum*)
- Subarticular tubercles on hands present but small (distinct from *C. nanum*, *C. poyntoni*, *C.* sp. A and *C.* sp. B)
- Outer metatarsal tubercle very small (distinct from *C. capense*)
- Tympanum not visible (distinct from *C.* sp. A and sometimes *C. nanum*)

Marius Burger

Colour variation.

Flat Caco

Platblikslanertjie

TRACK
115

Cacosternum platys Rose, 1950

LATIN: *plattus* = flat. Refers to the flattened appearance of the species.

Conservation status: Not threatened.

Flat Caco: Kleinmond, Western Cape.

Description
Maximum size: 22 mm. **Body:** head narrow; body wide. **Above:** grey to brown to green; often with dark spots or stripes; pale vertebral line sometimes present; dark band from eye to base of arm; pale band along jaw-line from under eye to base of arm; smooth to slightly granular. **Tympanum:** obscured. **Underside:** smooth; discrete small grey or black spots. **Forelimbs:** thin; long, subarticular tubercles small. **Hindlimbs:** thin; long; inner metatarsal tubercle small; outer metatarsal tubercle very small. **Sexual dimorphism:** male throat dark.

Average length
♀

Average length
♂

Maximum size: 22 mm

KEY ID POINTS

- Confined to the Western Cape south of 32° 30' latitude (distinct from other species except *C. capense*)
- Dorsum smooth to slightly granular (distinct from *C. capense*)
- Underside with discrete small grey to black spots but not on the throat (distinct from other species except *C. boettgeri*, *C. striatum*, *C.* sp. A and *C.* sp. B)
- Subarticular tubercles on hands present but small (distinct from *C. nanum*, *C. poyntoni*, *C.* sp. A and *C.* sp. B)
- Outer metatarsal tubercle small (distinct from *C. capense*)
- Tympanum not visible (distinct from *C.* sp. A and sometimes *C. nanum*)

Call
Series of pulsed chirps, starting slowly and gradually accelerating. Males call from concealed positions among vegetation at edge of water.

Habitat and habits
Western Cape region; in flooded grassland and seepages even at sea level.

Pale colour form: Noordhoek, Western Cape.

TADPOLE
Shape: Body oval. **Tail:** fin opaque; tapers to fine tip. **Colour:** cream to brown with golden stipples. **Eyes:** near lateral. **Nostrils:** small; fairly narrowly spaced; lateral margins of nostrils smaller than interorbital distance. **Spiracle:** below body axis; terminating in free tube; directed backwards. **Vent:** supramarginal; dextral. **Mouth:** near-ventral; single row of papillae behind; double row at mouth corners. **Jaw sheaths:** moderately built. LTRF: 4(2-4)/3. **Development:** hatch after two days; metamorphosis complete in less than three weeks.

Tadpole: lateral view.

Poynton's Caco

Poynton se blikslanertjie

Cacosternum poyntoni Lambiris, 1988

Named after eminent South African herpetologist, J.C. Poynton.

Conservation status: Data Deficient. This species is known from a single museum specimen discovered in a bottle in 1954 near Pietermaritzburg. It is probable that this species is an atypical *C. nanum*.

Mike Cooper

Poynton's Caco: illustration based on type specimen.

Probable average length

♀

Probable average length

♂

Maximum size: 15 mm

KEY ID POINTS

- Dorsum smooth with a distinct, bold, reticulated pattern of golden-brown blotches on creamy yellow background (distinct from other species)
- Underside with distinct, bold, reticulated pattern of golden-brown blotches on creamy yellow background (distinct from other species)

- Subarticular tubercles on hands well developed (distinct from other species except *C. nanum*, *C.* sp. A and *C.* sp. B)
- Outer metatarsal tubercle absent (distinct from other species except *C. poyntoni*, *C. striatum* and sometimes *C. boettgeri* and *C. namaquense*)
- Tympanum not visible (distinct from *C.* sp. B and sometimes *C. nanum*)

Description:

Maximum size: 15 mm. Above: bold reticulated pattern of golden-brown blotches on creamy yellow background, forming a more or less symmetrical pattern; pale line along upper lip from snout to base of arm; skin smooth. **Tympanum:** obscured. **Underside:** bold reticulated pattern of dark brown blotches on creamy yellow background. **Forelimbs:** tubercles prominent and single. **Hindlimbs:** fairly robust legs; webbing absent; blotches on ventral surface of thighs much darker than those on abdomen; inner metatarsal tubercle well developed and outer absent; toe tips slightly bulbous.

Call

Unknown.

Habitat and habits

Known from a single specimen collected at Town Bush Valley, Pietermaritzburg, which is situated in coast-hinterland bushveld.

TADPOLE

Unknown.

Striped Caco

Gestreepte blikslanertjie

Cacosternum striatum FitzSimons, 1947

LATIN: *striare* = streaked. Refers to the pair of dorsolateral dark stripes on the back.

Conservation status: Data Deficient.

Striped Caco: Franklin, KwaZulu-Natal.

Description

Maximum size: 21 mm. Above: light brown to orange-brown or greenish; pair of dorsolateral dark stripes running from behind eyes to groin; series of small, slightly elongated paravertebral skin ridges associated with dark markings, especially over front half of back; flanks and dorsal surface of limbs darkly spotted; dark broad facial band from snout through eye to base of

Average length
♀

Average length
♂

Maximum size: 21 mm

KEY ID POINTS

- Pair of dorsolateral dark stripes running from behind eyes to groin (distinct from other species)

- Known only from KwaZulu-Natal (distinct from other species except *C. boettgeri, C. nanum, C. poyntoni, C.* sp. A and *C.* sp. B)
- Dorsum smooth to slightly granular (distinct from *C. capense*)
- Underside smooth, immaculate white or with pale grey blotches (distinct from other species except *C. boettgeri, C. platys, C.* sp. A and *C.* sp. B)
- Tympanum not visible (distinct from *C.* sp. A

and sometimes *C. nanum*)
- Subarticular tubercles on hands present but small (distinct from *C. nanum, C. poyntoni, C.* sp. A and *C.* sp. B)
- Outer metatarsal tubercle absent (distinct from other species except *C. poyntoni, C. striatum* and sometimes *C. boettgeri* and *C. namaquense*)
- Pale line on back of thighs from heel to heel (distinct from other species)

arm; smooth to slightly granular. **Underside:** smooth, immaculate white or with pale grey blotches. **Tympanum:** not visible. **Hindlimbs:** pale line on back of thighs from heel to heel; toes without webbing. **Sexual dimorphism:** male throat dark.

Call
A protracted creak interspersed with three cricket-like chirps. Males call from concealed

positions among vegetation at water level, beginning in late afternoon and continuing all night.

Habitat and habits
Variety of grassland areas.

TADPOLE
Unknown, but probably very similar to the *C. boettgeri* complex.

Marius Burger

Two colour variations: Franklin, KwaZulu-Natal.

Rhythmic Caco

Ritmiese blikslanertjie

Cacosternum sp. A

TRACK
117

Conservation status: Data Deficient.

Marius Burger

Rhythmic Caco: KwaZulu-Natal midlands.

Description

Maximum size: 19 mm. **Body:** morphologically very similar to *C. boettgeri;* head acutely rounded; eyes protruding and visible from below. **Above:** colour varies greatly: combinations of dark grey, beige, reddish-brown, dark brown or green; dark brown vertebral band and pale vertebral line often present; dark facial band from snout through eyes to base of arm; white line along upper jaw from snout to base of arm; smooth with few irregular warts. **Tympanum:** obscured. **Underside:** immaculate white; occasional specimen with small dark spots; smooth. **Forelimbs:** no supernumerary tubercles on palm; subarticular tubercles well developed. **Hindlimbs:** inner metatarsal tubercle small, conical; outer metatarsal tubercle very small and additional tubercle at base of foot. **Sexual dimorphism:** male throat dark.

Average length
♀

Average length
♂

Maximum size: 19 mm

KEY ID POINTS

- Confined to the Mooi River area of KwaZulu-Natal (distinct from other species except *C. boettgeri* and *C. nanum*)
- Dorsum smooth to slightly granular (distinct from *C. capense*)
- Subarticular tubercles on hands well developed (distinct from other species except *C. nanum*, *C. poyntoni* and *C. sp. B*)
- Outer metatarsal tubercle small (distinct from *C. capense*)
- Tympanum not visible (distinct from *C. sp. A* and sometimes *C. nanum*)

- Underside immaculate or sometimes with black dots (distinct from other species except *C. boettgeri*, *C. platys*, *C. striatum* and *C. sp. B*)

Call

Distinctive series of single- and double-pulsed notes arranged in a rhythmic pattern and ending with a series of chirps.

Habitat and habits

Flat open terrain where there are shallow pools; flooded grassy patches in grassland in the vicinity of Mooi River in KwaZulu-Natal.

TADPOLE

Unknown.

Above and below: Two colour variations from KwaZulu-Natal midlands.

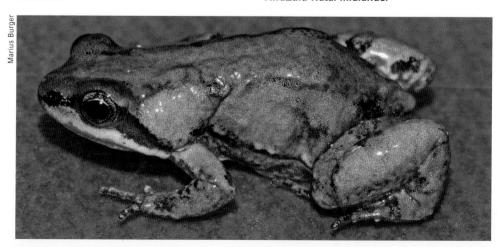

KwaZulu Caco

KwaZulublikslanertjie

Cacosternum **sp. B**

Conservation status: Unknown.

TRACK
118

KwaZulu Caco: Donnybrook, KwaZulu-Natal.

Marius Burger

Description

Maximum size: 28 mm. **Body:** more robust than other Caco species; eyes protruding; visible from below. **Above:** grey to dark brown; pale tan vertebral band bordered in black; pale vertebral line usually present; dark V-shaped interorbital bar pointing backwards; dark facial mask from snout through nostril and eye to base of arm; short pale skin ridge from the angle of the mouth to base of arm; skin smooth to finely granular. **Underside:** pale with large prominent black blotches that tend to fuse on abdomen; dense mottling over pectoral and gular regions;

Average length
♀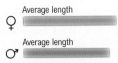

Average length
♂

Maximum size: 28 mm

KEY ID POINTS

- Only known from a few localities in central KwaZulu-Natal (distinct from other species except *C. boettgeri* and *C. nanum*)
- Dorsum smooth to slightly granular (distinct from *C. capense*)
- Underside with prominent large black blotches that tend to fuse (distinct from other species in KwaZulu-Natal except *C. nanum*)
- Subarticular tubercles on hands well developed (distinct from other species except *C. nanum*, *C. poyntoni* and *C.* sp. A)
- Outer metatarsal tubercle present as a pale spot (distinct from other species)
- Tympanum visible (distinct from other species except *C. nanum*)

Marius Burger

smooth. **Tympanum:** visible. **Forelimbs:** subarticular tubercles prominent. **Hindlimbs:** inner metatarsal tubercle small and conical; outer tubercle present as pale spot. **Sexual dimorphism:** male throat very dark.

Call

Similar to that of *C. nanum,* being a series of regularly repeated pulsed chirps, but the call duration is generally longer than that of *C. nanum* and includes slow-pulsed triple clicks.

Habitat and habits

Small area of central KwaZulu-Natal.

TADPOLE

Unknown.

Marius Burger

Dark colour form: Donnybrook, KwaZulu-Natal.

MICRO FROG

MIKROPADDA

Microbatrachella Hewitt, 1926

GREEK: *micros* = small; *batrachos* = frog; *ella* = diminutive. Refers to the very small size of the frog.

Only one species in the genus

Micro Frog

Mikropadda

TRACK
119

Microbatrachella capensis (Boulenger, 1910)

LATIN: *capensis* = of the Cape Province. Refers to the area where the frog occurs.

Conservation status: Critically Endangered. Restricted to four known subpopulations in fynbos wetlands of the southwestern Cape coastal lowlands – a total area of less than 10 km². Most suitable habitat has been destroyed by urban development and the few remaining populations are severely threatened.

Left: Micro Frog: Kleinmond, Western Cape.
Below left to right: Colour variations from Kenilworth, Western Cape.

Average length
♀

Average length
♂

Maximum size: 18 mm

Description

Maximum size: 18 mm; one of the smallest frogs in southern Africa. **Above:** usually brown but may be greenish to dark grey with darker markings; pale vertebral line often present; broad, light-coloured paravertebral bands common; dorsal skin slightly granular. **Pupil:** horizontal. **Tympanum:** normally not visible. **Underside:** smooth with varying degrees of black and white mottling. **Limbs:** legs are thin and short with the tibia less than half body length; toes webbed with two to three of the phalanges of the longest toe free of webbing. **Sexual dimorphism:** Male gular disc light brown and free of mottling; in female mottling extends onto the throat.

Call

Series of low-pitched *tshk-tshk* scratching sounds, about three per second. Males call in dense choruses at night from concealed positions among vegetation at water level, or may be more exposed on floating vegetation during daylight.

Habitat and habits

Undisturbed fynbos pools and vleis in the coastal lowlands of the Cape Flats, Betty's Bay, Kleinmond and Agulhas Plain. Suitable sites have darkly stained and slightly acidic water. Breeding takes place during the rainy season May to October with peak activity in July. Males congregate in large numbers at breeding sites to call and mate. When eggs are laid, clusters of up to 20 are attached to submerged vegetation just below the surface. The small tadpoles are benthic feeders.

DISTINCTIVE CHARACTERS

ADULT
- Tibia less than half body length
- Varying degrees of black and white mottling, from very prominent to almost absent
- Moderate webbing with two to three phalanges of the longest toe being free (distinct from sympatric species of *Cacosternum* and *Arthroleptella* which have no webbing)

TADPOLE
- Narrow medial gap in lower jaw papillae
- Vent paragyrinid
- Found in low-lying coastal Western Cape

TADPOLE

Length: up to 25 mm. **Shape:** body narrowly oval; anterior end of head rounded. **Tail:** tail fin rises gently; reaches highest point in middle of tail; terminates in sharp tip. **Colour:** brown to dark grey above; inner margin of nostrils and area between nostrils dark; below gill region transparent; abdomen white. **Eyes:** lateral. **Nostrils:** small; fairly narrow; close to tip of snout. **Spiracle:** paragyrinid, directed posteriorly at $10°$. **Vent:** marginal; dextral. **Mouth:** near-ventral; two rows of papillae laterally; single row with characteristic small medial gap below. **Jaw sheaths:** delicate. **LTRF:** 3(2-3)/3(1).

Tadpole: lateral view.

Mouthparts.

KLOOF FROG

KLOOFPADDA

Natalobatrachus Hewitt & Methuen, 1912

Named after Natal (now the province of KwaZulu-Natal) where the species occurs; GREEK: *batrachos* = frog.

Only one species in the genus

Kloof Frog

Kloofpadda

TRACK
120

Natalobatrachus bonebergi Hewitt & Methuen, 1912

Named after Father P. Boneberg of the Mariannhill Mission who was the first to collect this species in the early 1900s.

Conservation status: Endangered. Restricted to the coastal and gallery forests of northern Eastern Cape and eastern KwaZulu-Natal. Sugar plantations and housing developments have encroached upon the specialised habitat of the species.

Kloof Frog: Dukaduka Forest, KwaZulu-Natal.

Average length

♀

Average length

♂

Maximum size: 37 mm

Description

Maximum size: 37 mm. **Body:** slender; long, pointed snout overhanging an undershot jaw; longitudinal elevated skin ridges on the back. **Above:** brown to grey with small pale spots scattered over the back; often with pale vertebral line, which is sometimes superimposed on a broader vertebral band; pale triangular patch on top of snout; distinct dark facial band running from snout, through lower half of eye, over tympanum to base of arm; this band is bordered below by narrow white band along upper jaw. **Pupil:** horizontal. **Underside:** cream-coloured and usually freckled to some degree. **Forelimbs:** fingers with large T-shaped expanded tips. **Hindlimbs:** toes only slightly webbed; tips slightly less expanded than fingers. **Sexual dimorphism:** male fingers with conspicuous nuptial pads; vocal sac absent in males and the throat bulges only slightly while calling.

Call

Soft click at irregular intervals. Males call either from exposed elevated positions (1 to 2 m above water or ground) or from branches, leaves, rocks or partially concealed positions in holes or cracks in the ground or among rocks.

DISTINCTIVE CHARACTERS

ADULT
- Fingers unwebbed with terminal T-shaped expansions
- Snout pointed and overhanging the mouth
- Pale triangular patch on the snout

TADPOLE
- Distance between outer margins of nostrils greater than distance between inner margins of the eyes

Calling male: note small vocal sac.

Developing egg mass.

Female moistening egg mass with urine.

Habitat and habits

Dark kloofs and rocky stream-beds in closed canopy – never in open areas. Agile jumpers and good swimmers. Expanded adhesive toe tips allow easy movement over vertical rockfaces and slippery surfaces. Breeds in the warmer months October to May. Clutches of about 100 eggs are laid in clear masses attached to leaves, rocks or branches overhanging water, either close to or well above the water level in places generally inaccessible to most predators. Tadpoles develop inside the jelly mass and after about six days drop into water below. Adults are frequently found close to egg masses, and in dry conditions females urinate over the eggs to keep them moist.

Habitat: forest stream in Vernon Crookes Nature Reserve.

TADPOLE

Length: up to 41 mm. **Shape:** body oval; streamlined. **Tail:** very long; tail fin parallel and shallow, barely higher than body; dorsal fin starts off behind body; reaches deepest point in middle of tail. **Colour:** grey-brown above with specks of gold; fin transparent with small dark speckles; skin covering gill chambers is completely transparent. **Eyes:** near lateral. **Nostrils:** small; widely spaced, distance between outside edges of nostrils greater than between inside edges of eyes. **Spiracle:** just below body axis; directed dorsoposteriorly. **Vent:** supramarginal; dextral. **Mouth:** anteroventral; double row of small rounded papillae laterally and below. **Jaw sheaths:** moderate; flexed. **LTRF:** 5(2-5)/3 or 6(2-6)/3. **Behaviour:** often found among decaying organic matter in the bottom of pools.

Tadpole: lateral view.

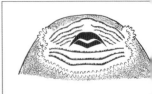

Mouthparts.

MARSH FROG

MOERASPADDA

Poyntonia Channing & Boycott, 1989

Named after South African herpetologist, J.C. Poynton.

Only one species in the genus

Montane Marsh Frog

Bergmoeraspadda

Poyntonia paludicola Channing & Boycott, 1989

LATIN: *paludicola* = marsh-dwelling.

Conservation status: Near threatened. The species is confined to marshy areas and seepage zones in mountain fynbos in the Western Cape. Although much of the habitat inhabited by this species is protected, distribution is restricted and knowledge of population dynamics is limited.

Montane Marsh Frog: Jonkershoek, Western Cape.

Average length

♀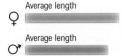

Average length

♂

Maximum size: 30 mm

DISTINCTIVE CHARACTERS

ADULT

- White or orange stripes running from eye to upper lip (distinct from other genera)
- Elevated granular region behind eyes (distinct from other genera, except toads)
- Tympanum not visible
- Fingers and toes without discs
- Mid-tarsal tubercle absent
- Moderate webbing between toes

Atherton de Villiers

TADPOLE

- Proportionally very long, shallow tail
- Numerous white-tipped tubercles covering the body and front third of tail
- Found in seeps on Western Cape mountains

Richard Boycott

Development stages.

Description

Maximum size: 30 mm. **Body:** squat with many wart-like protuberances giving a superficially toad-like appearance. **Above:** grey-brown; pale to reddish vertebral line often present; distinct pale ridge from the eye to the angle of the mouth; two or three evenly spaced pale lines from lower margin of eye to jaw; back is extremely granular and an elevated area behind the eyes resembles the parotoid glands of toads; elevated skin ridge runs from behind eyes to base of arm. **Pupil:** horizontal. **Tympanum:** not visible. **Underside:** with or without dark flecks. **Forelimbs:** fingers fringed with webbing. **Hindlimbs:** long, moderately webbed toes;

no outer metatarsal tubercle.
Sexual dimorphism: Female head
narrower than that of male; female
tibia shorter than that of male;
gular region darker in male.

Call
Between one and six brief croaks.
Throughout the year during
wet conditions males call from
concealed positions.

Habitat and habits
Shallow seepage zones, small
streams and marshy areas on
mountain slopes at altitudes
20 to 1 800 m where rainfall is
2 000 to 3 000 mm per annum.
Breeds from late summer (April)
to late winter (August).
Oviposition and eggs are
unknown. Tadpoles long and dark,
the body covered with numerous
small white-tipped tubercles.

Atherton de Villiers

*Habitat: mountain seep near Franschhoek Pass,
Western Cape.*

TADPOLE
Length: up to 32 mm. **Shape:** very long; streamlined; body elongated and oval. **Tail:** three
times as long as body; not higher than body; shallow parallel tail fin only begins behind
body; tapers to rounded tip. **Colour:** light brown with dark speckles; fins lightly pigmented;
numerous white-tipped tubercles cover body and front third of tail; tubercles absent below
level of nostrils and eyes; covering of gut coils darkly stippled. **Eyes:** near lateral. **Nostrils:**
periphery darkly pigmented with small posterio-medial flap. **Spiracle:** below; directed at
45°. **Vent:** dextral; marginal. **Mouth:** small; ventral; single row of small rounded papillae
below; multiple papillae at angle of mouth; no papillae above mouth corner. **Jaw sheaths:**
moderate. **LTRF:** 1/2 or 2(2)/2. **Behaviour:** found in very shallow water in seeps; often hides
in soft mud or slimy algae.

Richard Boycott

Tadpole: dorsolateral view.

RIVER FROGS

RIVIERPADDAS

Amietia Dubois 1987

Named after West African herpetologist, J-L. Amiet.

15 species, seven in southern Africa

Common River Frog: Potchefstroom, North West Province.

Southern African River Frogs are large and because two species are widely distributed and partly diurnal in their habits, they are commonly encountered and thus familiar to many people. Distinction between the species is not always obvious without careful examination of details such as webbing. Superficially, River Frogs can be confused with genera such as Grass Frogs *Ptychadena*, Stream Frogs *Strongylopus* and Golden-backed Frogs *Hylarana*, but they can be told apart by careful observation of webbing, leg length and dorsal ridges.

Most species live in close proximity to water. They are accomplished jumpers and swimmers because of their long, powerful legs and extensive webbing between toes and metatarsals. If threatened, they immediately take refuge in water.

Calling occurs by night and day, at any time of the year; it reaches a peak during autumn. Males of most species produce a double call, consisting of clicks and a croak.

Calling male: Bryanston, Gauteng.

They are generally heard calling singly or in small groups, but under suitable conditions large numbers of males may assemble and call. Eggs are laid in individual jelly capsules and deposited in shallow static or slow-flowing water. Tadpoles remain motionless for long periods but can swim rapidly if disturbed. Development may be slow in cold conditions and tadpoles can grow to a considerable size before metamorphosis takes place.

DISTINCTIVE CHARACTERS

ADULT
- Skin ridges on the back, if present, are broken and do not extend along the full length of the body (distinct from *Ptychadena*)
- Pupil horizontal
- Length of tibia more than half the length of the body (distinct from *Hildebrandtia* and *Hylarana*)
- Outer metatarsals separated by webbing (distinct from *Strongylopus*)

TADPOLE
- Muscular tails and thus strong swimmers
- Tail as high as, or higher than, body
- Spiracle constricted
- Vent marginal and dextral

KEY TO SPECIES

ADULT

1 Found north of Limpopo River 2
   Found south of Limpopo River 3
2 Tympanum less than half diameter of eye .... **Inyanga River Frog** *A. inyangae* (p.402)
   Tympanum more than half diameter of eye .... **Common River Frog** *A. quecketti* (p.396)
3 One or fewer phalanges of longest toe free of webbing 4
   One and a half or more phalanges of longest toe free of webbing 5
4 Head width half length of body .... **Maluti River Frog** *A. umbraculata* (p.404)
   Head width less than half length of body .... **Cape River Frog** *A. fuscigula* (p.400)
5 Found at high altitudes in Drakensberg-Maluti range 6
   Found other than at high altitudes in Drakensberg-Maluti range 7
6 Dorsal skin very warty .... **Phofung River Frog** *A. vertebralis* (p.408)
   Dorsal skin smooth .... **Drakensberg River Frog** *A. dracomontana* (p.398)
   or **Common River Frog** *A. angolensis* (p.396) (these two species are morphologically indistinguishable)
7 More than two phalanges of longest toe free of webbing .... **Van Dijk's River Frog** *A. vandijki* (p.406)
   Two or fewer phalanges of longest toe free of webbing ...... **Common River Frog** *A. angolensis* (p.396)

TADPOLE

1 Elygium or umbraculum present on eye; tadpole from high-lying parts of the Drakensberg 2
   No elygium or umbraculum present on eye, tadpole not from high-lying parts of the Drakensberg 4
2 Dorsal tail fin starts directly behind body .... *A. dracomontana* (p.398)
   Anterior part of dorsal fin very low 3
3 Anterior third of dorsal tail fin very low or absent; spiracle well below .... *A. umbraculata* (p.404)
   Anterior quarter of dorsal tail fin very low or absent; spiracle below .... *A. vertebralis* (p.408)
4 Seven labial tooth rows in lower jaw and six or seven in upper jaw .... *A. vandijki* (p.406)
   Three or four labial tooth rows in lower jaw and four in upper jaw 5
5 Tail fin broad, reaching deepest point at point two-thirds down tail; tapers to a rounded tip .. *A. inyangae* (p.402)
   Tail fin long, reaching deepest point shortly after middle; tapers to a pointed tip 6
6 Fin rises gradually from body; three labial teeth rows in lower jaw; tail tip not darker ....
   .... *A. angolensis* (p.396)
   Fin rises steeply from body; four labial teeth rows in lower jaw; tail tip often darker ....
   .... *A. fuscigula* (p.400)

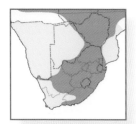

Common River Frog

Gewone rivierpadda

TRACK
122

Amietia quecketti (Boulenger, 1895)

Named after Mr FJ Queckett of Pietermaritzburg

Conservation status: Not threatened.

Common River Frog: Bryanston, Gauteng.

Identification

Maximum size: 90 mm. **Body:** streamlined with pointed snout; head narrow. **Above:** various shades of brown or green, scattered with circular dark blotches about the size of the eye; a pale vertebral line often present; lower parts of flanks reticulated grey or mottled; skin smooth with longitudinal, slightly elevated broken skin ridges. **Tympanum:** large, more than half the diameter of the eye. **Underside:** smooth; white with throat sometimes marbled grey, brown or black. **Hindlimbs:** long muscular legs barred, posterior surfaces mottled grey but never yellow; feet long; extensive webbing with two phalanges of the longest toe free of web. **Sexual dimorphism:** dark, swollen nuptial pad on male thumb during breeding season.

Average length
♀

Average length
♂

Maximum size: 90 mm

KEY ID POINTS

- Morphologically indistinguishable from *A. dracomontana* but can be identified by the call
- Head narrow; when viewed from above eyes protrude beyond the outline of head
- Tympanum more than half diameter of eye (distinct from *A. inyangae*)
- Head width approximately 58 to 66% of tibia length (distinct from *A. fuscigula*)
- Two phalanges of longest toe free of webbing (distinct from *A. fuscigula* and *A. umbraculata*)

Call
Rapid series of six or seven short rapid *kik-kik-kik-kik* clicks (sounding like a rattle), followed by a short *keroip* croak. Calling may be heard throughout the year. Males call during day and night from either partially concealed or exposed sites close to water's edge.

Habitat and habits
On the banks of slow-flowing streams or other permanent bodies of water in a wide range of wetland habitats in grassland, savanna and forest fringe. Frequently inhabit garden ponds and water features. If disturbed, quickly jump into the water and hide in soft mud.

Golden Gate, Free State.

TADPOLE
Length: up to 80 mm. **Shape:** body oval. **Tail:** long, very muscular, giving rise to strong swimmers; tail fin widening gradually from behind the body, reaching deepest point shortly after middle of tail; tapering to pointed tip. **Colour:** brown with darker mottling; tail and fins blotched; underside of tadpole white. **Eyes:** dorsolateral. **Nostrils:** small, oval, narrowly spaced. **Spiracle:** below body axis; directed backwards at $45°$; constricted. **Vent:** median; dextral. **Mouth:** near-ventral; single row of small rounded papillae above mouth corner and below; double row around mouth corners. **Jaw sheaths:** moderate to very strong. **LTRF:** 4(2-4)/3 or 4(2-4)/3(1-2). **Development:** completed in about 9 to 12 months but may take up to two years if food is in short supply or water is very cold.

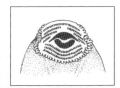

Tadpole: lateral view.

Mouthparts.

Drakensberg River Frog

TRACK
123

Drakensberg-rivierpadda

Amietia dracomontana (Channing, 1978)

LATIN: *draco* = dragon; *montana* = mountain. Named after the Drakensberg range where the species is found.

Conservation status: Not threatened. The distribution range is restricted to inaccessible high mountainous regions where there is little risk to the habitat.

Drakensberg River Frog: Sani Pass, Lesotho.

Description
Maximum size: 65 mm. **Body:** streamlined with pointed snout; head narrow. **Above:** dark to golden-brown or green with scattered circular dark blotches about size of eye; pale vertebral line often present; lower parts of flanks reticulated grey or mottled; skin smooth with longitudinal, slightly elevated broken

♀ Average length

♂ Average length

Maximum size: 65 mm

KEY ID POINTS

- Morphologically indistinguishable from *A. quecketti* but can be identified by the call
- Head narrow; when viewed from above, eyes protrude beyond the outline of head
- Head width approximately 58 to 66% of tibia length (distinct from *A. fuscigula*)
- Two phalanges of longest toe free of webbing (distinct from *A. fuscigula* and *A. umbraculata*)

skin ridges. **Tympanum:** large, more than half diameter of eye. **Underside:** smooth, white, sometimes with mottling on throat. **Hindlimbs:** long; webbing extensive with two phalanges of the longest toe free of web. **Sexual dimorphism:** Dark swollen nuptial pad on male thumb during breeding season.

Call

Long series of clicks at the rate of about ten per second, followed by harsh croak.

Males call from shallow water, often concealed by overhanging banks; they may also call some distance away from water.

Habitat and habits

Permanent streams in high montane grassland in KwaZulu-Natal and Lesotho. Adults and tadpoles are tolerant of extremely low temperatures and can survive snow or ice of winter.

TADPOLE

Shape: oval body. **Tail:** very muscular tail, thus ensuring strong swimming; tail long; tail fin shallow; climbing gradually; reaches its deepest point shortly after middle of tail; tapers to pointed tip. **Colour:** brown with darker mottling. **Eyes:** elygium present. **Nostrils:** small; oval; narrowly spaced. **Spiracle:** below body axis; directed backwards at 40° upwards; constricted. **Vent:** median; dextral. **Mouth:** near-ventral; single row of small rounded papillae above mouth corner and below; double row around mouth corners. **Jaw sheaths:** moderate. LTRF: 4(2-4)/3.

Head showing elygium on iris.

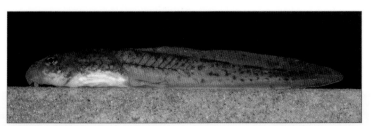

Tadpole: lateral view.

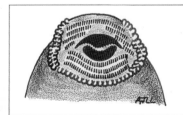

Mouthparts.

Cape River Frog

Kaapse rivierpadda

TRACK
124

Amietia fuscigula (Duméril & Bibron, 1841)

LATIN: *fusci* = dark; dusky; *gula* = throat. Refers to the characteristic dark mottling on the throat.

Conservation status: Not threatened.

Cape River Frog: Johannesburg, Gauteng.

Description

Maximum size: 125 mm. **Body:** robust with slightly rounded snout; **Above:** varying from light to dark brown to various shades of green and olive-brown; dark spots and pale vertebral line usually present; skin smooth with slightly elevated longitudinal broken skin ridges. **Tympanum:** large, only slightly smaller than the eye. **Underside:** smooth; white with dark mottling on the throat, sometimes extending over the belly. **Hindlimbs:** legs and feet long; webbing extensive with only ½ or I phalanx free of web; **Sexual dimorphism:** Dark swollen nuptial pad on male thumb during breeding season.

Average length

♀

Average length

♂

Maximum size: 125 mm

KEY ID POINTS

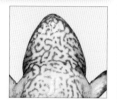

- ½ or 1 phalanx of the longest toe free of webbing (distinct from other species, especially *A. vandijki*)

- Head broad; when viewed from above, eyes are contained within the outline of the head
- Head width more than 66% of tibia length (distinct from other species except *A. vandijki*)

Call
Long series of taps followed by few harsh *kua-kua* groans. Single males call by day and night from partially concealed to fully exposed sites close to water, but in choruses the sound is louder, higher and more rapid.

Habitat and habits
Widespread around permanent rivers and streams in grassland, fynbos, and Karoo scrub, readily colonising farm dams and other artificial water bodies. Active during the day. When disturbed, jump from concealed positions into water to hide in soft mud on bottom.

Worcester, Western Cape.

TADPOLE
Length: usually around 85 mm but under certain conditions up to 165 mm. **Shape:** body oval; **Tail:** muscular and long, giving rise to strong swimmers; tail fin usually arising from body with steep curve; reaching deepest point shortly after middle of tail; tapers to pointed tip. **Colour:** body brown with darker mottling; tail and fins blotched; terminal fifth of tail sometimes dark grey to black; underside white. **Eyes:** dorsolateral. **Nostrils:** small; narrowly spaced; closer to snout than eyes. **Spiracle:** below body axis; directed backwards at 25°. **Vent:** marginal; dextral. **Mouth:** near-ventral; single row of small rounded papillae above mouth corner and below; double row around mouth corners. **Jaw sheaths:** moderate. **LTRF:** varies from 4(2-4)/3(1) to 5(2-5)/4(1). **Development:** complete after about 9 to 12 months; may take up to two years or even longer if food is in short supply or the water very cold.

Tadpole: lateral view.

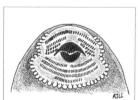

Mouthparts.

Inyanga River Frog

Inyanga-rivierpadda

Amietia inyangae (Poynton, 1966)

Named after the Inyanga District in the eastern highlands of Zimbabwe where the species is found.

Conservation status: Endangered because size and quality of suitable habitat is declining; total distribution range in Zimbabwe's eastern highlands is smaller than 5 000 km², including five locations that are less than 500 km².

Amietia johnstoni *Mt Mulanje, Malawi. Very similar to* A. inyangae. *No picture available.*

Description

Maximum size: 59 mm. **Body:** streamlined; acutely pointed head. **Above:** ground colour greenish-brown or grey but colouring often obscured by dense mottling or blotches; sometimes a dark V or triangle between eyes; no vertebral stripe; skin smooth with or without distinct skin ridges. **Tympanum:** small; less than half diameter of eye. **Underside:** smooth and white to

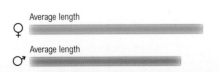

♀ Average length

♂ Average length

Maximum size: 59 mm

KEY ID POINTS

- Tympanum less than half diameter of eye (distinct from *A. queecketti*)
- Webbing extensive; two or fewer phalanges of longest toe free of web (distinct from *A. fuscigula* and *A. umbraculata*)
- Confined to eastern highlands of Zimbabwe (distinct from *A. fuscigula* and *A. vandijki*)
- Head narrow; when viewed from above, eyes protrude beyond outline of head. Head width 58 to 66% of tibia length (distinct from *A. fuscigula* and *A. vandijki*)

yellowish with grey mottling on throat and chest, occasionally extending over the abdomen. **Hindlimbs:** relatively short; toes of moderate length; webbing extensive with only two or fewer phalanges of the longest toe free of web. **Sexual dimorphism:** dark swollen nuptial pad on male thumb during breeding season.

Call
Quiet but distinct *quaak*. Males call day and night.

Habitat and habits
Rocky, fast-flowing streams, often close to waterfalls and rapids, among grass, ferns and small bushes.

TADPOLE

Length: up to 55 mm. **Shape:** body broad in dorsal view. **Tail:** fin deep; reaches deepest point two-thirds down length of tail; tapers sharply over terminal quarter; ends in rounded tip. **Colour:** dark grey-brown; speckled above; brownish-white below. **Eyes:** dorsolateral. **Nostrils:** narrowly spaced; distinct margin; margin indented medially midway between eyes and snout. **Spiracle:** below body axis; angled backwards at 45°. **Vent:** marginal, dextral. **Mouth:** near-ventral; single row of papillae borders mouth laterally and behind. **Jaw sheaths:** moderate to heavy; strongly curved. **LTRF:** usually 7(2-7)/4(1) but may vary from 4((2-4)/3(1) to 8(2-8)/5(1-2). **Development:** may be completed in little more than 30 days.

Tadpole: lateral view.

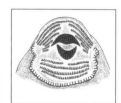

Mouthparts.

Maluti River Frog

Maluti rivierpadda

Amietia umbraculata (Bush, 1952)*; formerly known as*
Amietia vertebralis

LATIN: *umbraculum* = shade. Refers to the umbraculum in the
eye that shades the pupil.

Conservation status: Not threatened.

Maluti River Frog: Malibamatso River, Lesotho.

Identification

Maximum size: 150 mm. **Body:** large,
flattened; head very wide with enormous
gape; snout rounded; head wider than
half body length. **Above:** grey-brown
to greenish-brown with darker blotches
and pale patch in centre of back; short,
irregularly arranged skin ridges.
Pupil: horizontal with prominent
umbraculum. **Tympanum:** visible.
Underside: smooth; white with grey
vermiculations, especially on throat and
chest. **Hindlimbs:** toes fully webbed.
Sexual dimorphism: none recorded.

Average length

♀

Average length

♂

Maximum size: 150 mm

KEY ID POINTS

- Head and mouth very wide; head width half length of body and about as wide as length of tibia (distinct from other species)
- Toes fully webbed with no phalanges free of webbing (distinct from other species)
- Umbraculum in the eye (distinct from other species except *A. vertebralis*

Call

Long series of hollow knocking taps that may last for several seconds, followed by a low-pitched stuttering groan. Males call while almost submerged, occasionally from rocks in the stream-bed.

Umbraculum protecting eye from UV radiation.

Habitat and habits

Predominantly aquatic. Found in cold mountain streams and rivers at altitudes of 1 750 m and higher in Afromontane grassland in the Drakensberg. Intolerant of high temperatures, tadpoles and adult frogs can survive under ice when rivers are frozen over in winter. Preys mainly on invertebrates but can take larger prey items such as mice.

TADPOLE

Length: up to 50 mm. **Shape:** flattened; streamlined. **Tail:** muscular; dorsal fin slightly mottled; begins very low, rising up only about thirdway along tail; tail fin remains fairly shallow; parallel to ventral margin; ending in rounded tip. **Colour:** dark mottled brown above; pale below; underside white. **Eyes:** dorsolateral; prominent elygium on iris. **Nostrils:** narrowly spaced; inner margin elevated. **Spiracle:** below body axis; constricted. **Vent:** marginal; dextral. **Mouth:** ventral; oral disc wide, acting like a sucker to ensure firm grip on rocks in fast-flowing mountain streams; double row of papillae bordering mouth laterally and behind. **Jaw sheaths:** moderate but narrow. **LTRF:** Mostly 5(2-5)/4(1-2) and occasionally 6(2-6)/4(1-2). **Development:** metamorphosis is slow and may take up to a year, or even longer.

Tadpole: lateral view.

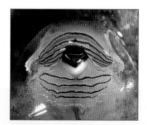

Mouthparts.

Van Dijk's River Frog

Van Dijk se rivierpadda

TRACK
126

Amietia vandijki (Visser & Channing, 1997)

Named after the South African herpetologist,
D.E. van Dijk.

Conservation status: Data Deficient. Distribution range (Swartberg and Langeberg) is
limited, but the extent to which the habitat is under threat is not known.

Atherton de Villiers

Van Dijk's River Frog: Marloth Nature Reserve, Swellendam, Western Cape.

Description

Maximum size: 56 mm. **Body:** heavy; wide
head. **Above:** grey-brown to greenish-brown
with darker blotches; large pale mark in middle
of back; prominent skin fold running from
back of eye to base of arm, obscuring upper
half of or entire tympanum. **Tympanum:** often
indistinct. **Underside:** smooth; white with
occasional darker markings. **Hindlimbs:** less
extensively webbed than other species in the
genus; two to three phalanges of the longest
toe free of webbing. **Sexual dimorphism:** dark
swollen nuptial pad on male thumb during
breeding season.

Average length
♀

Average length
♂

Maximum size: 56 mm

Call
A slow series of *chuck* notes followed by a harsh, pulsed croak.

Habitat and habits
Along rocky streams on steep, well-vegetated slopes and forest gorges in montane fynbos at medium to high altitudes in the Swartberg and Langeberg ranges.

Michael Cunningham

Habitat: Ladismith, Klein Swartberg, Western Cape.

KEY ID POINTS

- Skin fold from eye to base of arm partly obscuring the tympanum (distinct from other species)
- Pale mark in centre of back (distinct from other species except *A. vertebralis*)
- Two to three phalanges of longest toe free of webbing (distinct from *A. fuscigula* and *A. umbraculata*)

TADPOLE
Length: up to 65 mm. **Shape:** robust; oval. **Tail:** fin deep, reaching deepest point two-thirds down length of tail; tapers sharply over terminal quarter; ends in rounded tip. **Colour:** dark grey-brown; speckled above; brownish-white below. **Eyes:** dorsolateral. **Nostrils:** small; narrowly spaced; closer to snout than eyes. **Spiracle:** below body axis; directed towards back and tail. **Vent:** marginal; dextral. **Mouth:** near-ventral; single row of papillae bordering mouth laterally and behind. **Jaw sheaths:** moderate to heavy; strongly curved. **LTRF:** 7(2-7)/4(1). **Development:** complete in just over 30 days.

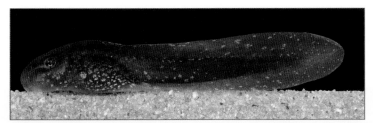

Tadpole: lateral view.

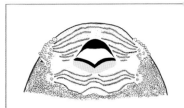

Mouthparts.

Phofung River Frog

Phofung rivierpadda

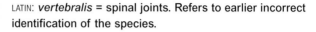

Amietia vertebralis (Hewitt, 1927)

LATIN: *vertebralis* = spinal joints. Refers to earlier incorrect identification of the species.

Conservation status: Not threatened.

TRACK
127

Phofung River Frog: Mont-aux-Sources, Lesotho.

Description

Maximum size: 65 mm. **Body:** snout rounded, giving a squat appearance; unlike other members of the genus; small umbraculum in eye. **Above:** light to dark brown; scattered dark markings; moderately to very warty. **Tympanum:** partially obscured by warts. **Underside:** white; mottling over gular region; smooth. **Hindlimbs:** thighs with dark bars; foot relatively short; webbing

Average length
♀

Average length
♂

Maximum size: 65 mm

KEY ID POINTS

- Head broad and snout very rounded (distinct from other species except *A. umbraculata*)
- Skin very warty
- Small umbraculum present in eye (distinct from other species except *A. umbraculata*)
- Back mottled grey and brown (distinct from other species)
- Webbing variable but generally extensive with two

to three phalanges of the longest toe free of webbing (distinct from *A. fuscigula* and *A. umbraculata*)

extensive but variable; two to three phalanges of longest toe free of webbing. **Sexual dimorphism:** male with darker throat; swollen nuptial pads on first finger of breeding male.

Call
Soft, irregular clucking sounds.

Habitat and habits
Often in seepage areas, along rocky banks of gently flowing streams; during breeding season near or in pools on the plateau and slopes in high grassland of the Drakensberg.

Note umbracula in eyes.

TADPOLE

Length: up to 55 mm. **Shape:** body oval. **Tail:** musculature robust; anterior fifth of dorsal fin rather shallow; tip of tail rounded. **Colour:** body and tail brownish-grey with dark blotches; fins finely stippled, with tip often darker; underside white. **Eyes:** dorsolateral; small elygium shields eye from harmful UV light. **Nostrils:** narrowly spaced. **Spiracle:** just below body axis; opening constricted. **Vent:** marginal; dextral. **Mouth:** ventral; double row of papillae below, three to four rows at mouth corner; single row above. **Jaw sheaths:** moderate. **LTRF:** 4(2-4)/3 or 4(2-4)/3(1-2). **Development:** slow; can survive in winter under ice of frozen mountain streams.

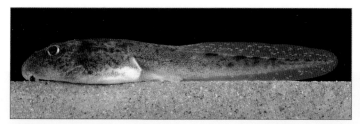

Tadpole: lateral view.

Mouthparts.

BULLFROGS

BRULPADDAS

Pyxicephalus Tschudi, 1838

GREEK: *pyxis* = box; *kephale* = head. Refers to the box-shaped head of the genus.

Three species, two in southern Africa

Giant Bullfrog: Bloemfontein, Free State.

Bullfrogs are the largest frogs in southern Africa and an adult Giant Bullfrog *P. adspersus* may weight more than 1 kg and be more than 240 mm long. The genus is recognisable by the exceptional size and distinctive heavy build of the adults, the flanged digging tubercle on the foot and the tooth-like projections in the lower jaw. The two southern African species are similar in overall appearance but can be distinguished in adulthood by the absence of head and facial markings in the case of the Giant Bullfrog. Other differences are given in the species descriptions.

Bullfrog numbers have declined by an estimated 80% in places where urbanisation has resulted in severe habitat loss. The Giant Bullfrog is consequently Red Data listed as Near Threatened.

Both species hibernate underground for much of the year and emerge only during the peak of the rainy season to forage and breed. Burrows are approximately 1 m deep in sandy soils (the preferred substrate) or about 300 mm deep in clay substrates. During hibernation they are encased in a parchment-like cocoon consisting of layers of cornified skin that reduces water loss; apart from the two nostrils, the entire body is enclosed and metabolism slows down to an absolute minimum. If conditions are

DISTINCTIVE CHARACTERS

ADULT

* Pupil horizontal
* Two bony projections (odontoids) in the lower jaw with a smaller central projection between them
* Upper jaw with a dense row of small recurved tooth-like bony projections
* Inner metatarsal tubercle is massive and flanged for digging
* Fingers lack webbing
* Fleshy webbing between toes

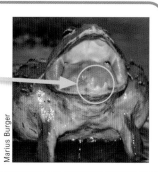

Marius Burger

TADPOLE

* Internarial distance less than six times the nostril diameter
* Body plump and the long coiled intestine seen prominently through abdomen wall
* Tadpoles form dense aggregations and keep to very shallow water
* First two labial tooth rows in upper jaw are continuous

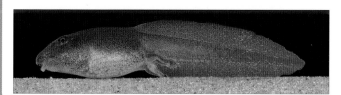 

extremely dry, they may remain cocooned underground for several years. After a series of rainy days ending in a substantial downpour, they emerge from hibernation.

Long distances often separate suitable breeding sites. In order to breed, Bullfrogs require shallow, rain-filled depressions that are seasonal but which retain water long enough for the tadpoles to metamorphose. Shallow, temporary water offers several advantages: the water is warmed by the sun and stimulates rapid development of tadpoles; aquatic predators are fewer in temporary pools. Shallow water is also necessary for the specialised egg-laying procedure in which the female straightens

Shedding cocoon after hibernation.

KEY TO SPECIES

ADULT

Upper jaw with irregular pale vertical bars	**African Bullfrog** *P. edulis* (p.416)
Upper jaw without irregular pale vertical bars	**Giant Bullfrog** *P. adspersus* (p.414)

TADPOLE

Two interrupted labial tooth rows in upper jaw	*P. adspersus* (p.414)
Three interrupted labial tooth rows in upper jaw	*P. edulis* (p.416)

her legs as she exudes a batch of eggs while the male simultaneously pushes her head underwater so that her hindquarters are elevated above the surface at the moment of oviposition. The male thus fertilises eggs in mid air and not underwater, ensuring a greater chance of fertilisation.

Suitable breeding conditions usually occur during November. The morning after a rainstorm, large numbers of adults gather in a lek (a gathering) or display arena where breeding behaviour is frenzied. Large males usually claim a territory in shallow water and defend it aggressively, jumping at each other with open jaws, occasionally inflicting injuries with their odontoids. Females cautiously approach the lek with only their eyes above water. If spotted, they are intercepted by the closest male which immediately goes into axillary amplexus. Other males try to dislodge the amplectant male, often with some success. Smaller males unable to defend a territory display satellite behaviour and try to intercept females as they approach a larger territorial male.

Spawning takes each pair about 15 minutes during which up to 4 000 eggs are scattered in 20 to 40 mm of water. After laying, the spent female prompts the male to release her by shaking her head from side to side and moving into deeper water. Normally by midday the mating is over and the frogs disperse. If the correct weather conditions reoccur, a second or third mating day may take place later in the year, usually in January or February.

Eggs develop rapidly. Small clusters of newly emerged black tadpoles can be seen within 36 hours. After two days these clusters merge into a large school that

Parental care: male digging canal to release tadpoles trapped in a dying pond.

Territorial fighting by males at the lek.

occupies very shallow warm water by day, moving to deeper water at night. During metamorphosis a territorial male shows deliberate parental care by remaining with the tadpoles and attacking potential intruders. He also saves tadpoles from desiccation if they become trapped in a pool that is drying up, by digging a canal to allow them to escape to deeper water. These canals can be as long as 18 m. Metamorphosis is completed in 18 to 33 days.

Before and after breeding, Bullfrogs forage in open grassland. Most prey consists of insects but a variety of comparatively large prey items, such as other frogs, lizards, snakes, small birds and rodents, are also taken. Newly metamorphosed froglets are voracious feeders and frequently cannibalise their siblings.

When breeding is over, males generally bury themselves within 100 m of the breeding site, but females may disperse for up to 1 km from the site in order to burrow. Both sexes appear to have strong philopatric instincts – the need to return to their old burrows. Juveniles migrate even further to integrate with other breeding populations.

Parental care: male protecting tadpoles.

Giant Bullfrog

Grootbrulpadda

Pyxicephalus adspersus Tschudi, 1838

LATIN: *adspersus* = scattered. Refers to the scattered white markings on the elevated skin ridges.

TRACK
128

Conservation status: Near Threatened. The specialised habitat is at risk from increasing urbanisation and agricultural activity.

Giant Bullfrog: Potchefstroom, North West Province.

Description

Maximum size: 245 mm long and weighing 1,4 kg; largest frog in southern Africa. **Body:** very large and stout with elongated dorsal ridges; very big specimens are flaccid and clumsy. **Above:** usually dark olive-green but may vary from grey to brown or (rarely) bluish; short dorsal skin ridges may be white or cream-coloured; head very broad. **Tympanum:** large with no white spot; the distance between eye and tympanum is about twice diameter of eye. **Underside:** smooth; white to creamy yellow; armpits and groin yellow; throat sometimes mottled. **Forelimbs:** flat tubercles on palms; well-developed subarticular tubercles. **Hindlimbs:** inner metatarsal tubercle massive and spade-like for digging into soil. **Sexual dimorphism:** male with bright yellow to orange at base of forelegs; male larger than female. **Juveniles:** distinctively marked bright green and black with a pale vertebral line from snout to vent.

Average length
♀

♂ Average length

Maximum size: 245 mm

KEY ID POINTS

- Upper jaw without irregular vertical pale bars (distinct from *P. edulus*)

- No white spot on tympanum (distinct from *P. edulus*)
- No pale interorbital bar (distinct from *P. edulus*)
- Eye to tympanum about twice the diameter of the eye (distinct from *P. edulus*)
- Large, spade-like inner metatarsal tubercle (distinct from other similar-sized genera)

Call
Very deep, prolonged *wooop*, reminiscent of lowing cattle. Males congregate in clusters; they call while sitting in shallow water, the vibrations of their large vocal sacs rippling the surface. If molested, they emit an open-mouthed cough or bray.

Habitat and habits
Seasonal shallow grassy pans, vleis and other rain-filled depressions in open flat areas of grassland or savanna and, at the limits of its distribution, in Nama Karoo and thicket. For much of the year the species remains buried up to 1 m underground.

Juvenile colour pattern.

TADPOLE
Length: up to 71 mm. **Shape:** robust; plump body. **Tail:** tail fin concave, deep and reaching deepest point just behind middle of tail. **Colour:** black initially, assuming a greyish colour at about 60 mm; underside grey anteriorly; abdominal skin transparent revealing coiled intestine. **Eyes:** dorsolateral. **Nostrils:** small; fairly narrowly spaced; directed anterolaterally; positioned close to eyes. **Spiracle:** well below; directed backwards at 20°. **Vent:** median; dextral. **Mouth:** double row of small rounded papillae above, laterally and below. **Jaw sheaths:** slender; strongly flexed. **LTRF:** 4(3-4)/3. **Development:** eggs develop rapidly; small black tadpoles emerge after only 36 hours; newly hatched tadpoles congregate in small clusters in shallow water; after two days individual clusters merge into one big school which keeps to very shallow warmer water during the day, moving to deeper water at night. **Development:** Complete metamorphosis within 18 to 33 days.

Tadpole: lateral view.

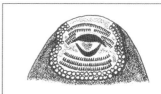

Mouthparts.

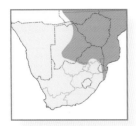

African Bullfrog

Kleinbrulpadda

TRACK
129

Pyxicephalus edulis Peters, 1854

LATIN: *edulis* = edible. Refers to the fact that some rural communities consume the species.

Conservation status: Not threatened.

African Bullfrog: Kruger National Park, Limpopo Province.

Description

Maximum size: 120 mm. **Body:** large and robust with elongated dorsal ridges. **Above:** grey to brown patches on a light brown background; pale vertebral line often present; head broad but snout more pointed than that of the Giant Bullfrog; upper lip with irregular pale-coloured vertical bars and pale bar between eyes. **Tympanum:** large with elliptical or crescent-shaped white spot; distance between eye and tympanum almost the same as diameter of eye. **Underside:** smooth, white to creamy yellow; throat sometimes mottled. **Hindlimbs:** inner metatarsal tubercle massive and spade-like for digging into soil. **Sexual dimorphism:** breeding male often bright green; male larger than female. **Juveniles:** distinctively marked bright green and black with a pale vertebral line from snout to vent.

Average length
♀

Average length
♂

Maximum size: 120 mm

Call

Short *whap-whap* at irregular intervals, like the yapping of a dog. Males call while sitting in shallow water with only the head and inflated vocal sac protruding.

Habitat and habits

Shallow temporary pans and marshy areas in open savanna woodland in eastern and southern Africa, including rice paddies in Mozambique. Adults are fossorial and remain buried for most of the year, emerging only during the breeding season.

Juvenile colour pattern.

KEY ID POINTS

- Upper jaw with irregular vertical pale bars (distinct from *P. adspersus*)
- White elliptical or crescent-shaped spot on tympanum (distinct from *P. adspersus*)
- Pale interorbital bar (distinct from *P. adspersus*)
- Distance from eye to tympanum is about the same as the diameter of the eye (distinct from *P. adspersus*)
- Large, spade-like inner metatarsal tubercle (distinct from other similar-sized genera)

TADPOLE

Length: up to 46 mm. **Shape:** rounded, plump-bodied. **Tail:** deep, concave tail fin reaches deepest point in middle of tail; terminates in blunt tip. **Colour:** body black; fin grey; often stippled with iridiophores; underside of tadpole anteriorly grey; skin covering abdomen semi-transparent revealing characteristic very long coiled intestine. **Eyes:** dorsolateral to near-lateral. **Nostrils:** small; narrowly spaced; midway between eyes and snout. **Spiracle:** below body axis; directed backwards at about 40°. **Vent:** median; dextral. **Mouth:** anteroventral; double row of small rounded papillae laterally above mouth corner and below; three to four rows at mouth corner. **Jaw sheaths:** slender; moderately flexed. LTRF: 5(3-5)/3. **Development:** eggs develop rapidly; small black tadpoles break from jelly capsules after 36 hours; tadpoles complete metamorphosis in about 30 days.

Tadpole: lateral view.

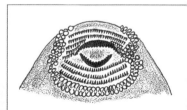

Mouthparts.

STREAM FROGS

LANGTOONPADDAS

Strongylopus Tschudi, 1838

GREEK: *strongylos* = round; *pus* = foot. Refers to the shape of the feet.

10 species, six in southern Africa

Banded Stream Frog: Muizenberg, Western Cape.

Stream Frogs are smooth and sleek and the majority have pointed snouts. Feet are at least as long as the distance from the tympanum to the tip of the urostyle. Toes are long and moderately to weakly webbed. Dorsal colouring is usually a pattern of contrasting stripes or blotches, often with a dark facial mask extending from the snout through the eye to the base of the arm or even further.

They are opportunistic and inhabit a wide variety of biomes, from low-lying flat areas to steep slopes at high altitudes. They remain active throughout most of the year and have an extensive breeding season that follows the first rains. Most species lay their eggs on damp or mossy banks on the edges of water bodies; here the eggs develop to an advanced stage, at which point further development is arrested. Then, when the eggs are flooded by rising water, the tadpoles emerge rapidly from their jelly capsules.

Two species are of conservation concern: *S. wageri* is listed as Near Threatened and *S. springbokensis* as Vulnerable.

DISTINCTIVE CHARACTERS

ADULT
- Pupil horizontal
- Long toes with reduced webbing
- Vertebral line or band usually present
- Tympanum prominent and about half the diameter of the eye

TADPOLE
- Internarial distance less than six times the nostril diameter
- Vent marginal and dextral
- Lower jaw sheath deep and pigmented to the base (all species except *S. wageri*)

KEY TO SPECIES

ADULT

1 Longitudinal pale and dark lines or bands on dorsum 2
   Dorsum pale or with scattered blotches 3
2 Two bold, dark brown to black paravertebral lines on a pale background ....
   .... **Striped Stream Frog** *S. fasciatus* (p.422)
   Light brown to olive-grey with longitudinal, broken, dark brown to black stripes or bands ....
   .... **Banded Stream Frog** *S. bonaespei* (p.420)
3 Confined to Namaqualand .... **Namaqua Stream Frog** *S. springbokensis* (p.428)
   Does not occur in Namaqualand 4
4 Facial mask not prominent .... **Clicking Stream Frog** *S. grayii* (p.424)
   Facial mask prominent 5
5 Webbing reduced; three to four toes free of web .... **Chimanimani Stream Frog** *S. rhodesianus* (p.426)
   Webbing moderate; fewer than three toes free of web .... **Plain Stream Frog** *S. wageri* (p.430)

TADPOLE

1 Tail higher than body; dorsal fin mottled; dorsal fin extending onto body; tail tip pointed .... *S. fasciatus* (p.422)
   Tail not higher than body; dorsal fin not mottled; dorsal fin not extending onto body 2
2 Ocular elygium present on eye; distal part of fin usually dark .... *S. wageri* (p.430)
   Ocular elygium not present on eye; distal part of fin usually not dark 3
3 Usually one divided and two undivided labial tooth rows in lower jaw 4
   Usually three undivided labial tooth rows in lower jaw 5
4 Two undivided and one divided tooth rows in upper jaw; more than one row of papillae laterally in lower jaw .... *S. rhodesianus* (p.426)
   One undivided and three divided tooth rows in upper jaw; one row of papillae in lower jaw ....
   .... *S. springbokensis* (p.428)
5 Body oval-shaped in dorsal view .... *S. grayii* (p.424)
   Body pear-shaped in dorsal view .... *S. bonaespei* (p.420)

Banded Stream Frog

TRACK
130

Gebande langtoonpadda

Strongylopus bonaespei (Dubois, 1980)

LATIN: *bonaespei* = good hope. Refers to the Cape of Good Hope, where the species occurs.

Conservation status: Not threatened.

Banded Stream Frog: Muizenberg, Western Cape.

Description

Maximum size: 35 mm. **Body:** slender; sharp snout. **Above:** light brown to olive grey; longitudinal, broken dark brown stripes; thin silver to orange vertebral line usually present, sometimes on broad, pale-coloured vertebral band; silver dorsolateral stripe, bordered by dark stripes, running from behind eye to groin; prominent white line running from below eye to base of arm; second less prominent line running from above eye over tympanum to base of arm; dark facial band running through eye; fine longitudinal skin ridges. **Tympanum:** small; not prominent. **Underside:** silvery gold;

♀ Average length
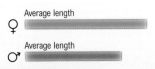

♂ Average length

Maximum size: 35 mm

smooth. **Forelimbs:** fingers slender; long. **Hindlimbs:** thighs barred; webbing reduced; four phalanges of longest toe free of webbing; fourth toe exceptionally long extending to level of eye when in sitting position. **Sexual dimorphism:** lateral margin of jaw dark in male.

Call

Harsh *ché-ché* squawk followed by a fast *e-e-e-e* crackle. Males usually call when well separated from one another, but large choruses have been reported early in winter. Males call from well-concealed positions among dense vegetation or in vegetation as high as 200 mm from the ground. Sporadic calling takes place throughout the day and increases around sunset.

Habitat and habits

Mountain ranges of the Western Cape, extending marginally into the Eastern Cape in montane fynbos and forest margins. Breeds in shallow pools in well-vegetated seasonal seepages and marshy areas. Eggs are scattered, grouped in clusters or laid in short rows of six to seven eggs on moist sites such as waterlogged soil or moss at the base of a grass tussock or restio. Tadpoles develop inside the egg capsules until they are ready to hatch. If the water level rises and covers them, tadpoles will break free from their capsules and swim off.

KEY ID POINTS

- Snout acutely pointed (distinct from *S. grayii* and *S. springbokensis*)
- Facial mask present (distinct from *S. springbokensis*)
- Prominent longitudinal stripes on dorsum (distinct from other species except *S. fasciatus*)
- Terminal four phalanges of fourth toe longer than head width (distinct from *S. springbokensis*)
- Webbing reduced, with four phalanges of longest toe free of web (distinct from *S. wageri*)

TADPOLE

Length: up to 35 mm. **Shape:** body and tail shallow; plump body; pear-shaped. **Tail:** not as deep as body; reaches deepest point about two-thirds along tail. **Colour:** body grey to dark with mottling; tail semi-transparent with sparse mottling. **Eyes:** near lateral. **Nostrils:** small; widely spaced; facing anterolaterally. **Spiracle:** well below body axis; directed backwards at $10°$; facing posteriorly. **Vent:** median; dextral; big. **Mouth:** ventral; three to four rows of papillae at and behind mouth corners; one row below. **Jaw sheaths:** moderate; deeply pigmented. **LTRF:** 4(2-4)/3.

Tadpole: lateral view.

Mouthparts.
Right: Oval body.

Striped Stream Frog

TRACK
131

Gestreepte langtoonpadda

Strongylopus fasciatus (Smith, 1849)

LATIN: *fasces* = bundle of rods bound together. Refers to the distinctive dark brown stripes of this species.

Conservation status: Not threatened.

Striped Stream Frog: Storms River Mouth, Eastern Cape.

Description

Maximum size: 50 mm. **Body:** slender; sharp snout. **Above:** two bold dark brown to black paravertebral lines running from behind eyes to vent; two to three shorter dorsolateral lines; broad vertebral band silvery to golden-yellow to orange-brown; ground colour between paravertebral line and first dorsolateral line usually darker, fading to pale cream or yellow along flanks; smooth and shiny except for slightly elevated skin ridges that underlie dark stripes; prominent white line running from below nostrils under eye and tympanum to base of arm; dark brown to black facial band bordering white line running from snout through eye and over tympanum to base of arm. **Tympanum:** not prominent; more than half eye diameter. **Underside:** pale white to yellow; smooth. **Forelimbs:** fingers slender;

Average length

♀

Average length

♂

Maximum size: 50 mm

KEY ID POINTS

- Striking dorsal pattern of pair of paravertebral dark lines with pair of shorter dorsolateral dark lines on pale background (distinct from other species except *S. bonaespei*)
- Webbing reduced, with three to four phalanges of longest toe free of web (distinct from *S. wageri*)

- Terminal four phalanges of fourth toe longer than head width (distinct from *S. springbokensis*)
- Snout acutely pointed (distinct from *S. grayii* and *S. springbokensis*)
- Facial mask present (distinct from *S. springbokensis*)

long. **Hindlimbs:** thighs with dark spots; not barred; webbing reduced to base of toes; three to four phalanges of longest toe free of webbing; toes long; inner metatarsal tubercle small, rounded; outer tubercle barely visible or absent; fourth toe extends to level of eye when in sitting position. **Sexual dimorphism:** lateral margin of jaw dark in male.

Call

High-pitched piercing *ik-ik-ik* chirp uttered singly, in pairs or in series of up to six at a time, followed by a series of rapid *ti-ti-ti* clicks. Males call from ground level or from slightly elevated positions on vegetation, mainly at night but also on overcast days. Call mainly in autumn and early winter.

Habitat and habits

Open grassy areas near dams, ponds or streams in forest, thicket, grassland and savanna, sometimes also in parks and gardens. Can tolerate disturbance. Active during day and night, throughout the year. Agile jumpers, able to clear considerable distances.

TADPOLE

Length: up to 70 mm. **Shape:** rounded plump body. **Tail:** long; fin moderately deep to deep, coming onto body. **Colour:** body dark brown above; fins yellow-brown with darker spots; fins have dark brown mottling with tip of tail usually dark grey and rounded; U-shaped pale line runs from nostrils to mouth; underside silvery. **Eyes:** near lateral. **Nostrils:** small; fairly narrowly spaced; edged in black. **Spiracle:** well below body axis directed backwards at about 25°. **Vent:** median; dextral. **Mouth:** near-ventral; single row of papillae below and above mouth corner; double row at mouth corner. **Jaw sheaths:** moderate to heavy; pigmented to base. **LTRF:** 3(2-3)/3. **Development:** completed in about five months.

Tadpole: lateral view.

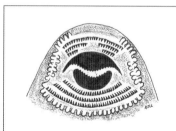

Mouthparts.

Clicking Stream Frog

Kliklangtoonpadda

TRACK
132

Strongylopus grayii (Smith, 1849)

Named after John Edward Gray, keeper of the Zoological Cabinet at the British Museum in the mid nineteenth century.

Conservation status: Not threatened.

Clicking Stream Frog: Keurbooms River, Western Cape.

Description

Maximum size: 50 mm. **Body:** snout not as sharp as some other Stream Frogs. **Above:** light brown to dark brown with scattered dark markings; may have pale to red-brown vertebral band; white line running from below eye and tympanum to base of arm; light brown to black facial band bordering a white line running from snout through eye, over tympanum, to base of arm; skin slightly granular with slightly elevated ridges. **Tympanum:** not prominent; more than half eye diameter. **Underside:** pale white; smooth. **Forelimbs:** fingers slender; long.

Average length
♀

Average length
♂

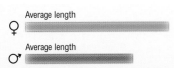

Maximum size: 50 mm

KEY ID POINTS

- Webbing reduced with four phalanges of longest toe free of web (distinct from *S. wageri*)
- Terminal four phalanges of fourth toe longer than head width (distinct from *S. springbokensis*)
- Dorsal colour pattern variable but dark spots on a light background common (distinct from *S. bonaespei* and *S. fasciatus*)
- Snout slightly pointed (distinct from other species except *S. springbokensis*)

Hindlimbs: thighs with dark bars; webbing reduced to base of toes; four phalanges of longest toe free of webbing; toes long; fourth toe does not extend beyond hand when in sitting position. **Sexual dimorphism:** male has gold pigmentation on lower jaw.

Call
Short, hollow tapping sound, monotonously regular. Large choruses suggest sustained crackling. Males call throughout day and night from a concealed position at base of vegetation.

Habitat and habits
Winter and summer rainfall areas; from sea level up to 3 000 m in fynbos and parts of the succulent Karoo, Nama Karoo, savanna, grassland, thicket and forest.

Colour variation.

Egg mass near water.

TADPOLE
Length: up to 50 mm. **Shape:** oval, plump body. **Tail:** not much deeper than body; terminates in blunt tip. **Colour:** greyish-brown above; fins mottled grey; terminal part of tail usually dark grey; bluntly rounded; underside white. **Eyes:** dorsolateral. **Nostrils:** small; widely spaced; slightly closer to eyes than snout. **Spiracle:** below body axis; directed backwards at about 25°; terminates in short tube. **Vent:** marginal; dextral. **Mouth:** double row of papillae below; three to four rows at mouth corner; single row above. **Jaw sheaths:** pigmented to base. **LTRF:** 4(2-4)/3(1).

Tadpole: lateral view.

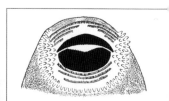

Mouthparts.

Chimanimani Stream Frog

TRACK
○
133

Chimanimani-langtoonpadda

Strongylopus rhodesianus (Hewitt, 1933)

Named after Rhodesia, the former name of Zimbabwe.

Conservation status: Vulnerable in view of habitat degradation. Occurs in an area of 20 000 km^2, and occupies less than 2 000 km^2; the species is known from only five locations.

Chimanimani Stream Frog: Chimanimani, Zimbabwe.

Description

Maximum size: 50 mm. **Body:** slender; pointed snout. **Above:** light brown or beige; round dark blotches on uniformly brown or orange background; usually with thin vertebral line; skin smooth with skin ridges. **Underside:** white; sometimes with grey spots; throat may be yellow; skin smooth. **Hindlimbs:** toes long, extending to level of snout when in sitting position; inner metatarsal tubercle small; outer tubercle absent; webbing reduced, three to four phalanges free of webbing. **Sexual dimorphism:** lateral margin of jaw dark in male.

Average length
♀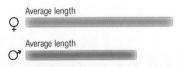

Average length
♂

Maximum size: 50 mm

Call
Short, medium-frequency trill; repeated once per second.

Habitat and habits
Dense grass in montane grassland and forest near streams and rivers in the eastern Zimbabwe highlands (Chimanimani Mountains) and Mt Gorongosa in Mozambique.

Richard Boycott

Colour variation: Chimanimani, Zimbabwe.

TADPOLE
Length: up to 36 mm. **Shape:** body plump; deep. **Tail:** fin reaches highest point in middle of tail; terminates in rounded tip. **Colour:** dark grey to red-brown above; transparent below. **Eyes:** dorsolateral. **Spiracle:** below body axis; directed backwards at $60°$. **Vent:** marginal; dextral. **Mouth:** near-ventral; three rows of papillae at mouth corner; double row at sides below; single row in middle below. **Jaw sheaths:** heavy; pigmented to base. **LTRF:** 3(3)/3(1).

KEY ID POINTS

- Snout acutely pointed (distinct from *S. grayii* and *S. springbokensis*)
- Facial mask present (distinct from *S. springbokensis*)
- Dorsal colour pattern variable: can be uniform brown or red-brown or spotted (distinct from *S. bonaespei* and *S. fasciatus*)
- Terminal four phalanges of fourth toe longer than head width (distinct from *S. springbokensis*)
- Webbing reduced with three to four phalanges of longest toe free of web (distinct from *S. wageri*)

Tadpole: lateral view.

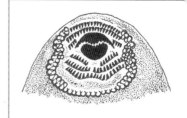

Mouthparts.

Namaqua Stream Frog

Namakwa-langtoonpadda

Strongylopus springbokensis Channing, 1986

Named after Springbok, a town in the Northern Cape, where this species was first identified.

Conservation status: Vulnerable as a result of limited and fragmented distribution and threats to its habitat.

Namaqua Stream Frog: Kamieskroon, Northern Cape.

Description

Maximum size: 44 mm. **Body:** snout fairly pointed. **Above:** yellowish-brown, with darker blotches edged with dark brown; narrow vertebral line often present; facial mask not prominent. **Tympanum:** distinct. **Underside:** smooth; immaculate. **Hindlimbs:** thighs with dark bars; toes short compared to most other species in group; webbing reduced; four phalanges of fourth toe free of webbing.

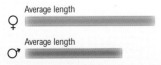

Average length
♀

Average length
♂

Maximum size: 44 mm

KEY ID POINTS

- Dorsal colour pale brown with irregular dark-edged brown markings (distinct from *S. bonaespei* and *S. fasciatus*)
- Webbing reduced with four phalanges of longest toe free of web (distinct from *S. wageri*)

- Terminal four phalanges of fourth toe shorter than head width (distinct from other species)
- Snout slightly pointed (distinct from other species except *S. grayii*)
- Facial mask absent (distinct from other species)

Sexual dimorphism: breeding male develops spines along back of arms; first finger develops margin of webbing giving it a paddle-like appearance; lateral margin of jaw dark in male.

Call

Series of two to seven melodious popping sounds. A short aggression call and male release call in the form of a series of long squeaking notes have been reported.

Habitat and habits

Confined to mountainous areas of Namaqualand in which it survives harsh conditions by keeping close to seeps and springs.

Marius Burger

Colour variation: Leliefontein, Northern Cape.

TADPOLE

Length: up to 30 mm. **Shape:** body oval; deep. **Tail:** not as deep as body; dorsal fin rises very gently; reaches deepest point in middle of tail. **Colour:** body uniformly brown above; transparent below; tail fins transparent. **Eyes:** dorsal to dorsolateral. **Nostrils:** narrowly spaced. **Spiracle:** above body axis; directed backwards at 45°. **Vent:** marginal; dextral. **Mouth:** near-ventral; papillae below; no papillae above mouth corner. **Jaw sheaths:** moderate; pigmented to base. LTRF: 4(2-4)/3(1-2).

Tadpole: lateral view.

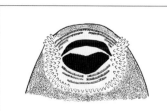

Mouthparts.

Plain Stream Frog

Wager se langtoonpadda

TRACK
135

Strongylopus wageri (Wager, 1961)

Named after the plant pathologist and naturalist Vincent A. Wager (1904–1989) who made a significant contribution to the knowledge of South African amphibians in the mid twentieth century.

Conservation status: Near Threatened.

Plain Stream Frog: Cathkin Park, Drakensberg, KwaZulu-Natal.

Description

Maximum size: 48 mm. **Body:** snout pointed. **Above:** plain; varies from beige, light brown to yellow-green to brick-red; slightly paler on snout; thin light vertebral line may be present; characteristic black facial mask runs from snout, over eye and tympanum to base of arm; mask sometimes continues along flanks as black line; prominent white line along upper jaw; back

Average length

♀

Average length

♂

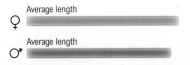

Maximum size: 48 mm

smooth. **Tympanum:** partially obscured by facial mask. **Underside:** pure white; smooth. **Hindlimbs:** thighs with light bars; webbing moderate; no more than three phalanges of longest toe free of webbing. **Sexual dimorphism:** lateral margin of jaw dark in male.

Call
A raucous *kuk-kuk-kuk-e-e-e* cackle. Males call in late afternoon and at night from concealed positions along the margin of breeding sites, such as streams and pools, or from under water.

Habitat and habits
Mistbelt forest at lower altitudes, and montane grassland at higher altitudes up to 2 000 m in the Drakensberg. Sensitive to habitat degradation. When disturbed, will dive into water and hide in silt.

TADPOLE
Length: up to 55 mm. **Shape:** body elongated; oval. **Tail:** muscular; fin rather shallow; usually same height as body; reaching highest point about thirdway from body; ends in tapered point. **Colour:** brown to dark brown; dorsal fin and posterior half of lower fin with faint reticulation; posterior section of tail characteristically dark; underside silvery white. **Eyes:** large; dorsolateral; elygium on iris. **Nostrils:** small; narrowly spaced; four times smaller than eye lens; nostril rim elevated. **Spiracle:** well below body axis. **Vent:** marginal; dextral. **Mouth:** near-ventral; one row of papillae at mouth angle; three rows below. **Jaw sheaths:** moderate; upper jaw sheath V-shaped; lower jaw sheath not deeply pigmented. **LTRF:** 4(2-4)3. **Development:** slow, completing metamorphosis in five to nine months; often seen sunning themselves in shallow water.

KEY ID POINTS

- Dorsum plain and varies from beige, light brown to yellow-green to brick-red (distinct from *S. bonaespei* and *S. fasciatus*)
- Webbing moderate with not more than three phalanges free of web (distinct from other species)
- Terminal four phalanges of fourth toe longer than head width (distinct from *S. springbokensis*)
- Snout acutely pointed (distinct from *S. grayii* and *S. springbokensis*)
- Facial mask very prominent (distinct from *S. grayii* and *S. springbokensis*)

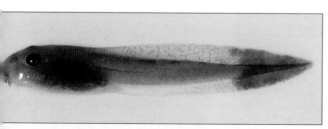

Tadpole: lateral view.

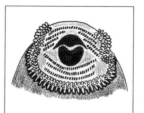

Mouthparts. Right: Head showing elygium on iris.

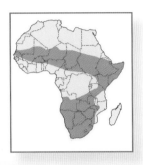

SAND FROGS

SANDPADDAS

Tomopterna Duméril & Bibron, 1841

GREEK: *tomus* = cut; *pterna* = heel. Refers to the deep groove behind the enlarged metatarsal tubercle.

10 species, eight in southern Africa

Cape Sand Frog: Durbanville, Western Cape.

Medium-sized, robust-bodied burrowing frogs that have a toad-like appearance in form and gait. Dorsal coloration is mottled white, grey or brown.

Distributed throughout subSaharan Africa, they inhabit a variety of biomes but avoid forested or extremely dry areas. They do, however, occur in the Kalahari. They are associated with sandy soils and are often found along seasonal river-courses as well as in temporary pans, ponds and farm dams.

Sand Frogs hibernate underground and dig themselves in backwards with a shuffling soil-displacement movement of the hindlegs. They call in dense choruses, often antiphonally.

DISTINCTIVE CHARACTERS

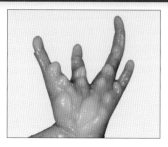

ADULT
- Pupil horizontal
- Squat, robust body
- No webbing on fingers
- Webbing reduced on toes
- Very prominent flange-like metatarsal tubercle for digging

TADPOLE
- Tail not as high as body
- Spiracle not constricted

- Prominent spur on developing foot
- Internarial distance less than six times the diameter of nostril
- Vent marginal and more or less dextral

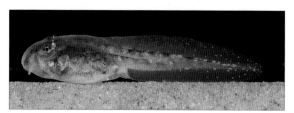

KEY TO SPECIES

ADULT

1   Glandular elevations below tympanum not fused to form a continuous ridge .... **Cape Sand Frog** *T. delalandii* (p.438)
    Glandular elevations below tympanum fused to form a continuous ridge **2**

2   Prominent glandular ridge from eye, over tympanum, to base of arm ... **Natal Sand Frog** *T. natalensis* (p.444)
    No glandular ridge from eye, over tympanum, to base of arm **3**

3   Subarticular tubercle under first finger double .... **Knocking Sand Frog** *T. krugerensis* (p.440)
    Subarticular tubercle under first finger single **4**

4   Each dark blotch on dorsum surrounded by ring of rounded warts ... **Beaded Sand Frog** *T. tuberculosa* (p.448)
    Warts scattered on dorsum **5**

5   Less than two phalanges of the fifth toe free of web .... **Russet-backed Sand Frog** *T. marmorata* (p.442)
    More than two phalanges of the fifth toe free of web **6**

6   Known only from Khorixas in Damaraland in northern Namibia; tympanum prominent ....
    .... **Damaraland Sand Frog** *T. damarensis* (p.436)
    Not restricted to Khorixas in Damaraland; tympanum obscured .... **Tremelo Sand Frog** *T. cryptotis* (p.434)
    or **Tandy's Sand Frog** *T. tandyi* (p.446) (morphologically and geographically indistinguishable)

TADPOLE

    Key to the tadpoles in this genus cannot be resolved because of variation and complexity.

Tremolo Sand Frog

Trillersandpadda

TRACK
136

Tomopterna cryptotis (Boulenger, 1907)

GREEK: *crypt* = concealed or hidden. Refers to the partially obscured tympanum.

Conservation status: Not threatened.

Tremolo Sand Frog: Suikerbosrand, Gauteng.

Description

Maximum size: 51 mm. Above: brown to green; dark-edged marbling with some dark spots on a pale background; vertebral pair of dorsolateral white lines usually present; pale scapular patch in shoulder region; granular skin ridge along jaw-line below tympanum; skin

Average length

♀

Average length

♂

Maximum size: 51 mm

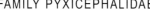

KEY ID POINTS

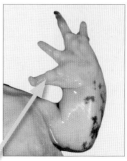

- Dorsum with asymmetrical irregular blotches (distinct from *T. tuberculosa*)
- Skin on back warty (distinct from *T. damarensis* and usually *T. marmorata* and *T. natalensis*)
- Pale scapular patch (distinct from *T. tuberculosa* and sometimes *T. natalensis*)
- Subarticular tubercle on first finger single (distinct from *T. krugerensis*)
- No continuous glandular ridge above tympanum from eye to base of arm (distinct from *T. natalensis*)
- Morphologically indistinguishable from *T. tandyi* but chromosome number and call differs

warty. **Tympanum:** present, partially obscured. **Underside:** white; skin smooth. **Forelimbs:** subarticular tubercle under first finger single. **Hindlimbs:** thigh with dark blotches; webbing reduced; 3½ phalanges of longest toe free of webbing; inner metatarsal tubercle large, flattened; outer metatarsal tubercle small or absent. **Sexual dimorphism:** throat of male with dark pigmentation along jaw-line.

Call
A series of rapid high-pitched metallic, but melodious, *ki-ki-ki-ki* notes, sometimes lasting several seconds. Males call from sites along edge of water and are extremely well camouflaged. They form dense choruses and call antiphonally.

Habitat and habits
Variety of habitats in savanna and grassland.

TADPOLE
Length: up to 37 mm. **Shape:** body plump; deep. **Tail:** fin shallow; usually not as deep or same depth as body; reaching highest point about thirdway from body; tapers to fine point. **Colour:** brown to dark brown; underside silvery white. **Eyes:** dorsal to dorsolateral. **Nostrils:** small; narrowly set; midway between eyes and snout. **Spiracle:** well below body axis; directed backwards at 45°; not constricted. **Vent:** marginal; dextral. **Mouth:** near-ventral; single row of papillae above mouth corner; double row of papillae laterally in lower jaw; three rows at mouth corner. **Jaw sheaths:** heavy. **LTRF:** 3(2-3)/3.

Tadpole: lateral view.

Damaraland Sand Frog

TRACK
137

Damara-sandpadda

Tomopterna damarensis Dawood & Channing, 2002

Named after the Damaraland area of Namibia where this species occurs.

Conservation status: Unknown (Data Deficient).

Alan Channing

Damaraland Sand Frog: Khorixas, Namibia.

Average length

♀

Average length

♂

Maximum size: 41 mm

KEY ID POINTS

- Dorsum with asymmetrical irregular blotches (distinct from *T. tuberculosa*)
- Skin on back smooth (distinct from *T. cryptotis, T. delalandii, T. krugerensis, T. tandyi* and *T. tuberculosa*)
- Pale scapular patch (distinct from *T. tuberculosa* and sometimes *T. natalensis*)
- Subarticular tubercle on first finger single (distinct from *T. krugerensis*)
- Lacks continuous glandular ridge above tympanum from eye to base of arm (distinct from *T. natalensis*)

Description

Maximum size: 41 mm. **Body:** stout; snout rounded; nostrils on slight projections. **Above:** reddish-brown with darker patches; dorsolateral line absent; uninterrupted glandular ridge below tympanum; three dark bands on eyelid; skin smooth. **Tympanum:** distinct. **Underside:** white; skin smooth; gular region slightly granular. **Forelimbs:** single subarticular tubercle under first finger. **Hindlimbs:** webbing reduced; at least three phalanges of longest toe free of webbing; inner metatarsal tubercle large, flattened; subarticular tubercle under first finger single. **Sexual dimorphism:** male with dark pigmentation along jaw-line.

Call

Series of high-pitched *tut-tut-tut-tut* notes produced at rate of about seven per second.

Habitat and habits

Arid wooded savanna.

TADPOLE

Unknown.

Habitat: Damaraland, Namibia.

Cape Sand Frog

Gestreepte sandpadda

TRACK
138

Tomopterna delalandii (Tschudi, 1838)

Named after the French naturalist, Pierre-Antoine Delalande, who collected zoological specimens during three visits to South Africa in the early nineteenth century.

Conservation status: Not threatened.

Cape Sand Frog: Hout Bay, Western Cape.

Description

Maximum size: 45 mm. **Body:** chubby. **Above:** grey with white markings and scattered dark patches; vertebral and pair of dorsolateral white lines often present; characteristic pale scapular patch in shoulder region; row of glands below tympanum not fused into ridge; skin warty. **Tympanum:** partially obscured. **Underside:** white; skin smooth. **Forelimbs:** short; well built; single subarticular tubercle under first finger. **Hindlimbs:** short; well built; thigh with dark blotches; webbing moderate; three phalanges of longest toe free of webbing; inner metatarsal tubercle large, flattened and used for digging; outer metatarsal tubercle small or absent. **Sexual dimorphism:** male with dark pigmentation along jaw-line.

Average length

♀

Average length

♂

Maximum size: 45 mm

KEY ID POINTS

- Dorsum with asymmetrical irregular blotches (distinct from *T. tuberculosa*)
- Skin on back warty (distinct from *T. damarensis* and usually from *T. marmorata* and *T. natalensis*)
- Pale scapular patch (distinct from *T. tuberculosa* and sometimes *T. natalensis*)
- Subarticular tubercle on first finger single (distinct from *T. krugerensis*)
- No continuous glandular ridge above tympanum from eye to base of arm (distinct from *T. natalensis*)

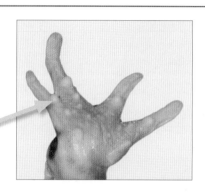

Call
Series of high-pitched metallic but melodious *ku-ku-ku-ku* notes sometimes lasting several seconds. Males camouflage themselves well and call from along the water's edge or in shallow water.

Habitat and habits
Lowlands and valleys in fynbos and succulent Karoo in the Western Cape and along the southern Cape coast.

Colour variation: Jeffrey's Bay, Western Cape.

TADPOLE
Length: up to 44 mm. **Shape:** body plump; deep. **Tail:** fin shallow, usually not as deep, or of same depth, as body; reaching highest point about thirdway from body; upper fin deeper than lower fin; fairly tapered point. **Colour:** brown with darker speckling; underside silvery white. **Eyes:** dorsal to dorsolateral. **Nostrils:** smaller than eye lens; midway between eye and snout; closer to eyes than tip of snout. **Spiracle:** well below body axis; directed backwards; not constricted; terminating in short free tube. **Vent:** marginal; dextral. **Mouth:** near-ventral; single row of papillae medially below; two to three rows at mouth corner. **Jaw sheaths:** heavy. **LTRF:** 2(1-2)/3(1).

Tadpole: lateral view.

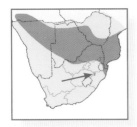

Knocking Sand Frog

Sandveld-sandpadda

Tomopterna krugerensis Passmore & Carruthers, 1975

Named after the Kruger National Park where this species was first identified.

Conservation status: Not threatened.

Knocking Sand Frog: Machayia Pan, Kruger National Park, Limpopo Province.

Description

Maximum size: 52 mm. **Body:** chubby. **Above:** cream to light brown with dark-edged brown blotches; usually without pale vertebral and dorsolateral lines; scapular patch in shoulder region

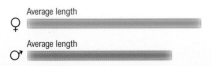

♀ Average length

♂ Average length

Maximum size: 52 mm

sometimes present but indistinct; granular skin ridge, sometimes interrupted, along jaw-line below tympanum; skin warty. **Tympanum:** obscured. **Underside:** white; skin smooth. **Forelimbs:** subarticular tubercles of at least first finger divided or partially divided on at least one hand. **Hindlimbs:** thigh with dark blotches; webbing moderate; not more than 3½ phalanges of longest toe free of webbing; inner metatarsal tubercle large, flattened and used for digging; outer metatarsal tubercle small or absent. **Sexual dimorphism:** male with dark pigmentation along jaw-line.

Call

Series of percussive, wooden *ta-ta-ta-ta* knocking notes repeated at rate of four or five per second.

Habitat and habits

Occupies a variety of habitats in savanna areas. Breeds in temporary rain pools and pans.

TADPOLE

Unknown.

KEY ID POINTS

- Dorsum with asymmetrical irregular blotches (distinct from *T. tuberculosa*)
- Skin on back warty (distinct from *T. damarensis* and usually from *T. marmorata* and *T. natalensis*)
- Pale scapular patch present but not prominent (distinct from *T. tuberculosa* and sometimes *T. natalensis*)
- Lacks continuous glandular ridge above tympanum from eye to base of arm (distinct from *T. natalensis*)

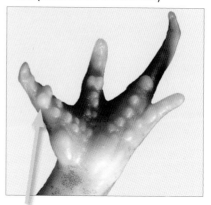

- Subarticular tubercle on first finger double (distinct from other species)

Colour variation: Nelspruit, Mpumalanga.

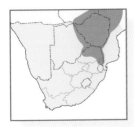

Russet-backed Sand Frog

Rooirugsandpadda

**TRACK
140**

Tomopterna marmorata (Peters, 1854)

LATIN: *marmor* = marble. Refers to the marbled pattern on the back.

Conservation status: Not threatened.

Russet-backed Sand Frog: Skukuza, Kruger National Park, Mpumalanga.

Description
Maximum size: 50 mm. **Above:** mottled maroon to reddish-brown, brown or grey; no vertebral or dorsolateral pale lines; pale scapular patch usually present; short granular skin ridge along jaw-line below tympanum is present but not prominent and not reaching base of arm; skin smooth to

Average length
♀

Average length
♂

Maximum size: 50 mm

granular. **Tympanum:** partially obscured. **Underside:** white with light grey pigmentation along jaw-line. **Forelimbs:** well-developed palmar and subarticular tubercles. **Hindlimbs:** thigh with dark blotches; webbing moderate; not more than three phalanges of longest toe free of webbing; well-developed palmar and subarticular tubercles; inner metatarsal tubercle large, flattened; outer metatarsal tubercle small, round or sometimes absent. **Sexual dimorphism:** Grey pigmentation along jaw-line usually darker in male.

Call
Rapid, piping notes repeated at a variable rate, sometimes lasting several seconds. Males call from exposed or semi-exposed positions.

Habitat and habits
Various habitats in subtropical savanna. Breeds in quiet areas of rivers or streams with sandy substrates.

TADPOLE
Unknown.

Habitat: sandy river bank in the Kruger National Park.

KEY ID POINTS

- Dorsum mottled maroon to reddish-brown, brown or grey (distinct from *T. tuberculosa*)
- Skin on back smooth to slightly granular (distinct from *T. cryptotis*, *T. delalandii*, *T. krugerensis*, *T. tandyi* and *T. tuberculosa*)
- Pale scapular patch (distinct from *T. tuberculosa* and sometimes *T. natalensis*)
- Lacks continuous glandular ridge above tympanum from eye to base of arm (distinct from *T. natalensis*)

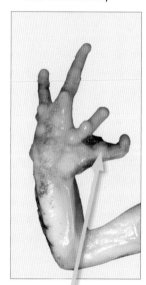

- Subarticular tubercle on first finger single (distinct from *T. krugerensis*)

Lanz von Horsten/IOA

Natal Sand Frog

Natalse sandpadda

Tomopterna natalensis (Smith, 1849)

Named after KwaZulu-Natal (formerly Natal) where this species was first identified.

TRACK
141

Conservation status: Not threatened.

Natal Sand Frog: Vredefort Dome, North West Province.

Description

Maximum size: 44 mm. **Body:** head more pointed than in other species of this genus. **Above:** variable, often with blotches of grey or brown; usually a dark bar between eyes; pale vertebral stripe sometimes present; scapular patch sometimes present; skin granular; one prominent granular ridge along upper jaw and a second from eye over tympanum to base of arm; pair of dark glandular skin elevations usually present in middle of back; skin smooth to granular. **Tympanum:** partially obscured to distinct. **Underside:** white; skin smooth. **Forelimbs:** subarticular tubercle under first finger single. **Hindlimbs:** webbing reduced; 3½ or more phalanges of longest toe free of webbing; inner metatarsal tubercle large, flattened; outer metatarsal tubercle small or absent. **Sexual dimorphism:** male with dark pigmentation over throat.

Average length

♀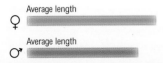

Average length

♂

Maximum size: 44 mm

KEY ID POINTS

- Dorsum with a pair of small, dark skin elevations in the middle of the back (distinct from other species)
- Skin on back smooth to slightly granular (distinct from *T. cryptotis*, *T. delalandii*, *T. krugerensis*, *T. tandyi* and *T. tuberculosa*)
- Pale scapular patch

sometimes present (distinct from *T. tuberculosa*)
- Subarticular tubercle on first finger single (distinct from *T. krugerensis*)
- Continuous glandular ridge above tympanum from eye to base of arm (distinct from other species)

Call

Series of high-pitched, penetrating but melodious *tut-tut-tut-tut* notes, sometimes lasting several seconds. Males call from exposed sites on mudbanks, bare sand or rocks along edge of water.

Habitat and habits

Variety of habitats in savanna and grassland. Often breeds in shallow permanent furrows, canals or streams in grassland and agricultural lands.

Colour variation: Skukuza, Kruger National Park, Mpumalanga.

TADPOLE

Length: up to 36 mm. **Shape:** body heavy; plump; slightly flattened. **Tail:** fin not as deep as body; reaching deepest point about thirdway from body; tapered point. **Colour:** body light brown to dark grey or black; stippled with gold above; fin transparent; dorsal fin slightly stippled; ventral fin transparent; gold to golden-white below. **Eyes:** dorsal to dorsolateral. **Nostrils:** small; half diameter of eye lens; narrowly spaced. **Spiracle:** just below body axis; not constricted; directed backwards at 70°. **Vent:** marginal; dextral. **Mouth:** near-ventral; single row of papillae above mouth corner, double row laterally behind; three rows at mouth corner. **Jaw sheaths:** heavy; moderately curved. LTRF: 4(2-3)/3 or 5(2–5)/3. **Development:** complete in just over two weeks; tadpoles sluggish, most of time lying at bottom of pools.

Tadpole: lateral view.

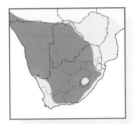

Tandy's Sand Frog

Tandy se sandpadda

TRACK 142

Tomopterna tandyi Channing & Bogart, 1996

Named after zoologist from the USA, Mills Tandy, who collected the first specimen.

Conservation status: Not threatened.

Tandy's Sand Frog: Burgersdorp, Eastern Cape.

Description

Maximum size: 54 mm. **Above:** brown to grey with darker and lighter patches; pale vertebral line and pair of pale dorsolateral lines usually present; broken granular skin ridge below tympanum; skin warty. **Tympanum:** partially obscured. **Underside:** white; skin smooth. **Forelimbs:** single subarticular tubercle under first finger. **Hindlimbs:** webbing reduced; three phalanges of longest toe free of webbing; inner metatarsal tubercle large, flattened and used for digging; outer metatarsal tubercle small, conspicuous.

Average length

♀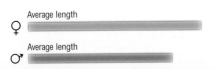

Average length

♂

Maximum size: 54 mm

KEY ID POINTS

- Dorsum with asymmetrical irregular blotches (distinct from *T. tuberculosa*)
- Skin on back warty (distinct from *T. damarensis* and usually from *T. marmorata* and *T. natalensis*)
- Pale scapular patch (distinct from *T. tuberculosa* and sometimes *T. natalensis*)
- Subarticular tubercle on first finger single (distinct from *T. krugerensis*)
- Lacks continuous glandular ridge above tympanum from eye to base of arm (distinct from *T. natalensis*)
- Morphologically indistinguishable from *T. cryptotis* but chromosome number and call differ

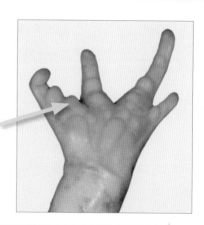

Sexual dimorphism: male with dark pigmentation along jaw-line.

Call

Series of rapid, high-pitched, metallic but melodious *ki-ki-ki-ki* notes that may last for several seconds. Males call from sites along the water's edge and are well camouflaged. They form large choruses and call antiphonally.

Habitat and habits

Nama Karoo grassland and savanna. Breeds in small streams, pans and farm dams as well as in temporary rain pools.

Colour variation: Burgersdorp, Eastern Cape.

TADPOLE

Length: up to 41 mm. **Shape:** body plump; ovoid. **Tail:** not as deep as body. **Colour:** tadpoles dark in clear water, mottled in muddy water. **Eyes:** dorsal. **Nostrils:** same size as eye lens; slightly closer to eyes than to snout. **Spiracle:** directed backwards at $45°$. **Vent:** marginal. **Mouth:** single row of papillae behind, double row behind mouth corners. **Jaw sheaths:** Moderate. **LTRF:** 3(2-3)/3.

Beaded Sand Frog

Skurwesandpadda

TRACK
143

Tomopterna tuberculosa (Boulenger, 1882)

LATIN: *tuberculum* = small rounded projection or protuberance. Refers to the rows of warts that surround the blotches on the back.

Conservation status: Not threatened.

Alan Channing

Beaded Sand Frog: South Luangwa National Park, Zambia.

Description

Maximum size: 45 mm. Above: colour varies from uniform dark to brown or pale with conspicuous almost symmetrical dark markings bordered by a thin white line; pale interocular band; pale vertebral line often present; granular skin ridge present along jaw-line below tympanum; each blotch on back surrounded by numerous prominent wart-like protuberances resembling a string of beads. **Tympanum:** partially obscured.

Average length
♀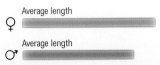

Average length
♂

Maximum size: 45 mm

KEY ID POINTS

- Dorsum with almost symmetrical dark markings bordered by a thin white line and a ring of bead-like skin elevations (distinct from other species)
- Skin on back warty (distinct from *T. damarensis* and usually *T. marmorata* and *T. natalensis*)

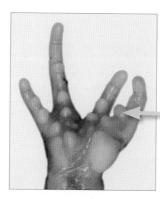

- No pale scapular patch (distinct from other species except *T. natalensis* that may have a similar patch)
- Subarticular tubercle on first finger single (distinct from *T. krugerensis*)
- Lacks continuous glandular ridge above tympanum from eye to base of arm (distinct from *T. natalensis*)

Habitat: vegetated pan in South Luangwa National Park, Zambia.

Underside: white; skin smooth.
Forelimbs: short, well developed with distinct bars; single subarticular tubercle under first finger. **Hindlimbs:** webbing reduced; 3½ to 4 phalanges of longest toe free of webbing; inner metatarsal tubercle large, flattened; outer metatarsal tubercle small, rounded.
Sexual dimorphism: male throat darkly pigmented.

Call
Continuous fast rattle. Males call from edge of water, very well camouflaged among pebbles.

Habitat and habits
Various habitats in upland savanna areas. Fossorial species that is seldom seen.

TADPOLE
Unknown.

GOLDEN-BACKED FROGS

GOUERUGPADDAS

Hylarana Rafinesque, 1814

GREEK: *hyla* = tree; LATIN: *rana* = frog. Refers to the climbing abilities of this genus, although neither of the southern African species is arboreal.

87 species, two in southern Africa

Alan Channing

Darling's Golden-backed Frog: Zimbabwe.

DISTINCTIVE CHARACTERS

ADULT
- Pupil horizontal
- Broad golden-brown or tan dorsal band (sometimes with dark markings) separated from dark flanks by pale dorsolateral stripes (distinct from similar species of *Ptychadena* and *Amietia*)
- Length of tibia less than half the body length (distinct from similar species of *Ptychadena* and *Amietia*)
- Distinct white line along upper lip to base of forearm
- Toes slightly dilated at tips

TADPOLE
- See tadpole of *H. galamensis* described on p.455. The tadpole of *H. darlingi* is unknown.

This large genus is distributed in two disjunct regions, namely East Africa and tropical Asia (from Sri Lanka, India, Nepal and southern China, extending through the Indo-Australian Archipelago into the Philippines, New Guinea and northern Australia).

Southern African members of Hylarana closely resemble some species of *Ptychadena* and *Amietia* but can be distinguished by having a shorter tibia and a clearly delineated dorsal pattern.

Golden-backed frogs are found only in the north of the southern African region, neither species occurring south of the Limpopo River. Darling's Golden-backed Frog *H. darlingi* occurs mainly in the central upland regions, while the Galam Golden-backed Frog *H. galamensis* is confined to the coastal plains.

The breeding habits of Darling's Golden-backed Frog *H. darlingi* are unknown. The Galam Golden-backed Frog *H. galamensis* breeds in still water, whether lakes, ponds or swamps. Up to 4 000 eggs are laid in a single layer of floating mass among vegetation in shallow water. Because of its equatorial distribution, it is not affected by seasonal changes and is active throughout the year, but especially during periods of rain.

KEY TO SPECIES

ADULT

Dorsum edged with pale line but without skin ridges .... **Darling's Golden-backed Frog** *H. darlingi* (p.452)

Dorsal pattern edged with skin ridges from eye to groin .... **Galam Golden-backed Frog** *H. galamensis* (p.454)

TADPOLE

The tadpole of only one species is known .... **Galam Golden-backed Frog** *H. galamensis* (p.455)

Darling's Golden-backed Frog

Darling se gouerugpadda

Hylarana darlingi (Boulenger, 1902)

Named after the nineteenth-century hunter and naturalist,
J. ffoliott-Darling.

Conservation status: Not threatened.

Darling's Golden-backed Frog: Zimbabwe.

Average length

♀

Average length

♂

Maximum size: 72 mm

KEY ID POINTS

- Broad dorsal band, plain or speckled (distinct from *H. galamensis*)
- Dorsum edged with pale line but without skin ridges (distinct from *H. galamensis*)
- Snout rounded (distinct from *H. galamensis*)
- Two to three phalanges of the fourth toe free of webbing (distinct from *H. galamensis*)
- Gular pouches in males not well developed (distinct from *H. galamensis*)

Description

Maximum size: 72 mm. **Body:** smooth, without dorsal or lateral skin ridges; streamlined with slightly pointed snout; distance from nostril to eye larger than distance between eyes. **Above:** broad golden, bronze or light brown band from snout to vent, plain or speckled; edges of band sharply delineated from dark-coloured flanks by a pale line that is not elevated into ridge; prominent white line from below nostrils along upper lip to base of arm; dark olive to black flanks may be mottled in juveniles. **Tympanum:** prominent; contained within the dark flank colour pattern. **Underside:** white with grey throat and chest and light spotting on ventral surfaces of thighs; juvenile underside whitish with grey spotting extending onto thighs; gular pouches not well developed. **Hindlimbs:** two to three phalanges of fourth toe free of webbing; toe tips slightly dilated. **Sexual dimorphism:** male with pair of vocal sac slits on either side of lower jaw.

Call

Rapidly accelerating barking sounds. Call rate in choruses accelerates to nearly double the normal rate and then stops abruptly. Males call while floating in shallow water among vegetation.

Habitat and habits

Grassland and open savanna but also occasionally on woodland margins or in evergreen lowland forests. Usually found near vleis, dams and streams, but often away from water in the daytime. Active throughout the year in moist conditions, but especially during the rainy season.

TADPOLE

Unknown.

Galam Golden-backed Frog

TRACK
145

Galam-gouerugpadda

Hylarana galamensis (Duméril & Bibron, 1841)

Named after Galam, the French name for Gajaga, a former
slave and gold station on the upper Senegal River.

Conservation status: Not threatened.

Alan Channing

Galam Golden-backed Frog: Mafia Island, Malawi.

Description

Maximum size: 86 mm. **Body:** smooth
with dorsolateral ridges outlining the
dorsal pattern; streamlined shape with
rounded snout; distance from nostril to eye
equal to distance between eyes. **Above:**
dorsum golden-coloured with grey or black
mottling; dorsum delineated from dark-
coloured flanks by elevated, pale-coloured
ridges from eye to groin; a second elevated

♀ Average length

♂ Average length

Maximum size: 86 mm

KEY ID POINTS

- Central dorsum gold-coloured with grey or black mottling and light edges (distinct from *H. darlingi*)
- Pale-coloured skin ridges along edges of dorsum from eye to groin and along lower flanks (distinct from *H. darlingi*)
- Snout rounded (distinct from *H. darlingi*)

- 2½ to slightly more than three phalanges of fourth toe free of webbing (distinct from *H. darlingi*)
- Gular pouches in males well developed and visible in vocal sac slits (distinct from *H. darlingi*)

ridge along lower flank; dark olive-brown flanks sometimes mottled, especially in juveniles; prominent white line from below nostrils, along upper lip, to base of arm. **Tympanum:** prominent with pale outline. **Underside:** speckled but less so in large individuals; dark baggy gular pouches. **Hindlimbs:** 2½ to slightly more than three phalanges of the fourth toe free of webbing; toe tips slightly dilated. **Sexual dimorphism:** male with a visible pair of vocal sac slits.

Call
Muffled, nasal snore. Males gather at permanent water bodies and call close to one another.

Habitat and habits
Adapts well to modified habitats. Strongly aquatic and found at permanent lakes, small rivers, ponds and swamps. Up to 4 000 eggs laid in a single layer of floating mass among vegetation in shallow water.

TADPOLE
Length: up to 60 mm. **Shape:** body plump; deep. **Tail:** not much longer than tadpole; very deep. **Colour:** two dark longitudinal lines start at oral corners, running backwards and fading out in middle of body; in older tadpoles markings fade to leave brown or beige coloration; body and tail covered in prominent brown spots. **Eyes:** dorsolateral. **Nostrils:** narrowly spaced. **Spiracle:** above; directed backwards and upwards at 70°. **Vent:** marginal; dextral. **Mouth:** one to two rows of papillae below; multiple larger papillae at mouth corner. **Jaw sheaths:** moderate. **LTRF:** 1/2.

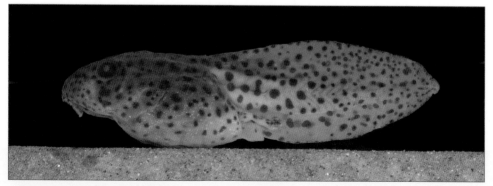

Tadpole: lateral view.

FOAM NEST FROGS

SKUIMNESPADDAS

Chiromantis Peters, 1854

GREEK: *chiro* = hand; LATIN: *manto* = to wait or to stay.
The name may refer to the grasping capability of the hand.

15 species, one in southern Africa

Foam Nest Frog.

Foam Nest Frogs are found in the African tropics, south of the Sahara, and in Southeast Asia (northeastern India, Myanmar, Thailand, Vietnam, Laos, China).

This an arboreal genus found in open savanna woodland and closed forest areas of Africa and eastern Asia. The frogs have long slender limbs with large discs on both toes and fingers. The southern African species frequently seeks refuge in cool places in buildings such as verandas and bathrooms. During the night frogs leave these retreats to forage and breed, returning to them before dawn. In the breeding season they can also be seen sitting fully exposed on branches, with feet tucked under the body in order to prevent desiccation. When doing so, the skin becomes chalky white

Tadpoles developing in foam nest.

DISTINCTIVE CHARACTERS

• See specific description.

or pale grey, thus reflecting light and heat. In extremely hot conditions they secrete sweat droplets in order to cool themselves through evaporation. To retain further water, nitrogen is excreted in the form of uric acid.

Breeding takes place October to February. As darkness descends, males select call sites in trees overhanging water. When one male begins calling, the others move closer to it and join in, squeaking and croaking. On the approach of a female, a male clasps her and the pair positions itself on a branch directly overhanging water. Soon, a number of other males arrive and jostle the amplectant pair. They

Les Minter

Habitat: nests in tree; Hans Merensky Nature Reserve, Limpopo Province.

may contribute to the fertilisation of the eggs as they are laid (polyandry). At first the female releases an oviducal secretion which she and the males churn into a froth with their hindlegs. After about 15 minutes she begins to deposit eggs into the foam, all the while secreting more of the foam-making fluid. Up to about 1 200 large cream-coloured eggs are laid in the foam nest. Constructing the nest lasts most of the night, during which time the female descends to water level once or twice in order to rehydrate herself. During these breaks she usually sheds her amplectant partner and another male may mate with her when she returns. On the following night the female usually returns alone to add more foam to the nest. Nests of different mating groups are sometimes fused and as many as 20 females with 50 attendant males have been observed collaborating in nest-making.

Foam nests hang suspended over water while the tadpoles develop inside. The outer crust of a nest hardens, insulating the tadpoles from temperature extremes and desiccation. It may also offer some protection from predation although birds, monkeys and the Greater Leaf-folding Frog *Afrixalus fornasinii* have been observed raiding nests. After four to six days the tadpoles wriggle to the bottom of the foam where the crust softens and allows them to drop into the water. Even after they have been vacated the bright meringue-like nests are conspicuous around dams and waterholes in the bushveld throughout summer. Where trees are not available, bridges and culverts and similar structures may serve as nesting sites.

Nest construction.

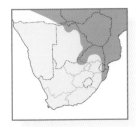

Southern Foam Nest Frog

Grootgrysskuimnespadda

Chiromantis xerampelina Peters, 1854

GREEK: *xero* = dry; LATIN: *ampelidae* = of the vine. Refers to the grey, dry appearance of the frog, resembling dry wood.

TRACK
146

Conservation status: Not threatened.

Southern Foam Nest Frog: Mkuzi Game Reserve, KwaZulu-Natal.

Description

Maximum size: 85 mm. **Body:** pelvic girdle protrudes to give a characteristic hump and an undernourished appearance.

Above: dark grey to whitish, varying to brown with scattered dark markings; capable of considerable colour change from light to dark depending on surrounding

♀ Average length

♂ Average length

Maximum size: 85 mm

environment and disturbance; dorsal markings more conspicuous on darker-coloured specimens; dorsal skin granular but soft with scattered warts; granular skin ridge extends from behind eye, over tympanum, to base of arm. **Pupil:** horizontal in large protruding eyes. **Tympanum:** distinct. **Underside:** throat and chest white with a variable extent of grey speckling; pinkish on belly; granular. **Forelimbs:** fingers arranged in opposing pairs; outer pair larger than inner pair; moderately webbed with large, marginally grooved, sucker-like terminal discs. **Hindlimbs:** toes with terminal discs; extensively webbed with only two phalanges of the longest toe free of webbing. **Sexual dimorphism:** male with whitish nuptial pads on two fingers; female much larger than male.

Call

Subdued series of discordant croaks or squeaks. Males call from trees or tall grass next to or overhanging bodies of water.

Habitat and habits

Found around seasonal or permanent bodies of open water in a variety of bushveld vegetation types in the savanna biome. Males are not aggressive towards each other.

KEY ID POINTS

- Pupil horizontal
- Fingers arranged in opposing pairs with the outer pair better developed
- Toes and fingers with terminal discs

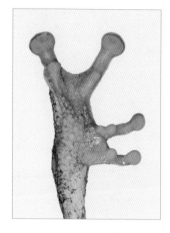

- Toes extensively webbed
- Thin granular skin ridge from behind eye over tympanum to the base of the arm

TADPOLE

Length: up to 55 mm. **Shape:** oval. **Tail:** fin deepest midway along its length, tapering sharply to acute point; upper fin almost twice as deep as lower fin. **Colour:** body uniformly brown to orange-brown; fins semi-transparent with specks of grey and orange; whitish below. **Eyes:** dorsolateral; interorbital space greater than internarial distance. **Nostrils:** small; narrowly spaced; closer to snout than eye. **Spiracle:** short free tube; well below body axis; directed backwards at $30°$. **Vent:** marginal; dextral. **Mouth:** anteroventral. **Papillae:** Narrow medial gap in the lower jaw papillae. **Jaw sheaths:** moderate; not strongly flexed. LTRF: 3(2-3)/3.

Tadpole: lateral view.

GLOSSARY

A

Aestivate State of inactivity similar to hibernation, but triggered by heat and/or drought.

Agonistic behaviour Aggression, threats, posturing or ritual display between two rival males to establish dominance.

Allopatric Having separate and mutually exclusive areas of geographical distribution.

Alti-montane High-lying parts of mountains.

Amphibian Adapted for life both in water and on land.

Amplexus Sexual embrace of amphibians. The grasping by the male of the female's body usually with the forelimbs but in some species by adhesion.

Anterolateral Directed towards front and side.

Antiphonal Regular spacing or alternation of the calls of two or more frogs or choruses of frogs in such a way that the calls do not overlap.

Anura/Anurans One of the three orders of living amphibians to which all frogs, including toads, belong.

Apomorphic Trait characterising an ancestral species and its descendents.

Aposematic Warning coloration or markings that signal to a predator that an organism is toxic, dangerous or distasteful.

Arthropod Segmented invertebrate organism with limbs or other appendages on one or more segments.

Asperities Small, spine-like, keratinised outgrowths of the skin of certain frogs, especially the genera *Afrixalus* and *Heleophryne*. These are believed to serve a tactile function during courtship.

Axial Pivotal or central line (axis) around which a body rotates or is symmetrical.

B

Benthic Ecological region at the lowest level of a water body (close to the bottom).

Biome Climatically controlled group of plants and animals with a characteristic composition and distributed over a wide area, for example, grassland, desert, savanna.

Body axis Imaginary horizontal line along the midline of tadpole viewed from the side.

BP Before the present.

Buccal cavity Interior of the mouth.

Bushveld Tropical savanna ecoregion of southern Africa.

C

Canthal Pertaining to the angle at which the top of the snout and the upper jaw meet. The canthal ridge may be rounded or sharply angular.

Canthus rostralis Angle between the upper surface and side of the head, between the eye and snout.

Cerebellum Pair of spherical structures situated in hindbrain. Regulates muscle tone and posture.

Cerebral hemisphere One of two lobes extending from the forebrain. Mainly concerned with co-ordination.

Choanae Internal opening of the nostrils.

Chorus Group of calling frogs.

Chromatophores Pigment cell or group of cells which, under the control of the nervous system or hormones, can be altered in shape or colour.

Cladistics Hierarchical classification of species based on evolutionary ancestry.

Cloaca Dual functional opening for the excretory and reproductive tracts.

Cocoon Outer covering of dried mucus and layers of shed skin produced by some species of frogs during aestivation or hibernation in order to reduce water loss.

Coelenterates = Cnidarians Taxonomic group of animals including sea anemones and jellyfishes.

Columella Rod-shaped bone connecting the tympanum to the inner ear. Transmits sounds and other vibrations detected by the tympanum.

Conspecific Belonging to the same species.

Cornea Transparent covering of the front of the eye.

Cornify Convert into hardened, horny tissue.

Cryptic species One that is extremely similar to another in external appearance. These similar species do not interbreed and can usually be separated on the basis of behavioural or molecular differences.

D

Desiccation Process of drying up.

Detritus Any fine particulate debris of organic or inorganic origin.

Dextral On the right-hand side.

Diameter of the eye Widest external distance across the eye.

Diameter of tympanum Width of tympanum, including the tympanic ring.

Diencephalon Part of the forebrain that functions as a signalling centre for the regulation of body activities.

Digital disc Expanded disc or pad at the end of a finger or toe.

Distal Refers to the part of an organ furthest from its point of attachment to the body.

DNA (Deoxyribonucleic acid) The genetic material of all organisms that determines inherited features. Characteristically organised into linear sequences of genes.

Dorsal/Dorsum Upper surface of the body.

Dorsolateral Referring to the upper, dorsal flanks of a specimen.

Dorsoposterior Directed up and backwards towards the dorsum and the posterior end of the body.

E

Ectoderm Outer layer of embryonic epithelium in multicellular animals, which gives rise to the epidermis and nervous system; in coelenterates it is the outer layer of epithelium.

Ectotherm Animal that derives its body heat primarily from the surrounding external environment.

Ecotone Boundary line or transitional interface between two different plant or animal communities or ecological systems.

Elygium Pigmented layer arising from the iris, distal to the pupil, or a pigmented layer in the skin above the eye, which shades the pupil.

Emergent vegetation Aquatic plants with underwater roots, and stems and leaves growing above the water level.

Endemicity Endemic or restricted to a specific geographical region.

Endoderm Inner layer of embryonic epithelium in multicellular animals, which gives rise to the digestive tract, respiratory tract and associated glandular epithelium.

Endorheic basin Closed drainage basin that allows no outflow to rivers and streams.

Epidermis Outer layer or layers of the skin, derived from the embryonic ectoderm. In vertebrates it is a non-vascular stratified tissue, often hardened into keratin.

Epithelium Cellular tissue covering a free surface or lining of a tube or cavity.

Explosive breeding Occurs when an organism breeds rapidly as soon as environmental conditions are favourable.

F

Femoral gland Swollen and often differently coloured raised area situated on the legs. Plays a role in reproduction.

Filamentous Thread-like in structure.

Fossorial Characterised by digging or burrowing.

G

Gastrulation Stage in early embryo-genesis involving extensive cell movement, and in which the gut cavity is formed and the three primary layers of the animal body (ectoderm, mesoderm and endoderm) are developed.

Genus Taxonomic group of closely related species. Similar and related genera are grouped into families.

Gosner stages Embryological development stage of tadpoles.

Gravid Describes a female with eggs.

Gula/Gular Upper part of the throat. In many frog species the vocal sac is situated in this area.

Gular disc Area of thickened skin below the throat of male frogs which protects the vocal sac or expands with the vocal sac when the frog calls.

Gular slit Pair of slits bordering the gular disc from whence vocal sacs appear while the frog is calling.

H

Hierarchy Social system in which members of the group are organised in ranks so that, in any encounter, one is dominant and aggressive, and another submissive.

Holotype = Type specimen Name-bearing specimen housed in a museum-type collection.

Hyaline Clear, transparent and free from inclusions.

Hybrids/Hybridisation Offspring produced when two different species cross.

I

Infratympanic ridge Glandular ridge, often continuous with the thickened skin of the upper lip, extending below the tympanum to the base of the forearm.

Inner and outer metatarsal tubercles Tubercles at the bases of the first (inner) and fifth (outer) toes.

Inselberg Isolated rocky hill or mountain.

Interdigital Area between fingers or toes.

Internarial distance Shortest distance between the inner margins at the rims of the nostrils.

Interorbital Between the eye sockets.

Invaginable proboscis Snout or trunk that folds in within itself.

Iridiophores Opaque, milky or iridescent pigment cells.

Iris Circular pigmented contractile disc in the eye with a variable aperture.

J

Jacobson's organ Auxiliary olfactory sense organ found in the roof of the mouth of several reptiles and other animals.

K

Keratin Hard, bony tissue.

Keratodont/Labial teeth Minute tooth-like scrapers that tadpoles use to scrape off algae and other food particles.

L

Lachrymal gland Tear gland.

Larva Tadpole (in the case of frogs).

Lateral Referring to the sides or flanks of an animal.

Lateral line organ Group of sensory cells located in the skin along the flanks of fish and certain amphibians enabling them to perceive movement in water.

Lek Gathering place where males of a species gather to display and attract females for breeding.

Lipophore Pigmented cell containing oil droplets.

M

Marginal At, or near, the margin, edge, or border.

Medulla oblongata Bulbous part of the spinal cord directly behind the brain. Regulates respiration, blood pressure and heartbeat.

Melanophores Black or darkly pigmented cells.

Mesic Having a temperate, moist climate.

Mesoderm Layer of embryonic cells lying between ectoderm and endoderm.

Mesonephros Primitive kidney in amphibians and some other lower vertebrates.

Metamorphosis Change in form and structure undergone by an animal – from embryo to adult stage.

Metatarsal Area of the foot between ankle and toes.

Mid-tarsal tubercle A tubercle present on the posterior surface of the tarsus, at approximately the mid point. It occurs in the genus *Phrynobatrachus*.

Morphology Form and structure of an organism. Also refers to the study of form and structure.

Musculature System or arrangement of muscles as a whole.

N

Nektonic Free swimming in an aquatic environment.

Nictitating membrane Translucent upper half of the lower eylid. Protects the eye under water.

Nostril/Nare External opening from nasal cavity.

Notachord Flexible rod-shaped structure found in all embryos and some adults of the chordates resembling a vertebral column in structure and function.

Nuptial pad Elevated roughened areas of skin on the thumb or forearm of male frogs, which become enlarged during the breeding season and provide an efficient grip during amplexus.

O

Odontoid Projection resembling a tooth.

Olfactory lobe Lobe that projects from the anterior side of each cerebral hemisphere. Concerned with the sense of smell.

Olfactory tract Tract of olfactory fibres that transmits messages pertaining to smell.

Omosternum Part of the pectoral girdle that projects forwards from the medial articulation of the clavicles in some frogs. It may be bony (ossified) or composed of cartilage.

Ontogeny Course of development of an individual from egg to adult.

Opercularis muscle Small muscle that connects the shoulder bones to the operculum (a movable disc in the ear) and transmits ground vibrations to the inner ear.

Optic lobe Part of the brain where visual signals are received and interpreted.

Oral disc Fleshy disc bordering the mouth of a tadpole – usually bearing papillae, labial tooth rows and jaw sheaths.

Outer metatarsal tubercle Tubercle at the base of the fifth (outer) toe.

Ovarian follicles Female reproductive cells in the ovary that form the basic unit of female reproductive biology.

Oviposition Egg-laying.

P

Palmar tubercles Tubercles of various sizes, shapes and distinctiveness on the ventral surfaces of the hands and feet, excluding those under the digits.

Papillae Small, nipple-like fleshy projections around the oral disc.

Paragyrinid Refers to the position of the spiracle when situated low on the left side of a tadpole.

Paravertebral Alongside the spinal column.

Parotoid glands Large swellings or raised areas on the side of the head behind the eyes. They produce secretions that may be poisonous.

Pathogens Organisms producing, or capable of producing, disease.

Phalanges (sing. phalanx) Bones forming the fingers or toes (digits).

Philopatric Tendency of a migrating animal to return to a specific location.

Phylogeny Evolutionary history and line of descent of a species of a higher taxonomic group. *See also* **Ontogeny**.

Physiology Part of biology dealing with the functions and activities of organisms, as opposed to their structure.

Pinial gland Gland in the brain that secretes the hormone melatonin, which controls day-night rhythm.

Plesiomorphic Ancestral condition of a variable character.

Poisonous Containing a toxic or lethal substance that would be harmful if absorbed by ingestion or through the skin. *See also* **venomous**.

Polymorphism Having more than one form.

R

Retina Light-sensitive layer at the back of the eye.

Rostral and mental Referring to the anterior and posterior borders, respectively, of the oral disc.

Rostrodonts = Jaw sheaths Pair of keratinised beak-like mouthparts present in many tadpoles.

S

Sacral Refers to the part of the anatomy at and around the upper pelvic region.

Seep/Seepage Wet area, usually of limited extent, where surface water oozes slowly out of the ground, sometimes forming small puddles on sloping ground.

Sensory papillae Structures in the inner ear that detect sound waves and transmit signals to the nerves, which relay messages to the brain.

Septum Wall between two cavities.

Serpentine Snake-like.

Sexual dimorphism Marked differences in shape, size, morphology, colour, etc., between male and female of a species.

Sinistral On the left-hand side.

Snout-vent length Measurement from tip of the snout to posterior border of the vent.

Species In sexually reproducing organisms, a group of interbreeding individuals not normally able to interbreed with other groups.

Spectrogram Two-dimensional representation of a sound, showing the variation of frequency through time; also known as a sonogram.

Spiracle Opening allowing the exit of water pumped through the respiration system of a tadpole. May be single or paired; mid ventral (medial), ventrolateral; lateral (sinistral).

Subarticular tubercles Rounded wart-like elevations under the joints of fingers and toes.

Subdigital tubercle Tubercle underneath a finger or toe.

Subspecies Recognisable, geographically distinct subdivision of a species that may interbreed with other subspecies within the same species.

Supramarginal Refers to a position above the margin (for example, where the vent of a tadpole is higher than the margin of its tail).

Sympatric Occurring in broadly overlapping areas of geographical distribution.

Syntopic Sharing the same habitat within the same geographical range.

T

Tarsal fold Ridge or fold of skin extending along the tarsus from the tibiotarsal articulation (ankle) to the base of the toes.

Tarsus/Tarsal Elongated part of the foot between the heel and the base of the toes.

Taxon (pl. taxa) Members of any particular taxonomic group, for example, a particular species, genus, or family.

Taxonomy Science of classification.

Terrestrial Living or found on land, as opposed to in rivers, lakes or oceans or in the atmosphere.

Territorial call Call by a male frog to signal his presence to other conspecific males. In some species the advertisement call, or a component of it, fulfils this function. In others, a separate territorial call is produced.

Tetrapod Four-footed vertebrate animal.

Thornveld Southern African vegetation type with grass and scattered trees of which the acacia thorntree is the dominant group.

Tibiotarsal Lower leg, including the foot to the base of the toes.

Trophic Pertaining to feeding and nutrition.

Tubercle Small, rounded protuberance.

Tympanum Eardrum or tympanic membrane. In amphibians it is usually visible as a circular shape behind the eye.

Type/Holotype A specimen with all the characteristics common to a large number of individuals (for example, a species) and serving as the basis for classification. A primary model, the actual specimen described as the original of a new genus or species.

U

Umbraculum Small, translucent, pigmented area of the cornea in the eye that projects over the pupil to shade it from direct sunlight. It occurs in certain species of frogs and tadpoles, particularly those living at high altitudes.

Urostyle Unsegmented bone forming the posterior part of vertebral column – sometimes incorrectly referred to as the tailbone.

Utricle Part of the inner ear containing the receptors for dynamic body balance.

V

Venomous Capable of injecting a harmful or lethal substance into a victim by means of fangs, sting or other method. *See also* **Poisonous**.

Vent (also the Cloaca) Terminal orifice in amphibians which serves both reproductive and anal (excretory) functions.

Vent tube Tube that releases digested matter from intestines.

Venteroposterior Directed down and backwards towards both the ventral and rear end of the body.

Ventral/Venter Underside of the body.

Ventrolateral Along the sides of the venter.

Vermiculation Convoluted, worm-like markings on the body of a frog.

Vertebral Referring to structures situated near or connected with the backbone.

Vlei Area of flat, swampy ground with predominantly grassy vegetation that may be inundated seasonally or all year round.

Vocal sacs Extension of the mouth cavity in frogs, inflated during sound production. Presence or absence, number and shape may be of diagnostic value.

Vomerine teeth Teeth borne on a pair of bones (vomers) in the roof of the mouth.

W

Width of the upper eyelid Measured as the greatest width, usually about mid point.

Wolfian duct Embryonic duct that develops into the excretory duct in males, and degenerates in females.

X

Xantophore Lipophore in which alcohol-soluble oil droplets have a yellow or yellowish hue.

SPECTROGRAMS

By definition, spectrograms are visual images of sounds. They show accurately the structure of the advertisement call of each species and are more precise than words. Because each advertisement call is unique, spectrograms make definitive species identification possible even when morphological characters may be uncertain.

Spectrograms are not difficult to read or understand. Three essential elements determine the structure of a call.

FREQUENCY

High-pitched whistles or squeaks appear towards the top of the spectrogram while low-pitched, booming sounds appear lower down. Many frog calls are made up of a mixture of high and low-pitched sounds and their component parts are therefore spread over the height of the spectrogram. Frequency is determined by the wavelength of the sound and is measured in kilohertz (kHz) on the vertical axis of the graph.

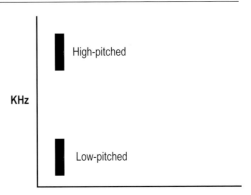

DURATION AND PULSE

The length of time for each part of the call to be emitted and the duration of the whole call is shown horizontally across the width of the spectrogram. A long, slow call stretches across the width of the spectrogram, a short, sharp click appears as a spot or narrow vertical strip. A protracted, pure flute-like tone extends unbroken across the spectrogram. A call that is made up of short, closely spaced pulses or vibrations appears as a series of short marks. The horizontal scale is in seconds or fractions of a second.

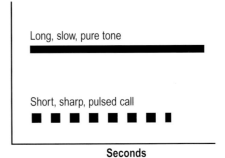

AMPLITUDE

The density of the spectrogram pattern reflects how loudly or softly each part of the call is made. Dense, black marks indicate loud sounds; lighter grey patterns indicate softer sounds.

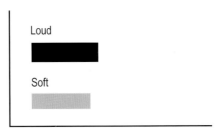

The track number on each spectogram refers to the relevant track on the accompanying CD.

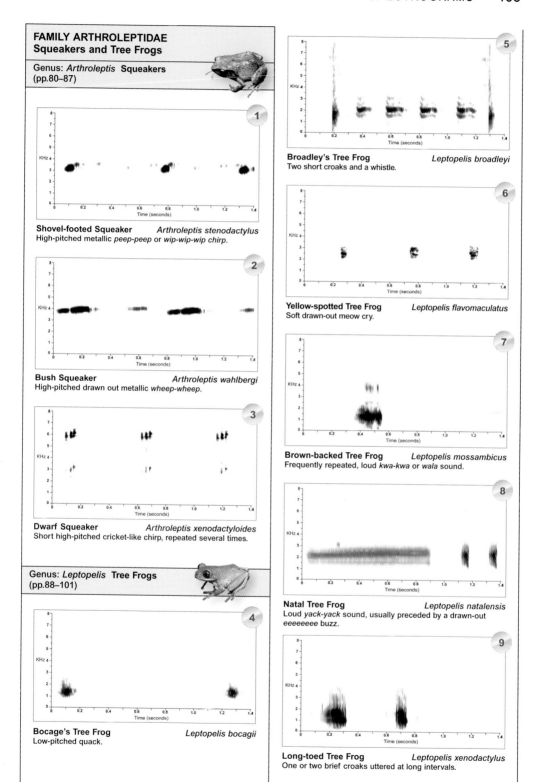

FAMILY ARTHROLEPTIDAE
Squeakers and Tree Frogs

Genus: *Arthroleptis* Squeakers
(pp.80–87)

Shovel-footed Squeaker   *Arthroleptis stenodactylus*
High-pitched metallic *peep-peep* or *wip-wip-wip chirp*.

Bush Squeaker   *Arthroleptis wahlbergi*
High-pitched drawn out metallic *wheep-wheep*.

Dwarf Squeaker   *Arthroleptis xenodactyloides*
Short high-pitched cricket-like chirp, repeated several times.

Genus: *Leptopelis* Tree Frogs
(pp.88–101)

Bocage's Tree Frog   *Leptopelis bocagii*
Low-pitched quack.

Broadley's Tree Frog   *Leptopelis broadleyi*
Two short croaks and a whistle.

Yellow-spotted Tree Frog   *Leptopelis flavomaculatus*
Soft drawn-out meow cry.

Brown-backed Tree Frog   *Leptopelis mossambicus*
Frequently repeated, loud *kwa-kwa* or *wala* sound.

Natal Tree Frog   *Leptopelis natalensis*
Loud *yack-yack* sound, usually preceded by a drawn-out
eeeeeeee buzz.

Long-toed Tree Frog   *Leptopelis xenodactylus*
One or two brief croaks uttered at long intervals.

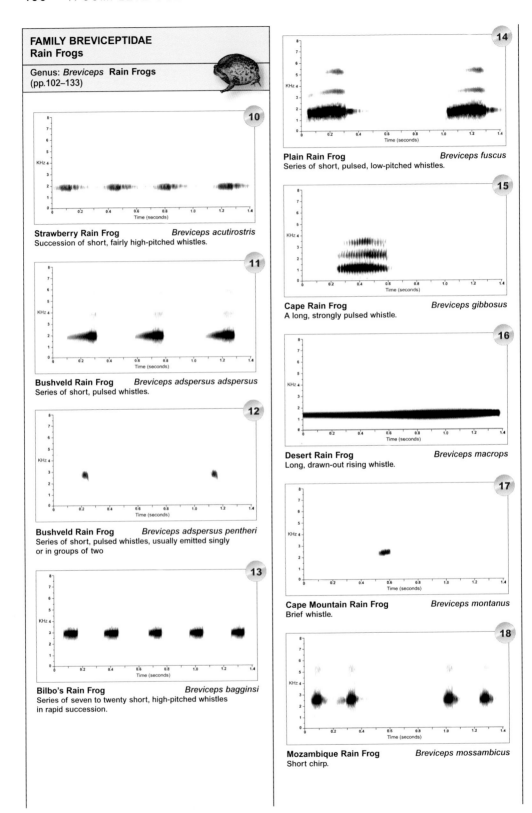

FAMILY BREVICEPTIDAE
Rain Frogs

Genus: *Breviceps* Rain Frogs
(pp.102–133)

Strawberry Rain Frog   *Breviceps acutirostris*
Succession of short, fairly high-pitched whistles.

Bushveld Rain Frog   *Breviceps adspersus adspersus*
Series of short, pulsed whistles.

Bushveld Rain Frog   *Breviceps adspersus pentheri*
Series of short, pulsed whistles, usually emitted singly
or in groups of two

Bilbo's Rain Frog   *Breviceps bagginsi*
Series of seven to twenty short, high-pitched whistles
in rapid succession.

Plain Rain Frog   *Breviceps fuscus*
Series of short, pulsed, low-pitched whistles.

Cape Rain Frog   *Breviceps gibbosus*
A long, strongly pulsed whistle.

Desert Rain Frog   *Breviceps macrops*
Long, drawn-out rising whistle.

Cape Mountain Rain Frog   *Breviceps montanus*
Brief whistle.

Mozambique Rain Frog   *Breviceps mossambicus*
Short chirp.

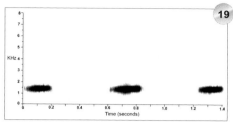

Namaqua Rain Frog   *Breviceps namaquensis*
Short low-pitched whistle, repeated.

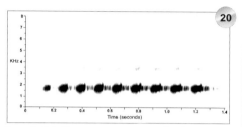

Power's Rain Frog   *Breviceps poweri*
Series of short whistles.

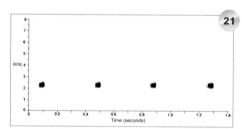

Sand Rain Frog   *Breviceps rosei rosei*
Short, moderately pitched chirp.

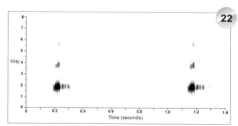

Sand Rain Frog   *Breviceps rosei vansoni*
Short, moderately pitched whistle.

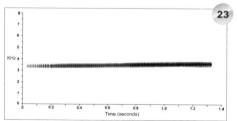

Whistling Rain Frog   *Breviceps sopranus*
Long, drawn-out, high-pitched whistle.

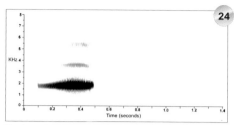

Northern Forest Rain Frog *Breviceps sylvestris sylvestris*
Series of short, pulsed whistles.

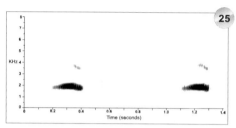

Northern Forest Rain Frog *Breviceps sylvestris taeniatus*
Series of short soft, evenly spaced whistles.

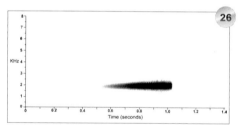

Plaintive Rain Frog   *Breviceps verrucosus*
Protracted, moderately pitched mournful whistle.

FAMILY BUFONIDAE
Toads

Genus: *Amietophrynus* Typical Toads
(pp.136–155)

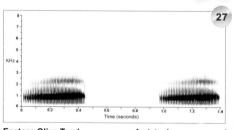

Eastern Olive Toad   *Amietophrynus garmani*
Loud, braying *kwââ-kwââ* often antiphonally.

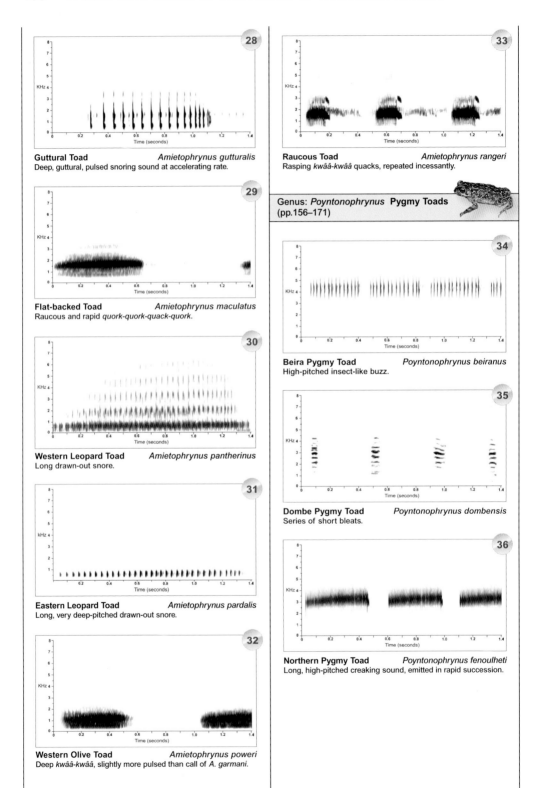

28

Guttural Toad   *Amietophrynus gutturalis*
Deep, guttural, pulsed snoring sound at accelerating rate.

29

Flat-backed Toad   *Amietophrynus maculatus*
Raucous and rapid *quork-quork-quack-quork*.

30

Western Leopard Toad   *Amietophrynus pantherinus*
Long drawn-out snore.

31

Eastern Leopard Toad   *Amietophrynus pardalis*
Long, very deep-pitched drawn-out snore.

32

Western Olive Toad   *Amietophrynus poweri*
Deep *kwââ-kwââ*, slightly more pulsed than call of *A. garmani*.

33

Raucous Toad   *Amietophrynus rangeri*
Rasping *kwââ-kwââ* quacks, repeated incessantly.

Genus: *Poyntonophrynus* Pygmy Toads
(pp.156–171)

34

Beira Pygmy Toad   *Poyntonophrynus beiranus*
High-pitched insect-like buzz.

35

Dombe Pygmy Toad   *Poyntonophrynus dombensis*
Series of short bleats.

36

Northern Pygmy Toad   *Poyntonophrynus fenoulheti*
Long, high-pitched creaking sound, emitted in rapid succession.

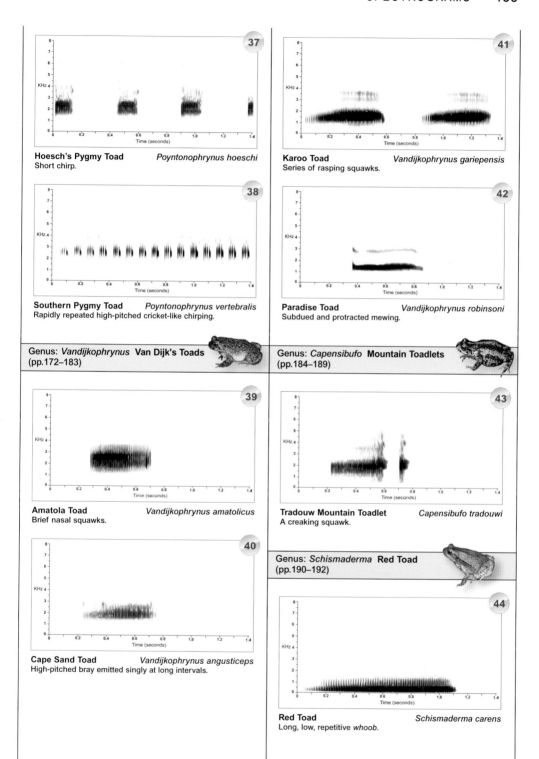

Hoesch's Pygmy Toad *Poyntonophrynus hoeschi*
Short chirp.

Karoo Toad *Vandijkophrynus gariepensis*
Series of rasping squawks.

Southern Pygmy Toad *Poyntonophrynus vertebralis*
Rapidly repeated high-pitched cricket-like chirping.

Paradise Toad *Vandijkophrynus robinsoni*
Subdued and protracted mewing.

Genus: *Vandijkophrynus* **Van Dijk's Toads** (pp.172–183)

Genus: *Capensibufo* **Mountain Toadlets** (pp.184–189)

Amatola Toad *Vandijkophrynus amatolicus*
Brief nasal squawks.

Tradouw Mountain Toadlet *Capensibufo tradouwi*
A creaking squawk.

Genus: *Schismaderma* **Red Toad** (pp.190–192)

Cape Sand Toad *Vandijkophrynus angusticeps*
High-pitched bray emitted singly at long intervals.

Red Toad *Schismaderma carens*
Long, low, repetitive *whoob*.

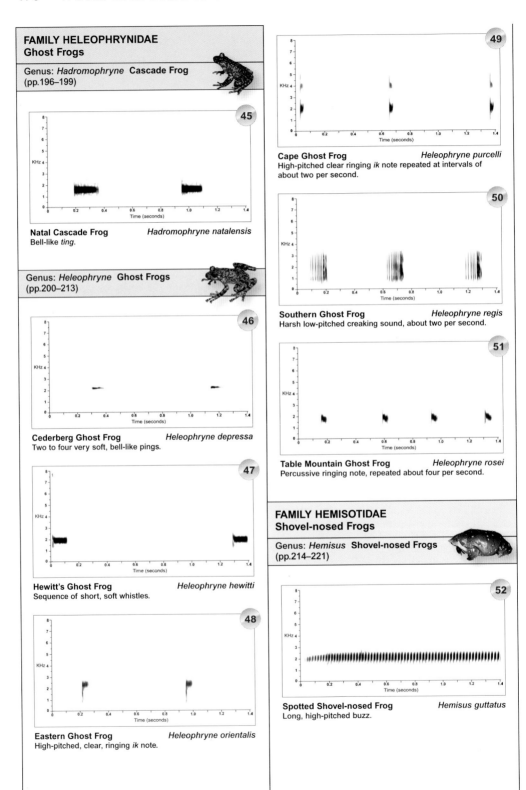

FAMILY HELEOPHRYNIDAE
Ghost Frogs

Genus: *Hadromophryne* **Cascade Frog**
(pp.196–199)

45

Natal Cascade Frog   *Hadromophryne natalensis*
Bell-like *ting*.

Genus: *Heleophryne* **Ghost Frogs**
(pp.200–213)

46

Cederberg Ghost Frog   *Heleophryne depressa*
Two to four very soft, bell-like pings.

47

Hewitt's Ghost Frog   *Heleophryne hewitti*
Sequence of short, soft whistles.

48

Eastern Ghost Frog   *Heleophryne orientalis*
High-pitched, clear, ringing *ik* note.

49

Cape Ghost Frog   *Heleophryne purcelli*
High-pitched clear ringing *ik* note repeated at intervals of
about two per second.

50

Southern Ghost Frog   *Heleophryne regis*
Harsh low-pitched creaking sound, about two per second.

51

Table Mountain Ghost Frog   *Heleophryne rosei*
Percussive ringing note, repeated about four per second.

FAMILY HEMISOTIDAE
Shovel-nosed Frogs

Genus: *Hemisus* **Shovel-nosed Frogs**
(pp.214–221)

52

Spotted Shovel-nosed Frog   *Hemisus guttatus*
Long, high-pitched buzz.

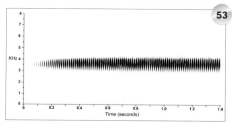

Mottled Shovel-nosed Frog   *Hemisus marmoratus*
Long, high-pitched buzz lasting up to five seconds.

FAMILY HYPEROLIIDAE
Reed Frogs

Genus: *Afrixalus* **Leaf-folding Frogs**
(pp.222–235)

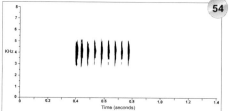

Golden Leaf-folding Frog   *Afrixalus aureus*
Short, repeated buzz.

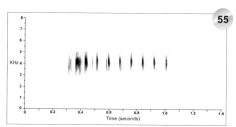

Snoring Leaf-folding Frog   *Afrixalus crotalus*
Series of indistinct clicks or rattles.

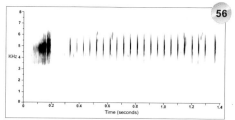

Delicate Leaf-folding Frog   *Afrixalus delicatus*
High-pitched *zick*, interspersed with buzzing.

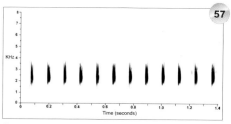

Greater Leaf-folding Frog   *Afrixalus fornasinii*
Burst of loud, rapidly repeated *clacks*.

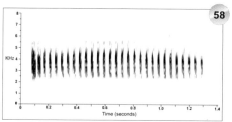

Knysna Leaf-folding Frog   *Afrixalus knysnae*
Soft, insect-like trill, lasting for about one or two seconds.

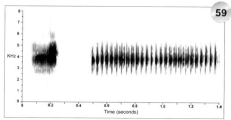

Natal Leaf-folding Frog   *Afrixalus spinifrons spinifons*
Short *zip*, followed by a longer trill of about five seconds.

Genus: *Hyperolius* **Reed Frogs**
(pp.236–271)

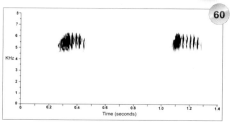

Sharp-nosed Reed Frog   *Hyperolius acuticeps*
Harsh, insect-like *dzeee-dzeee* chirp.

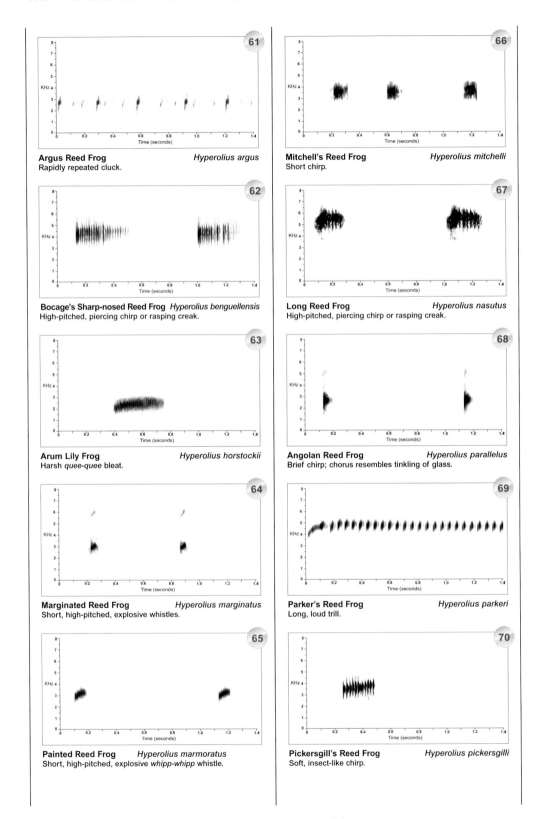

Argus Reed Frog   *Hyperolius argus*
Rapidly repeated cluck.

Bocage's Sharp-nosed Reed Frog *Hyperolius benguellensis*
High-pitched, piercing chirp or rasping creak.

Arum Lily Frog   *Hyperolius horstockii*
Harsh *quee-quee* bleat.

Marginated Reed Frog   *Hyperolius marginatus*
Short, high-pitched, explosive whistles.

Painted Reed Frog   *Hyperolius marmoratus*
Short, high-pitched, explosive *whipp-whipp* whistle.

Mitchell's Reed Frog   *Hyperolius mitchelli*
Short chirp.

Long Reed Frog   *Hyperolius nasutus*
High-pitched, piercing chirp or rasping creak.

Angolan Reed Frog   *Hyperolius parallelus*
Brief chirp; chorus resembles tinkling of glass.

Parker's Reed Frog   *Hyperolius parkeri*
Long, loud trill.

Pickersgill's Reed Frog   *Hyperolius pickersgilli*
Soft, insect-like chirp.

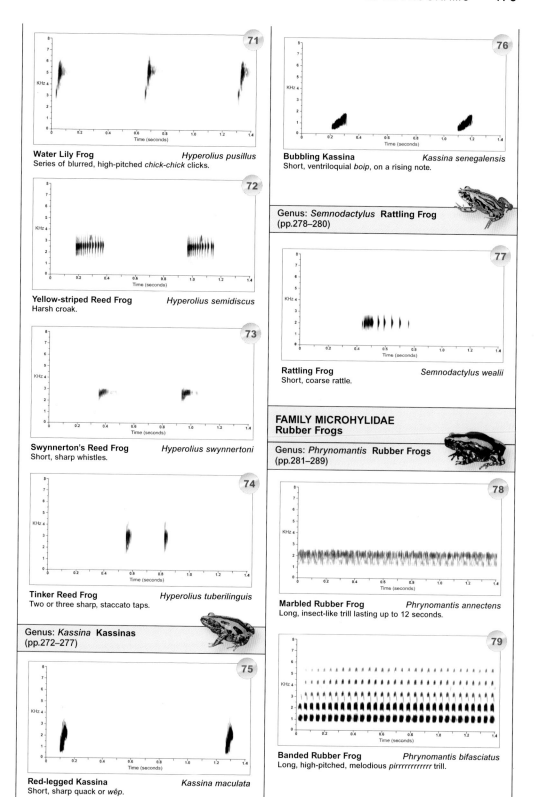

Water Lily Frog   *Hyperolius pusillus*
Series of blurred, high-pitched *chick-chick* clicks.

Yellow-striped Reed Frog   *Hyperolius semidiscus*
Harsh croak.

Swynnerton's Reed Frog   *Hyperolius swynnertoni*
Short, sharp whistles.

Tinker Reed Frog   *Hyperolius tuberilinguis*
Two or three sharp, staccato taps.

Genus: *Kassina* Kassinas
(pp.272–277)

Red-legged Kassina   *Kassina maculata*
Short, sharp quack or *wép*.

Bubbling Kassina   *Kassina senegalensis*
Short, ventriloquial *boip*, on a rising note.

Genus: *Semnodactylus* Rattling Frog
(pp.278–280)

Rattling Frog   *Semnodactylus wealii*
Short, coarse rattle.

**FAMILY MICROHYLIDAE
Rubber Frogs**

Genus: *Phrynomantis* Rubber Frogs
(pp.281–289)

Marbled Rubber Frog   *Phrynomantis annectens*
Long, insect-like trill lasting up to 12 seconds.

Banded Rubber Frog   *Phrynomantis bifasciatus*
Long, high-pitched, melodious *pirrrrrrrrrrr* trill.

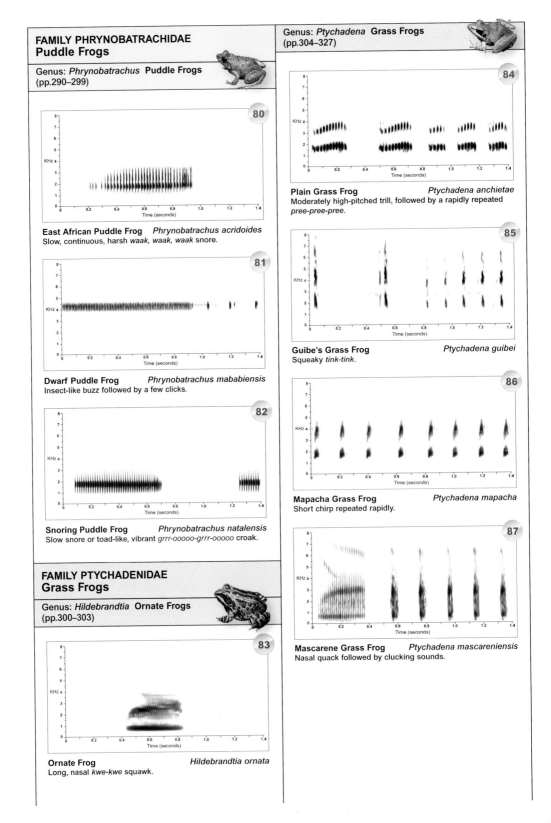

FAMILY PHRYNOBATRACHIDAE
Puddle Frogs

Genus: *Phrynobatrachus* Puddle Frogs
(pp.290–299)

80

East African Puddle Frog   *Phrynobatrachus acridoides*
Slow, continuous, harsh *waak, waak, waak* snore.

81

Dwarf Puddle Frog   *Phrynobatrachus mababiensis*
Insect-like buzz followed by a few clicks.

82

Snoring Puddle Frog   *Phrynobatrachus natalensis*
Slow snore or toad-like, vibrant *grrr-ooooo-grrr-ooooo* croak.

FAMILY PTYCHADENIDAE
Grass Frogs

Genus: *Hildebrandtia* Ornate Frogs
(pp.300–303)

83

Ornate Frog   *Hildebrandtia ornata*
Long, nasal *kwe-kwe* squawk.

Genus: *Ptychadena* Grass Frogs
(pp.304–327)

84

Plain Grass Frog   *Ptychadena anchietae*
Moderately high-pitched trill, followed by a rapidly repeated
pree-pree-pree.

85

Guibe's Grass Frog   *Ptychadena guibei*
Squeaky *tink-tink*.

86

Mapacha Grass Frog   *Ptychadena mapacha*
Short chirp repeated rapidly.

87

Mascarene Grass Frog   *Ptychadena mascareniensis*
Nasal quack followed by clucking sounds.

SPECTROGRAMS   475

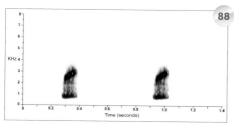

Broad-banded Grass Frog   *Ptychadena mossambica*
Series of *kwe-kwe* clucks.

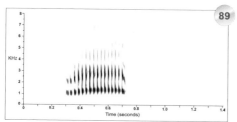

Sharp-nosed Grass Frog   *Ptychadena oxyrhynchus*
Series of moderately high-pitched, penetrating trills.

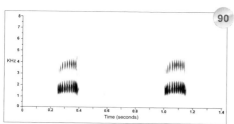

Striped Grass Frog   *Ptychadena porosissima*
Three or four short, bird-like, rasping chirps, *pree-pree.*

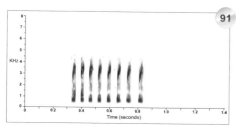

Schilluk Grass Frog   *Ptychadena schillukorum*
Very rapid bursts of three to six explosive chucks.

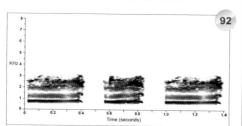

Speckled-bellied Grass Frog   *Ptychadena subpunctata*
Soft croaks in rapid succession.

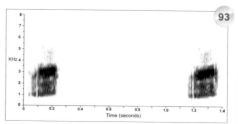

Dwarf Grass Frog   *Ptychadena taenioscelis*
Short, nasal bleats.

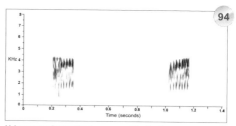

Udzungwa Grass Frog   *Ptychadena uzungwensis*
A repetitive *prrrrp.*

FAMILY PIPIDAE
Platannas

Genus: *Xenopus* Platannas
(pp.328–337)

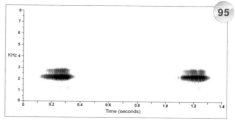

Cape Platanna   *Xenopus gilli*
Series of short, rapidly pulsed, metallic buzzes.

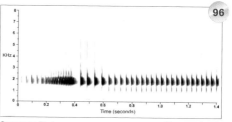

Common Platanna   *Xenopus laevis*
Constant undulating, snoring sounds.

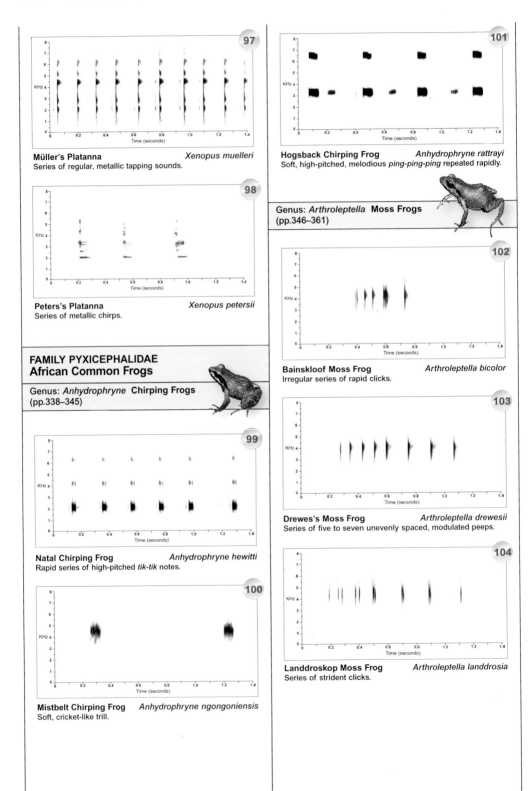

Müller's Platanna   *Xenopus muelleri*
Series of regular, metallic tapping sounds.

Peters's Platanna   *Xenopus petersii*
Series of metallic chirps.

FAMILY PYXICEPHALIDAE
African Common Frogs

Genus: *Anhydrophryne* **Chirping Frogs**
(pp.338–345)

Natal Chirping Frog   *Anhydrophryne hewitti*
Rapid series of high-pitched *tik-tik* notes.

Mistbelt Chirping Frog   *Anhydrophryne ngongoniensis*
Soft, cricket-like trill.

Hogsback Chirping Frog   *Anhydrophryne rattrayi*
Soft, high-pitched, melodious *ping-ping-ping* repeated rapidly.

Genus: *Arthroleptella* **Moss Frogs**
(pp.346–361)

Bainskloof Moss Frog   *Arthroleptella bicolor*
Irregular series of rapid clicks.

Drewes's Moss Frog   *Arthroleptella drewesii*
Series of five to seven unevenly spaced, modulated peeps.

Landdroskop Moss Frog   *Arthroleptella landdrosia*
Series of strident clicks.

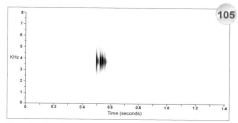

Cape Peninsula Moss Frog *Arthroleptella lightfooti*
High-pitched chirp.

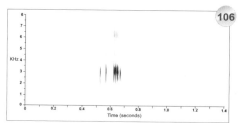

Rough Moss Frog *Arthroleptella rugosa*
Rough chirp and occasionally a rattling sound.

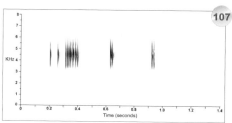

Northern Moss Frog *Arthroleptella subvoce*
Repertoire of several notes: a chirp of four to six pulses is
followed by two to six double clicks.

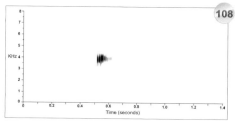

De Villiers's Moss Frog *Arthroleptella villiersi*
High-pitched chirp.

Genus: *Cacosternum* **Cacos**
(pp.362–385)

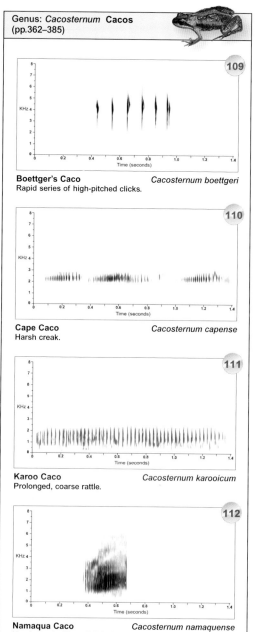

Boettger's Caco *Cacosternum boettgeri*
Rapid series of high-pitched clicks.

Cape Caco *Cacosternum capense*
Harsh creak.

Karoo Caco *Cacosternum karooicum*
Prolonged, coarse rattle.

Namaqua Caco *Cacosternum namaquense*
Harsh creak with a slightly rising note.

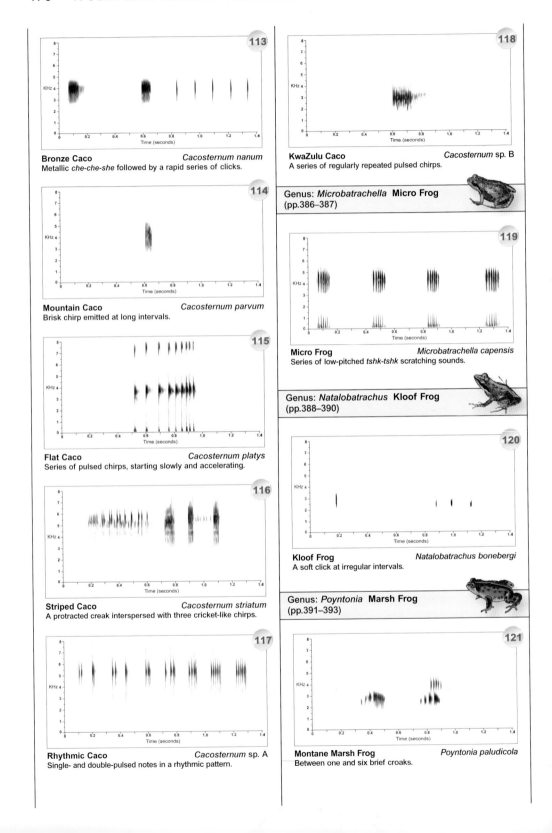

Bronze Caco   *Cacosternum nanum*
Metallic *che-che-she* followed by a rapid series of clicks.

Mountain Caco   *Cacosternum parvum*
Brisk chirp emitted at long intervals.

Flat Caco   *Cacosternum platys*
Series of pulsed chirps, starting slowly and accelerating.

Striped Caco   *Cacosternum striatum*
A protracted creak interspersed with three cricket-like chirps.

Rhythmic Caco   *Cacosternum* sp. A
Single- and double-pulsed notes in a rhythmic pattern.

KwaZulu Caco   *Cacosternum* sp. B
A series of regularly repeated pulsed chirps.

Genus: *Microbatrachella* **Micro Frog**
(pp.386–387)

Micro Frog   *Microbatrachella capensis*
Series of low-pitched *tshk-tshk* scratching sounds.

Genus: *Natalobatrachus* **Kloof Frog**
(pp.388–390)

Kloof Frog   *Natalobatrachus bonebergi*
A soft click at irregular intervals.

Genus: *Poyntonia* **Marsh Frog**
(pp.391–393)

Montane Marsh Frog   *Poyntonia paludicola*
Between one and six brief croaks.

Genus: *Amietia* River Frogs
(pp.394–409)

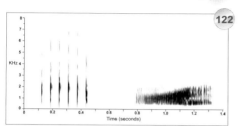

Common River Frog   *Amietia angolensis*
Six or seven, short rapid *kik-kik-kik-kik* clicks (sounding like a rattle), followed by a short *keroip* croak.

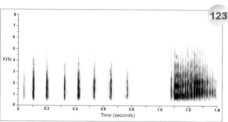

Drakensberg River Frog   *Amietia dracomontana*
Long series of clicks followed by a harsh croak.

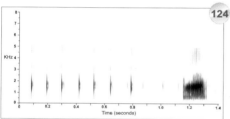

Cape River Frog   *Amietia fuscigula*
Long series of taps followed by a few harsh *kua-kua* groans.

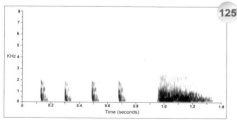

Maluti River Frog   *Amietia umbraculata*
Long series of hollow taps followed by a low-pitched groan.

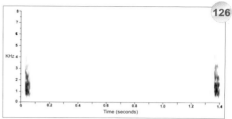

Van Dijk's River Frog   *Amietia vandijki*
A slow series of chucks followed by a harsh, pulsed croak.

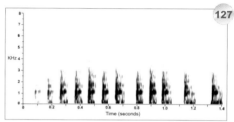

Phofung River Frog   *Amietia vertebralis*
Soft, irregular clucking sound.

Genus: *Pyxicephalus* Bullfrogs
(pp.410–417)

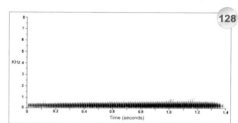

Giant Bullfrog   *Pyxicephalus adspersus*
Very deep, prolonged *wooop*, reminiscent of lowing cattle.

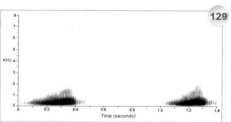

African Bullfrog   *Pyxicephalus edulis*
Short *whap-whap* at irregular intervals, like the yapping of a dog.

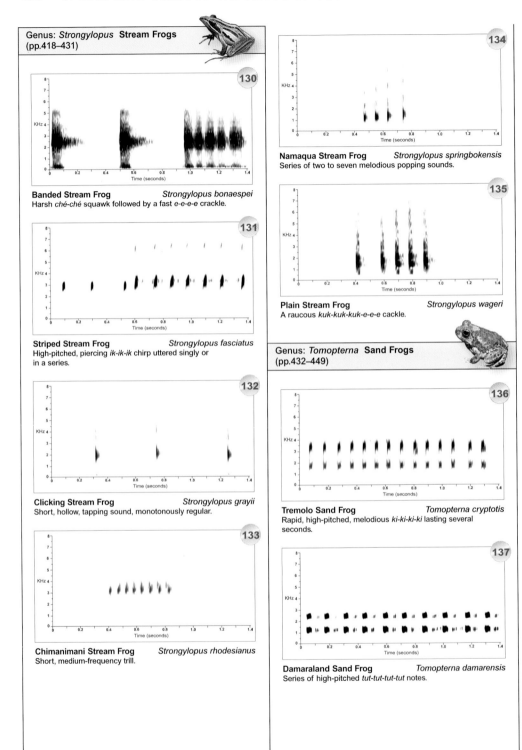

Genus: *Strongylopus* Stream Frogs
(pp.418–431)

130

Banded Stream Frog   *Strongylopus bonaespei*
Harsh *ché-ché* squawk followed by a fast *e-e-e-e* crackle.

131

Striped Stream Frog   *Strongylopus fasciatus*
High-pitched, piercing *ik-ik-ik* chirp uttered singly or
in a series.

132

Clicking Stream Frog   *Strongylopus grayii*
Short, hollow, tapping sound, monotonously regular.

133

Chimanimani Stream Frog   *Strongylopus rhodesianus*
Short, medium-frequency trill.

134

Namaqua Stream Frog   *Strongylopus springbokensis*
Series of two to seven melodious popping sounds.

135

Plain Stream Frog   *Strongylopus wageri*
A raucous *kuk-kuk-kuk-e-e-e* cackle.

Genus: *Tomopterna* Sand Frogs
(pp.432–449)

136

Tremolo Sand Frog   *Tomopterna cryptotis*
Rapid, high-pitched, melodious *ki-ki-ki-ki* lasting several
seconds.

137

Damaraland Sand Frog   *Tomopterna damarensis*
Series of high-pitched *tut-tut-tut-tut* notes.

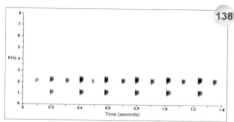

Cape Sand Frog *Tomopterna delalandii*
Series of melodious *ku-ku-ku-ku* notes lasting several seconds.

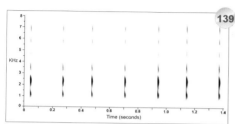

Knocking Sand Frog *Tomopterna krugerensis*
Series of percussive, wooden *ta-ta-ta-ta* knocking notes.

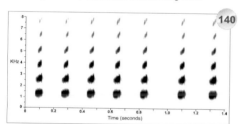

Russet-backed Sand Frog *Tomopterna marmorata*
Rapid piping notes repeated at a variable rate.

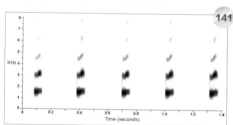

Natal Sand Frog *Tomopterna natalensis*
Series of penetrating but melodious *tut-tut-tut-tut* notes.

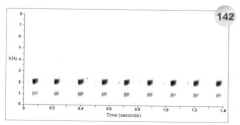

Tandy's Sand Frog *Tomopterna tandyi*
Series of rapid, melodious *ki-ki-ki-ki* notes.

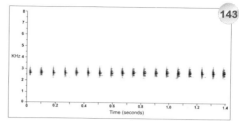

Beaded Sand Frog *Tomopterna tuberculosa*
Continuous fast rattle.

FAMILY RANIDAE
European Common Frogs

**Genus: *Hylarana* Golden-backed Frogs
(pp.450–455)**

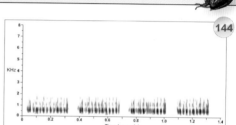

Darling's Golden-backed Frog *Hylarana darlingi*
Rapidly accelerating barking sounds.

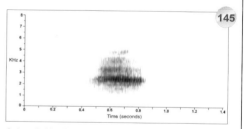

Galam Golden-backed Frog *Hylarana galamensis*
Muffled, nasal snore.

FAMILY RHACOPHORIDAE
Foam Nest Frogs

**Genus: *Chiromantis* Foam Nest Frogs
(pp.456–459)**

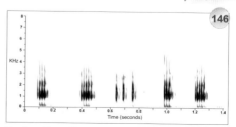

Southern Foam Nest Frog *Chiromantis xerampelina*
Subdued series of discordant croaks or squeaks.

The calls on the accompanying CD are recorded as MP3 files
and can only be played on MP3-compatible equipment.

Track list of southern African frog calls

Track	Species		Credit
	SQUEAKERS	*Arthroleptis*	
1	Shovel-footed Squeaker	*A. stenodactylus*	MCm
2	Bush Squeaker	*A. wahlbergi*	NP
3	Dwarf Squeaker	*A. xenodactyloides*	MCm
	TREE FROGS	*Leptopelis*	
4	Bocage's Tree Frog	*L. bocagii*	BS
5	Broadley's Tree Frog	*L. broadleyi*	MCm
6	Yellow-spotted Tree Frog	*L. flavomaculatus*	LdP
7	Brown-backed Tree Frog	*L. mossambicus*	HB
8	Natal Tree Frog	*L. natalensis*	MJ
9	Long-toed Tree Frog	*L. xenodactylus*	NP
	RAIN FROGS	*Breviceps*	
10	Strawberry Rain Frog	*B. acutirostris*	LM
11	Bushveld Rain Frog	*B. adspersus adspersus*	LM
12	Bushveld Rain Frog	*B. adspersus pentheri*	LM
13	Bilbo's Rain Frog	*B. bagginsi*	LM
14	Plain Rain Frog	*B. fuscus*	LM
15	Cape Rain Frog	*B. gibbosus*	LM
16	Desert Rain Frog	*B. macrops*	LM
17	Cape Mountain Rain Frog	*B. montanus*	LM
18	Mozambique Rain Frog	*B. mossambicus*	LM
19	Namaqua Rain Frog	*B. namaquensis*	LM
20	Power's Rain Frog	*B. poweri*	BS
21	Sand Rain Frog	*B. rosei rosei*	LM
22	Sand Rain Frog	*B. rosei vansoni*	MB
23	Whistling Rain Frog	*B. sopranus*	LM
24	Northern Forest Rain Frog	*B. sylvestris sylvestris*	LM
25	Northern Forest Rain Frog	*B. sylvestris taeniatus*	LM
26	Plaintive Rain Frog	*B. verrucosus*	LM
	TYPICAL TOADS	*Amietophrynus*	
27	Eastern Olive Toad	*A. garmani*	LdP
28	Guttural Toad	*A. gutturalis*	LdP
29	Flat-backed Toad	*A. maculatus*	NP
30	Western Leopard Toad	*A. pantherinus*	AdV
31	Eastern Leopard Toad	*A. pardalis*	NP
32	Western Olive Toad	*A. poweri*	LdP
33	Raucous Toad	*A. rangeri*	LdP
	PYGMY TOADS	*Poyntonophrynus*	
34	Beira Pygmy Toad	*P. beiranus*	MPI
35	Dombe Pygmy Toad	*P. dombensis*	AC
36	Northern Pygmy Toad	*P. fenoulheti*	HB
37	Hoesch's Pygmy Toad	*P. hoeschi*	AC
38	Southern Pygmy Toad	*P. vertebralis*	HB
	VAN DIJK'S TOADS	*Vandijkophrynus*	
39	Amatola Toad	*V. amatolicus*	NP
40	Cape Sand Toad	*V. angusticeps*	MC
41	Karoo Toad	*V. gariepensis*	LdP
42	Paradise Toad	*V. robinsoni*	HB
	MOUNTAIN TOADLETS	*Capensibufo*	
43	Tradouw Mountain Toadlet	*C. tradouwi*	NP
	RED TOAD	*Schismaderma*	
44	Red Toad	*S. carens*	NP
	CASCADE FROG	*Hadromophryne*	
45	Natal Cascade Frog	*H. natalensis*	RB
	GHOST FROGS	*Heleophryne*	
46	Cederberg Ghost Frog	*H. depressa*	MCm
47	Hewitt's Ghost Frog	*H. hewitti*	RB
48	Eastern Ghost Frog	*H. orientalis*	RB
49	Cape Ghost Frog	*H. purcelli*	NP
50	Southern Ghost Frog	*H. regis*	NP
51	Table Mountain Ghost Frog	*H. rosei*	AdV
	SHOVEL-NOSED FROGS	*Hemisus*	
52	Spotted Shovel-nosed Frog	*H. guttatus*	LM
53	Mottled Shovel-nosed Frog	*H. marmoratus*	LM
	LEAF-FOLDING FROGS	*Afrixalus*	
54	Golden Leaf-folding Frog	*A. aureus*	RT
55	Snoring Leaf-folding Frog	*A. crotalus*	MPI
56	Delicate Leaf-folding Frog	*A. delicatus*	NP
57	Greater Leaf-folding Frog	*A. fornasinii*	NP
58	Knysna Leaf-folding Frog	*A. knysnae*	HB
59	Natal Leaf-folding Frog	*A. spinifrons*	NP
	REED FROGS	*Hyperolius*	
60	Sharp-nosed Reed Frog	*H. acuticeps*	NP
61	Argus Reed Frog	*H. argus*	NP
62	Bocage's Sharp-nosed Reed Frog	*H. benguellensis*	MPI
63	Arum Lily Frog	*H. horstockii*	NP
64	Marginated Reed Frog	*H. marginatus*	MPI
65	Painted Reed Frog	*H. marmoratus*	NP
66	Mitchell's Reed Frog	*H. mitchelli*	MPI
67	Long Reed Frog	*H. nasutus*	LdP
68	Angolan Reed Frog	*H. parallelus*	LdP
69	Parker's Reed Frog	*H. parkeri*	DM
70	Pickersgill's Reed Frog	*H. pickersgilli*	MB
71	Water Lily Frog	*H. pusillus*	NP
72	Yellow-striped Reed Frog	*H. semidiscus*	NP
73	Swynnerton's Reed Frog	*H. swynnertoni*	MPI
74	Tinker Reed Frog	*H. tuberilinguis*	MCm
	KASSINAS	*Kassina*	
75	Red-legged Kassina	*K. maculata*	MCm

76	Bubbling Kassina	*K. senegalensis*	NP
	RATTLING FROG	***Semnodactylus***	
77	Rattling Frog	*S. wealii*	NP
	RUBBER FROGS	***Phrynomantis***	
78	Marbled Rubber Frog	*P. annectens*	NP
79	Banded Rubber Frog	*P. bifasciatus*	NP
	PUDDLE FROGS	***Phrynobatrachus***	
80	East African Puddle Frog	*P. acridoides*	LM
81	Dwarf Puddle Frog	*P. mababiensis*	NP
82	Snoring Puddle Frog	*P. natalensis*	PB
	ORNATE FROGS	***Hildebrandtia***	
83	Ornate Frog	*H. ornata*	HB
	GRASS FROGS	***Ptychadena***	
84	Plain Grass Frog	*P. anchietae*	NP
85	Guibe's Grass Frog	*P. guibei*	LdP
86	Mapacha Grass Frog	*P. mapacha*	AC
87	Mascarene Grass Frog	*P. mascareniensis*	NP
88	Broad-banded Grass Frog	*P. mossambica*	NP
89	Sharp-nosed Grass Frog	*P. oxyrhynchus*	NP
90	Striped Grass Frog	*P. porosissima*	NP
91	Schilluk Grass Frog	*P. schillukorum*	DM
92	Speckled-bellied Grass Frog	*P. subpunctata*	AC
93	Dwarf Grass Frog	*P. taenioscelis*	NP
94	Udzungwa Grass Frog	*P. uzungwensis*	AC
	PLATANNAS	***Xenopus***	
95	Cape Platanna	*X. gilli*	MP
96	Common Platanna	*X. laevis*	AE
97	Müller's Platanna	*X. muelleri*	AE
98	Peters's Platanna	*X. petersii*	AC
	CHIRPING FROGS	***Anhydrophryne***	
99	Natal Chirping Frog	*A. hewitti*	NP
100	Mistbelt Chirping Frog	*A. ngongoniensis*	PB
101	Hogsback Chirping Frog	*A. rattrayi*	NP
	MOSS FROGS	***Arthroleptella***	
102	Bainskloof Moss Frog	*A. bicolor*	AT
103	Drewes's Moss Frog	*A. drewesii*	AT
104	Landdroskop Moss Frog	*A. landdrosia*	AT
105	Cape Peninsula Moss Frog	*A. lightfooti*	AT
106	Rough Moss Frog	*A. rugosa*	AT
107	Northern Moss Frog	*A. subvoce*	AT
108	De Villiers's Moss Frog	*A. villiersi*	AT
	CACOS	***Cacosternum***	
109	Boettger's Caco	*C. boettgeri*	LdP
110	Cape Caco	*C. capense*	RB
111	Karoo Caco	*C. karooicum*	AdV
112	Namaqua Caco	*C. namaquense*	LdP
113	Bronze Caco	*C. nanum*	MB
114	Mountain Caco	*C. parvum*	MB
115	Flat Caco	*C. platys*	LdP
116	Striped Caco	*C. striatum*	MB

117	Rhythmic Caco	*C. sp A*	MB
118	KwaZulu Caco	*C. sp B*	MB
	MICRO FROG	***Microbatrachella***	
119	Micro Frog	*M. capensis*	LdP
	KLOOF FROG	***Natalobatrachus***	
120	Kloof Frog	*N. bonebergi*	PB
	MARSH FROG	***Poyntonia***	
121	Montane Marsh Frog	*P. paludicola*	MCm
	RIVER FROGS	***Amietia***	
122	Common River Frog	*A. angolensis*	NP
123	Drakensberg River Frog	*A. dracomontana*	AC
124	Cape River Frog	*A. fuscigula*	NP
125	Maluti River Frog	*A. umbraculata*	AC
126	Van Dijk's River Frog	*A. vandijki*	MCm
127	Phofung River Frog	*A. vertebralis*	MCm
	BULLFROGS	***Pyxicephalus***	
128	Giant Bullfrog	*P. adspersus*	NP
129	African Bullfrog	*P. edulis*	NP
	STREAM FROGS	***Strongylopus***	
130	Banded Stream Frog	*S. bonaespei*	AC
131	Striped Stream Frog	*S. fasciatus*	NP
132	Clicking Stream Frog	*S. grayii*	NP
133	Chimanimani Stream Frog	*S. rhodesianus*	NP
134	Namaqua Stream Frog	*S. springbokensis*	HB
135	Plain Stream Frog	*S. wageri*	AC
	SAND FROGS	***Tomopterna***	
136	Tremolo Sand Frog	*T. cryptotis*	NP
137	Damaraland Sand Frog	*T. damarensis*	AC
138	Cape Sand Frog	*T. delalandii*	NP
139	Knocking Sand Frog	*T. krugerensis*	NP
140	Russet-backed Sand Frog	*T. marmorata*	HB
141	Natal Sand Frog	*T. natalensis*	NP
142	Tandy's Sand Frog	*T. tandyi*	AC
143	Beaded Sand Frog	*T. tuberculosa*	AC
	GOLDEN-BACKED FROGS	***Hylarana***	
144	Darling's Golden-backed Frog	*H. darlingi*	AC
145	Galam Golden-backed Frog	*H. galamensis*	AC
	FOAM NEST FROGS	***Chiromantis***	
146	Southern Foam Nest Frog	*C. xerampelina*	HB

CREDITS: Key to recorders of frog calls

PB P. Bishop	AdV A. de Villiers	MPI M.
RB R. Boycott	LdP L. du Preez	Pickersgill
HB H. Braack	AE A. Elepfandt	BS B. Sternstedt
MB M. Burger	MJ M. Jennions	RT R. Toms
AC A. Channing	LM L. Minter	AT A. Turner
MC M. Cherry	DM D. Moyer	
MCm M.	NP N. Passmore	
Cunningham	MP M. Picker	

INDEX

**Brown-backed Tree Frog
with eggs.**

Les Minter